# THE REVELS PLAYS

*Former editors*
Clifford Leech 1958–71
F. David Hoeniger 1970–85

*General Editors*
E. A. J. Honigmann, J. R. Mulryne, David Bevington
and Eugene M. Waith

# POETASTER

Jonson's ambitious satirical comedy is the most devastating and funniest assault mounted in the 'War of the Theatres'. However, its satire reaches beyond the derisive lampooning of rival dramatists: set in ancient Rome, *Poetaster* offers the first and one of the most subtle statements in English of the Augustan cultural ideal. Jonson contrasts Augustus' wise rule with an English polity dominated (like the stage) by malice, intrigue and envy. In a clear and closely argued introduction to this new edition, Tom Cain examines these different strands so skilfully interwoven by Jonson, and argues for a reassessment of *Poetaster* as one of the most ideologically interesting of all early modern plays.

The detailed explanatory notes guide the reader through the personal and political allusions which gave the play its immediate satirical impact, and gloss the numerous classical references.

Tom Cain is Head of the Department of English Literary & Linguistic Studies at the University of Newcastle upon Tyne.

# THE REVELS PLAYS

THE REVELS PLAYS

# POETASTER

## BEN JONSON

edited by Tom Cain

MANCHESTER
UNIVERSITY PRESS

Manchester and New York

*Distributed exclusively in the USA and Canada
by* St. Martin's Press

Introduction, critical apparatus, etc.,
© Tom Cain 1995

*Published by* Manchester University Press
Oxford Road, Manchester M13 9NR, UK
*and* Room 400, 175 Fifth Avenue,
New York, NY 10010, USA

*Distributed exclusively in the USA and Canada*
*by* St. Martin's Press, Inc.,
175 Fifth Avenue, New York, NY 10010, USA

*British Library Cataloguing-in-Publication Data*
A catalogue record for this book is available
from the British Library

*Library of Congress Cataloging-in-Publication Data*
Jonson, Ben. 1573?–1637.
Poetaster / Ben Jonson: edited by Tom Cain.
p. cm.—(The Revels plays)
Includes index.
ISBN 0-7190-1549-9
1. Rome—History—Augustus, 30 BC–14 AD—Drama.
2. Poets. Latin—Drama. I. Cain, T. G. S. (Thomas Grant Steven)
II. Title. III. Series.
PR2617.A2C35 1995
822'.3—dc20 94-12613
CIP

ISBN 0 7190 1637 1 *paperback*

Paperback edition published 1996

Printed in Great Britain
by Biddles Limited, Guildford and King's Lynn

# Contents

# Illustrations

# General Editors' Preface

The series known as the Revels Plays was conceived by Clifford Leech. The idea for the series emerged in his mind, as he explained in his preface to the first of the Revels Plays in 1958, from the success of the New Arden Shakespeare. The aim of the new group of texts was 'to apply to Shakespeare's predecessors, contemporaries and successors the methods that are now used in Shakespeare editing'. The plays chosen were to include well known works from the early Tudor period to about 1700, as well as others less familiar but of literary and theatrical merit: 'the plays included,' Leech wrote, 'should be such as to deserve and indeed demand performance.' We owe it to Clifford Leech that the idea became reality. He set the high standards of the series, ensuring that editors of individual volumes produced work of lasting merit, equally useful for teachers and students, theatre directors and actors. Clifford Leech remained General Editor until 1971, and was succeeded by F. David Hoeniger, who retired in 1985.

The Revels Plays are now under the direction of four General Editors, E. A. J. Honigmann, J. R. Mulryne, David Bevington and E. M. Waith. The publishers, originally Methuen, are now Manchester University Press. Despite these changes, the format and essential character of the series will continue, and it is hoped that its editorial standards will be maintained. Except for some work in progress, the General Editors intend, in expanding the series, to concentrate for the immediate future on plays from the period 1558–1642, and may include a small number of non-dramatic works of interest to students of drama. Some slight changes have been forced by considerations of cost. For example, in editions from 1978, notes to the introduction are placed together at the end, not at the foot of the page. Collation and commentary notes will continue, however, to appear on the relevant pages.

The text of each Revels play, in accordance with established practice in the series, is edited afresh from the original text of best authority (in a few instances, texts), but spelling and punctuation are modernised and speech headings are silently made consistent. Elisions in the original are also silently regularised, except where metre would be affected by the change; since 1968 the '-ed' form is used for non-syllabic terminations in past tenses and past participles ('-'d' earlier), and '-èd' for syllabic ('-ed' earlier). The editor emends, as distinct from modernises, his original only in instances where error is patent, or at least very probable, and correction persuasive. Act divisions are given only if they appear in the original or if the structure of the play clearly points to them. Those act and scene divisions not found in the original are provided unobtrusively in small type and in square brackets. Square brackets are also used for any other additions to or changes in the stage directions of the original.

Revels Plays do not provide a variorum collation, but only those variants which require the critical attention of serious textual students. All departures of substance from 'copy-text' are listed, including any relineation and those changes in punctuation which involve to any degree a decision between alternative interpretations; but not such accidentals as turned letters, nor necessarily additions to stage directions whose editorial nature is already made clear by the use of brackets. Press corrections in the 'copy-text' are likewise included. Of later emendations of the text, only those are given which as alternative readings still deserve attention.

One of the hallmarks of the Revels Plays is the thoroughness of their annotations. Besides explaining the meaning of difficult words and passages, the editor provides comments on customs or usage, text or stage-business–indeed, on anything he judges pertinent and helpful. Each volume contains a Glossarial Index to the Commentary, in which particular attention is drawn to meanings for words not listed in *OED*.

The Introduction to a Revels play assesses the authority of the 'copy-text' on which it is based, and discusses the editorial methods employed in dealing with it; the editor also considers his play's date and (where relevant) sources, together with its place in the work of the author and in the theatre of its time. Stage history is offered, and in the case of a play by an author not previously represented in the series a brief biography is given.

It is our hope that plays edited in this fashion will promote further scholarly and theatrical investigation of one of the richest periods in theatrical history.

E. A. J. HONIGMANN
J. R. MULRYNE
DAVID BEVINGTON
E. M. WAITH

In memory of Hana

# Preface

This book has suffered more than its fair share of interruptions and vicissitudes, human and mechanical, but work on it has almost always been an enjoyable activity. Too many debts have been incurred over the years for them to be adequately acknowledged here, but it is a pleasure to mention some. A special tribute is due to Ernst Honigmann: few editors can have had the benefit of a general editor as learned and as patient, and his wisdom and experience have saved me from many blunders, classical as well as modern. The list of copies of the 1616 folio in Appendix 2 indicates how much I owe to how many librarians who cannot be mentioned individually. Special thanks are due, however, to the staff at the Victoria and Albert Museum, who transferred the Dyce quarto of *Poetaster* to the British Library for collation with the copies there, to the librarians at Eton, Westminster and Winchester, who were particularly helpful, and most of all to the staff of the Robinson Library at the University of Newcastle-upon-Tyne. I must acknowledge too the patience as well as the learning of many colleagues in the School of English and the Department of Classics at Newcastle, amongst whom Jeremy Paterson, Jonathan Powell, Hermann Moisl and Rowena Bryson have been especially helpful, as have, further away, Kelsey Thornton, James A. Riddell and Margarita Stocker. As ever, I am grateful to Robert Orme, for hospitality, for many hours of discussion, and for use of his splendid library. Most of all though I must thank my family. My children have not only put up with the fruitless importunity of editing without complaint but have aided and abetted it in practical ways. But my greatest debt is, as always, to my wife Lynn, whose love and understanding has supported me throughout.

TOM CAIN
*Newcastle-upon-Tyne, 1994*

# Abbreviations

Place of Publication is London unless otherwise stated.

Finkelpearl  Philip J. Finkelpearl, *John Marston of the Middle Temple* (Harvard, 1969).

Fleay, *Biographical Chronicle*  F. G. Fleay, *A Biographical Chronicle of the English Drama, 1559–1642*, 2 vols (1891).

Gair  Reavley Gair, *The Children of St Paul's: The Story of a Theatre Company, 1553–1608* (Cambridge, 1982).

Greg, *BEPD*  W. W. Greg, *A Bibliography of the English Printed Drama to the Restoration*, 4 vols (1939–56).

Gurr  Andrew Gurr, *Playgoing in Shakespeare's London* (Cambridge, 1987).

*HLQ  Huntington Library Quarterly.*

*HMC*  Historical Manuscripts Commission, Reports.

Hall, *Poems  The Collected Poems of Joseph Hall*, ed. A. Davenport (Liverpool, 1949).

Hasler  P. W. Hasler, *The House of Commons 1558–1603*, 3 vols (1981).

Hayes  Gerald R. Hayes, *Musical Instruments and their Music 1500–1750 II: The Viols, and Other Bowed Instruments* (Oxford, 1930).

Hillebrand  H. N. Hillebrand, *The Child Actors* (New York, 1964).

Honigmann, *Myriad-minded Shakespeare*  E. A. J. Honigmann, *Myriad-minded Shakespeare* (1989).

Honigmann, *Shakespeare's Impact*  E. A. J. Honigmann, *Shakespeare's Impact on his Contemporaries* (1982).

*Hoskyns*  Louise Brown Osborn, *The Life, Letters, and Writings of John Hoskyns 1566–1638* (New Haven, 1937).

Kay  W. David Kay, *Jonson, Horace, and the Poetomachia* (unpublished Ph.d. thesis, Princeton University, 1968).

King  Arthur H. King, *The Language of Satirised Characters in 'Poetaster'* (London, 1941).

Lavin  J. A. Lavin, 'Printers for Seven Jonson Quartos', *Library*, 5, XXV (1970), 331–8.

*MLQ  Modern Language Quarterly.*

*MLR  Modern Language Review.*

McPherson  David McPherson, 'Ben Jonson's Library and Marginalia', *SP*, LXXI (Texts and Studies, 1974), 1–106 (refs are to catalogue numbers).

Manningham  *The Diary of John Manningham of the Middle Temple*, ed. Robert P. Sorlien (Hanover, N.H., 1976).

Maus  Katharine Eisaman Maus, *Ben Jonson and the Roman Frame of Mind* (Princeton, N.J., 1984).

*N&Q  Notes and Queries.*

Nason  A. H. Nason, *Heralds and Heraldry in Ben Jonson's Plays* (New York, 1907).

*OED  The Oxford English Dictionary* (1st ed., Oxford, 1882–1933).

*PQ  Philological Quarterly.*

*Parnassus Plays  The Three Parnassus Plays (1598–1601)*, ed. J. B. Leishman (1949).

Partridge, *Slang*  Eric Partridge, *A Dictionary of Slang and Unconventional English*, 2 vols (5th ed., 1961).

Platz  Norbert H. Platz, 'Ben Jonson's *Ars Poetica*: An Interpretation of *Poetaster* in its Historical Context', *Salzburg Studies in English Literature*, XII (1973), 1–42.

*RES*   *Review of English Studies.*
Riggs   David Riggs, *Ben Jonson, A Life* (Cambridge, Mass., 1989).
Rudyerd, *Prince d'Amour*   Benjamin Rudyerd, *Le Prince d'Amour, Or the Prince of Love* (1660).
*SB*   *Studies in Bibliography.*
*SEL*   *Studies in English Literature.*
*SP*   *Studies in Philology.*
*Sh.S*   *Shakespeare Survey.*
*STC*   *A Short-Title Catalogue of Books Printed in England, Scotland, & Ireland and of English Books Printed Abroad 1475–1640*, 2nd ed., begun by W. A. Jackson and F. S. Ferguson, completed by Katherine F. Pantzer, 3 vols (1986–91).
Sharpe   Robert Boies Sharpe, *The Real War of the Theatres: Shakespeare's Fellows in Rivalry with the Admiral's Men, 1594–1603* (Boston and London, 1935).
Sidney, *Apology*   Sir Philip Sidney, *An Apology for Poetry: or, The Defence of Poetry*, ed. Geoffrey Shepherd (Manchester, 1973).
Small   R. A. Small, *The Stage Quarrel between Ben Jonson and the so-called Poetasters* (Breslau, 1899).
Smith, *Blackfriars*   Irwin Smith, *Shakespeare's Blackfriars Playhouse* (New York, 1964).
*TLS*   *Times Literary Supplement.*
*Weever*   E. A. J. Honigmann, *John Weever* (Manchester, 1987)
Womack   Peter Womack, *Ben Jonson* (Oxford, 1986).
*YES*   *Yearbook of English Studies.*

## 2   CLASSICAL

Unless otherwise stated, citations, translations and quotations from classical authors are from the editions in the Loeb Classical Library, which are not listed separately. The historical Horace is abbreviated 'Hor.' throughout the notes to distinguish him from the character in *Poetaster* and *Satiromastix*; abbreviations of classical titles follow those used in the *Oxford Classical Dictionary* (Oxford, 1970). The following abbreviations are also used:

Bond   *Q Horatii Flacci Poemata, scholiis sive annotationibus a J. Bond illustrata* (1606).
Godwyn   Thomas Godwyn, *Romanae historiae anthologia: An English exposition of the Romane antiquities. For the use of Abingdon Schoole* (Oxford, 1614).
Heinsius   *Q. Horatii Flacci Opera. Cum Animadversionibus & Notis Danielis Heinsii* (Lyons, 1612).
*Iliad*   *The Iliad of Homer*, trans. Richmond Lattimore (Chicago and London, 1951).
Lewis and Short   Charlton T. Lewis and Charles Short, *A Latin Dictionary* (Oxford, 1879).
Rosinus   Johannes Rosinus, *Romanorum Antiquitatum libri decem* (Basileae, 1583).
Turnebus   Adrianus Turnebus, *Adversariorum Tomi III* (Argentinae, 1599).

### 3  WORKS BY JONSON, MARSTON, DEKKER
### AND SHAKESPEARE

Unless otherwise indicated, references to Jonson's plays are to Herford and Simpson's text. The following abbreviations are used:

*Alc.*    *The Alchemist.*
*BF*    *Bartholomew Fair.*
*C is A*    *The Case is Altered.*
*Cat.*    *Catiline.*
*Christmas*    *Masque of Christmas.*
*Conv.*    *Conversations.*
*CR*    *Cynthia's Revels.*
*D is A*    *The Devil is an Ass.*
de Vocht    *Poetaster*, ed. Henry de Vocht, *Materials for the Study of the Old English Drama*, IX (Louvain, 1934).
*Disc.*    *Discoveries.*
*EH*    *Eastward Ho!*
*E Highgate*    *The Entertainment at Highgate.*
*EMI*    *Every Man in His Humour.*
*EMO*    *Every Man out of His Humour.*
*Engl. Gr.*    *English Grammar.*
*Ep.*    *Epigrams.*
*F*    *The Workes of Beniamin Jonson (1616).*
*F2*    *The Workes of Benjamin Jonson (1640).*
*FI*    *Fortunate Isles.*
*G*    *The Works of Ben Jonson*, ed. W. Gifford, Esq., 9 vols (1816).
*H&S*    *Ben Jonson*, ed. C. H. Herford, Percy and Evelyn Simpson, 11 vols (Oxford, 1925–52).
*Hadd.*    *The Haddington Masque.*
*Hym.*    *Hymenaei.*
*K. Ent.*    *The King's Coronation Entertainment.*
*ML*    *The Magnetic Lady.*
Mallory    *Poetaster*, ed. Herbert S. Mallory, *Yale Studies in English*, XXVII (New York, 1905).
*Merc. Vind.*    *Mercury Vindicated.*
*NI*    *The New Inn.*
*NW*    *News from the New World in the Moon.*
Nicholson    *Ben Jonson*, ed. Brinsley Nicholson and C. H. Herford, 3 vols, vol. I (1893).
*PR*    *Pleasure Reconciled to Virtue.*
Parfitt    *Poetaster*, ed. George Parfitt (Nottingham, 1979).
Penniman    *Poetaster and Satiromastix*, ed. Josiah H. Penniman (Boston and London, 1913).
*Q*    *Poetaster or The Arraignment (1602).*
*SS*    *The Sad Shepherd.*
*Sej.*    *Sejanus.*
*SW*    *The Silent Woman.*
*S of N*    *The Staple of News.*
*T of T*    *The Tale of a Tub.*
*UV*    *Uncollected Verse.*

*Und. Underwoods.*
*Volp. Volpone.*
Whalley   *The Works of Ben Jonson*, ed. Peter Whalley, 7 vols (1756).

Titles of Shakespeare's plays are abbreviated as in Onions, *Shakespeare Glossary*, p.x; quotations and references are from *The Riverside Shakespeare*, ed. G. Blakemore Evans *et al* (Boston, 1974). Unless otherwise indicated, references to Marston's plays are to the edition by Wood (see below). This has no line numbering: references are to vol. and page numbers. References to his poems are to the edition by Arnold Davenport (Liverpool, 1961). References to Dekker's plays are to *The Dramatic Works*, ed. Fredson Bowers, 4 vols (Cambridge, 1953–61). The following abbreviations are used:

*1 Ant.*   *Antonio and Mellida: The First Part.* ed. G.K. Hunter (Regents Renaissance Drama Series, 1965).
*AR*   *Antonio's Revenge*, ed. W. Reavley Gair (Revels Plays, Manchester, 1978).
*Hist.*   *Histriomastix. Or, The Player Whipt.*
*JD's Ent.*   *Jack Drum's Entertainment.*
*Scourge*   *The Scourge of Villainy.*
*S-M*   *Satiromastix, or The Untrussing of the Humorous Poet.*
*WYW*   *What You Will.*
Wood   *The Plays of John Marston*, ed. H. Harvey Wood, 3 vols (Edinburgh and London, 1934–9).

# Introduction

## I THE PLAY

### *1 Critical reputation and place in Jonson's career*

Poetaster has not been acted on the commercial stage since it was performed by the Children of the Chapel in 1601-2.[1] What reputation it has now, nearly four hundred years after that first controversial run at the Blackfriars Theatre, is as an early, somewhat flawed experiment by Jonson in satirical comedy, of little interest except to specialist students of his career, or the dwindling band of scholars still interested in the 'War of the Theatres'.[2] Why, then, should it claim the attention of a wider audience? The answer is that *Poetaster* is one of the most ideologically interesting of English Renaissance plays, the first and still one of the most powerful statements of an Augustan literary programme in English, and a comedy constructed with a deftness, intelligence and humour that calls out for a reassessment of its place in Jonson's *oeuvre*, one that places it alongside that handful of his plays that still do reach a wider audience than the specialist scholarly one.[3]

*Poetaster* was Jonson's second play for the boy actors at the Blackfriars, and his most accomplished play to date: the interest in the role of poetry, and of language in general, present in the earlier plays is brought into sharp focus, without the plotless longeurs or the complacency of the other 'comicall satyres', *Every Man Out* (1599)[4] and *Cynthia's Revels* (1600). Though not returning to the more conventional comic plotting of *The Case is Altered* (1597-8) or *Every Man In* (1598), its action is carefully structured, and it manages more adroitly than did the quarto version of the latter the shared themes of filial strife and the rejection of false poets, the young Ovid's enthusiasm for poetry being more carefully, if sympathetically, placed than that of his counterpart, Lorenzo Jr. The climactic judgement scene which dismisses fools and knaves from an ordered, at least part-rational society links *Poetaster* to both earlier and later plays by Jonson (not only comedies);[5] but the most obvious anticipation of the later work comes in the committed and scholarly reconstruction of a classical Rome which was to be converted to tragic uses in *Sejanus* (1603) and *Catiline* (1611). *Poetaster* is linguis-

I

tically of great interest, and not only for its onslaught on neologisms and vulgarisms introduced by Marston. Jonson's mastery of the rhythms, structures and inflexions of a wide variety of naturalistically conceived speech forms, already evident in previous plays, is deployed more comprehensively in its prose than before or after, making it the most linguistically varied of all Jonson's plays (King, p. xiii); while the more formal rhetoric of Caesar, in particular, in praise of poetry (e.g. IV.vi.33–46, V.i.17–32) achieves a poetic *energia* never eclipsed in the later work. Here Jonson sets out powerfully and persuasively that unequivocal link between the 'good poet' and the 'good man' that is so important to him, but which is much more familiar in its prose formulation in the Epistle to *Volpone* (1606), or in its restatement by the other great humanist poet of early modern England, John Milton.[6]

*Poetaster* has suffered from the partial nature of most of the critical attention it has received, and from the belief that modern readers or auditors would not find comic interest in a play which demands two areas of knowledge which they lack—a knowledge of the particular context of Jonson's London, especially of his rival playwrights, and a knowledge of the poetry and politics of Augustan Rome. That the latter was taken for granted from Jonson's time until this century is partly due to his influence, not least through this play. The difficulties posed for a modern audience in these respects are not, however, different in kind from those successfully negotiated in later 'Augustan' texts in which classical and contemporary worlds are set in comparative tension with each other. 'What! Man hath nothing given him in this life, without much labour' as Crispinus tells Horace (III.i.272–3): if the play is worth the labour, then late Elizabethan London and Augustan Rome can be recovered sufficiently for a modern audience to inhabit the two cities.

The frequently reductive criticism *Poetaster* has received presents a different kind of problem. For a century after it was resurrected in Gifford's pioneering edition, it was read exclusively as the leading play in the Poetomachia, that sequence of plays in which Marston, Dekker and Jonson lampooned each other with increasing bitterness, and which so fascinated Victorian scholars. For many of them, *Poetaster* was no more than a *pièce à clef* to be quarried for speculative identification of the play's protagonists with contemporary writers: to over-simplified identification of Horace with Jonson, or Crispinus and Demetrius with Marston and Dekker, was added 'proof' that Ovid was Chapman, Donne or Shakespeare, or alternatively that Virgil was Shakespeare, and so forth.[7] The critical reaction to all this was predictable, and was given theoretical support by the dominance of humanistic, Leavisite criticism in Britain, and the New Criticism in America: neither school was interested in whether or not Ovid was a portrait of Donne or Daniel. Neither New Historicists nor Cultural Materialists have found such questions any more pressing. Thus from the early twentieth century onwards emphasis has shifted from the play as part of the War of the Theatres to assessment of it as that entity beloved of the New Criticism, 'a meaningful work of art worth studying in its own right' (Platz, p. 1). The lampooning of individuals being too petty, undignified and ephemeral to have any part in the transcendent significance of a meaningful work of art, most twentieth-century critics have ignored the attacks on Marston and Dekker, or pushed them, embarrassed, to one side as a triviality which obscures the real, serious purpose of the play.[8] That 'purpose' has usually been taken to be either a satire on Ovidian lust, or an *ars poetica* by Jonson, or a combination of the two, but the thematic and structural unity demanded of the free-standing work of art has never been convincingly established in these readings. If, as Campbell argued, 'the essential plot' concerns Ovid, then we are left with a long, eventful and ideologically important last act in which he is not referred to, even by implication; if the 'essential plot' is that of Horace, then the main protagonist does not appear until Act III, and plays only a minor part in Act IV, to re-emerge in the last act. It seems clear that either this is a badly made play, or that the wrong questions are being asked about purpose and unity.

## 2    The general and the particular

Twentieth-century emphasis on *Poetaster's* wider meanings has undoubtedly been an important corrective, establishing that this is a serious play about the poet in society, that Horace is not just a self-projection of Jonson, that Crispinus is a generic poetaster as well as a caricature of Marston: but it has left an anaemic if genteel play which can only be resuscitated by recognising that the personal satire and parody that modern critics have sought to marginalise are at its very heart, specific and then-living examples of the virtues, vices and follies that are Jonson's theme. Far from the two readings of the play, as personal lampoon or as 'meaningful work of art', being mutually exclusive, the two are interdependent, a point that can be made more strongly by saying that an *ars poetica* which did not apply to Jonson's particular predicament in 1601 would not only be of limited use to him but would make a very dull play, of doubtful interest to an audience then or now: this is, after all, one of the 'satires that gird and fart at the time' (III.iv.194–5). In conceiving his reply to the attacks on him by Marston in the form of a statement of his own Augustan values, Jonson inevitably combined the personal with the general in a way that we do not need to disentangle. In representing Marston and Dekker as foolish, venal and motivated by envy he was both settling personal scores, and simultaneously exploring larger issues. Thus, for example, Horace's impassioned outburst to Caesar, when the latter assumes that Horace's poverty will make him 'likeliest to envy or to detract' (V.i.78–99), is both a response to Marston's accusations that Jonson's satire is motivated by poverty and envy, and a wider vindication of 'knowledge' rather than wealth or status as the 'nectar' that keeps judgement free from malice. The personal and general are linked in this way throughout the play, part of a debate about the satirist's function, which is seen in different ways by each of the participants in the Poetomachia: Jonson's Horace, the urbane satirist and confidant of statesmen and emperor, stands against Marston's more obviously bitter, Juvenalian voice, and Dekker's typically unclassical defence of the institutions under attack: the Court, the law, the adult actors and the City.[9] That the warring parties in this debate should be caricatured, and that real bitterness should be evident, only adds urgency to the argument, making the issues seem to matter more than would a genteel presentation of generic poetasters (and generic 'good poets'). Lampooning also represents a gain in comic impact, not least in encouraging that specificity of concrete 'observation'—'That's he, in the embroidered hat there, with the ash coloured feather' (III.iii.1–2)—which in Jonson's greatest comedies balances the drive towards an authoritative moral overview of human folly.

*Poetaster* is, then, not just about Ovid and courtly misdemeanours or the art of poetry, any more than it is 'just about' Jonson, Marston and Dekker. Indeed, it is more than usually reductive to argue that a play by so intelligent a writer as Jonson is essentially 'about' any one topic, or to look for the simple thematic unity such an approach implies.[10] *Poetaster* is clearly about the role of the poet in society, but it is also about (among other things) the corrosive power of envy and detraction, about language, its use and abuse, its struggle, for Jonson, towards singleness of meaning, and its disturbing tendency to fracture into multiple meanings which, especially in the mouth of Tucca, threaten the authority of the humanist arbiter; in this sense it is a play about authority, as it is also in its statement of Augustanism, the first and still one of the most subtle such in English.[11] The authority is that of the author, but also here of the prince, whose responsible authority both sanctions and is sanctioned by the poet, and replaces the false authority of Ovid's father, of Tucca over his pages, of Lupus in his office as tribune. All these themes and more emerge, but it would falsify the play if they were to be stressed at the expense of the play's contemporaneity and personal satire. Its 'application', routinely denied by Jonson, but undoubtedly part of its purpose and appeal, extends beyond the comic humiliation of Marston and Dekker to the satire on lawyers and actors, and to political satire in what I take to be daring reference to the Essex rebellion. Such satire shows the Augustan moralist at work on the material provided by his own society in a drama deeply engaged with the here and now, applying the values of Horace's Rome to the London of 1601. The elusive 'unity' of the play is the product of the interlocking of all these elements, a unity acutely described by Jonson himself in *Discoveries* (adapting Heinsius), not of an action 'one, and intire', but a conceptual unity which 'beginnes to be one, as those parts grow, or are wrought together . . . : compos'd of parts, which laid together in themselves, with an equall and fitting proportion, tend to the same end' (2751–61).[12]

These parts are not laid together in a conventional plot, and Jonas A. Barish rightly points to a lack of 'causal linkage' in this, as in other Jonson plays.[13] But they are 'wrought together' into a far more carefully shaped play than Herford and Simpson, for whom it was 'the least well made' of all his comedies, allowed (*H&S*, I, 421). *Poetaster* retains its dramatic impetus throughout in a way that *Every Man Out* and, especially, *Cynthia's Revels*, had signally failed to do. The first act introduces Ovid, the second Crispinus, the third Horace, their careers, and those of Tucca, Lupus, Histrio and Demetrius, Albius and Chloe, becoming interwoven in such a way that the lack of causal linkage does not lead to disintegration into arbitrarily connected episodes. A different kind of structuring, one of elegant symmetry, can be seen in the last two acts: in Act IV Ovid presides over a 'feast of sense' which is interrupted by Caesar, led by Lupus, who thus brings about Ovid's banishment. This pattern is adroitly reversed in Act V, where Virgil presides over a feast of the spirit, which is again interrupted by Lupus, who this time brings

1   Heroic Virtue (Hercules) treads down Envy.
Christoffel Jegher, woodcut after Peter Paul Rubens,
*modello* for Banqueting House ceiling.

about his own downfall, and that of Tucca, Crispinus and Demetrius. The final product is a tightly structured play that handles its serious themes surely and amusingly, the latter a simple but important point that is not always mentioned. Crispinus' vomiting up of a sequence of Marstonisms in the final scene, the brilliantly accurate parodies of Marston and Dekker in the two 'poems', the ludicrously sinister machinations of Lupus, and, most of all, the grotesquely inventive language of Tucca, whom King rightly calls 'the greatest character-creation of Jonson's early period' (p. 218), are aspects of a comic inventiveness that stands comparison with the better-known comedies. If this is an *ars poetica* and a political and social satire combined, it is a highly comic one: *Poetaster* may not have the carnivalesque generosity of *Bartholomew Fair*, but its Horatian, Lucianic humour is more genial than its origins lead one to expect, and Gibbons is right to point to its 'wonderfully preposterous and grotesque farce'.[14] Despite the personal attacks, the play is pervaded by Jonson's optimism, his belief that satire can teach; the sanguine tone is thrown into sharp relief by the bitterness, more Juvenalian than Horatian, of the 'Apologetical Dialogue' and the *Ode. To himselfe* (*Und.* XXIII), in both of which he is clearly bruised by 'the wolf's black jaw and the dull ass's hoof' (l. 226) as represented by *Satiromastix*.[15]

## 3  Classical imitation: London and Rome

Jonson's decision to set his play in 'Augustus Caesar's times', when 'wit and arts were at their height in Rome' ('Apologetical Dialogue', ll. 88–9) involved more than making a simple contrast between Augustan Rome and late Elizabethan London. He wanted also to show the continuities: even then, 'Virgil, Horace and the rest / Of those great master spirits did not want / Detractors' (ll. 90–2). There may be no 'parallel' in merit between himself and Virgil or Horace, but they had their Crispinus and Demetrius as he had his Marston and Dekker. Then, too, were malicious lawyers with a 'cheverel conscience' which advanced them over 'better men' (I.ii.129–32), informers, slanderers, actors appealing to 'all the sinners i'the suburbs' (III.iv.198–9), genuine poets betraying their vocation, poetasters with no idea of a poetic vocation, philistines regarding poetry as 'idle fruitless studies' (I.ii.137), courtiers forgetting their social, moral and religious obligations, and even merchants drawn absurdly out of their sphere by their wives' social ambitions. Set in Rome, the vices of the play are necessarily of Rome

as well as London, and, as the notes to this edition show, are often
described (or exemplified) in Roman writers: *Poetaster* is built
around a series of detailed 'imitations' of Horace and other classical,
mainly Latin, writers. Because these are so frequent, varied and
integral to the whole concept of the play, I have not included a
separate list of 'sources': all the classical echoes found by myself or
earlier editors are given in the notes, and virtually all are available in
modern translations. In some cases, as in Virgil's reading in V.ii,
Jonson translates directly; in others, notably III.v, he is very close to
doing so; but in most cases imitation is less simple: the whole of III.i
and ii, and the opening of III.iii, for example, is a successful
expansion into dramatic form of the 78 lines of Horace *Sat.* I.ix,
with Horace's unnamed boor particularised as a caricature of John
Marston, without the scenes ever losing touch with their model (see
especially III.i.161–79 and 180–6 and notes). In V.iii the fourteen
lines of *Sat.* I.x 78–91 are contracted into the eight lines of 448–54
(see note). More often, the allusion is much briefer: outside of the
scenes which are direct imitations of Horace, the notes record over
thirty such echoes of Horace, with Ovid, Martial (who provides both
the motto on the title-page and the four lines *Ad Lectorem* after the
*dramatis personae*) and the younger Seneca being the next most
frequently utilised. Whether or not all these echoes, some of them
tantalisingly brief, would have been recognised in the theatre, their
cumulative effect, especially for an audience whose education had
been almost entirely in Latin, is to build for the first time on the
English stage a convincing incarnation of the Augustan ethos,
annexing its values to the English tradition like, as Oldham was
to say, 'some mighty Conqueror in Poetry'.[16] Katharine Maus
describes well how Jonson assimilated a distinctive 'Roman frame of
mind' from his favourite Latin authors—Horace, Seneca, Cicero,
Juvenal and Quintilian: all moralists who shaped an outlook on
literature and life utterly distinct from his friends Shakespeare and
Donne.[17] In this play at least, Ovid, Virgil, Martial and the elder
Seneca should be added to the list, as should the Greeks Plutarch,
Lucian and, a more shadowy figure beyond him, Aristophanes. All
are transmuted into the comic vision of a society which 'hath
somewhat in it *moris antiqui*',[18] but in which we also see that nothing
changes; the new world imitates the old, but those who comprehend
the past imitate it deliberately and discriminatingly, as poets,
statesmen or even monarchs. Those who do not, imitate it only by
unwittingly repeating its follies and vices.

The first production by the Children of the Chapel reinforced the conflation of the two cities: anachronistic clothes and customs infiltrated Jonson's Augustan world, the satirised characters at least being dressed in contemporary costume. Crispinus and Demetrius wore clothes which probably parodied Marston's and Dekker's: Crispinus wears threadbare satin sleeves over a cheap 'rug' undershirt, with 'ample velvet bases' (III.i.67–9), and an 'embroidered hat' with an 'ash coloured feather' (III.iii.1–2). Dekker later implied that the feather at least was Marston's, and added more that cannot be derived from the text: 'Now sir, if the writer be a fellow that hath either epigramd you, or hath had a flirt at your mistris, or hath brought either your feather or your red beard, or your little legs, &c. on the stage'.[19] The beard (III.i.29), given the boy actor's age, must have been a comic version of Marston's.[20] Dekker too was probably recognisable in a cloak covering a 'decayed' doublet (III.iv.318–20). Tucca has a sword in a velvet scabbard (I.i.26), and a leather 'jerkin' (I.ii.185), Chloe wears 'bumrolls' and a 'whalebone bodice' (II.i.65–6), and lives in a London merchant's house, with bay windows and a gallery (II.i.108–10, 124). The costume of this group may have clashed with those who embody 'Augustan' values, rather as a 1595 drawing of a performance of *Titus Andronicus* shows both stage-Roman and contemporary costume.[21] This would underline the distinctions the play makes, presenting the Augustan characters as well-mannered time travellers. It is more likely, however, that all actors wore contemporary costume: there is no clue to what Horace, Augustus, Virgil or Julia wear, but Ovid dons the cap and gown of an Elizabethan law student in I.i.5–6, and the chains which Ovid's father and Maecenas wear are Elizabethan flagon chains (V.iii.38) not Roman *torques*. In either case, a Roman play acted partially or wholly in English dress would elicit a powerful synchronic effect, highlighting continuities and differences between the cities. There emerges a timeless city, in which exist simultaneously the ideal moral city and the degenerate city which had been linked to satire for generations.[22] In the resulting 'comicall satyre' Jonson expounds the poet's social role and responsibilities, projecting the Horatian ideal of a tolerant and urbane moralist whose disinterested wisdom is heeded by the greatest of monarchs, as opposed to the sensuous indulgence of Ovid, or those otherwise worthy poets misled by him, Gallus and Tibullus.

## 4 Jonson and Horace

Jonson's time at Westminster would have given him a good grounding in Latin, and perhaps a little Greek, but he seems to have begun a systematic programme of reading in classical authors sometime around 1599 (Riggs, pp. 57–8). If he came to it at this time, he must have read the opening of Suetonius' *Life* of Horace with an excited sense of recognition. Horace's father was a freed slave, lowborn as Jonson's stepfather had been; as Jonson had been taunted over his stepfather's (and his) profession of bricklaying, so Horace had been over his father's profession, 'a dealer in salted provisions'. Horace had fought at Philippi, Jonson in the Low Countries. After the defeat there, Horace gradually gained patronage as a writer, as did Jonson from the late 1590s. Horace had, with Virgil and Varius, been a poetic innovator and reformer (judiciously imitating earlier writers) like Jonson and Chapman in the 1590's. The bricklaying and the military service are not to be interpreted as *imitatio*, but must have seemed a promising start to a programme of 'self-fashioning'. It is hard now to appreciate the humanist commitment to *imitatio* as a strategy not only for writing but for living and dying by. Burckhardt tells a revealing story of a conspiracy against the Medici, foiled because the conspirators relied on classical models, leaving a fatal trail of literary clues.[23] Translating the humanist Buchler into *Discoveries*, Jonson set down a principle which he so fully endorsed that his admirers frequently identified him as a reincarnation of Horace:

> The third requisite in our *Poet*, or Maker, is *Imitation*, to bee able to convert the substance, or Riches of an other *Poet*, to his owne use. To make choise of one excellent man above the rest, and so to follow him, till he grow very *Hee*: or, so like him, as the Copie may be mistaken for the Principall.　　　　　　　　　　　　(*H&S*, VIII, 638; ll. 2466–71)

This, and its succeeding warning against servile imitation, was genuinely 'commonplace', traceable to Petrarch's 1366 letter to Boccaccio, and thence back to Seneca, Quintilian and Horace himself. Erasmus, Vives, and others endorsed the strategy, their warnings against slavish copying notwithstanding.[24] Jonson also knew that '*One*, though hee be excellent, and the chiefe, is not to bee imitated alone. For never no Imitator, ever grew up to his *Author*' (*Discoveries* ll. 884–6), and *Poetaster* offers an alternative Augustan model in Virgil, to whose praise V.i.100–41 is devoted. But despite Virgil's exalted status in the play (strategically necessary to enable him to vindicate Horace), and Jonson's lifelong admiration for him, a closer affinity with Horace is clear here, as in all his work, partly, as Robert B. Pierce suggests, because Horace was 'master of both the theory and practice of the poetic craft'.[25] In this spirit *Discoveries* offers as 'masters... *Horace*, and (hee that taught him) *Aristotle*' who 'deserve to bee the first in estimation' (2509–11).

This affinity with Horace is proclaimed by contemporaries from before *Poetaster* to the memorial poems of *Jonsonus Virbius*. The first reference, Weever's epigram of 1599 addressed to Marston and Jonson, associates Marston, ironically, with '*Horace*'[s] vaine', and Jonson's 'rich' style seems swept up in the same association (*H&S*, XI, 362). For his and Dekker's collaborator, Chettle, he is 'our English Horace' in 1603, while in 1605 Thomas Smith praises 'the elaborate English *Horace*... even our Lawreat worthy *Beniamen*'. On becoming a 'Son of Ben', Thomas Randolph felt instantly related to 'the whole quire' of classical poets, but especially to the '*Latin lyre* / That is so like thy *Horace*',[26] the same possessive terminology Jonson uses in the second *Ode. To himselfe* written after the failure of *The New Inn*: 'Leave things so prostitute, / And take the *Alcaick* Lute; / Or thine owne *Horace*' (*H&S*, VI, 493, ll. 41–3).

What so attracted him to Horace? In *Discoveries*, after quoting Heinsius on the 'true critic' Jonson adds his own endorsement: 'Such was *Horace*, an Author of much Civilitie; and (if any one among the heathen can be) the best master, both of vertue, and wisdome; an excellent, and true judge upon cause, and reason; not because he thought so; but because he knew so, out of use and experience' (2590–5). The lost commentaries on Jonson's translation of the *Ars Poetica* would have provided more detail, but the moral and literary qualities that make up 'Civilitie' are glossed in the detailed praise of his 1606 editor, John Bond, who was almost certainly acquainted with Jonson (see p. 45), and who gives as explicit an insight as we can hope to get into the thinking of the circle to which they both belonged. For Bond, Horace is 'perfect in all numbers: a poet crammed with a rich variety of matter, of elegant and polished language'. He provided Augustus' favourite reading because he 'described not only justice, invincible greatness of soul, frugality, moderation, reverence for God [*sic*], duty towards parents, endurance of poverty and worldly contempt' but also attacked 'dishonesty, injustice, cowardice, prodigality, lust, luxury, avarice, and virtually every vice'. This combination of eloquence with powerful moral credentials makes him 'without argument the foremost in merit (Homer always excepted) among all the Greek and Latin poets, in whom pleasantness so contends with usefulness, that he holds the reader enticed, ensnared once for all by his charm, nor does he ever let go'.[27] Jonson frequently quotes Horace's briefer version of this formula in the *Ars Poetica* (in Jonson's translation): 'Poets would either profit, or delight, / Or mixing sweet, and fit, teach life the right'.[28]

For Jonson, then, Horace was more than the great poet-critic: he was also the great poet-moralist, a satirist more controlled and urbane than Juvenal or Persius. His style was plain, perspicuous and unaffected, close to ordinary educated speech (cf. *Sat.* I.iv.41–2) yet, as Bond says, held the reader enticed: it was also the style which Augustus preferred (Suetonius, *Divus Augustus* LXXXV). Its balance, rhetorical decorum, moral focus and control was quintessentially 'Augustan'; the other great Augustan poet of *Poetaster*, Virgil, had less to offer in practical terms to an English writer committed to a programme that could 'raise the despised head of poetry again and, stripping her out of those rotten and base rags wherewith the times have adulterated her form, restore her to her primitive habit, feature, and majesty' (*Volpone*, Epistle, ll. 121–4). Nevertheless, Jonson offers an example of Virgilian epic in *Poetaster*, as he does an Ovidian love scene: in both cases, though, he is continuing to imitate Horace, who developed the *recusatio*, the poem which in refusing to adopt a certain style actually exemplifies that style, as a way of coming to terms with the limitations he imposed on his own poetic range. In 1601 Jonson addressed a *recusatio* to Sir John Salusbury, the *Proludium* (*H&S*, VIII, 108) which treats the Ovidian elegy in just this Horatian way.

Jonson never quite became a second Horace: his frequent and unstoical lapses from moderation and urbanity were, like Tolstoy's lapses from celibacy and vegetarianism, signals of a temperament at odds with its dearest ideals. Curiously, a number of personal characteristics which Jonson did share with Horace are not exploited in *Poetaster*: the Horace of the play is more austere than the historical Horace, who, like Jonson, is always ready to celebrate his friendships, his love of good food and wine. As Dekker pointed out, Horace was (unlike Jonson at this date) 'a goodly, Corpulent Gentleman' (*Satiromastix* V.ii.261–2); though Jonson's Horace is a 'little fat' figure (IV.vii.24), he is also an embattled one, the moralist who represents the will in that struggle with the appetite which

permeates Jonson's drama. Jonson's vision of Rome in *Poetaster* is
Apollonian, a culture imposing clear moral order on the world, and
on the individual, with the Dionysian alternative caricatured in
Tucca's irresponsible hedonism. There is, as has been said, little of
the carnivalesque in the play: instinct and appetite are not seen,
as they are in *Bartholomew Fair*, as vital and positive but as limiting,
whether in Tucca's 'skeldering' greed, Ovid's sensuality or Crispinus'
wooing of Chloe. Given the objectives of the play, this was inevi-
table: the carnivalesque vision accepts and celebrates an imperfect
world, in which all is in metamorphosis. Jonson could at times
embrace this vision, but his Augustan world is one of absolute values
offered in the clear, authoritative language of the committed
humanist. Even in this world, though, there is rebellion: Tucca's
Falstaffian characteristics, ostensibly negative and subject to sober
condemnation, continually threaten to escape their Horatian bounds,
so much so that King sees him as 'the most important character, the
centre of energy, in *Poetaster*' (p. 218), which judged in King's
linguistic terms he certainly is. But he never quite becomes a
Falstaffian Lord of Misrule, nor does his 'tumbling' language,
hugely energetic though it is, have the more innocent, celebratory
qualities of that of his predecessor, Juniper in *The Case is Altered*
(Juniper was the model for the 'ranting host of the Garter' in *Merry
Wives* (II.i.189) and Simon Eyre in *The Shoemaker's Holiday*).[29] If
Jonson is both fascinated and repelled by this anti-Augustan figure,
the banquet of the gods also combines two activities he always
treated, and indulged in, with fascinated disapproval—feasting and
dressing-up (compare the fantasies of Mammon and Volpone, the
bizarre activities of Nick Stuff and his wife in *The New Inn*, and the
real-life dressing-up by Jonson described in *Conversations* 306–11).
But Horace dominates, and the banquet falls well short of the
'positive, triumphant, liberating element' Bakhtin finds in Rabelaisian
feasting, just as Tucca is not allowed to be a truly Rabelaisian
character.[30] Horatian satire is moderated less by the spirit of satur-
nalia than by Aristophanic, Plautine and Lucianic comedy, close
enough in spirit for Horace to associate his work with such comedy
in *Sat.* I.iv.1–16, where he traces satire back through Lucilius
to Aristophanes and the Greek 'comoedia prisca', and in *Sat.*
I.x.15–16, where it is recommended as a model.[31] Aristophanes'
satire on Euripides in *Frogs* must, indeed, have seemed to Jonson to
provide a specially authoritative model for his attack on Marston, a
sanction whose weight would have been increased by the fact that

not only Horace but Augustus 'took great pleasure in the Old Comedy' (*Divus Augustus* LXXXIX).

## 5   *The poet and the ruler*

Jonson had been preoccupied with the difficult relationship between poet and ruler since the controversial ending of *Every Man Out* brought Macilente face to face with an actor playing the Queen. *Cynthia's Revels* staged the fantasy of a collaboration between a Jonsonian moralist and the Queen in the satiric cleansing of her court. In emphasising Elizabeth's innocence of those corruptions which Richard Martin and others of his circle were to attack in the parliament of October 1601 (see pp. 43–6), Jonson followed a convention adopted both in the Commons and in Donne's *Satire V*, written two or three years earlier:

> Greatest and fairest Empress, know you this?
> Alas, no more than Thames' calm head doth know
> Whose meads her arms drown, or whose corn o'er flow.          (ll. 28–30)

Less hypocrisy than necessary convention, the explanation was the traditional one of bad counsellors, used from *Magnificence* onwards, notably in that play which so interested the Essex conspirators, and Elizabeth herself, *Richard II*. The role of truth-telling satirist condemning the court but not the Queen was at best uneasy, however, and the move to Augustus' court allowed implicit criticism of Elizabeth, contrasted with the ideal prince, patron of poets, who encouraged freedom of speech (*Divus Augustus* LIV–LVI) and brought peace and prosperity after factionalism, rebellion and (in Rome, though not yet in England) civil war. Envy's discomfiture in the prologue as she finds she cannot 'apply' a play set in Rome proclaims Jonson's new-found freedom for his satire, and announces the beginning of the first serious programme of 'Augustanism' in English.

The importance of what Howard Erskine-Hill calls the 'Augustan Idea' in subsequent centuries clarifies the historical significance of *Poetaster*: transcending literary quarrels and oblique commentary on factionalism at Court, it makes a statement about the nature of poetry and its role in society that was to have far-reaching effects over the next two centuries.[32] The relationships between Horace, Virgil and Augustus that Jonson dramatises idealistically to make his statement have surprisingly strong historical sanction. Augustus' admiration for Horace, described in Suetonius' *Life* of Horace, is confirmed in the *Epistle* to Augustus (II.i); Bond invokes their relationship in his dedication to Prince Henry, whose father was welcomed as Britain's Augustus.[33] Jonson paraphrased Suetonius (not just Heinsius, his main source) in *Discoveries* 2613–18; Horace was 'a man so gratious, and in high favour with the Emperour, as *Augustus* often called him his wittie *Manling*, (for the littlenes of his stature;) and (if wee may trust Antiquity) had design'd him for a Secretary of Estate; and invited him to the P[a]lace, which he modestly praid off, and refus'd'. The secretaryship Augustus offered was less powerful than 'Secretary of Estate' suggests, but Jonson's exaggeration is significant in its desire to show how differently poets were valued in Augustan Rome, when '*Poetrie*, and the *Latin* Language were at the height' and when a poet like Horace was 'inwardly familiar with the censures of great men, that did discourse of these things daily amongst themselves' (*Discoveries* 2609–13).

Virgil's relationship with Augustus was as close as that of Horace; his First and Fourth *Eclogues* had both alluded to the then Octavian, and, according to the *Life* by Aelius Donatus (a probable source for Jonson) he read the *Georgics* to Augustus 'on the emperor's way back to Rome after the victory at Actium'. The third book promised an epic with Caesar at its centre (l. 20), and Augustus followed the composition of the *Aeneid* with the intense interest Jonson attributes to him in V.i.69–74:

> And Augustus, when he was away on his campaign against the Cantabriges, wrote begging the poet, in terms which mixed entreaty with good-natured menace, to send him . . . 'either the preliminary outline, or any specimen passage' that he liked. But it was only long afterwards, when the poem was substantially complete [cf. V.i.72–4] that Virgil would recite any of it to the emperor, and then three books only, the second, fourth and sixth—the last of these to the great distress of Octavia, who being present at the recitation is said to have fainted at the words referring to her son *tu Marcellus eris* . . . , and was only with difficulty revived.[34]

Jonson's Virgil is, however, almost too perfect to be a model for contemporary poets. Though Horace emphasises that Virgil's poetry is 'rammed with life' (V.i.136), and Tibullus that lines from it could be used to serve 'at any serious point' in one's life (V.i.122), he is a godlike figure (as he had been throughout the Middle Ages) whose mind cannot be painted by mere 'fleshly pencils' (i.e. brushes: V.i.115). Horace judges him

> of a rectified spirit,
> By many revolutions of discourse
> In his bright reason's influence refined
> From all the tartarous moods of common men,
> Bearing the nature and similitude
> Of a right heavenly body; most severe
> In fashion and collection of himself,
> And then as clear and confident as Jove.                    (V.i.100–7)

This supernatural clarity and confidence is evident in his role as judge, and in his language, which if it is not always as clear as claimed (see V.iii.341–8) is certainly confident, with an authority that is only partly dependent on Caesar's power. Peter Womack argues that in Jonson's three comical satires the unifying moral view, and the language of authority, can be validated only by the absolute monarch, who sanctions Crites, Virgil and Horace, and who transforms Macilente.[35] Here, though, Jonson goes out of his way to establish that Virgil ranks even higher than Augustus in the order of things, by placing him, as he reads his epic, above the *princeps*: it is, admittedly, Augustus himself who insists that he takes his place 'above best kings' (V.ii.27), but authority is vested in Virgil, as to a lesser extent in Horace, by his status as a great vatic poet whose relation to the stern ethical values of Rome, and Roman law, is that of the confident interpreter of a tradition. Augustus, the 'president' (V.i.39) in two senses, is here an enabler, an exemplary prince who encourages these values in the sun of his discerning rule.

Jonson takes minor liberties with Roman history in such matters as the age and friendship of his Roman poets (all the principal historical characters except Augustus and Julia were dead well before Ovid's banishment in AD 8). Nowhere, however, is he more selective than in portraying Augustus, avoiding intimations of sexual corruption (even Suetonius admits 'he gave himselfe overmuch to the deflowering of young maides'), and ignoring the evidence of Gibbon's 'subtle tyrant'. Jonson follows that humanist tradition exemplified by Sir Thomas Elyot, which saw Augustus as a 'most noble emperour . . . in whom reigned all nobilitie', a pattern for princes.[36] Tacitus' critical republican view, very probably known to Jonson in 1601, and used in *Sejanus* (1603), is never invoked. The most notable departure from Suetonius involves making Ovid, not Augustus, responsible for the 'dinner of the twelve gods'. This banquet features prominently in Suetonius' list of the emperor's vices (*Divus Augustus* LXX) and Jonson must have expected the

change to be noted, perhaps anticipating that his audience, following
Elyot, would remember the historical banquet as the turning point
in Augustus' career, teaching him frugality 'so would he be to all
men the general example of living' (III.xxii). Jonson, however,
makes Augustus over-react: even the wisest ruler can find that
passion 'everts' (overturns) his soul, and only courageous plain
speaking from wise counsellors, the 'learned heads' that he has
advanced (V.i.52–3), prevents him from rash action. This traditional role of the humanist counsellor, schooled in morality as in
eloquence, was close to Jonson's heart. He told Drummond that 'he
heth a minde to be a churchman, & so he might have favour to make
one Sermon to the King, he careth not what yrafter sould befall him,
for he would not flatter though he saw Death' (*Conversations* 330–2).
This was not entirely fantasy, as his presumably brief meeting in
Paris with Cardinal Duperron shows: Duperron, maker of popes and
adviser of kings, showed Jonson his 'free translations' of Virgil;
Jonson told him 'that they were naught' (*Conversations* 69–71). In
the *Panegyre* for the opening of James's first parliament, Themis
takes the king aside and lectures him on his responsibilities, and the
failings of his predecessors: 'And all so justly, as his eare was joy'd /
To heare the truth, from spight or flattery voyd' (ll. 92–3). Horace
shows the same 'free and wholesome sharpness' to Augustus, who is,
like James, wise enough to prefer it to flattery (V.i.94–6). Thus a
picture emerges of an ideal ruler, a strong Prince attentive to good
counsellors, for 'the good Counsellors to Princes are the best
instruments of a good Age. For though the *Prince* himselfe be of
most prompt inclination to all vertue: Yet the best *Pilots* have need
of *Mariners*, beside Saylēs, Anchor, and other Tackle' (*Discoveries*
1245–9).

## 6   The poet and the commonwealth

Apart from this direct role in government, Jonson's humanist poet
has an important formative influence on the commonwealth at large.
In *Poetaster* three types of genuine poet are distinguished. Ovid,
Tibullus, Gallus and Propertius are love poets whose art cannot
shape their society, except insofar as its eroticism may undermine
it. Virgil and Horace use poetry, as Augustus says, to

> so mould Rome and her monuments
> Within the liquid marble of her lines
> That they shall stand fresh and miraculous,
> Even when they mix with innovating dust.

In her sweet streams shall our brave Roman spirits
Chase and swim after death with their choice deeds
Shining on their white shoulders.                    (V.i.21–7)

Virgil, the 'master of the *Epick* poeme' (*New Inn* I.vi.134) stands
more aloof from the everyday world than 'Material Horace', whose
satires and epistles deal in plain language with the characteristically
Roman virtues and vices—moderation, frugality, duty, cowardice,
avarice, lust—enumerated by Bond. When he attempts heroic verse
'I feel defects in every faculty' (III.v.20). Characteristically, whereas
Ovid recites alone, behind his philistine father's back, and Virgil
reads in a formal, hieratic setting, Horace is first seen composing
while walking through Rome.[37] Jonson uses Horace's own words to
describe the honourable motivation of his art in the translation of
*Sat.* II.i that he added to *F*, and gives Virgil the task of justifying
the 'sharpness' of Horatian satire, which is 'forced out of a suffering
virtue / Oppressèd with the licence of the time' (V.iii.363–4). This
'wholesome sharp morality', born of 'modest anger', is essential
for the state: only when it grows from envy or malice is satire
irresponsible and a danger to society. Such malice is introduced in
Envy's prologue, exemplified in the 'poems' of Crispinus and
Demetrius, and evident in the 'sinister application' (V.iii.135) of
Horace's work. The importance of 'application' to Jonson, rather
than the historical Horace, is indicated by the number of times here
and in other plays he defends himself against 'wrestings, comments,
applications' (Ind. 24). Real dangers faced the Elizabethan satirist:
Horace had not been imprisoned for writing satire, as Jonson had
been in 1597, and was to be again in 1605.[38] It also springs from
misunderstanding the nature of true satire, which has 'a general
scope and purpose' that is reformative, but not 'particular' in terms
of attacking individuals for private revenge (V.iii.138–9). The
quotation from Martial in the 'Apologetical Dialogue', 'My books
have still been taught / To spare the persons and to speak the vices'
(ll. 71–2) may appear pure hypocrisy in a play which so clearly
attacks two individual writers, and (as Jonson admits in the 'Apologetical Dialogue', ll. 128–33) several identifiable actors. To some
extent the defence hinges on 'naming', as in Erasmus's *Epistola
Apologetica* from which Jonson copied into *Discoveries*: '*Whilst* I
name no persons, but deride follies; why should any man confesse,
or betray himselfe?' (2304–5). But, applied to *Poetaster*, this is a
complacent piece of evasion and the real defence is indicated the first
time the lines from Martial are quoted. Jonson adds them to his

version of Horace *Sat.* II.i (III.v.133–4), and follows with a more significant addition, that the man whose motives are honourable *can* 'tax in person a man fit to bear / Shame and reproach' (ll. 138–9), and the court will dissolve in laughter. Here Horace's poetry 'functions as the law should: in open court, it exposes and punishes the vices of men'.[39] In a society where lawyers are ignorant, greedy and malicious (I.ii.115–34), and exemplified by the tribune Lupus, it is the 'honest satyr' who exposes folly and vice.

### 7 Ovid

The play opens not, as might be expected, with Horace, or the poetaster of the title, Crispinus, but Ovid: this early introduction of another poet who is to be rejected has been seen as a confusing flaw,[40] but this is a misapprehension, based on the notion that the original audience saw a play called *Poetaster*, when in fact they saw a play called *The Arraignment* (Ind. 3). It would, in any case, have taken a dim-witted member of the audience to assume that Ovid was to be presented as a poetaster: the suffix indicates a fake, one who only partially resembles a poet, one of the few sins of which Ovid had never been accused. If, on the other hand, some had assumed that Ovid was the person to be arraigned, they would not have been entirely mistaken. But most of the audience, and Jonson's first readers, would probably have seen the opening as a graceful if double-edged tribute to Marlowe, whose translation Ovid is heard composing in the play's first words. These lines are from a banned edition published with John Davies's *Epigrams* (making it doubly familiar to an Inns audience) and thus constituted an open challenge to Elizabethan censorship.[41] They are appropriate to the memory of the recently-dead (1593) poet, and are valedictory in another sense, in that before the end of the play both Ovid himself and his English followers, of whom Marlowe loomed largest in 1601, are to be rejected. Marlowe's career, with its climb to friendships at Court, its rebellious unconventionality, and even its mysterious ending, may well have seemed to Jonson to have had much in common with that of Ovid. Certainly the sympathy embodied in the Marlowe allusion remains with Ovid throughout the play, even when his failings as man and poet are clarified. This is, though, always the Ovid of the 'banquet of sense' tradition, and Jonson makes him chairman of a 'feast of sense' in IV.v. His life and poetry are erotic, focused on individual gratification, not the social and moral issues Horace takes up, nor the heroic morality and historical sweep of Virgil. Neverthe-

less, Jonson saw Ovid as inspired, and shows him first as a young
poet assailed by philistinism and ignorance, seemingly continuing
the role of Lorenzo junior in the quarto of *Every Man In*. Unlike
Lorenzo, however, he does not stand up to his father—'I will be
anything, or study anything' (I.ii.102); but if this, and his duplicity
in keeping his poetry secret, are disturbing, his defence of poetry at
the end of I.ii. is unequivocally Jonsonian.

Misgivings deepen in I.iii, with the poet unable to control his gift
(ll. 8–9). Tibullus warns Ovid that his passion will make him lose
himself—as it does. He condones, as Tibullus does not, Propertius'
excessive grief and lack of stoical self-knowledge. By the end of the
scene he is firmly placed as a gifted but misguided young poet, lost
in a sensual 'labyrinth'. The banquet of the gods must be considered
in this context. It is preceded by the satire of Chloe's schooling in
courtly manners (IV.i), which is followed by Tibullus and Gallus
arriving to take the two women to that very Court for the banquet.
Even Cytheris is dubious about its 'fiction', and the poets' defence is
not convincing: Gallus' playful remark about 'the sacred breath of a
true poet' (IV.ii.32–3) only reminds us that this witty game involves
abuse of their 'divine spirits' (ll. 26–7). The occasion is also socially
dubious, with Chloe and Albius to be installed in 'honours equal';
Horace's brief appearance recalls a world of more securely based
values, before Tucca and Crispinus are added to the guest list,
despite Tibullus and Gallus having seen through them.

If this prelude apparently damns the banquet as, at best, misguided levity, Jonson denies us a simple judgement, and retains
sympathy for Ovid, by interpolating the scene between Lupus and
Histrio (IV.iv). If Lupus condemns the banquet, can we? His
ludicrous reaction is based on two objections: that 'these poets' are
profaning the gods (l. 16), which, since it is also Augustus' objection, must be taken seriously, and that the 'crown and sceptre'
involve rebellion. The latter point is certainly absurd, its echoes of
*Richard II* (see p. 42) implying that that too could only be seen as
seditious by the malicious or paranoid, the Lupuses of 1601.
The emphasis of the banquet is on 'licence', a licence partially
reminiscent of the Middle Temple Christmas revels, at which
*Poetaster* may well have been performed (see p. 29): Ovid presides
like a Lord of Misrule—Richard Martin's role—and what follows is,
on the part of Ovid, Julia and the courtier poets, a witty acting-out
of the banquet of the gods in the *Iliad*. It is hard, though, to accept
the claim that it is a *'feast of sense, / As free from scandal as offence'* (ll.

192–3), a sentiment Horace echoes in his judgement that it involved 'innocent mirth / And harmless pleasures, bred of noble wit' (IV.viii.12–13). This may be intended to show Horace's generosity of judgement, the fact that he is 'the worst accuser under heaven' (V.iii.170), but it is far from telling the whole story. The banquet may be innocent and harmless in that it is not treasonable, but the licence is specifically sensual, condoning adultery. Augustus, despite his own early indulgence in just such a banquet, had moved to strengthen ties of marriage, and stamp out such casual adultery by the *Lex Iulia* of 18 BC, which brought adultery within the criminal law. The fiction 'bred of noble wit' involves not just a general abuse of noble wit, therefore, but a specific challenge to his policies. The sensuality might have been emphasised by the acting, if it was still as described in a now-lost attack: 'Even in her maiesties chappel do these pretty upstart youthes profane the Lordes Day by the lascivious writhing of their tender limbs, and gorgeous decking of their apparell, in feigning bawdie fables gathered from the idolatrous heathen poets'.[42] 'Feigning bawdie fables' is not, for Jonson, the business of the poet, though it may have been for Ovid and Marlowe: the Tudor moralist's phrase echoes those of Jonson's favourite Latin moralists, Seneca and Cicero, who both complained of Homer and other poets (including Horace) showing the gods indulging in human vices. More to the point here, Quintilian had hinted that Ovid did the same thing, being 'lascivus' in his treatment of the heroic.[43] As Katharine Maus points out, Jonson consistently equates Ovidian metamorphosis with vice (p. 90), a highly problematic attitude for a dramatist, dependent on the metamorphoses of actors, to take up. That Tucca, the habitual corrupter of mythology, should be so close to Ovid emphasises his culpability, as does the descent into drunken stupor, with the liberated senses so dulled that they have to be revived by song.

The banquet scene, then, finally places Ovid outside of the true Augustan tradition, which has no place for the celebration of the erotic, or for the uncertainties of metamorphosis, and outside Augustus' own moral laws. Augustus' reaction is in this sense historically plausible: Ovid and Julia *were* banished (in Ovid's case, 'relegated'), and this offers a dramatically neat explanation. Even Augusus' over-reaction has a 'historical' basis: from Suetonius onwards, his bitterness at his family's licentiousness is emphasised; he 'even thought of putting [Julia] to death' (*Divus Augustus* LXV), the source of his wild threat in IV.vi.12–13.

Augustus' two speeches after his passion has cooled (IV.vi.30–58, and 61–77) clarify matters, justifying the treatment of Ovid on the grounds that he lacks that wider 'knowledge' of his civic and moral obligations, and 'virtue' in general, that Horace too deems necessary for the poet. Quoting Seneca on liberality and worthiness (as he quoted him on his gratitude to Martin), Jonson makes Augustus relate virtue to 'knowledge'. Mockery of the gods is mockery of the poet's obligations. With a nice irony, Jonson uses Ovid's own description of the poet's inspiration in Caesar's speech (see IV.vi.33n). Inspiration notwithstanding, Ovid's 'knowledge is mere ignorance' (l. 69): Augustus 'will prefer for knowledge none but such / As rule their lives by it' (ll. 73–4), stoical poets like Horace and Virgil who can 'becalm / All sea of humour with the marble trident / Of their strong spirits' (ll. 74–6). One cannot be a 'good poet without first being a good man' (*Volpone*, Epistle, ll. 21–2).

In scenes which invoke *Tristia* and *Romeo and Juliet*, Ovid's farewell to Julia is the occasion for the rejection of romantic comedy and tragedy from Jonson's Augustan poetic. These scenes have something in common with the *recusatio*: serious parody exploits the emotions of Ovidian romance with considerable sympathy even as it implicitly criticises them. Ovid has apparently rejected the stoic values described by Augustus, his obstinacy in this respect perhaps suggested by a literary judgement made by the elder Seneca that 'he was well aware of his faults—and enjoyed them' (*Controversiae* II.ii.12). He sees the Court (still dissociated in its vices from the monarch) as a magic circle: outside it, all is meaningless; within, virtue and vice become relative, validated by the Court, not by any absolute. He dissuades Julia from suicide by the dubious argument that love belongs only to flesh and blood 'whose quintessence is sense' (IV.x.38), and that physical beauty is more 'plausible' (gratifying) 'Than spiritual beauty can be to the spirit' (40–1). Nevertheless, Julia is given a powerful defence of Ovid's 'virtue' (a good example of the deluding 'witchcraft' of love) and an equally powerful attack on her father's 'tyranny' over both Ovid and her own mind. Anne Barton (p. 84) has doubts about Julia and Ovid's 'to-ing and fro-ing' in this scene, since Jonson uses such indecisiveness elsewhere (as by Albius in II.i) for comic effect. These doubts are partially answered by echoes of Juliet's coming and going in *Romeo and Juliet* II.i, and more tellingly by the echoes of Ovid's indecision in leaving his wife: 'Thrice I touched the threshold, thrice did something call me back' (*Tristia* I.iii.55–6). The sentiments of this scene could have been rendered absurd by the boy actors parodying adult romantic drama, but there is surely more sympathy than mockery in Julia's speeches in particular. The lovers are not let off the hook, however: the language they are given is dominated by the 'illusion' of love (IV.x.101) and its grandiose imagery distorts their vision of the world. Ovid's final Marlovian/Chapmanesque words are those of the defiant, irredeemably sensual lover: 'The truest wisdom silly men can have / Is dotage on the follies of their flesh' (IV.x.108–9).

In turning his back on Ovid, Jonson was making a powerful assertion of the need to break from the fashionable Ovidian poetry and drama of the years immediately preceding *Poetaster*. If the audience were invited to identify Ovid primarily with Marlowe (to whom Jonson owed a great deal more than is always recognised), many would also have shared Francis Meres's view that 'the sweete wittie soule of *Ovid* liues in mellifluous & hony-tongued *Shakespeare*, witnes his *Venus* and *Adonis*, his *Lucrece*, his sugred Sonnets among his priuate friends, &c'.[44] Lesser poets—among them Marston in *Pigmalion's Image*, despite his disavowal—had followed Marlowe and Shakespeare in writing Ovidian narrative poems which exploited the erotic freedom sanctioned by the form, while Donne had turned to the *Amores* as a model for his early elegies. But Jonson's friend Chapman, both in his continuation of *Hero and Leander* (1598) and in the puzzling *Ovid's Banquet of Sense* (1595), had turned away from this tradition, and Jonson probably had the latter poem especially in mind when he wrote the banquet scene in *Poetaster*.[45] The Ovid being rejected is as much the Ovid of the 1590s in England as the historical Ovid of Augustan Rome. If a new English Augustanism is to be established through the imitation of the great poets of classical Rome, the one who has been most influential for the previous decade has to be excluded as a model.

## 8  Satire and calumny

The War of the Theatres was in part a debate about the proper nature of satire and its motivation. Horatian satire, in Jonson's version, springs from an acute moral sensibility that must speak out (cf. III.v.43–9, 85–9); it is the natural expression of the man of 'merit', (V.iii.351, 610) whose integrity cannot be compromised. Jonson draws a powerful distinction between this and false satire which comes from the 'grosser spirit', whose 'bleared and offended sense' (V.iii.345–6) cannot recognise such merit, and so calumniates it out of spite and envy. After *poet* and its derivatives (which occur fifty-five times), the key words in *Poetaster* are, in fact, *envy*, *spite*, *malice* and *detraction* on the one hand (together, they and their derivatives occur forty times in the play) and *merit* (seventeen times, mostly associated with Virgil and Horace) on the other. Merit is, at this stage in Jonson's career, a matter of assertion rather than achievement (it is important throughout *Poetaster* to recall that he is a relative newcomer). It is also complacently self-sustaining, since not to recognise it is not to have it. Dekker objected in *Satiromastix* to the arrogance of Jonson's high moral claims:

> *Thy pride and scorne made her* [his muse] *turne Saterist,*
> *And not her love to vertue* (as thou Preachest).           (V.ii.216–17)

but part of Jonson's successful strategy in linking his stance to Horace's is to gain access to the high ground in this dispute: by avoiding, outside of the 'Apologetical Dialogue', the harsher language of Juvenalian satire, Jonson attempts to avoid the moral questions that, for Renaissance theorists, such satire provoked. The common distinction between Horatian and Juvenalian satire is neatly encapsulated in Lambinus's edition of Horace. His annotation of the opening lines of *Sat.* II.i. says that satire should be 'courtly and urbane', 'it should point out and admonish the morals and vices of mankind through play and jest, not harshly, not solemnly, not insolently, abusively, irascibly, as do Persius and Juvenal'.[46] Not only is the motivation of such satire suspect, pandering to its readers' more disreputable appetites, it is simply bad form to be so obviously angry. The stance of Macilente, even of Asper and Crites, had been much closer to Juvenal's, as had the authorial voice of Marston's satire: throughout *Poetaster*, Jonson tries to capture a Horatian urbanity, emphasising Horace's restraint when confronted with the nightmarish importunacy of Crispinus, and his unwillingness to 'accuse' Crispinus and Demetrius in V.iii. Such un-Jonsonian temperance has led some to see Horace as ineffectual, less clearly the author's mouthpiece than one might expect,[47] but it is here a positive attribute, the measured urbanity of a satirist whose 'sharpness' only emerges when 'forced out of a suffering virtue'. The return to a more Juvenalian anger and disgust in the 'Apologetical Dialogue' brings with it a sombre moral intensity that is rarely evident in the play itself. Only in the moment when Horace turns on Demetrius is the tone of the Dialogue anticipated:

And why, thou motley gull, why should they fear? . . .
Now thou curl'st up, thou poor and nasty snake,
And shrink'st thy pois'nous head into thy bosom.
Out viper, thou that eat'st thy parents, hence.
Rather such specklèd creatures as thyself
Should be eschewed and shunned: such as will bite
And gnaw their absent friends.                    (V.iii.316–24)

Compared with the image of Marston and Dekker as 'vile
ibids . . . That make their mouths their clysters, and still purge /
From their hot entrails' ('Apologetical Dialogue', ll. 206–8), however, Horace's bitter serpent imagery is positively restrained. It
emphasises how much Demetrius, in particular, is falsely motivated
by pure envy and malice. He and Crispinus are far from being even
Juvenalian satirists, and consequently their works are libels (another
word that echoes through *Poetaster*), a serious crime in Roman law,
originally punished by execution.

## 9   Poetasters and language

The intrusion of the poetasters with Lupus, Tucca and Histrio paves
the way for Jonson's Lucianic denouement by uniting Crispinus and
Demetrius with the enemies of poetry. Lupus has destroyed Ovid
with Histrio's help: now he seeks, with the poetasters' support, to do
the same to Horace. There is ironic symbolism in their cutting off
Virgil in full flow: not only does he represent poetry at its most
exalted but he has been reading about the attack by the giants on the
gods, interpreted in the Renaissance as an allegory of barbarism's
attack on learning. The passage deals with the monster 'fame', close
companion of envy and detraction (see V.ii.75n), and with Dido's
misuse of language: 'She calls this wedlock, and with that fair name /
Covers her fault' (V.ii.72–3). Such verbal duplicity is serious
because language and morality are so closely related that

> *There* cannot be one colour of the mind; an other of the wit. If the mind be
> staid, grave, and compos'd, the wit is so; that vitiated, the other is blowne,
> and deflowr'd. . . . Wheresoever, manners, and fashions are corrupted,
> Language is. It imitates the publicke riot. The excesse of Feasts, and
> apparell, are the notes of a sick State; and the wantonnesse of language, of
> a sick mind.                                    (*Discoveries* 948–58)

This translates Seneca, whose proverbial 'Man's speech is just like
his life' was a cornerstone of Jonson's credo. In the same passage,
Seneca explains how the 'hunt for novelties in speech' grows in 'the

mind [that] has acquired the habit of scorning the usual things of life; now it summons and displays obsolete and old-fashioned words; now it coins even unknown words or misshapes them; and now a bold and frequent metaphorical usage is made a special feature of style' (*Ep.* CXIV, 3, 11). The relationship of *Poetaster* to the whole passage is obvious, and Jonson's adoption of its values is a good example of how thoroughly he assimilated the 'Roman frame of mind'. His friend and 'loving Father' John Florio[48] related the demand for simplicity and clarity explicitly to Augustus in the Preface to his translation of Montaigne (1603): '*If to write obscurely be perplexedly offensive, as* Augustus *well judged . . .*'. Tucca's language, with its vaunting but misdirected inventiveness and its use of inappropriate mythological names, is the note 'of a sicke minde', as perhaps is his stutter (I.ii.178–9).[49] Until the final act, his is the dominant voice of corruption but, as Seneca says, the gratuitous coining of words is another sign of moral sickness, and, for the final purging of society's ills, it is Crispinus, the inventor and distorter of words, who must be ritually purged.

Though the source for the vomiting of words is Lucian's *Lexiphanes*, and perhaps the memory of a lost play by Lyly, staged when Jonson was sixteen or seventeen (see p. 39), Seneca is again suggestive in associating linguistic with physical dissipation. For Jonson physical and mental over-indulgence have a more than metaphorical relationship. Horace is a 'well-digested' man; it is Crispinus who suffers from 'inflation', pseudo-psychological terms that retain a physical dimension, as is shown when Crispinus brings up a group of 'Terrible windy words', synonyms for flatulence, the 'gross fumes' of which were still associated with psychological disorder (see V.iii.490–1). In *The Case is Altered* Juniper's words are similarly 'forc't. As though they were pumpt out on's belly' (I.iv.19): as 'Gut's' belly actually turns food into lust (*Ep.* CXVIII), Crispinus' turns it into neologisms and vulgarisms. The linkage is analogous to that between sexual indulgence and food in the fantasies of Volpone and Mammon. The vomited words are dealt with in detail in the notes to V.iii.269–86, 460–515; not all are Marston's: some are coined by Jonson himself to suggest the flatulence of Marston's style, and to parody the process by which his neologisms were invented; some come from Harvey (some of whose vocabulary is used by Juniper, Tucca's and Crispinus' predecessor as a misuser of words) and one or two from Shakespeare.[50]

The mention of Harvey, and of Lyly's lost contribution to the

Marprelate war (in which he, Nashe and others had defended the established church against the Puritan attacks of 'Martin Marprelate'), are reminders that the battle over 'inkhorn terms' was not new: before Nashe and Harvey had attacked each other over their use in the 1590s (in a battle that, like those earlier ones between humanist scholars of the fifteenth and earlier sixteenth centuries, provided another sanctioning model for the Poetomachia), the rhetoricians Wilson and Puttenham had both warned against 'straunge ynkehorne termes', Wilson's *Arte of Rhetorique* (1553) providing a parody inkhorn letter, and Puttenham's *Arte of English Poesie* (1589, but written earlier) doggedly searching for English equivalents to words like 'audacious' and 'theatre', and providing new 'English' paraphrases (such as 'cooko-spel' for *epizeuxis*) for the Greek terminology of rhetoric.[51] In these debates, the need for foreign, usually Latin, loanwords to fill a lexical gap, especially in the sciences, was always admitted. Translation, both of the classics and the Bible, made the need more urgent: prefaces to the Catholic New Testament of 1582 (which the convert Jonson may have read in the late 1590s) and to the Authorised Version of 1611 both defended the use of Latin and Hebrew words. Florio extended this to Montaigne's French in the spirited introduction to his translation of the *Essais*; Jonson's annotated copies of both Puttenham's and Florio's books are now in the British Library (McPherson, 147, 129). What was generally condemned was the 'peevish affectation' (Puttenham) which introduced what Jonson calls 'wild, outlandish terms' (V.iii.537) where a good native word was available, or the almost opposite violation of decorum which brought words like 'chilblained', 'clumsy' and 'barmy' into the literary lexicon (see V.iii.278–80 and notes). Seneca's views probably weighed heaviest with Jonson, but he was on strong humanist ground in attacking Marston's style in these terms (humanist scholars like Cheke and Ascham being prominent in the anti-inkhorn movement), and Marston's vocabulary, in both the verse satires and the plays, presented an obvious target, which he exploited brilliantly in the devastatingly accurate parody of V.iii.269–86. He was not, however, being merely reactionary, nor even over-authoritarian. King notes (p. 62) that most of the 'Crispinisms still seem wrong to us': 'Jonson's satire . . . shows how deeply in touch he was with the fundamental tendency of English style. That satire of Crispinus is not a mere episode in the Stage Quarrel: it is one of the important steps towards the establishment of standard literary English.'

## 2   DATE AND CONTEXT

### *1   Date*

*Poetaster* has usually been dated in spring or summer 1601,[52] but it
is more likely that Jonson began his 'fifteen weeks' work (cf. Ind.
14–15) in summer with a view to an autumn opening. The limits
are fixed by the entry of *Satiromastix*, which post dates it, in the
Stationers' Register on 11 November 1601 and, more tentatively, by
a probable Court performance of *Cynthia's Revels* in the previous
January or February (see n. 72). *Satiromastix* may have been entered
after it had been on stage for a relatively short time, or it may have
been a 'blocking entry' made by the Chamberlain's Men while
Dekker's play was still new because (most unusually) it was due to
be acted by the Paul's Boys also.[53] Simpson believed a reference to
the winter 'proved' *Poetaster* was first performed in spring 1601
(*H&S*, IX, 189), but this is by no means certain. Histrio speaks as if
it is *currently* winter, with Jonson possibly thinking as he wrote of a
play running once-weekly through the Michaelmas/winter season of
1601–2: 'O, it will get us a huge deal of money captain, and we have
need on't, for this winter has made us all poorer than so many
starved snakes. Nobody *comes* at us' (III.iv.326–8; my italics). The
spring/summer dating also conflicts with an apparent allusion noted
in the same edition twenty-five years earlier (*H&S*, I, 29) to
Weever's *The Whipping of the Satire* (entered 14 August 1601).[54]
Weever attacks Marston, Guilpin and Jonson as 'the Satirist, the
Epigrammatist, and Humorist'; in *Poetaster* Tucca swears 'I'll have
the slave whipped one of these days for his satires and his humours,
by one cashiered clerk or another' (IV.iii.117–8). Possibly here, as
probably in V.iii.155, 592, and 'Apologetical Dialogue', l. 42,
Jonson refers only to Marston's *Scourge*, or anticipates the whipping
Dekker was to give him in *Satiromastix* V.ii.241–5; but the specificity
with which Tucca echoes Weever's terms suggests otherwise. These
allusions to whipping come relatively late in the text: if the play was
nearing completion after mid-August, then Histrio's reference is to
the winter of 1601–2, which must certainly also be the winter
referred to in the epilogue to *Satiromastix* (ll. 27–8). A series of
performances over the Michaelmas/winter season of 1601–2 would
explain how the 'Apologetical Dialogue' could have been written
after *Satiromastix* which in its current form it evidently was, since it
takes up at least one of Dekker's specific accusations (ll. 180–1; cf.

*Satiromastix* V.ii.201–3), and yet be acted (if only once) at the end of a production of *Poetaster*. Chambers noted this, and suggested it was spoken in December, 'between the two S.R. entries' (i.e. of *Satiromastix* in November and of *Poetaster* on 21 December 1601: *ES*, III, 366). An earlier production must remain a possibility, but if the play was produced in spring 1601, it would have been late spring: Lent closure is likely to have been enforced in the aftermath of Essex's execution (Lent ran from 25 February to 4 April, and the Children of the Chapel were included in a Lenten prohibition of 11 March, 1601: Chambers, *ES*, IV, 332). In any case, the allusions to the Essex rebellion (see pp. 40–4) imply that Jonson's fifteen weeks' work did not begin until after February, pointing to completion in early June. Since the Inns' long vacation (and the close of the London 'season' generally) ran from the end of Trinity Term in late May or early June till late September, when Michaelmas Term began, this would have been a bad time to open a play. Many of the Blackfriars audience left London during the summer, and it is highly probable that the indoor theatres closed for much of this time (see p. 40). A new production was much more likely in late September or October: this date would not only accommodate the reply to *Satiromastix* in the 'Apologetical Dialogue', and make better sense of Histrio's use of the present tense in 'nobody comes at us': it would coincide suggestively with Marston's unexplained absence from his rooms in the Middle Temple, for which he was fined and expelled on 14 October. Satire on Marston would also have made *Poetaster* a topical play for the Middle Temple Revels of Christmas 1601/2; satire on their own members was by no means unknown in the Revels under Richard Martin, as John Davies, hitherto his great friend, found to his cost in the Revels of 1597–8.[55] That *Poetaster* may have been written with an eye to those revels, rather than the usual Court performance at Christmas, is also suggested by the satire on the law, on Ovid as an Elizabethan law student (see esp. I.i.5–6), and, of course, by the 'arraignment' in V.iii. Other strong reasons for linking the play with the Middle Temple are given below (pp. 44–7). Evidence for a performance there is inevitably circumstantial, but it is worth adding that, as the leader of the revels, the dedicatee of *Poetaster*, Richard Martin, would have been the natural ambassador to Popham to apologise for the play's satire, and that *Twelfth Night*, to which, it is argued below (pp. 36–8), *Poetaster* responds, was performed at those same revels, on 2 February 1602.[56]

## 2  The War of the Theatres

'There was for a while', Rosencrantz tells Hamlet, 'no money bid for argument, unless the poet and the player went to cuffs in the question' (*Hamlet* II.ii.354–6), and *Poetaster* cannot be understood unless it is placed in the wider context of what Dekker called '*that terrible* Poetomachia, *lately commenc'd betweene* Horace the second, *and a band of leane-witted* Poetasters' (*Satiromastix*, '*To the World*', ll. 7–9). That the *ad hominem*, lampooning aspect of *Poetaster* was, contrary to the wishes of many twentieth-century critics, central to its conception is confirmed by Jonson's recollection of it nearly twenty years later when he told Drummond in 1619 that 'he had many quarrells with Marston beat him & took his Pistol from him, wrote his Poetaster on him the beginning of ym [them] were that Marston represented him jn the stage' (*Conversations*, *H&S*, I, 140, ll. 284–6). A note by Drummond in his copy of *F* confirms this: against *Ep*. LXVIII which begins 'Playwright, convict of public wrongs to men, / Takes private beatings, and begins again', he wrote 'Marstone once beaten by the author'.[57] The quarrel was thus serious, lasted for some time ('beginning' and 'begins again') and became violent at at least one point: it was not purely a matter of gaining publicity for rival theatrical companies, or a good-humoured 'flyting'. The bitter 'Apologetical Dialogue' confirms this, referring again to Jonson's representation on the stage, speaking of 'their manners that provoked me then' ('To the Reader', ll. 8–9), of 'black vomit' (24), of the actors who presented the plays of his 'whippers' as 'servile apes' (43), of 'excrement' and 'base filth' motivated by hunger, malice or ignorance (81).

The origins of the War are obscure. Jonson's statement that 'three years / They did provoke me with their petulant styles / On every stage' ('Apologetical Dialogue', ll. 83–5), if written in 1601,[58] takes the beginnings of the quarrel back to 1598. Marston, then twenty-two, had been a member of the Middle Temple for six years, and that year published his first collections, *The Metamorphosis of Pigmalions Image. And Certaine Satyrs* (entered 27 May) and *The Scourge of Villanie* (entered 8 September). He was prolific and, as will be seen, combative, but nothing is known from that year which Jonson could have construed as a provocation on the stage. Jonson, twenty-six in 1598, had been a writer and actor for Henslowe in 1597 and 1598, and had had *Every Man in His Humour* performed by the Chamberlain's Men in September 1598. He too was combative: on 22 September that year he fought and killed an ex-colleague, Gabriel

Spencer, one of Henslowe's actors. In prison awaiting trial, and fearing the death sentence, he converted to Roman Catholicism; he was allowed to plead 'benefit of clergy' (by proving that he could read Latin). He was branded and released, but with his goods confiscated, on 6 October. Poverty thus became an urgent problem; by January 1599 he was back in jail, for debt, but was free by March/April, when his second son, Joseph, was conceived. He seems, at what must have been a desperate period for him, to have returned briefly to his other trade of bricklaying.[59]

The order of 1 June 1599 commanding that 'noe *Satyres* or *Epigrams* be printed hereafter' (Arber, *SR*, III, 677–8) blocked Marston's career as a satirical poet. By September 1599 a series of entries in Henslowe's *Diary* (p. 124) shows that 'mr. maxton the new poete' (interlined with caret 'mr. mastone') was probably collaborating with Jonson, Dekker and Chettle on a play for Henslowe.[60] Slightly later in 1599 *Every Man out of His Humour* was performed at the Globe: it can be dated by the folio title-page, by references (III.iv.33 and V.vi.79) to *Julius Caesar* (performed September 21 1599) and to 'this yeere of Iubile [i.e. 1600], comming on' (II.iii.243). In it Marston's language in *Scourge* and his first play *Histriomastix* is satirised as 'fustian', with *Histriomastix* named. *Histriomastix* is the first extant play in which Marston could have 'represented [Jonson] in the stage'. The evidence for its dating, and even for its authorship, is complex and uncertain, but it was probably written for a Michaelmas re-opening of the Paul's Boys, whose premises were available from autumn 1599, its first performances only just preceding *Every Man Out*.[61] Marston was closely associated with the Paul's Boys from that date, writing his two *Antonio* plays, *Jack Drum's Entertainment* and *What You Will* for them in 1599–1601; in late 1601 or early 1602 they also performed *Satiromastix*, of which Marston was an aider and abetter but probably not a writer. Jonson's 'three years' thus probably exaggerates the duration of the attacks on him, and hence his patience: 'two years they did provoke me' would not strike the right note of dignified forbearance. The presumed collaboration for Henslowe suggests the quarrel began in or after September 1599, either through two aggressive personalities working closely together, or in the aftermath of the relatively mild exchange in *Histriomastix* and *Every Man Out*.

To describe the satire in *Histriomastix* as mild is, however, to beg the question: does the scholar-poet Chrisoganus 'represent' Jonson, and if he does, is this lampoon or eulogy? Chrisoganus is not a consistent caricature of Jonson, but then scarcely any representations in the Poetomachia before *Poetaster* and *Satiromastix* are. He is, though, a 'translating-scholler' who 'can make / A stabbing *Satir*, or an *Epigram*' (Wood, III, 258). If one adds that he is a stoic moralist and a dramatist who, despite his poverty, writes slowly, and looks down on the actors and the 'common sort / Of thickskin'd auditors' as opposed to the 'hearings of judiciall eares' and nevertheless charges £10 for a play (273) the picture seems close enough. Marston probably took the name from the epigram '*Of Chrysogonus*' in his cousin Everard Guilpin's *Skialetheia* (entered September 1598). Guilpin seems to aim at Jonson as 'Chrisogonus', not so much 'golden born' as 'golden faced' (cf. *Satiromastix* I.ii.285, 320, 367–8) and making 'villanous faces' of the kind alluded to in *Satiromastix* (see e.g. III.i.55, 255; IV.iii.92–9; V.ii.265, 300). But even when read with Guilpin's epigram in mind, Marston's portrait is not obviously hostile: some of Chrisoganus' speeches are unequivocally noble (e.g. pp. 288, 289), and at times he could represent Marston himself. This in itself, however, might have been enough to anger Jonson, the implied solidarity seeming to claim too much for Marston (see also 'Apologetical Dialogue', ll. 80–3 and note). There is, moreover, always a disturbing element in mimicry, even when flattering; as Anne Barton points out it attacks the 'freedom and individuality of the original' (p. 60). Much depends on how the part was played, especially by a boy actor whose incongruity in the part may, intentionally or not, have intensified the element of parody.

Jonson replied mildly in *Every Man Out*, glancing at Marston in Puntarvolo's greeting to Carlo Buffone, 'how doest thou, thou grand scourge; or second *untrusse* of the time?',[62] and giving Clove some of Marston's language. Clove's fustian consists largely of words of a pretentiously philosophical or scientific nature, joined together to make nonsense. Such fustian was a staple of Inns of Court revels, signalling how much the 'comicall satyres' with their use of legal terminology and judgement scenes, are aimed at an Inns audience.[63] Dekker later warned Jonson 'not to bumbast out a new Play, with the olde lynings of Iestes, stolne from the Temples Reuels' (*Satiromastix* V.ii.295–6). Clove's fustian is also the first sign in the Poetomachia of a highly developed interest in the use and misuse of words. Like references to clothing—Jonson/Horace's black perpetuana, Marston/Crispinus' velvet—but far more fundamentally, neologisms, affectations and catachreses run through subsequent plays, culminating in Crispinus' vomiting of Marstonisms in *Poet-aster*. In an age of new coinings and new meanings for old words this comes as no surprise: a word like 'element', unremarkable to a modern reader, still had sufficient novelty in its figurative use (see *OED*, *sb*. 12) for Feste, the 'corrupter of words', to mock Jonson's alleged abuse of it (*Twelfth Night* III.i.36, 58–9) as Dekker does in *Satiromastix* (I.ii.187 and V.ii.327).[64]

*Jack Drum's Entertainment* (1600) is more aggressive.[65] As with *Histriomastix*, there is scepticism about how far it contains, in Brabant senior, a caricature of Jonson. Brabant is unlike Jonson in being a rich man who 'will not stick to spend some 20. pound / To grope a gull' (Wood, III, 190), but to argue that this discrepancy means that Brabant has nothing to do with Jonson is to demand point by point correspondence between caricature and target of a very literal kind. Critics from Campbell on have emphasised that characters in these plays are types, not satirical versions of actual persons, but the truth is that they are both: Brabant Senior is the type of 'a satirist who misconceives his critical function' (Campbell, p. 163); but he is a satirist who is described as Jonson/Horace is in *Satiromastix* I.ii.320 as a 'gull-groper'. His first words are 'You shall see his humour' (191), while his second speech invites Planet to 'observe' a gull (192). Jonson had used 'observe' in *Every Man Out*, and his comic strategy had been criticised as mere 'observation' (cf. *Poetaster* IV.iii.104–7). He deflected the charge in the Induction to *Cynthia's Revels* (l. 183) and in *Poetaster* associates observation with Crispinus, who will 'observe, till I turn myself to nothing but obser-vation' (II.i.161–2). On Brabant Senior's next entrance he again begins with 'observe', but this time stresses 'compliment' (209), which also occurs in *Every Man Out*. Jonson again dissociates him-self from it in *Poetaster*, giving it to Envy (Ind. 20), Crispinus (II.ii.209), Tucca (III.iv.84) and Cytheris (IV.i.27–8).[66] Brabant Senior's language, then, is Jonson's, enough in itself to make the identification clear; Marston intensified the quarrel, however, by ridiculing Brabant as 'The Prince of Fooles, unequald Ideot' with a 'perpetuall grin' (190), lampooning the facial contortions Guilpin's epigram and *Satiromastix* also mock. Brabant is as dismissive of contemporary poets as Jonson talking to Drummond nearly twenty years later: 'they are all Apes & gulls, / Vile imitating spirits, dry heathy Turffes' (221). He explicitly attacks the Paul's Boys, whose plays 'do not sute the humorous ages backs' (234); Planet, Marston's commentator, condemns him as a 'bumbaste' wit, 'puft up with

arrogant conceit' (229). It is disingenuous to argue that many in an
essentially *coterie* audience in 1600 would not have 'applied' the
character to Jonson, who is condemned for just such arrogance in
*Satiromastix* (e.g. V.ii.216–22). Brabant is finally humiliated by
cuckolding himself, introducing his wife to an intended gull as a
'loose lascivious Curtezan' (222). Jonson told Drummond, in a
passage immediately following the account of his quarrel with
Marston, that 'a man made his own wyfe to Court him, whom he
enjoyed two yeares erre he knew of it' (*Conversations* 290–1). This
passage begins 'In his youth given to Venerie' (*Conversations* 287),
referring back to before 1600. It is hard to believe this is coincidence,
and that because the roles are reversed in the play and the time
shorter, the episode, and the whole character of Brabant, bear 'no
relation to the historical Jonson'.[67]

Dekker and Marston both believed that the shapeless and com-
placent *Cynthia's Revels* took up the 'particular and private' quarrel.
In *Satiromastix* Dekker quotes Crites' description of Hedon and
Anaides in *Cynthia's Revels*, making Horace apply the words to
Crispinus and Demetrius, that is, to Marston and himself: 'The one
a light voluptuous Reueler, / The other, a strange arrogating puffe, /
Both impudent, and arrogant enough' (*Satiromastix* I.ii.163–5; cf.
*Cynthia's Revels* III.iii.25–7). It seems 'inconceivable that Dekker
should be mistaken' (Small, p. 38), but his claim has been disputed.[68]
As in *Jack Drum's Entertainment*, confusion arises where a satirical
type is given some of the attributes of a historical figure, but is not
wholly consistent. Neither character is a realistic portrait of Marston
or Dekker, indeed neither is a literary figure, and without their
evidence any identification would be very tenuous; but a single
mannerism or article of dress would have been enough to turn
generic type into caricature, and internal support for the identifications comes in Hedon's promise to 'speake all the venome I can
of him [Crites]; and poyson his reputation' (III.ii.46–7), while
Anaides says he will 'giue out, all he does is dictated from other
men ... and that I know the time, and place where he stole it'
(III.ii.60–2), anticipating *Poetaster*'s 'devised' abuse of Horace and
the accusation of plagiarism (III.iv.322–38, IV.iii.116–28, and
V.iii.304–7). Crites, arguably too idealised to be a self-portrait even
of Jonson, nevertheless strongly resembles him: his 'poore coate' is
specifically the perpetuana mocked in *Satiromastix* IV.iii.235, and
'he smells all lamp-oyle, with studying by candle-light' (III.ii.11–12),

as Lampatho Doria does in *What You Will*, and as Jonson presents himself in *Poetaster* ('Apologetical Dialogue', 199–200).

*What You Will*[69] shows that Marston also perceived *Cynthia's Revels* as a further attack. He too parodies Crites' speech in *Cynthia's Revels* III.iii.18–31 (see Wood, II, 249–50), and answers the play in some detail. The elaborate intertextuality this involves signals yet another escalation of hostilities by Marston. The quarrel had only been incidental in their previous work, but in *What You Will* Lampatho Doria (the fool who smells of the lamp) is onstage for almost half the play. The Induction attacks Jonson's scorn of adverse criticism (232), and Lampatho is a 'ragg'd Satyrist' motivated by 'malice, Enuie, grinning spight' (249), and, of course, he wears black (246). He is a scholar 'Devote to mouldy customs of hoary eld' (246), and, like Horace in *Satiromastix*, has a simple-minded admirer, Simplicius Faber, who may be a caricature of John Weever.[70] When Simplicius praises his verses he responds, as in the Epilogue to *Cynthia's Revels*: 'faith 'tis good'. Lampatho is also a backbiter, a hypocrite who will fawn on a patron and then ridicule him, a recurrent charge against Jonson in *Satiromastix* (see esp. IV.i.61–3, V.ii.317–21).

*What You Will* suggests that the moral vision and motivation of the poor scholar—Asper, Macilente, Crites—who has been Jonson's satiric *persona* is distorted by his poverty and status. Marston's gentility, contrasting with Jonson's 'yeoman' status, is another recurrent theme of the War.[71] Marston offers an alternative satiric stance, that of the *dégagé* (if hardly urbane) gentleman, Quadratus, who splendidly defends '*Phantasticknesse*', condemned in *Cynthia's Revels* (e.g. Palinode, l. 5), as a function 'Even of the bright immortal part of man' (250). There is a reference, poignant in view of what is to come, to Jonson's objections to Marston's neologisms:

> Qua. A *foutra* for thy hand, thy heart, thy braine,
>   Thy hate, thy malice, Envie, grinning spight!
>   Shall a free-borne that holdes *Antypathy*——
> Lam. *Antypathy*?
> Qua. I *Antypathy*,
>   A native hate unto the curse of man. (249)

The first *OED* example, from Holland's *Pliny* (also 1601), shows it was then still an 'outlandish' word, 'which the Greeks call antipathie'. In a still more direct reference to the Poetomachia, Quadratus in-

sults Lampatho's Muse by soaking a poem in wine. Lampatho's response—'Ile be reveng'd'—is answered 'How pree-thee? in a play?'
(278). Lampatho's play is a comedy, *Temperance*, of which the Duke
not unreasonably asks 'What sot elects that subject for the Court?'
(290). It is, more or less, just what Jonson had offered the Court in
*Cynthia's Revels*, an ill-judged play to give there at any time,
but positively quixotic if, as is possible, it was performed on
Quinquagesima Sunday, three days before Essex's execution.[72] It
was probably one of the plays 'misse-likt at Court', at which Horace/
Jonson has to swear not to 'cry Mew like a Pusse-cat, and say
you are glad you write out of the Courtiers Element' (*Satiromastix*
V.ii.324–6).

### 3 'Twelfth Night' and 'Poetaster'

*What You Will* was probably performed in the spring/summer of
1601, when Jonson apparently learnt of Dekker's intention to inten-
sify the attack still further; before *Satiromastix*, however, he may
well have had to contend with another attack from the Chamberlain's Men, in the form of a second *What You Will*, Shakespeare's
*Twelfth Night, or What You Will*. That Shakespeare contributed
more to the Poetomachia than the *Hamlet* reference (II.ii.337–62) to
'an aery of children, little eyases' that have forced the adult players
to tour, is inferred from a Cambridge play, *The Second Part of the
Return from Parnassus*, in which a barely-literate Kempe and Burbage
praise Shakespeare at Jonson's expense: 'Why heres our fellow *Shakespeare* puts them all downe, I and *Ben Jonson* too. O that *Ben Jonson*
is a pestilent fellow, he brought vp *Horace* giuing the Poets a pill,
but our fellow *Shakespeare* hath giuen him a purge that made him
beray his credit.'[73] Much ink has been spilt on this passage, *Troilus
and Cressida* (Ajax), and *Twelfth Night* (Malvolio) being the leading
cathartic contenders. Both are more plausible than Penniman's (and
Leishman's) view that the reference is not to a Shakespeare play but
to one performed by his company—*Satiromastix*.[74] There is a strong
case for arguing that *Twelfth Night* satirises Jonson, but that it seems
to have been written before *Poetaster*. Since Kempe's speech implies
that the 'purge' came after *Poetaster*, it follows either that *Twelfth
Night* is not the purge but a form of pre-medication, or (more likely,
in my view) that the student author(s) are referring to the Middle
Temple performance of *Twelfth Night* in February 1602. If this is so,
it gives much more weight to Riggs's observation that the 'purge'

may be found in the character of Malvolio, who 'has a number of traits in common with . . . Ben Jonson' that a *coterie* audience in the Middle Temple could have recognised (Riggs, pp. 84–5).

Shakespeare's mockery of Jonson's use of 'element' in *Twelfth Night* (see p. 33) has usually been taken to echo Dekker's in *Satiromastix*, placing *Twelfth Night* after it, late in 1601;[75] but Jonson's language was not private, and *Twelfth Night* could have satirised it before *Poetaster* or *Satiromastix* were written. Certainly Jonson seems to be be replying to Shakespeare by making Albius echo *Twelfth Night* when asking his courtly guests to 'draw near and accost' his banquet (II.ii.83) and then answering Julia's request to see his jewels: 'At your ladyship's service. [*Aside*] I got that speech by seeing a play last day, and it did me some grace now; I see 'tis good to collect sometimes. I'll frequent these plays more than I have done, now I come to be familiar with courtiers' (II.ii.86–90).

'At your ladyship's service' is italicised in *Q*, its equivalent to quotation marks. The only play likely to have been on 'last day' combining a mannered use of 'accost' with such a 'speech' is *Twelfth Night*, in which Malvolio says 'Here, madam, at your service' (I.v.299) and Sir Toby and Sir Andrew debate the meaning of 'accost' (I.iii.49–59, cf. also III.ii.21). Although Cornwallis indicates that 'at your service' was an overused phrase in 1600,[76] earlier in the same scene in *Twelfth Night* in which 'accost' occurs, another fashionable word, 'confine', is also misunderstood (I.iii.8–11); in *Poetaster*, Histrio, probably a representative of Shakespeare's company, uses 'confine' twice, the second time in a stilted, almost incomprehensible manner best explained as parodying *Twelfth Night*'s affected 'Confine yourself within the modest limits of order'. This becomes Histrio's 'Jupiter and the rest of the gods confine your modern delights, without disgust' (III.iv.315–6; cf. III.iv.133–4). Albius may echo *Twelfth Night* again when he says 'I have read in a book that to play the fool wisely is high wisdom' (IV.v.48–9): though proverbial, the nearest contemporary version (though not yet 'in a book') is in *Twelfth Night* III.i.60–1, 'This fellow is wise enough to play the fool / And to do that well craves a kind of wit'.[77] It has been plausibly argued that *Twelfth Night* was conceived in part as an 'Ovidian' riposte to the criticism of romantic comedy in *Every Man Out* (III.vi.195–201), and that it was intended to be acted at the Middle Temple Revels, with Orsino reminding the audience of Richard Martin as the 'Prince d'Amour'.[78] Three other factors add

to the argument for regarding *Twelfth Night* as a contribution to the
War, and for placing it before *Poetaster*. First, there are several
references to other Jonsonian or Marstonian words and themes in
their plays before *Poetaster*. Second, there is a possible allusion in
*Poetaster* III.iv.302–5 to Pope's playing of Sir Toby: 'let him not
beg rapiers nor scarfs in his over-familiar playing face, nor roar out
his barren bold jests with a tormenting laughter, between drunk and
dry' (cf. *Twelfth Night* I.iii.36–40, 76, I.v.41–5, 116). Finally, this
is the only Shakespeare play that was published (in the Folio of
1623, for the first time) with an alternative title. It has been suggested (see Arden ed., p. xxxiii) that this was because his original
choice, *What You Will*, was pre-empted by Marston; this is a rather
thin argument, but it bears more weight if the two plays were,
indeed, produced almost simultaneously in the first five months of
1601, making a change impracticable.

## 4  The children's companies

The majority of the plays in the War were performed by the boys'
companies at St Paul's and the Blackfriars. It is clear that boy actors
must have added to the impact of the comic caricature, but in other
respects a performance acted entirely by boys is difficult to recreate
in the imagination. A number of facts about the children's companies can, however, be marshalled to give some idea of what a
performance would have been like, and what may have led Jonson to
write for the Children of the Chapel Royal.[79] The boys themselves
were at this date in their teens, or slightly younger: of the actors in
*Poetaster*, Field was fourteen, Pavy about twelve, in 1601. They were
recruited, often forcibly, for their talents as actors and musicians,
and writers seem to have been confident in their abilities, making
few concessions for their age. Their musical abilities were exploited,
both in songs and dances in the plays themselves (though there are
no dances in *Poetaster*), and in instrumental and vocal music before
the play, and between acts (act intervals were observed, as they were
not by the men's companies). Also exploited were the special pri-
vileges belonging to the 'private' theatres: neither Paul's nor Blackfriars was subject to the jurisdiction of the City authorities, and both
had a close relationship with the court. Thomas Heywood condemned the 'Abuse lately crept into the Quality [i.e. actors] as an
inveighing against the State, the Court, the Law, the Citty, and their
Governements, with the particularizing of private Mens Humors (yet

alive)' and 'The Liberty which some arrogate to themselves, Com-
mitting their Bitternesse, and liberall Invectives against all Estates,
to the Mouthes of Children, supposing their juniority to be a Pri-
viledge for any rayling, be it never so violent'.[80] Lyly, writing for
the boys' companies in an earlier phase, had exploited the same
freedom, and had anticipated both the 'particularizing of private
Mens Humors' and the emetic punishment found in *Poetaster*,[81] but
the association of satire with the Blackfriars was especially strong in
the years following its reopening in 1600: the scope of the satire in
*Poetaster* itself is discussed below, but to it must be added Daniel's
*Philotas*, Day's *Isle of Gulls*, Jonson's, Marston's and Chapman's
*Eastward Ho!*, the lost play 'of the Silver Mines' which ridiculed
James I, and Chapman's *The Widow's Tears*, *Monsieur D'Olive*,
and his two-part *Byron* play, all of which involve pointed political
satire.[82]

Prices at the Blackfriars ranged from sixpence to two shillings and
sixpence, contrasting with a penny to sixpence at 'public' amphitheatres like the Globe, and suggesting that the playwrights' claims
that they addressed a 'choice selected influence' were accurate.[83] A
significant proportion of this well-heeled audience was from the Inns
of Court, a short walk or boat ride away, with a large student
population of overwhelmingly gentry status, some scarcely older
than the oldest boy actors. They provided an eager audience for (and
most of the writers of) the satires, dramatic and non-dramatic, of the
period, and would be more likely than those at the amphitheatres to
pick up personal allusions: there is evidence that the writers were
catering for regular patrons,[84] Marston was a notable member of the
Middle Temple, and Jonson well-known there since the successful
publication of *Every Man Out*. A satirist like Jonson, looking for a
more discerning audience than that of the Admiral's or even the
Chamberlain's Men, would have been attracted by this one. He was
probably also able to control the performance of his plays in a way
that must have been impossible when writing for Henslowe or the
Chamberlain's Men. Jonson seems, in addition, to have enjoyed
working with children: he is almost unique in taking pains, in *F*,
to list the boy actors in his plays; he taught Nathan Field Latin
(*Conversations* 164-5) and wrote a moving epitaph, not long after
*Poetaster*, on Salomon Pavy (*Ep*. CXX) as well as those on his own
son and daughter, all pointing towards a tenderness that is at odds
with the aggressive personality that emerges from other accounts,

and which helps explain the affection of younger literary followers like Herrick.

The boys' companies played a maximum season of six months, probably between Michaelmas and May/June, with a break for Lent. They performed only once, or at most twice, a week (hence Histrio emphasises that 'All the sinners i' the suburbs come and applaud our action *daily*' (III.iv.198–9)). The size of the Blackfriars company in 1601 was at least twenty (the number on stage in IV.vi) with doubling accounting for the total of thirty-three parts in the play as performed then (thirty-six if we include the 'Apologetical Dialogue', in which it seems unlikely that Jonson would have played himself in conversation with two child actors). Their acting, under Jonson's influence, must have been more naturalistic than at Paul's, where the boys tended 'to recite and symbolise, to posture rather than portray'.[85] This technique would suit Marston's drama, but would betray the acutely recorded speech rhythms of much of the comic prose in *Poetaster*, and the transparent seriousness of the verse spoken by Horace, Virgil and Augustus (and by Crites in *Cynthia's Revels*). A posturing, exaggerated style would work for some comic characters, especially for Tucca, whose mannerisms and stutter would have appeared more absurd played by a boy. But, as Barish points out, this 'marvel of strangeness' is achieved 'despite its evident realism, and the fact that it was apparently copied from life, from a certain Captain Hannam' (see below, pp. 48–9).[86] Parodic mimicry must have here combined with realism, as probably also happened in the impersonations of Marston and Dekker. The case for a relatively naturalistic delivery is confirmed by the obviously parodic performances of extracts from the adult repertory by Tucca's pages in III.iv. Here the comic discrepancy of 'child-actors consciously ranting in oversize parts'[87] is exploited, but it would only have point in a performance that as a whole avoided such a style.

## 5  The Essex rebellion

The Blackfriars audience's taste for topical satire would have been satisfied in *Poetaster* by the opportunity for 'application' of the play to a subject more dangerous to both writer and company than the lampooning of playwrights, actors or even lawyers. The Earl of Essex's rebellion on 8 February and his execution on Ash Wednesday, 25 February, had been the dominant events of 1601 in English domestic politics. Although it has been argued that *Cynthia's Revels* and *Sejanus* refer to Essex,[88] the allusions in *Poetaster* have been largely overlooked amidst arguments about the identification of writers.[89] Jonson believed comedy should be 'neere, and familiarly allied to the time' (*Every Man Out* III.vi.200), and some of *Poetaster*'s major themes are immediately relevant: the dangers of 'detraction', its relation to satire, and of malicious misinterpretation, 'wrestings, comments, applications, / Spy-like suggestions, privy whisperings' (Ind. 24–5). Jonson knew the system of informers only too well: in prison in 1599 'his judges . . . placed two damn'd Villans to catch advantage of him' (*Conversations* 256–60). It has long been recognised that this sinister aspect of late Elizabethan England forms a serious subtext of *Sejanus*, but Barish's description of the latter representing 'a whole nation turning into a race of spies and eaves-droppers, a situation in which informers were encouraged to bring charges in hopes of inheriting their victims' property, in which innocent remarks, half-remarks and non-remarks were made pre-texts for accusations of treason'[90] needs no modification to fit the satiric world of *Poetaster*, where Lupus and Tucca accuse Horace and Maecenas of treason in order to 'beg their land betimes' (V.iii.48). The difference is a ruler who listens to the counsel of poets and statesmen rather than informers. The banquet of the gods, the libels by Crispinus and Demetrius, and Horace's emblem which Lupus steals and maliciously misreads, all find parallels in the Essex re-bellion, the background to which was notable for both factions' circulation of 'libels', including letters reputedly written by Essex, which were stolen, then had forged passages added.[91] Donne, who like many of Jonson's circle had been sympathetic to Essex, probably reflected the views of most of them when writing to Wotton, formerly Essex's secretary, that the Earl's problem was 'the weakness of innocency';[92] he was a man who, though rash, was condemned by gossip, malicious innuendo and conspiracy. Essex's sensitivity to libel makes him sound like a character from *Poetaster*: 'The prating tavern haunter speaks of me what he lists; they print me and make me speak to the world, and shortly they will play me upon the stage.' The echoes of this letter to the Queen of 12 May 1600 in speeches by Lupus and Tucca (I.ii.39–52, III.iv.200–4) are coinci-dental, but the centrality of calumny to *Poetaster* is not. One of Essex's major problems before the rebellion was his loss of access to the Queen: he saw her surrounded by 'base-born upstarts', and founded his defence on the claim that he simply wanted to put his own case to her.[93] Access to the monarch by those who tell the truth rather than flatter and detract is another of *Poetaster*'s themes.

Lord Chief Justice Popham, almost certainly the 'greatest Justice' of Jonson's dedication, played a prominent part in the suppression of the rebellion: he was one of the Privy Councillors who, on the morning of the rebellion, were imprisoned at Essex House until the rebellion had failed. He conducted several interrogations, and was one of the court which arraigned Essex and Southampton. His interrogations included that of Augustine Phillips, representative of the Chamberlain's Men, who had performed *Richard II* at the request of a group of the rebels. As Lupus interrogates the player Histrio in *Poetaster* IV.iv in search of conspiracy and rebellion, so Popham and his two fellow judges examined the player Phillips:

> He sayeth that on Fryday last was senyght or Thursday, Sr Charles Percy Sr Jostlyne Percy and the L[ord] Montegle wth some thre more spake to some of the players in the presens of this exa[minant] to have the play of the deposyng and kyllyng of Kyng Rychard the Second to be played the Satedy next promysyng to geve them xls more then their ordynary to play yt. Wher this exa[minant] and hys freindes were determyned to have playd some other play holdyng that play . . . to be so old & so long out of use as that they shold have small or no cumpney at yt. But at their request this exa[minant] played yt accordyngly.[94]

Monteagle was a patron of Jonson (see *Ep.* LX) and, like him, a Catholic; the two Percys were Catholics, and members of the Middle Temple,[95] a connection that would make the allegory of IV.iv particularly obvious to Inns members. It must, though, have been clear to all who knew of Phillips's interrogation and remembered *Richard II*: the crucial lines when Richard gives the crown and sceptre, the emblems of kingship, to Bolingbroke (IV.i.204–5) are ludicrously echoed by Lupus: 'A crown and sceptre? This is good. Rebellion now!' (IV.iv.21).

Another powerful magistrate whose role in 1601 resembled that of Lupus was Henry Brooke, 8th Lord Cobham. Especially hated by Essex, Cobham had, like Lupus, clashed with the players for their representation in *1 Henry IV* of his namesake, Sir John Oldcastle, who after the Brooke family's complaints became Sir John Falstaff (when Essex was not referring to Cobham as the 'sycophant' or 'my lord Fool' he and Southampton called him 'Sir John Falstaff').[96] Shakespeare retaliated with 'Mr. Brooke' (later 'Mr. Broome') in the *Merry Wives of Windsor*, at which point Lupus's complaint 'They

will play you or me, the wisest men they can come by still. Me! Only
to bring us into contempt with the vulgar, and make us cheap'
(I.ii.45–8) becomes Cobham's as well.[97] Other writers showed
hostility to Cobham, both Nashe and Jonson punning on the 'cob'
(the head of a herring) in *Lenten Stuffe* and *Every Man Out*. Such
punning may even continue in a tortuous form in the epithet 'cropshin' which Tucca applies to Lupus: this was an inferior herring.
Cobham was thought (like Lupus) to have used libels to influence
the Queen: at Essex's arraignment (*Poetaster*'s subtitle, under which
it was performed, is here suggestive) he intervened to make an un-
necessarily vehement denial that he had used forged letters, 'neither
used he any such means of accusing the Earl to the Queen as the
Earl of Essex pretended against him'. However, Lupus is not a
straightforward satirical portrait of Cobham or Popham, so much as
a topical presentation of a malicious informer, the danger of his type
emphasised by Horace's and Maecenas' warnings against flattery and
malice (IV.viii.8–24, 28–31). The 'asinine wolf' is Jonson's version
of Sidney's sly wolf, who can 'make justice the cloak of tyranny',
and of Spenser's Blatant Beast, itself derived from Virgil's Fame
(*Poetaster* V.ii.75n). Elsewhere in *The Faerie Queene* Spenser represents 'malicious *Envie*' riding on 'a ravenous wolfe' (I.iv.30). In
the repressive atmosphere of 1601, the threat the wolf represented
would have been clear enough.

This is especially so for those many members of the audience who
had been subjects of the Privy Council's letter to 'the severall Innes
of Courte' ordering that 'the gentlemen & others might be ready
upon all occasions with their armour & weapons, and especially that
the yonger sorte might be commaunded to keepe themselves within
the houses to answere all occasions of service'.[98] Essex House was
immediately next door to the Middle Temple, and there was a well-
justified fear that the 'younger sort' might side with Essex: he was
more popular with them than the Cecil–Cobham faction, often for
religious as much as political reasons. Many Catholics like Jonson
had looked to Essex for support, his tolerant policy holding together
a curious following of puritans, freethinkers and loyal Catholics.
With the exception of Sir John Salusbury (see Appendix 1, pp.
283–4), the sympathies of Jonson's circle at the Inns at this time
were probably with Essex and Southampton: the radical sentiments
of Martin and Hoskyns in particular are similar to those of Edwin
Sandys, another Middle Templar who was, like Martin, close to

Southampton in the immediately following years, all three active in the Virginia Company.[99] Chamberlain later mentions Martin as the lover of Lettice Rich, daughter of Essex's sister Penelope (II, 247). At court, Jonson's patrons, the Earls of Bedford and Rutland, sided with the Essex faction, as did Sir Henry Neville (*Ep.* CIX), Monteagle, and Sir Robert Cotton's patron (later Jonson's enemy) Henry Howard. The young Earl of Pembroke, a major patron in later years, may already have been helping Jonson: his Sidney connections associated him, too, with the Essex group.[100] All this points to Jonson's sympathy towards Essex, the critical references to Actaeon in *Cynthia's Revels* notwithstanding.[101] Essex's rebellion remained a forbidden topic for several years: Daniel's *Philotas* (1604) and Chapman's *Byron* plays (1608) ran into trouble over allusions, and *Troilus and Cressida* may have been withdrawn from performance in case of 'application'. Fulke Greville, an Essexian with more to lose, destroyed his *Antony and Cleopatra* 'seeing the like instance not poetically, but really fashioned in the Earl of *Essex* then falling'.[102] In 1601 even Jonson's original title, *The Arraignment*, might have seemed subversive (only in 1616 does it become the less politically 'applicable' *His Arraignment*) and in this climate it is highly probable that part of the 'innocence' that Richard Martin vouched for on Jonson's behalf was of allusion to the Essex rebellion.

## 6  The Middle Temple and 'Poetaster'

Martin and Popham were, like Marston, Middle Templars.[103] Jonson had addressed his plays and much of his non-dramatic poetry to Inns members at least since *Every Man Out*, and, as has been argued, his move to the Blackfriars was surely influenced by its attraction of more members of the Inns than the public amphitheatres. The Inns provided both the writers of and the main audience for the satires and epigrams of these years, but while even their love poetry (as in Donne's *Songs and Sonets*) subverted the tropes and rhythms of courtly poetry, Inns members seem at first sight committed to the social and economic structures of which courtly poetry was a manifestation. Closer scrutiny reveals a more critical view of the court, especially in the group with whom Jonson was closely associated. In *Discoveries*, the court is contrasted to the Inns as 'the Inne of *Ignorance*' (2303), while Donne's fourth satire is a powerful attack, and an assertion of his independence (see esp. ll. 160–8). Of Jonson's probable circle of friends and patrons at the Inns in 1598–1602, only

Salusbury qualifies as a courtier, one of what Stone calls the élite gentry.[104] The most prominent—Martin, Donne, Hoskyns, Rudyerd, Overbury—were not courtiers by birth, title or inherited wealth or land, though they were, as Donne said, 'none's slave' (*Satire IV*, l. 162); they made their way by their own abilities. Their careers shared a period at Oxford in the 1580s, a long attachment to an Inn (except Donne the Middle Temple), prominence in their Inn's revels, and a period as an MP, marked in the cases of Martin, Hoskyns and Rudyerd by their ability as speakers critical of aspects of royal power (Donne reserved his oratory for the pulpit). Other wits and satirists have broadly similar backgrounds—Marston himself, Guilpin and Davies, plus such distinguished lawyer-politicians as Selden, Sandys, and Hakewill.[105] Their allegiances lay with the common law, the church and the House of Commons, rather than the court, and it was for such an audience that *Poetaster* was written. That it should also be so hostile to the law as a profession is less paradoxical than it might seem: mockery of lawyers was predictably traditional in the Inns revels, while a more serious critical note is struck in Martin's only published work, his welcome to James I, which looks forward to a future free from corrupt lawyers.[106] Law did not always restrain this group, which, with the partial exception of Donne, shows a high degree of violence and recklessness. Violence, however, was endemic among the gentry and aristocracy; this group took it further than most, as did the Essex circle, but Finkelpearl exaggerates in characterising Martin and Hoskyns as 'troublemakers, more or less serious disciplinary problems'.[107] Their recklessness at least had principle: they spoke their minds in the Commons when others failed to (Hoskyns being jailed for a year as a result), and the fiercely principled Jonson, who had killed a man in single combat in Flanders, another in a duel, and had been imprisoned for the rash satire of *The Isle of Dogs*, would have been at home in this milieu.

A wider circle, whose meetings at the Mitre Tavern a few years later are well documented, included Henry Goodyere, Christopher Brooke, John Davies of Hereford, Inigo Jones, the merchants Lionel Cranfield and Arthur Ingram, and John Bond, editor of Horace, and outspoken MP for Taunton in 1601 and 1604. Because he almost certainly knew Jonson, probably at this time, I have used his 1606 edition of Horace, as well as Heinsius's edition which Jonson used later, for the notes to this edition; it is impossible to establish which of the many available pre-1601 editions Jonson actually used for *Poetaster*.[108] In his Commons speeches in 1601 Bond applied his Latin to contemporary politics, a process entirely to Jonson's taste. Beyond this Mitre circle, Jonson became familiar to a large number of Inns men after publication of *Every Man Out*, his plays being more read there than any other dramatist's.[109] Dekker and Marston accuse him of exploiting these admirers; he must have shaped the views of many, but the outspokenness of the leading figures amongst them must also have helped form his own satirical stance. They are the 'assembly' whose 'shine' and 'grace' dazzles Envy in *Poetaster* (Ind. 11–13), the audience in *Cynthia's Revels* 'Who can both censure, understand, define what merit is' (Prologue, ll. 16–17). David Norbrook has argued that Jonson's work after 1603 increasingly supports crown and court, but the position is, as Norbrook allows, more complex: in 1601 his values probably closely resembled those which Martin, Bond, Davies and Hakewill were articulating in Parliament, which met in October, at about the time *Poetaster* was probably first staged. While they attacked corruption, monopolies and other abuses of the royal prerogative, Jonson evoked an ideal prince who encouraged freedom of speech, listened to wise poet-advisers and scornfully punished informers and flatterers.[110]

The charismatic Richard Martin, the dedicatee of *Poetaster*, was a leading figure in this group.[111] According to Rudyerd

> Fortune never taught him to temper his owne wit or manhood. His company, commonly weaker than himself, put him into a just opinion of himself of his owne strength. Of a noble and high spirit, as farre from base and infamous strains as ever he was from want . . . soe eloquent in ordinary speech, by extraordinary practise, and los of to much tyme, that his judgment, which was good, studdy could not mend it.[112]

Aubrey reports that 'He was a very handsome man, a graceful speaker, facetious and well-beloved'; Wood adds there was 'none more admired by Selden, Serjeant Hoskins, Ben Jonson &c than he', and that he left 'various poems' of which he had not seen a copy.[113] Martin was the regular Prince d'Amour, the Lord of Misrule of the Middle Temple Christmas Revels. He was, however, much more than the 'frivolous' friend of Donne and Jonson (Bald, p. 190). In October 1601, around the time he interceded with Popham on Jonson's behalf, Martin became MP for Barnstaple. He 'took to the House as a duck to water', clashing repeatedly with government spokesmen, and on one occasion courageously humiliating Cecil. Neale's account of the 1601 debates shows him, supported by Davies, Bond and Hakewill, opposing Privy Councillors on monopolies, fines for recusancy and Exchequer reform, all sensitive issues because touching the royal prerogative, speaking strongly but eloquently, and wishing 'perdition on oppressors of the people'.[114] His impact as an MP may well have helped his successful intercession for Jonson over *Poetaster*. His eloquence made him the choice of the Sherriffs of London and Middlesex to welcome the new king in 1603; Martin took the chance to give James an elegant but, by the standards of the time, a remarkably open warning of what to expect from the English court, in words that recall, and help explain, *Poetaster's* emphasis on the dangers posed by 'the moths and scarabs of a state' (IV.viii.15):

> here flattery will essay to undermine, or force your Majesties strongest constancie and integrity: base assentation the bane of virtuous Princes, which (like *Lazarus* dogs) lick even the Princes soares, a vice made so familiar to this age by long use, that even Pulpits are not free from that kind of treason? A treason I may justly call it most capitall, to poyson the fountaine of wisedome and justice, whereat so many kingdomes must be refreshed. (*A Speach delivered to the King's Majestie*, sig.A4v).

Though he reminds James of the latter's recent comparison of Elizabeth to Augustus (cf. Erskine-Hill, p. 107) the clear message of Martin's speech is that recent experience has been of corruption and oppression which James will set right.

Martin was a leading speaker in the 1604 Parliament,[115] but he did not stand for the Addled Parliament of 1614, 'for feare of being transported and doing himself harme'. 'Loth to venter his rising fortune upon his slipperie tongue', he nevertheless addressed the House as counsel for an Essexian group of peers who were major stockholders in the Virginia Company, a focus for opposition to the crown. He rapidly turned the opportunity into a political event, attacking the inertia of the Commons, and 'ripping up what had passed since theyre sitting, taxing them for theyre slow proceding . . . and schooling them what they shold do'.[116] Martin's outspokenness should be set in the context of the longer political careers of his associates Hoskyns, Hakewill and Sandys, who were by 1614 leading figures in the increasing parliamentary hostility to the crown. Later their role was assumed by John Pym, himself at the Middle Temple from 1602, and a member of that 1614 parliament.[117]

### 7  Captain Hanham

Apart from Jonson's statement that he had 'writ his Poetaster' on
Marston, the only contemporary identification of a character in the
Poetomachia is Dekker's:

> A second Cat-a-mountaine mewes, and calls me Barren, because my braines
> could bring foorth no other Stigmaticke than Tucca, whome Horace had put to
> making, and begot to my hand: but I wonder what language Tucca would have
> spoke, if honest Capten Hannam had bin borne without a tongue? Ist not as
> lawfull then for mee to imitate Horace, as Horace Hannam?[118]

Grudgingly accepting that this refers explicitly to personal satire,
Campbell bleakly opined that 'because we must forever remain in
complete ignorance of Captain Hannam, Dekker's allegation, if true,
can have no significance for us'.[119] Such pessimism suited Campbell,
but is unfounded. Four candidates exist for 'Captain Hannam',
though their pursuit would be pointless were not two—possibly
all—related to Thomas and James Hannam or Hanham, senior
members of the Middle Temple in the 1590s, and through Thomas
to Chief Justice Popham, adding a strong personal dimension to his
interest in Poetaster.

Thomas Hanham the elder (d. 1593), a prominent lawyer and MP,
married Popham's daughter Penelope, and succeeded Popham as
Recorder of Bristol. He and his cousin James (d. 1597) were senior
benchers of the Middle Temple. Thomas's first son, John, was a
student there, but it is his second son, Captain Thomas Hanham (b.
1576), who is one possible model for Tucca.[120] Another is 'Captain
Rafe Hamon', 'gentleman porter of Munster', who in August 1601
desired 'one of the companies that now go into Ireland' and who may
be the Ralph Hannam who married Agnes Coquin in Westminster in
1575.[121] He may also be identical with the third, and most likely,
candidate, the 'captayne Haname' who twice pawned linen to
Henslowe in 1593 (Henslowe misspells the name 'hamame' once, as I
am assuming Cobham did: see Diary, pp. 147, 149). The fourth
candidate, Captain Jack Hanham, proposed in H&S, IX, 53, was
the elder Thomas's brother. He sailed on Drake's expedition to the
West Indies in 1585, as Simpson notes, but he also died on it:[122]
Jonson, only thirteen then, could hardly have copied his mannerisms,
however memorable. The relative youth of Jack's nephew, Captain
Thomas Hanham, who was twenty-five in 1601, counts against him.
Though his case is strong because he was connected by family with

the Middle Temple (though Ralph may also have been, he was not Popham's grandson), Thomas's career does not suggest Tucca's: he was a pioneer coloniser of America, member of one of two companies (that headed by Popham) granted a patent in 1606 to colonise Virginia. After one abortive attempt Popham sent 'out another shippe, wherein Captayne Thomas Hanam went Commander'. Purchas, who tells the story, says 'Reader, I had by me the Voyage of Captain Thomas Hanham, (written by himselfe) unto Sagadahoc'.[123] Thomas stayed until 1620, then returned to succeed his brother at Dean Court, Wimborne Minster. In 1640 a local clergyman, Richard Bernard, dedicated his *Common Catechisme* to him, praising his piety. Though he certainly cannot be ruled out, the pious coloniser, explorer and writer is not a promising model for Tucca.

The most plausible candidate is thus the Captain Hanham of Henslowe's *Diary*, of whom nothing is known except that he was hard up in January and February 1593, and had some high-quality linen: his use of Henslowe as pawnbroker, however, suggests familiarity with actors and writers. Since Jack Hanham was dead, and the younger Thomas Hanham only seventeen in 1593, Henslowe's Hanham can in the absence of other 'Captain Hanhams' be very tentatively identified with Ralph. Apart from his marriage and possible Irish connections, nothing is known of Ralph either, but Popham and the elder Thomas Hanham both had an interest in Irish settlement which may have involved more indigent members of the family.[124] Ralph's request for command of a company in Ireland fits well with Gallus' contemptuous version of Tucca's military experience: 'He's one that hath had the mustering or convoy of a company now and then' (V.iii.194–5). From one of these men, if we are to believe Dekker, Jonson drew the extraordinary and yet utterly convincing speech-patterns that make Tucca one of the most compelling *milites gloriosi* in drama.

The editorial principles employed in this edition are described in Appendix 1, which sets out the textual history of the play. In the commentary I have made use where possible of the classical scholarship of Jonson's time, on the grounds that the modern reader often needs to know what Jonson and his readers believed about the classical world, not what has been discovered since. Those anti-

50    POETASTER

quarian writers most frequently cited are given in the list of Abbreviations, p. xi.

I have used the first edition of the *Oxford English Dictionary* throughout; the commentary was virtually completed before the second edition became available, but the quotations from early periods are, in any case, little changed in the new *OED*, and a spot check has not led me to make any alterations.

NOTES

1 *H&S* (IX, 189–90) record a single revival by William Poel, performed in London on 26 and 27 April, 1916, and in Pittsburgh, by students, the following October.
2 Platz is representative in saying (p. 1) the war is 'dead and buried, and nowadays hardly anyone who is interested in the Elizabethan period wants to resurrect it'.
3 Cf. the description by J. A. Bryant, Jr of the narrowness and unrepresentativeness of the Jonson canon as currently anthologised and taught: 'On Reconsidering Ben Jonson', *Sewanee Review*, XCV (1987), 614–19.
4 Dates are of first performance, where known, not of publication.
5 For discussion of Jonson's use of such scenes, see Jonas A. Barish, 'Feasting and Judgement in Jonsonian Comedy', *Renaissance Drama*, n.s. V (1972), 3–51, and Maus, pp. 126–7.
6 *Volpone* (Revels, ed. Parker) ll. 21–2 (see below, p. 22); Milton, *Apology [for] Smectymnuus*, in *Works* (New York, 1931–8), III.i.303: 'he who would not be frustrate of his hope to write well hereafter in laudable things, ought him selfe to bee a true Poem, that is a composition, and patterne of the best and honourablest things'. Cf. IV.vi.42–6n.
7 See e.g. Robert Cartwright, *Shakespeare and Jonson, Dramatic versus Wit Combats* (1864), F. G. Fleay, *Life and Work of William Shakespeare* (1886), and *Biographical Chronicle* (1891); somewhat less wildly conjectural than Fleay is J. H. Penniman, *War of the Theatres* (Philadelphia, 1897), slightly modified in his introduction to his edition of *Poetaster* and *Satiromastix*. Small's *Stage Quarrel* is much the best of such Victorian investigations. Good later accounts are Alfred Harbage, *Shakespeare and the Rival Traditions* (New York, 1952), pp. 90–119, M. C. Bradbrook, *The Growth and Structure of Elizabethan Comedy* (1955), pp. 103–25, Kay, pp. 158–251, and Barton, pp. 58–91. Sharpe, *The Real War of the Theatres*, hypothesises a battle between the adult companies.
8 See Campbell, pp. 109–34, esp. pp. 110–12; King, pp. 59–60; Ralph W. Berringer, 'Jonson's *Cynthia's Revels* and the War of the Theatres', *PQ*, XXII (1943), 1–22; E. W. Talbert, 'The Purpose and Technique of Jonson's *Poetaster*', *SP*, XLII (1945), 225–51; Eugene M. Waith, 'The Poet's Morals in Jonson's *Poetaster*', *MLQ*, XII (1951), 13–29; Ralph Nash, 'The Parting Scene in Jonson's *Poetaster*', *PQ*, XXXI (1952), p. 62; Edward B. Partridge, 'Ben Jonson: The Makings of the

Dramatist (1596–1602)' in *Elizabethan Theatre, Stratford upon Avon Studies*, IX (1966), 221–44; Platz, p. 1; James D. Mulvihill, 'Jonson's *Poetaster* and the Ovidian Debate', *SEL*, XXII (1982), 239–55; Joseph A. Dane, 'The Ovids of Ben Jonson in *Poetaster* and *Epicoene*' in *Drama in the Renaissance*, ed. C. Davidson, C. J. Gianakaris and J.H. Stroupe (New York, 1986), pp. 103–15; Barton, pp. 58–91, 181–4 is a notable exception to the trend, as in part is Kay.

9  Cf. Bevington, pp. 283–4.

10  Cf. Richard Levin, *New Readings vs. Old Plays* (Chicago and London, 1979), pp. 1–77.

11  For an excellent discussion of language and authority in Jonson, see Womack, esp. pp. 19–20, 50–60, 76–107, 112–13; for Augustanism, see Erskine-Hill esp. pp. 108–21.

12  The best account of *Poetaster*'s structure is by Freda L. Townsend, *Apologie for Bartholmew Fayre: The Art of Jonson's Comedies* (New York and London, 1947), pp. 53–7; see also Campbell, p. 112, and Nash, 'The Parting Scene in Jonson's *Poetaster*', p. 62. For the theoretical background to Jonson's idea of unity, see Daniel J. Quigley, *Ben Jonson's Conceptual Unity*, Ph.D. thesis, University of Notre Dame, 1988.

13  Barish, pp. 80–1.

14  Brian Gibbons, *Jacobean City Comedy* (2nd ed., 1980), p. 60.

15  Cf. Robert C. Jones, 'The Satirist's Retirement in Jonson's "Apologetical Dialogue"', *ELH*, XXXIV (1967), 447–67, for discussion of the implications of the 'Dialogue' for the rest of Jonson's work.

16  'Upon the WORKS of BEN. JOHNSON' (1678), in *H&S*, XI, 538–45 (l. 180); cf. Dryden, 'He invades Authors like a Monarch, and what would be theft in other Poets, is onely victory in him' (*Of Dramatick Poesie*, 1668, pp. 49–50, in *H&S*, XI, 515).

17  See Maus, esp. pp. 22–46.

18  The phrase is in a note sent with the 'Epitaph' on Cecilia Bulstrode, 1609 (*UV* IX).

19  *Gull's Hornbook* (1609), in Chambers, *ES*, IV, 368.

20  Here the Blackfriars practice differed from St Paul's, where false beards were apparently frowned on: Gair, pp. 143–4; see also below pp. 39–40. For the beard, see also II.ii.76–7.

21  Plate 9 in *The Riverside Shakespeare*.

22  See e.g. Earl Miner, 'In Satire's Falling City', in *The Satirist's Art*, ed. James H. Jensen and Malvin R. Zirker, Jr (Bloomington, Indiana and London, 1972), pp. 3–27.

23  Jacob Burckhardt, *The Civilisation of the Renaissance in Italy*, trans. Middlemore (1944), p. 37.

24  Petrarch, *Epistolae* ed. Fracassetti (Florence, 1859), Lib. XXXIII, Ep. xix; Seneca, 'Ad Lucilium', *Ep.Mor.* 84; Quintilian *Inst.* X.ii.18; Horace *Epist.* I.xix, 21–34; cf. E. H. Gombrich, *Norm and Form* (1966), p. 122. See R. R. Bolgar, *The Classical Heritage and its Beneficiaries* (New York, 1964), pp. 265–75 for the importance of imitation in general, and of Erasmus' *De Copia Verborum et Rerum* in particular; cf. *Vives on Education*, trans. R. Foster Watson (Cambridge, 1913), p. 198.

25 'Ben Jonson's Horace and Horace's Ben Jonson', *SP*, LXXVIII (1981), 20–31, p. 29.

26 Henry Chettle, *England's Mourning Garment* (1603), sig. D2v, also quoted in Erskine-Hill, p. 122; Sir Thomas Smith, *Voiage and Entertainment in Rushia* (1605), the latter in *H&S*, XI, 374. Randolph, *A gratulatory to Mr. Ben. Iohnson for his adopting of him to be his Son* (*H&S*, XI, 390, ll. 13–14).

27 Bond, *Horace*, A2v: 'Poetam (audeo dicere) omnibus numeris absolutum: Poetam multiplici rerum copia refertum, verborum elegantia perpolitum . . . Hinc est, quod Divus *Augustinus* inprimis jubet legendum esse hunc Poetam: quippe non modo justitiam, invictam animi magnitudinem, parsimoniam, continentiam, religionem in Deum, pietatem in parentes, patientiam paupertatis, & contemptionem rerum humanarum summis laudibus prosequatur; sed contra, perfidiam, injustitiam, metum, prodigalitatem, libidinem, luxuriam, avaritiam, atque omnia fere vitia acerbe carpat, vituperet, exagitet. . . . *Horatius* sine controversia omnibus Poetis & Graecis & Latinis (*Homerum* semper excipio) est merito anteponendus, in quo sic suavitas cum utilitate contendit, ut lectorem suis illecebris semel captum semper teneat irretitum, nec demittat unquam.'

28 Horace, *Ars P*, 333–4 in Jonson's translation (*H&S*, VIII, 327), ll. 477–8, also quoted as title-page mottoes of *Volpone* and *Staple of News*; for the eight further echoes of these lines, or the similar lines 343–4 of the *Ars P*, in Jonson see *H&S*, IX, 420–1.

29 *Shoemaker's Holiday* is dated July 1599. *Merry Wives* is variously dated between 1597 and 1602, so it is just possible that Shakespeare had Tucca as well as Juniper as model. The question arises, of course, as to whether Hanham was a model for Juniper, or whether Dekker (see p. 48) was overstating his importance as a model for Tucca. Tucca's language is well treated by Barish, pp. 123–9.

30 Mikhail Bakhtin, *Rabelais and His World*, trans. Hélène Iswolsky (Cambridge, Mass., 1968), p. 300.

31 Cf. also the 'Epistle to Augustus' (*Epist.* II.i), esp. ll. 145–76. For Lucian see Douglas Duncan, *Ben Jonson and the Lucianic Tradition* (Cambridge, 1979), esp. pp. 119–43; he wrote, of course, later than Horace.

32 Erskine-Hill, esp. pp. 164–359; for *Poetaster*, see pp. 108–21.

33 Bond, *Horace*, A2v. See also Tenney Frank, 'On Augustus' References to Horace', *CP*, XX (1925), 26–30.

34 W. A. Camps, *An Introduction to Virgil's Aeneid* (Oxford, 1969) gives the *Life* as Appendix I, pp. 115–20; it was probably based closely on a lost *Life* by Suetonius. For this passage, see p. 118. The victory at Actium and Augustus' 'triple triumph' in Rome are depicted by Vulcan on Aeneas' shield (*Aeneid* VIII, 675–731).

35 *Ben Jonson*, pp. 58–9.

36 Suetonius, *The Historie of Twelve Caesars*, trans. Holland (1606), p. 70. Elyot, *The Boke Named the Governour*, I.xxii; cf. Erskine-Hill, pp. 54–8.

37  Cf. Alexander Leggatt, *Ben Jonson His Vision and His Art* (London and
    New York, 1981), p. 95.

38  Malicious 'application' of a satiric dramatist who sounds like Jonson is
    threatened by Envy in the Epilogue added to *Mucedorus* some time after
    *Poetaster*: see *The Shakespeare Apocrypha*, ed. C. F. Tucker Brooke
    (Oxford, 1908), p. 125, ll. 29–53. Riggs (p. 76) makes the point that the
    informers' methods in *Poetaster* are similar to those used against Jonson
    over *The Isle of Dogs* in 1597, *Poetaster* becoming a fantasy of revenge.
    Richard Dutton, *Mastering the Revels* (1991), argues that, whatever the
    vicissitudes of Jonson's career, censorship was less repressive than is
    usually assumed.

39  Leggatt, *Ben Jonson*, p. 95.

40  By Swinburne, *A Study of Ben Jonson* (1889), p. 25, and by *H&S*, IX,
    538.

41  Cf. Erskine-Hill, pp. 111–12; there has been a general and unjustified
    assumption of plagiarism by Jonson. The elegy was first published in the
    two undated 'Middleburgh' editions of the 1590s, probably in fact
    printed in Britain: see Fredson Bowers, 'The Early Editions of Marlowe's
    *Ovid's Elegies*', *SB*, XXV (1972), 149–72. The third edition has the
    *Poetaster* version printed after the Marlowe one, but there is no evidence
    that Jonson claimed it as his. The variants in the 'Jonson' version are
    generally more faithful to the original, and are usually assumed to be
    Jonson's revisions of Marlowe; it is possible, however, that they simply
    come from a different MS version. Roma Gill and Robert Kreuger, 'The
    Early Editions of Marlowe's Elegies and Davies's Epigrams', *Library*, 5,
    XXVI (1971), 242–9, show that revisions, argued to be Marlowe's own,
    are made between the earlier two editions; these are lesser than, but
    similar in kind to, those in the *Poetaster* version. Nashe had access to a
    MS in the 1590s, since he quotes in *The Unfortunate Traveller* from
    another elegy not printed until the third edition. James A. Riddell, 'Ben
    Jonson and Marlowe's "Mighty Line"' in *A Poet and a filthy Play-
    maker*, ed. Friedenreich, Gill and Kuriyama (New York, 1988), pp.
    37–48, shows that the text of the Jonson version in the third edition was
    set up from *Q*, so must have come out in 1602 at the earliest. Jonson
    uses Ovid's structure here (six Greek and six Latin poets) in the elegy on
    Shakespeare, where six English poets are set against six classical ones
    (*UV* XXVI, ll. 20–35).

42  *The Children of the Chapel Stript and Whipt* (1569), quoted in Hillebrand,
    p. 86, n. 42.

43  See Seneca *De brevitate vitae* xvi.5; *De vita beata*, xxvi.6; Cicero *Tusc.*
    I.xxvi.65 (quoted IV.v.n and IV.v.13–14n); Quintilian *Inst.* X.i.88. Cf.
    Maus, pp. 89–90.

44  *Palladis Tamia. Wits Treasury* (1598), ff. 281v–2r.

45  Cf. Frank Kermode, 'The Banquet of Sense', *Bulletin of the John
    Rylands Library*, LXIV (1961–2), 68–99, and articles by Mulvihill and
    Dane cited in n. 5.

46  'Est autem satyrae lex, ut comiter, & urbane, & per ludum, ac iocum,
    mores, vitiaque hominum, notet, ac reprehendat: non aspere, non serio,

non petulanter, non contumeliose, non iracunde, ut Pers. & Iuvenal', *Q. Horatii Flacci Sermonum, seu Satyrarum* (Frankfurt, 1596 ed.), p. 116.

47 Cf. *H&S*, I, 422; Richard Dutton, *Ben Jonson: to the First Folio* (Cambridge, 1983), pp. 48–9.

48 Described thus by Jonson in his inscription in the *Volpone* quarto in the British Library; for Augustus, see *Montaigne's Essays*, ed. L. C. Harmer, Everyman ed., 3 vols (1965), I, p. 8.

49 For Tucca's use of names 'to subjugate individuals' like a nervous dramatist, see Barton, p. 184. For stuttering as a symptom of mental disorder, see Burton, *Anatomy* I, p. 383.

50 The fullest discussion of Marston's language in relation to *Poetaster* is in King, Chapter 1.

51 See Manfred Gorlach, *Introduction to Early Modern English* (Cambridge, 1991), pp. 149–74; Gorlach usefully assembles many of the relevant texts, pp. 215–60.

52 Small, p. 38 (June); Mallory, p.xxx (July); *H&S*, IX, 189 ('early in the year'); Chambers, *ES*, III, 366 gives 'late spring or early autumn'.

53 Chambers (*ES*, II, 207) believed that *Satiromastix* had been on the stage 'not long before' it was entered to John Barnes 'vppon condicion that yt be lycensed to be printed'. Barnes presumably did not obtain licence, since it was printed in 1602 for Edward White, later than *Poetaster* since in the epistle *To the World* Dekker invites his readers to '*read his* Arraignement [i.e. *Poetaster*] *and see*' (l. 29); the wording of the entry to Barnes may be compared to that for *Troilus and Cressida* to James Roberts 'when he hath gotten sufficient aucthority for yt'. It is likely that *Satiromastix* opened for the Michaelmas season only slightly later than *Poetaster*, with Dekker either having detailed information about Jonson's MS or hurriedly inserting the material which responded to *Poetaster* after seeing an early performance. Haste would explain why 'Horace' is dragged into a play set in William Rufus's reign. This is the only instance I have found of a play being acted almost simultaneously, and apparently by agreement, by a boys' and an adult company: *The Malcontent* was 'stolen' by the King's Men: see Ind.72–80, and Introduction pp. xli–xlvi, ed. G. K. Hunter (Revels, Manchester, 1975).

54 The allusion is noted also by Honigmann, *Weever*, p. 40. Weever's pamphlet was quickly answered by Nicholas Breton's *No Whipping, nor tripping, but a kind friendly snipping* (entered 16 September) and by *The Whipper of the Satire his penance in a white sheet* (6 November), almost certainly by Everard Guilpin: see Arnold Davenport, ed., *The Whipper Pamphlets (1601)* (Liverpool, 1951); these pamphlets form a minor prose counterpart to the war going on in the theatres.

55 See Finkelpearl, pp. 50–5.

56 See Manningham, pp. 48, 265.

57 The copy is in the University Library, Dundee; another note confirms that *Ep.* XLIX also refers to Marston: there he is accused of mistaking obscenity for wit. Cf. J. R. Barker, 'A Pendant to Drummond of Hawthornden's *Conversations*' *RES*, XVI (1965), 284–8.

58 Even if, as is possible, the Dialogue belongs to early 1602, the statement remains problematical.

59 He became a freeman of the Company of Tilers and Bricklayers at this time; see Riggs, p. 53.

60 See Small, pp. 90–2; Chambers, *ES*, II, 171; Greg thought the addition a forgery (*Henslowe's Diary*, 2 vols (1904–8), I, xxxviii) but Foakes and Rickert accept it. All the payments are 'earnests' (advances), but Henslowe was not always accurate in his terminology. If the payments were divided as described, Marston would have received £2 10s, £1 more than Jonson or Chettle, £1 10s more than Dekker, perhaps in itself enough to start a debate on the nature of satire. For a dissenting view on the play involved, see K. G. Cross, 'The Authorship of *Lust's Dominion*', *SP*, LV (1958), 39–61.

61 For different views on date and authorship, see P. J. Finkelpearl, 'John Marston's *Histrio-Mastix* as an Inns of Court Play: A Hypothesis', *HLQ*, XXIX (1966), 223–34; James P. Bednarz, 'Representing Jonson: *Histriomastix* and the Origin of the Poets' War', *HLQ*, LIV (1991), 1–30, and Kay, pp. 204–5; for the Paul's opening, see Gair, p. 118. Gair's evidence is stronger than Michael Shapiro's, who posits 1597 in *Children of the Revels* (New York, 1977), pp. 18–19.

62 This led Fleay and Penniman to identify Carlo, untenably, with Marston (Fleay also managed to identify him with Dekker in the same book, *Biographical Chronicle*). Simpson (*H&S*, IX, 399–406) gives an excellent analysis of the limits of personal identification in *Every Man Out*, concluding that only Carlo Buffone (Charles Chester) and possibly Shift are what Jonson called 'particular' and 'personal' (*Poetaster* V.iii.139, *Volpone*, Epistle, l. 53). Jasper Mayne claims such satire is not '*nature*' to Jonson, and defends him against those who said he began such quarrels: 'who say thy *wit* lay in thy *Gall*. / That *thou* didst quarrell first, and then, in spight, / Didst' gainst a *person* of such *vices* write: / That 'twas *revenge*, not *truth*, that on the *Stage* / *Carlo* was not presented, but *thy Rage*', '*To the Memory of* BEN. JOHNSON', ll. 107–12 (*H&S*, XI, 454). Mayne's evidence is important, but hearsay: not born until 1604, he cannot have known Jonson until the early 1620s at best.

63 The fullest list of Marstonisms in *EMO* is in Small, p. 45; cf. also *H&S*, IX, 449–50. For the revels, see Finkelpearl, chapters 3 and 4, Christopher Baker, *Ben Jonson and the Inns of Court* (unpublished Ph.D. thesis, University of North Carolina, 1974), chapter 1, and the account of the 1597–8 revels by Benjamin Rudyerd, *Le Prince d'Amour* (1660). The best surviving example of a fustian speech is John Hoskyns's 'Tufftafity' speech from these revels; see *Hoskyns*, pp. 100–2.

64 For *Twelfth Night*, see pp. 36–8.

65 The title-page does not attribute the play to Marston, but 'all critics have recognized the style . . . and some of the vocabulary is vomited in *Poetaster*' (Chambers, *ES*, IV, 21). It can be dated firmly from internal evidence: it is set at Whitsun (Wood, III, 182), and it is becoming light at 3 a.m. (195); there are references to Kempe's Morris which ended 11 March 1600 (182), and 'womens [i.e. leap] yeere': all point to a date in early summer of 1600 (a leap year).

66 For 'observe', see *Every Man Out* II.iii.78, 224, 314; II.iv.55 and III.iv.100; for 'compliment', II.ii.19, 84 and IV.iv.75; Hoskyns warns

against 'compliment' as a 'perfumed term' in a passage from *Directions for Speech and Style* copied by Jonson in *Disc.* (*H&S*, VIII, 632, 2274–7; *Hoskyns*, p. 121), and it is mocked by Donne in *Satire IV*: 'in his tongue, called compliment' (*Donne*, p. 37, l. 44). For the association of specific words with Jonson, see *Satiromastix* II.ii.11–20, esp. 18–20: 'Master Asinius Bubo, you have eene Horaces wordes as right as if he had spit them into your mouth.'

67 Kay, p. 170; Campbell is categorical that 'he is not Ben Jonson' (p. 163); Kay follows him in 'eliminating' *Jack Drum's Entertainment*, along with *Cynthia's Revels* and (with more reason) *Patient Grissell* from the Poetomachia (pp. 171–2). Chambers, like Barton (pp. 61–2), has 'little doubt that the critical Brabant Senior is Jonson' (*ES*, IV, 21).

68 Notably by Campbell, quoted approvingly by Simpson (*H&S*, IX, 507–8), and by Berringer, 'Jonson's *Cynthia's Revels* and the War of the Theatres'.

69 *What You Will* was not entered until August 1607, and was printed that year; it clearly postdates *Cynthia's Revels*, but does not respond to *Poetaster*, so belongs to the period from December 1600 to October 1601. Small argues that it was heavily revised after *Poetaster*, some of the untraced words vomited by Crispinus having been in the original, but his evidence rests on confusions which could equally well be a result of foul papers being used as copy.

70 See *Weever*, pp. 42–9; Honigmann also identifies Weever with Shift in *Every Man Out*, a suggestion lent support by Jasper Mayne's hint that Shift, like Carlo, was a historical figure: 'And the just *indignation thou* wert in / Did not expose *Shift*, but his *tricks* and *ginne*' (*H&S*, XI, 454). Cf. Kay, p. 93: 'the relationship [between Lampatho and Simplicius] must have some foundation in fact'.

71 Cf. *Poetaster* II.i.87–102; Jonson is classified as 'yeoman' at his trial in 1599: Fleay, *Biographical Chronicle*, I, 143.

72 Both *Every Man Out* and *Cynthia's Revels* were probably performed at Court; Chambers identifies *Cynthia's Revels* as the 'showe wth musycke and speciall songes p'pared for the purpose' given by the Children of the Chapel on 6 January 1601 (*ES*, III, 364; IV, 113, 166), a date accepted by *H&S* (IX, 188), but as Kay points out (p. 101) there are problems: the small payment of £5, half the normal rate for a full play, the unusually detailed description, and the three full-length plays also given that day, the most ever recorded (*ES*, IV, 113), make it likely this was a special Twelfth Night 'show' and not a play, which leaves 22 February as the only *recorded* date for a court performance by the Chapel Children in 1601. *Liberality and Prodigality* has been assigned to this date, since its 'crime' (V.v) takes place on 4 February 1601 (see Fleay, *Biographical Chronicle*, II, 323, Chambers, *ES*, IV, 26), but this is hardly conclusive. On 22 February Essex's confession and sentence were announced in every church: see E. M. Tenison, *Elizabethan England*, XI (Leamington Spa, 1956), p. 496. Actaeon's 'fatall doome' for 'presuming farre' (V.xi.15–16) *could* thus be a last minute reference to the death sentence, Essex and Southampton having been found guilty on 19 February.

73 *Parnassus Plays*, p. 337, ll. 1769–73. *The Second Part of the Return* was performed in late 1601 or late 1602 (pp. 24–6). Like Lyly's lost plays of the 1580s (see p. 39 and n. 81), these plays involved personal satire comparable to that in *Poetaster* (*Parnassus Plays*, pp. 61–92).

74 For recent discussion see Honigmann, *Myriad-minded Shakespeare*, Chapter 7 and Riggs, pp. 84–5. Cf. *Parnassus Plays*, pp. 369–71. For the probable addition to *Hamlet* of the passages dealing with the Poetomachia after *Poetaster* had been performed, see Harold Jenkins, ed., Arden *Hamlet*, pp. 1–7, and Honigmann, 'The Date of *Hamlet*', *Sh.S*, IX (1956), 24–34.

75 *Twelfth Night*, Arden, ed. J. M. Lothian and T. W. Craik (1975), p. xxxv; cf. Jenkins, *Hamlet*, p. 2.

76 *Essayes*, Sir William Cornwallis the Younger, ed. Don Cameron Allen (Baltimore, 1946), p. 71.

77 Mallory (p. 212) cites Jocob Feis, *Shakespere and Montaigne* (1884), p. 159 as first noting Albius' speech as a possible allusion to *Twelfth Night*.

78 Henk Gras, '*Twelfth Night*, *Every Man Out of his Humour*, and the Middle Temple Revels of 1597–98', *MLR*, LXXXIV (1989), 545–64; cf. Honigmann, *Shakespeare's Impact*, pp. 100–3 for the argument that *Twelfth Night* precedes *EMO*.

79 The information that follows is largely derived from Gair, Hillebrand and Gurr.

80 Quoted in Hillebrand, p. 269.

81 Nashe, *Return of Pasquill* (1589), says that in an unnamed comedy, 'Martin [Marprelate] would have forced' the figure of Divinity 'but myssing of his purpose, he left the print of his nayles upon her cheekes, and poysoned her with a vomit, which he ministered unto her to make her cast uppe her dignities and promotions'. See R. W. Bond, *The Complete Works of John Lyly* (1902), III, 585n. That Lyly lampooned recognisable individuals is confirmed by a letter of 1585 printed by F. P. Wilson, *MLR*, XV (1920), 79–82, p. 82.

82 See Albert H. Tricomi, *Anticourt Drama in England, 1603–1642* (Charlottesville, Va, 1989), pp. 3–50.

83 Marston, *Jack Drum's Entertainment*, Wood, III, 179; Gurr, pp. 72–9.

84 Gair, pp. 130, 170.

85 Gair, p. 145.

86 Barish, p. 126.

87 R. A. Foakes, 'John Marston's Fantastical Plays: *Antonio and Mellida* and *Antonio's Revenge*', *PQ*, XLI (1962), p. 236.

88 Riggs, pp. 69–70; Annabel Patterson, *Censorship and Interpretation* (Madison, Wis., 1984), pp. 50–6; Jonas Barish, ed., *Sejanus* (New Haven and London, 1965), p. 16; Margot Heinemann, 'Rebel Lords, Popular Playwrights, and Political Culture: Notes on the Jacobean Patronage of the Earl of Southampton', *YES*, XXI (1991), 63–86, p. 64.

89 Chambers is, as so often, an exception, asking 'Can the Aesop episode be a reminder of the part played by Augustine Phillips in the Essex innovation?' (*ES*, I, 385; cf. II, 206–7); Erskine-Hill (p. 111) and Dutton,

*Mastering the Revels*, pp. 138–9 also note the allusion in Lupus's allega-
tions of treason; Sharpe has much speculation on the adult companies'
connections with Essex, but none on those of the children's companies;
Bevington (pp. 279–88) and Platz give the best accounts to date of the
play's general political implications, but do not relate it to the Essex
affair. Riggs suggests that Essex and Southampton were social 'counterparts' of Ovid (p. 75), but this overestimates the latter's social standing
(cf. IV.x.5–10), and underestimates the political importance of the two
peers.

90  *Sejanus*, ed. Barish, p. 16. For the spy network slightly later, see B.N.
de Luna, *Jonson's Romish Plot: A Study of 'Catiline' in its Historical
Context* (Oxford, 1967). Cf. V.iii.39–40, 48–9.

91  For a detailed but highly partisan account of the Essex rebellion see
Tenison, *Elizabethan England* XI, *passim*; a good recent account is
Mervyn James, 'At a Crossroads of Political Culture: the Essex revolt,
1601' in his *Society, Politics and Culture* (Cambridge, 1986), pp. 416–65.

92  Quoted in Bald, p. 108.

93  James, *Society, Politics and Culture*, p. 446.

94  *CSPD Elizabeth*, CCLXXVIII, p. 578, 18 February 1601; text here
from the original document, SP 12/278/85.

95  See Wilfrid R. Prest, *The Inns of Court Under Elizabeth I and the Early
Stuarts* (1972), p. 179.

96  Clare, p. 95 n. 43; cf. Sharpe, pp. 69–72.

97  The name 'Broome' may not have improved matters: see E. A. J.
Honigmann, 'Sir John Oldcastle: Shakespeare's Martyr', in *'Fanned and
Winnowed Opinions': Shakespearean Essays presented to Harold Jenkins*
(1987), pp. 118–32 (pp. 128–9).

98  *Acts of the Privy Council*, 1600–1, 8 February.

99  Heinemann, 'Rebel Lords', p. 66; she notes that Jonson's friend Selden
was arrested and interrogated along with Sandys and Southampton for
organising 'mischievous opposition' in Parliament. For the Virginia
Company, Susan M. Kingsbury, *The Records of the Virginia Company of
London* (Washington, 1933), III, 68, 80–90.

100 Jonson's letter to him in 1605 implies that the connection is of some
years' standing: 'You have euer been free and Noble to mee' (*H&S*, I,
199).

101 The list of contemporary 'wits' in *Discoveries* is also significant: Sidney,
Hooker, Essex ('noble and high'), Raleigh, Saville, Sandys, Egerton and
Bacon (*H&S*, VIII, 591). This view is contrary to that of de Luna,
*Jonson's Romish Plot*, that Jonson was an apologist for the anti-Essex
faction: see e.g. pp. 20, 24–5, 100–5.

102 Chambers, *ES*, III, 275–6; Clare, pp. 127–31, 143–4. Greville is
quoted in Honigmann, *Myriad-minded Shakespeare*, p. 117, where the
argument on unintended Essex allusions in *Troilus* is advanced.

103 Though Popham would have resigned membership on appointment to
the bench, he kept close contacts with his old Inn, helping to arrange a
masque for the Queen in 1602, and leaving money to buy plate in his
will.

104 Lawrence Stone, *The Crisis of the Aristocracy: 1558–1641* (Oxford, 1965), p. 62. The precise date of Jonson's first acquaintance with some of these men cannot be established, but references to Hoskyns, Martin, Donne and Overbury at least suggest that he knew them well by the late 1590s: see e.g. Riggs, pp. 56–7.

105 A list of prominent members of the Middle Temple and other Inns is in Finkelpearl, pp. 261–4; cf. also Baker, *Ben Jonson and the Inns of Court*, chapter 1.

106 Richard Martin, *A Speach delivered to the King's . . . Majestie* (1603), sig. B1r. For a discussion of attitudes to Roman civil law, see Brian P. Levack, 'Law and Ideology: The Civil Law and Theories of Absolutism in Elizabethan and Jacobean England' in *The Historical Renaissance*, ed. Heather Dubrow and Richard Strier (Chicago and London, 1988), pp. 220–41. Bevington argues (p. 287) that Jonson is interested only in the humanist aspect, and has a patrician contempt for the law: but *Poetaster* does show the legal system (admittedly run by poets) working under Caesar's guidance.

107 For widespread use of violence among gentry and aristocracy, see Stone, *Crisis of the Aristocracy*, pp. 223–34, 242–50; amongst the Essex-Southampton group in particular, James, *Society, Politics and Culture*, pp. 429–32. For the Martin–Jonson group, see Finkelpearl, pp. 46–8 and Riggs, p. 57.

108 For the Mitre/Mermaid circle, see I. A. Shapiro, 'The "Mermaid Club"', *MLR*, XLV (1950), 6–17; cf. also *CSPD*, lxvi, p. 2, and Bald, 193–4; Bald is wrong in thinking that 'John' is a mistake for 'Thomas' Bond: the former was certainly one of this group. Donne later became MP for Taunton following John Bond: the seat was largely in the gift of Sir Edward Phelips, who was also closely associated with this group. Martin defended Bond's attacks on JPs in the 1601 parliament. Bond's *Horace* was popular throughout the seventeenth century. For Jonson's use of Heinsius in his translation of the *Ars Poetica*, see W. D. Briggs, *Anglia*, XXXVIII (1914), 116–18; he met Heinsius in Leiden in 1613 (Riggs, p. 191). The edition that survives from Jonson's library is that of Bernardino Partenio (Venice, 1584), now in Cambridge University Library (McPherson, 85), but the satires important to *Poetaster* are not marked, and it may well have been bought after the fire which damaged many of his books in 1623.

109 Gurr, pp. 75–6, quoting Frances Lenton, *The Young Gallant's Whirligigg* (1629), p. 4: 'Instead of *Perkins* pedlers French, he sayes / He better loves *Ben: Iohnsons booke of Playes*.'

110 Norbrook, *Poetry and Politics in the English Renaissance* (1984), pp. 16–17, 175–94.

111 The fullest accounts of Martin are in *DNB*, Hasler, III, 22–3 and Manningham, pp. 311–12. Bald, Finkelpearl and Menna Prestwich, *Lionel Cranfield: Politics and Profits under the Early Stuarts* (Oxford, 1966) add details. For Martin's part in the 1601 parliament, see J. E. Neale, *Elizabeth I and her Parliaments 1584–1601* (1957), pp. 369–432 *passim*.

112  *Prince d'Amour*, pp. 89–90.
113  *Brief Lives*, ed. Andrew Clark, 2 vols (Oxford, 1898), II, 48. Anthony
     Wood, *Athenae Oxonienses*, ed. P. Bliss, 4 vols (1813–20), II, 250–1.
114  Hasler, III, 22–3; Neale, pp. 380, 382–3, 398, 402 and 418–19.
115  Bald, p. 145: 'The choice and usuall Speakers are, *Bacon, Edwin Sands,
     Yelverton, Martin*'.
116  Chamberlain, I, 525, 531; see also Michael Strachan, *Sir Thomas Roe
     1581–1644: A Life* (1989), p. 50.
117  Cf. Finkelpearl, pp. 62–9. Pym was, like Martin, a west countryman;
     both went to Broadgates Hall, Oxford. For the broader ideological
     context of such opposition, see Johan Sommerville, *Politics and Ideology
     in England 1603–1640* (1986) and the review by Kevin Sharpe, 'Culture,
     Politics and the English Civil War' in his *Politics and Ideas in Early
     Stuart England* (1989), pp. 279–316.
118  *Satiromastix*, 'To the World', ll. 29–35
119  Campbell, p. 110, n. 7.
120  For the Hanham family, see John Hutchins, *History and Antiquities of
     Dorset* (3rd ed., 1868), I, 398–9 and III, 231; *Visitation of Dorsetshire,
     1623, Harleian Soc.*, XX (1885), 50–1; *Middle Temple Records*, ed.
     Charles Henry Hopwood (1904), I, 372, 383; *Wills Proved in the Prero-
     gative Court of Canterbury 1584–1604, Index Library*, XXV (1901);
     Hasler, II, 248–9.
121  *HMC*, IX, Salisbury, XI, p. 320, Cobham to Cecil; Foster, *London
     Marriage Licences 1521–1869* (1887), 17 February 1575.
122  Richard Hakluyt, *Principal Navigations Voyages Traffiques & Discoveries
     of the English Nation* (1927), VII, pp. 77, 108.
123  Samuel Purchas, *Hakluytus Posthumus or Purchas his Pilgrimes* (Glasgow,
     1906), XIX, 269–70, 296; see also *Purchas his Pilgrimage, or Relations of
     the World and the Pilgrims Observed* (2nd ed., 1614), pp. 755–6 for a
     similar summary of Hanham's account. John Latimer, *Annals of Bristol
     in the Seventeenth Century* (Bristol, 1900), pp. 27–8, makes it clear that
     Hanham went as 'commander', not 'master' of the ship: he was a
     military not a naval captain.
124  *CSP Ireland*, CXLII, 4 March 1588/9, Popham on 'the undertakers in
     Cork', including himself and Hanham.

# POETASTER

## or

# The Arraignment:

*As it hath beene sundry times priuately acted in the* Blacke Friers, *by the children of her Maiesties* Chappell.

Composed, by *Ben. Iohnson.*

*Et mihi de nullo fama rubere placet.*

LONDON

¶ Printed for M. L. and are to be sould in Saint Dunstans Church-yarde.

1602.

2   The title-page of the first edition of *Poetaster* (1602).

# POETASTER

## OR

# The Arraignment

## *A Comical Satire*

To                                                                              5
THE VIRTUOUS,
AND MY WORTHY
FRIEND,
Mr. Richard Martin.

Sir,   A thankful man owes a courtesy ever, the unthankful        10
but when he needs it. To make mine own mark appear, and
show by which of these seals I am known, I send you this

---

3. The] *Q*; His *F*.   4. *A . . . Satire*] *F*; *not in Q*.   5–21. To . . . Ben
Jonson.] *F; not in Q*.   8. FRIEND,] *Corr. F*; FRIEND. *uncorr. F*.

---

1. *POETASTER*] The suffix *-aster* indicates an incomplete resemblance,
hence here an imitation, 'petty or paltry poet' (*OED*). It is not classical
Latin, but is first recorded in a Latin letter of Erasmus (25 March 1521; see
*Collected Works*, VII, 175, trans. R. A. B. Mynors (Toronto, 1988)). Forms
(*poetastre, poetastro*) appear in French, Italian, Spanish and Portuguese during the sixteenth century, but the first recorded use in English is by J. in *CR*
II.iv.15: 'your ignorant *Poetasters* of the time, who when they have got
acquainted with a strange word, neuer rest till they have wroong it in'. It is
used of Crispinus in III.iv.111, 295 and V.iii.176, 211; Tucca calls Gallus
and Tibullus poetasters in IV.iii.99; cf. *Volp.* Epistle, l. 13, and *S-M*
II.ii.12: 'I doe not thinke but to proceede Poetaster next Commencement'.
   3. *The Arraignment*] trial, indictment; both the play as a whole, and the
actual trial in V.iii. 'The' was replaced by 'His' in *F*, but is retained here
both because of its possible associations with Essex's arraignment, *the*
arraignment of 1601–2 (see p. 44), and because it is the title used in the play
itself (Ind.3).
   4. Comical Satire] first used by J. on the title-page of the three quartos of
*EMO* (all 1600), but added to the title-pages of *CR* and *Poetaster* only in *F*.
In 1600 the use of the term challenged the order of 1 June 1599 'That noe
*Satyres* or *Epigrams* be printed hereafter' (Arber, *SR*, III, 677–8).
   9. *Richard Martin*] See pp. 46–7.
   10–11. *A thankful . . . it*] *H&S* note the paraphrase of Seneca *Ben.*
III.xvii.3: 'The grateful man delights in a benefit over and over, the un-
grateful man but once.'

62

piece of what may live of mine, for whose innocence, as for the Author's, you were once a noble and timely undertaker to the greatest Justice of this kingdom. Enjoy now the delight of  15
your goodness, which is to see that prosper, you preserved; and posterity to owe the reading of that, without offence, to your name, which so much ignorance and malice of the times then conspired to have suppressed.

Your true lover,  20
Ben Jonson.

The Persons of the Play.

AUGUSTUS CAESAR.

21. Ben Jonson] *This ed.;* BEN. IONSON *F.*    The Persons . . . Play.] *F;*
THE PERSONS THAT ACT. *Q, numbering the characters. F (and Subst. Q)
dispose the characters in two columns thus:* AVGVSTVS CÆSAR. | LVPVS. /
MECŒNAS. | TVCCA. / MARC. OVID. | CRISPINVS. / COR. GALLVS. |
HERMOGENES. / PROPERTIVS. | DE. FANNIVS. / FVS. ARISTVS. | ALBIVS. /
PVB. OVID. | MINOS. / VIRGIL. | HISTRIO. / HORACE. | PYRGVS. /
TREBATIVS. | LICTORS. / IVLIA. / CYTHERIS. / PLAVTIA. / CHLOE. /
MAYDES.

---

13. *innocence*] J. was accused of attacking the law, soldiers and actors: see 'Apol. Dial.', 68–70. For allusions to the Essex rebellion, see pp. 40–4.

14. *undertaker*] guarantor; cf. *SW*, Ded., 10 (*H&S*). See p. 29 for the suggestion that Martin may have intervened as Prince d'Amour responsible for the Middle Temple Revels.

15. *the greatest Justice*] The courts of Queen's Bench and Common Pleas both had Lord Chief Justices at this time, but the Chief Justice of the Queen's Bench was given precedence, and would therefore be the 'greatest'. This position was held by Sir John Popham from 1592 to 1607. His connections with the Middle Temple, the Hanham family, and the Essex rebellion all point to him as the person referred to (see pp. 42–3, 48–9).

19. *suppressed*] Any action against *Poetaster* would normally have been brought in Popham's court, but none is known. Since the court could not force a litigant to drop proceedings at Martin's behest, it follows that the threat of legal action, if there was one, was initiated by the court itself. In view of Popham's probable reasons for disliking the play, however, it is more likely that he would have used his influence as Privy Councillor and Lord Chief Justice to have the play suppressed without reference to the courts.

Further information on some of the characters will be found in the Introduction and Commentary.

1. *AUGUSTUS CAESAR*] 63 BC to AD 14; first emperor of Rome, undisputed master of the empire after the defeat of Mark Antony at Actium (31 BC).

MAECENAS.
MARC[US] OVID.
[TIBULLUS.]
COR[NELIUS] GALLUS.                             5
PROPERTIUS.
FUS[CUS] ARISTIUS.
PUB[LIUS] OVID.
VIRGIL.

2. MAECENAS] *Subst. Parfitt; Mecœnas Q;* MECŒNAS *F (so throughout).*
4. TIBULLUS] *Penniman; not in Q, F.*     7. ARISTIUS] *G; Aristius Q;*
ARISTVS *F.*

---

2. *MAECENAS*] Gaius Maecenas, died 8 BC, friend and counsellor of
Augustus, patron of many poets, including Virgil, Horace and Propertius.

3. *MARC[US] OVID*] father of the poet, who says (*Tristia* IV.x.77–84)
he died before his son's banishment in AD 8.

4. *[TIBULLUS]* Albius Tibullus, poet of equestrian family, *c.* 54–19
BC, friend of Horace, who addressed *Odes* I, 33 to him, and of Gallus. Ovid,
whose *Amores* III.ix is an elegy on his death, never met him.

5. *COR[NELIUS] GALLUS*] born *c.* 69 BC. poet and first prefect of
Egypt. Committed suicide in 26 BC after falling out of favour with Augustus.
Virgil's tenth *Eclogue* is a pastoral elegy praising him, but recently discovered
poetry by him has proved disappointing. Verse wrongly attributed to him
was in *Chorus Poetarum Classicorum* (Lyons,1616), II, 3263; J.'s copy is in the
British Library (McPherson, 40).

6. *PROPERTIUS*] Sextus Propertius, elegiac poet, born *c.* 51 BC,
patronised by Maecenas.

7. *FUS[CUS] ARISTIUS*] friend of Horace, mentioned in *Odes* I, 22
and *Sat.* I.ix.

8. *PUB[LIUS] OVID*] Publius Ovidius Naso, poet of equestrian
family, 43 BC to AD 18. Trained for the law, but did not practise it for long.
He was suddenly banished for life in 8 AD (sixteen years after Horace's death)
for reasons which remain obscure. Some Renaissance scholars believed that
an affair with the emperor's daughter Julia (see 24n) was the cause of his
banishment.

9. *VIRGIL*] Publius Virgilius Maro, epic and pastoral poet, 70–19 BC.
Patronised by Maecenas and Augustus. He read three books of the *Aeneid* to
Augustus and his family in 23 BC (see p. 15). Horace mentions him fre-
quently in affectionate terms.

HORACE.                                                    10
TREBATIUS.
LUPUS.
TUCCA.
CRISPINUS.

11. TREBATIUS] *F; not in Q.*

10. *HORACE*] Quintus Horatius Flaccus, poet, 65–8 BC. Patronised by Maecenas from about 39 BC; Augustus also showed strong favour towards him, see pp. 14–15.

11. *TREBATIUS*] Gaius Trebatius Testa, lawyer, *protégé* of Cicero; he may have died before Hor. addressed *Sat.* II.i, translated by J. in III.v below, to him.

12. *LUPUS*] Latin 'wolf'. A Lupus is mentioned by Hor. *Sat.* II.i as a figure attacked by the earlier satirist Lucilius (see J.'s version, III.v.110). He is given the *praenomen* Asinius in I.ii.147. Dekker replies by calling Horace's acolyte in *S-M* 'Asinius Bubo'. Fleay surmised 'Lupus was certainly someone named Wolf' (*Biographical Chronicle*, I, 367), but it is more likely that J. simply used the name to suggest its owner's dangerous malice. See also pp. 42–3.

13. *TUCCA*] given the *praenomen* Pantilius in I.i.30. In Hor. *Sat.* I.x.78, the 'bug Pantilius' (Greek, 'all-plucking') is associated as an annoyance with the 'backbiter' Demetrius and the 'inept' Fannius. Tucca is a name used in Martial's *Epigrams* (I.xviii, VI.lxv, VII.lxxvii, IX.lxxv, XI.lxx, XII.xli, XII.xciv) for a rather different character, and by Everard Guilpin in *Skialetheia* (1598), sig. B8v, for a character who responds to erotic verse thus: 'Which read to Captaine *Tucca*, he doth sweare, / And scratch, and sweare, and scratch to heare / His own discourse discours'd: and *by the Lord* / *It's passing good: oh good*! at every word / When his Cock-sparrow thoughts to itch begin, / He with a shrug swearest *a most sweet sinne.*' The specificity of this, and the characteristics shared with J.'s Tucca, support the view that a contemporary figure is the model for both. For Dekker's identification of him with 'Captain Hannam', see pp. 48–9.

14. *CRISPINUS*] Rufus Laberius Crispinus: a poetaster largely identified here with John Marston, first recognised by *G* (see III.iv.161n). 'Rufus' probably for Marston's red hair (cf. II.ii.76–81 and p. 9). Laberius was a writer of mimes mentioned by Hor. (*Sat.* I.x.6), and said by Aulus Gellius to write 'excessively ignoble and foul language' (*Noctes Atticae* xix.13). Crispinus was a stoic teacher mentioned several times by Hor. as a prolific poetaster (see esp. *Sat.* I.i.120, I.iv.14). It is also the name of a gallant in Juvenal I, 26–30.

HERMOGENES.                                                    15
DE[METRIUS] FANNIUS.
ALBIUS.
MINOS.
HISTRIO.
PYRGI.                                                        20

---

20. PYRGI] *G; Pyrgus Q, Subst. F* .

---

15. *HERMOGENES*] Hermogenes Tigellius, a singer and smooth courtier frequently mentioned with contempt by Hor. (see esp. *Sat.* I.ii.3, I.iii.4, I.ix.25 and I.x.80–90). J. adds character traits not in Hor., but strikingly similar to those of John Dowland, described as 'immensely self-centred and highly emotional, with a just appreciation of his own powers, but with an almost childishly irritable reaction to criticism; subject from time to time to attacks of melancholy' (Diana Poulton, *John Dowland* (1982), pp. 43–4). Dowland had left England in August 1598, but was probably sufficiently well-known to be lampooned in this way.

16. *DE[METRIUS] FANNIUS*] largely identified with Thomas Dekker (first by *G*, see III.iv.161n). Based on two characters in Hor.: Fannius is a bad poet ('ineptus') (*Sat.* I.iv.21, I.x.79–80) while Demetrius is a 'monkey' in *Sat.* I.x.18 and a 'backbiter' in I.x.78–9 (V.iii.323–33n and 448–54n).

17. *ALBIUS*] J.'s citizen goldsmith became a stock figure of Jacobean city comedy. He probably took the name from Hor. *Sat.* I.iv.28, a character who beggars his family by collecting bronzes, and hence a foolish wealthy man.

18. *MINOS*] An apothecary. King Minos was after his death a judge in the underworld. The name applied to an apothecary probably contains an allusion now irrecoverable. *H&S* surmise a tradesman who had Marston arrested for debt, but the arrest is in Hor. *Sat.* I.ix.74–8.

19. *HISTRIO*] Latin, 'an actor'; for parallels with contemporaries, see p. 42.

20. *PYRGI* ] Tucca's pages. From Greek, *pyrgos* a tower, with ironic reference to the size of the boy actors. *Pyrgopolinices*, 'one who conquers cities with towers', is the central figure in Plautus' *Miles Gloriosus*; aspects of Tucca's character derive from him, and the names of his pages acknowledge Plautian influence. Pyrgopolinices' servant addresses him in much the same contemptuous tone as Tucca's pages. *Pyrgus* was also an alternative name for the *turricula*, a dice box: cf. Martial XIV.xvi, and Turnebus VI.iii.164 and XXVII.iii.949–50 (J. owned the 1581 ed., and consulted it for *Sej.*; see *H&S*, I, 270). In J.'s copy of Scriverius' 1619 ed. of Martial (Folger Shakespeare Library), the word 'fritillus' (dice box) in epigram XIII.i is reported to be glossed 'pyrgus' by J. Renaissance editors of Horace read 'pyrgus' for 'phimus' in *Sat.* II.vii.16; Bond's note glosses it 'vasculum' (vessel) for dice. Thus the pages are siege towers to storm Tucca's objectives (*H&S*), and his means of gambling: with them, he hopes to 'skelder' money

LICTORS.

[LUSCUS.]

[EQUITES ROMANI.]

JULIA.

CYTHERIS.

PLAUTIA.                                                       25

CHLOE.

MAIDS.

[ENVY.]

[PROLOGUE.]                                                    30

21. LICTORS] *F; Lictor Q.*     22. LUSCUS] *Whalley; not in Q, F.*
23. EQUITES ROMANI] *H&S; not in Q, F;* Equites, &c. *G.*     27.
CHLOE] *F; Chloë Q (normally thus throughout).*     29–30. ENVY. PRO-
LOGUE] *This ed.; not in Q, F.*

from his victims. Cf. also the 'ordinary gallants page' in *WYW* (1601), who is
kept 'as his adamant to draw metell after to his lodging' (Wood, II, 270).
    21. *LICTORS*] attendants who carried the *fasces* (bundles of rods) before
a Roman magistrate, and exercised his powers of arrest: cf. Turnebus
XI.ix.328, quoting Cicero *Q.Fr.* I.i.13.
    23. *EQUITES ROMANI* ] members of the equestrian order, and at-
tendants on the emperor. According to Turnebus, there were six divisions of
the order (XI.ix.329).
    24. *JULIA*] only child of Augustus (39 BC to AD 14) exiled in 2 BC
because of her adulteries. Her daughter, also Julia, was exiled in AD 9 for the
same reason, and Ovid hints that she, or another member of Augustus'
family, was in some way the cause of his banishment in AD 8 (*Tristia* II,
102–6). *H&S* note that the misidentification of the elder Julia as Ovid's
mistress may stem from Sidonius Apollinaris, a writer of the fifth century
(*Carmina* XXIII, 158–61). That J. had this passage in mind is confirmed by
*Und.* XXVII, 17–20, which imitate Sidonius: 'Or hath Corinna, by the name
/ Her Ovid gave her, dimmed the fame / Of Caesar's daughter, and the line /
Which all the world then styled divine?' Chapman accepts this tradition in
the introduction to *Ovid's Banquet of Sence* (1595), as does Sandys in the life
of Ovid prefixed to his translation of the *Metamorphoses* (1640).
    25. *CYTHERIS*] a dancer, mentioned by Ovid (*Amores* I.xv.29) and
Virgil (*Eclogues* X) as the mistress of Gallus, who addressed her under the
pseudonym of Lycoris. Cf. *Und.* XXVII, 15–16.
    26. *PLAUTIA*] supposed mistress of Tibullus, whom he addresses
under the pseudonym of Delia. Cf. *Und.* XXVII, 10.
    27. *CHLOE*] The name is used by Hor. several times in the *Odes.* The
'haughty ('arrogantem') Chloe' of *Odes* III, 26 may have suggested the name
to J. Three of Martial's epigrams (III.liii, IV.xxviii and IX.xv) attack a
Chloe.

## THE SCENE
## ROME.

Ad Lectorem.

*Ludimus innocuis verbis, hoc iuro potentis*
*Per Genium Famæ, Castalidumque gregem:*                    5
*Perque tuas aures, magni mihi numinis instar,*
*Lector, inhumana liber ab Invidia.*                    Mart.

---

1–2. *THE SCENE* **ROME**] *F; not in* Q.     3–7. Ad . . . Mart.] *Q; not
in F; after* **ROME** *F2 adds list of actors given in F at end of play.*

3. *Ad Lectorem*] To the Reader.
4–7. Ludimus . . . Invidia.] slightly     adapting     Martial     VII.xii.9–12
(Martial has 'innocui: scis hoc bene' in the first line): 'We play with harmless
words: I swear by the genius of mighty Fame, and the Castalian choir, and
by your ears, which are to me like a great deity, reader, free from churlish
envy' (my translation; whether reader or poet is free is left nicely ambiguous). The same epigram (l. 4) supplied the motto on the title-pages of Q and
F (see Plate 2): 'And fame won from another's blush does not please me.'
The context is important for J., in that Martial is claiming innocence ('my
page has not wounded even those it justly hates') and misrepresentation:
'What does this avail me when certain folk would pass off as mine darts wet
with the blood of Lycambes [see 'Apol. Dial.', 148–9n], and under my name
a man vomits his viperous venom who owns he cannot bear the light of
day?' Dekker retorted modestly with Martial XIII.ii.4–8 in *S-M*, 'Ad
Detractorem'.

*After the second sounding.*

*[Enter]* ENVY. *Arising in the midst of the stage.*

*Envy.* Light, I salute thee, but with wounded nerves,
　　Wishing thy golden splendour pitchy darkness.
　　What's here? *Th' Arraignment?* Ay, this, this is it

---

0.1. *After . . . sounding*] F; *not in* Q.　0.2. ENVY] *Subst. F; LIVOR Q.*
*Arising . . . stage*] F *in margin; not in* Q.　3. *Th'Arraignment*] *Subst. F;*
*Th'arraignment* Q.

---

0.1. *Second sounding*] second of three trumpet calls announcing the beginning of a play. *CR* and *EMO* both have introductory speeches 'After the
second sounding'; it is not clear where the sounding was made for the indoor
theatres. Cf. Dekker, *Gull's Hornbook*: 'the quaking prologue . . . is ready to
giue the trumpets their Cue that hees vpon point to enter' (in Chambers, *ES*,
IV, 367).

0.2. *ENVY*] Marston had personified Envy in *Hist.* (Wood, III, 277;
acted 1599; see pp. 31–2); *Troil.* II.iii.20–1, 'I have said my prayers, and
devil Envy say amen' may refer to *Poetaster* (Small, p. 142). 'Envy' carried a
stronger sense of malice, ill-will, than it does today: cf. *OED*, 1. Several
contemporary verse satires, including Marston's *Scourge*, open or close with
addresses to Envy or Detraction. For criticism of J.'s use of the prologue 'to
mainetaine *Contempt* / Gainst common *Censure*' see *WYW* (Wood, II, 232).
For the influence of earlier personifications of Envy, see C.R. Baskervill,
*English Elements in Jonson's Early Comedy* (Austin, Texas, 1911), pp. 155,
286–9.

*Arising . . . stage*] There was probably a single winch-operated trap centre
stage at the Blackfriars: cf. the rise of Echo in *CR* I.ii.14–18, Scylla's ghost in
*Cat.* I.1–3, and Asdrubal in Marston's *Sophonisba* (Wood, II, 52). It was
probably the hiding place in *C is A* III.v.13; Marston uses it for descents (as J.
here in l. 58) in *Sophonisba* (Wood, II, 38 and 39). Dekker parodies J.'s use in
*S-M* IV.i.142–3: 'So, now arise sprite ath Buttry; no Herring-bone I'll not pull
thee out, but arise, dear Echo rise, rise, devil or I'll conjure thee up'.

1–2. *Light . . . darkness*] This and much of the following imagery derives
from Ovid's Envy in *Met.* II, 760–801, 'wrapped in thick, black fog'. Ovid's
'Invidia' is female, the *Livor* of Q masculine. J. is probably also recalling
Plutarch, 'On Envy and Hate': 'like sore eyes, [Envy] is disturbed by everything resplendent' (*Moralia*, 537). Mallory quotes Coleridge, *Shakespeare, Ben
Jonson, Beaumont and Fletcher* (1874), p. 226, raising the remote possibility
that 'Satan's address to the sun in the *Paradise Lost* [IV.32–6]' may have been
suggested by these lines.

1. *nerves*] feelings, courage (*OED*, 8b, citing this as first example).

3. Arraignment] The title under which the play was performed, and was
known to Dekker (*S-M, To the World*, 29). Envy reads from a title board,
probably on an upper storey of the tiring-house façade; William Percy's notes

That our sunk eyes have waked for all this while:
Here will be subject for my snakes and me.                              5
Cling to my neck and wrists, my loving worms,
And cast you round in soft and amorous folds
Till I do bid uncurl: then break your knots,
Shoot out yourselves at length, as your forced stings
Would hide themselves within his maliced sides                         10
To whom I shall apply you. Stay! The shine
Of this assembly here offends my sight;
I'll darken that first, and out-face their grace.
Wonder not if I stare: these fifteen weeks

---

for properties needed for his *Faery Pastorall* (intended for St Paul's) include
'Highest, aloft, and on the Top of the Musick Tree the Title . . . Beneath him
pind on Post of the Tree The Scene' (Chambers, *ES*, III, 137). Cf. *CR*, Ind.
40–2: 'First, the title of his play is CYNTHIAS *Reuels*, as any man (that hath
hope to be saued by his booke) can witnesse; the *Scene*, GARGAPHIE'. It is
less likely that Envy is reading from a playbill, though these were used; cf.
*Hist.*, Wood, III, 285: 'Enter *Belsh* setting uppe billes, Enter to him a
*Captaine.* / *Capt.* Sirra what set you up there? / *Belsh.* Text billes for Playes.'
They were also fixed to the doors of theatres (*ibid*, 282).

4. *waked*] stayed awake waiting for (*OED*, *v*. 2).

5. *snakes*] Envy was traditionally represented with snakes: cf. Ovid *Met*. II,
768–70, and Plate 1. Spenser places a coiled snake in Envy's bosom: *Faerie
Queene* I.iv.31.

6–10.] Together with l. 44, these lines suggest that the boy playing Envy
was festooned with snakes he was able to manipulate; Henslowe lists a snake
among the props of the Admiral's men (*Diary*, p. 320).

6. *worms*] snakes; cf. *MND* III.ii.71, 'Could not a worm, an adder, do so
much?'

9. *forced*] forcefully impelled.

10. *maliced*] threatened: cf. *EMO* V.xi.61: 'I am so farre from malicing
their states, / That I begin to pitty 'hem' (*H&S*).

11. *shine*] The 'shine' is figurative of the audience's accomplishments, but
also literal: unlike the public playhouses, the Blackfriars presented plays in
artificial (candle) light: cf. Smith, *Blackfriars*, pp. 301–3. *WYW* opens with
three gallants who 'sit a good while on the Stage before the Candles are
lighted . . . Enter *Tier-man* with lights' (Wood, II, 231).

12. *offends*] hurts. See ll. 1–2n for the link between envy and sore eyes.

13. *darken*] Cf. *Cat*. I.313 S.D.: 'A darkness comes over the place':
together with this passage, it makes clear that the auditorium lighting was
dimmed by some or all candles being extinguished at the beginning of the play;
stage lighting could have been altered between acts.

14. *fifteen weeks*] See pp. 28–9; cf. Dekker *S-M* I.ii.362–4, where Tucca
says of an epithalamium composed by Horace: 'What wut end? wut hang thy

(So long as since the plot was but an embrion) 15
Have I with burning lights mixed vigilant thoughts
In expectation of this hated play,
To which, at last, I am arrived as Prologue.
Nor would I you should look for other looks,
Gesture or compliment from me than what 20
The infected bulk of Envy can afford:
For I am ris here with a covetous hope,
To blast your pleasures and destroy your sports
With wrestings, comments, applications,
Spy-like suggestions, privy whisperings, 25
And thousand such promoting sleights as these.
Mark how I will begin: the scene is—ha!

---

18. at last] *In parentheses in Q, F.*     21. The infected] *G;* Th' infected *Q,* *F.*     22. ris] *This ed.;* risse *Q, F.*     27. scene] *G;* Scene *Q; Scene F.* is—] *This ed.;* is, *Q, F.*

---

selfe now? Has he not writ Finis yet *Iacke?* what will he bee fifteene weekes about this Cockatrice's egge too? has hee not cackeld yet? Not laide yet?' (*G*). J. replies in *Volp.* Prol. 9–18, esp. 15–16: 'And, though he dares give them five lives to mend it / 'Tis known five weeks fully penned it.'

15. *embrion*] original and etymologically more correct form of 'embryo'; cf. *Alc.* II.iii.83.

21. *bulk*] breast, trunk; cf. *Ham.* II.i.94–5: 'He raised a sigh so piteous and profound / As it did seem to shatter all his bulk' (*H&S*). Ovid says Envy's breast is green with gall (*Met.* II, 777).

*afford*] supply from its own resources.

22. *ris*] risen: cf. *Engl. Gr.* I.xix.30, where 'ris, rise or risen' are all given as examples of the 'participle past'.

24. *wrestings*] twisting of meanings.

*comments*] contrived interpretations, falsehoods; cf. V.iii.74, 101.

*applications*] maliciously applying satire to a particular case, cf. V.iii.135 and *Volp.* Epistle, 60–2: 'Application is now grown a trade with many, and there are that profess to have a key for the deciphering of everything'. See pp. 18, 40–4.

26. *promoting*] informing (*OED*, 8); cf. Drayton, *The Owl*, 545, 'Steps in this false spie, this promoting wretch' (*Poems*, ed. Buxton, I, 95.)

27. *scene*] setting; reading from a locality board (see note to l. 3). Slightly earlier such labels had been placed on the doors from which actors entered; cf. Sidney, *Apology*, p. 124: 'What child is there, that coming to a play, and seeing *Thebes* written in great letters upon an old door, doth believe that it is *Thebes?*' Cf. also *Troil.* Prol. 1: 'In Troy, there lies the scene.'

'Rome?' 'Rome?' and 'Rome?' Crack eye-strings, and
   your balls
Drop into earth! Let me be ever blind!
I am prevented; all my hopes are crossed,                          30
Checked and abated; fie, a freezing sweat
Flows forth at all my pores, my entrails burn!
What should I do? 'Rome'! 'Rome'! O my vexed soul,
How might I force this to the present state?
Are there no players here? No poet-apes,                           35
That come with basilisks' eyes, whose forkèd tongues
Are steeped in venom, as their hearts in gall?

---

28. 'Rome?' . . . 'Rome?'] *This ed.; Rome? . . . Rome? Q;* ROME? . . .
ROME? *F.* 33. 'Rome!' 'Rome!'] *This ed; Rome: Rome? Q;* ROME?
ROME? *F.*

---

28. '*Rome . . . Rome*'] 'The rage of Envy is excited because the scene is not
laid in London, and among the poet's contemporaries [and she therefore
cannot 'apply' the play maliciously to them]; a little patience, however, would
have rendered her fury unnecessary' (*G*). Chambers (*ES*, III, 154) takes the
repetition of 'Rome' to indicate three separate locality boards, a plausible
interpretation despite the smallness of the Blackfriars stage, with a label on
each of the three doors of the tiring-house, or with one placed centrally over a
tiring-house door, and two more on the boxes along each side of the stage (see
l. 71n).
   *eye-strings*] ocular nerves, whose breaking was thought to cause blindness.
The shock of grief or anger could break them: cf. *Cym.* I.iii.17, 'I would have
broke mine eye-strings, crack'd them', and Marston, 1 *Ant.* I.i.3–4: 'Veins,
sinews, arteries, why crack ye not'. In *EMO* Macilente has the same symp-
toms of envy: I.i.25–32, again related to Plutarch's metaphoric linking of envy
and sore eyes (see ll. 1–2n). Elkiah Crooke, *Microcosmographia* (1613) gives the
medical details.
   29. *blind*] Latin *invidia* is derived from *invidere*, to look maliciously at
(Lewis and Short, s.v. 'invideo'). Blindness would thus disable envy even
more than does the 'shine' of l. 11.
   30. *prevented*] anticipated.
   34. *force*] distort the meaning of.
   35. *here?*] i.e. in the audience.
   *poet-apes*] Those who ape poets, as Crispinus does. First used by Sidney,
*Apology*, p. 141; cf. *Ep.* LVI, 'On Poet-ape', and *S-M* II.ii.42–3: 'these
Twynnes, these *Poet-apes*', and V.ii.339 (as Crispinus crowns Horace with
nettles): '*All Poets shall be Poet-Apes but you*' (Penniman).
   36. *basilisks*] A fabulous serpent, hatched from a cock's egg (cf. *EMO*
I.ii.220); also called a cockatrice (cf. III.iv.192, IV.iii.64, and IV.v.53, 109).

Either of these would help me; they could wrest,
Pervert, and poison all they hear or see
With senseless glosses and allusions.                          40
Now if you be good devils, fly me not:
You know what dear and ample faculties
I have endowed you with: I'll lend you more.
Here, take my snakes among you, come and eat,
And while the squeezed juice flows in your black jaws,         45
Help me to damn the Author. Spit it forth
Upon his lines, and show your rusty teeth
At every word or accent; or else choose
Out of my longest vipers, to stick down
In your deep throats, and let the heads come forth             50
At your rank mouths, that he may see you armed
With triple malice, to hiss, sting and tear
His work and him; to forge, and then declaim,
Traduce, corrupt, apply, inform, suggest:
O, these are gifts wherein your souls are blest.               55
What! Do you hide yourselves? Will none appear?
None answer? What, doth this calm troop affright you?
Nay, then I do despair: down, sink again.

*[She begins to descend.]*

54. inform] *G; enforme Q, F; enforce F2.*     58.1 S.D.] *This ed.; Descends
slowly. G, after 61.*

---

38-9. *wrest ... poison*] echoing Marston, *Scourge*, 'To him that hath
perused me', 5–14.

41. *good devils*] Still addressing the players or poet-apes Envy hopes to find
in the audience.

44. *come and eat*] Ovid represents Envy 'eating snakes' flesh, the proper
food of her venom' (*Met.* II, 769; so *H&S*).

46. *damn*] i.e. hiss.

47. *rusty teeth*] Ovid describes them as *robigine*, rusty; Martial describes an
envious man as having 'rusty teeth' ('robiginosis ... dentibus', V.xxviii.7;
*H&S*).

50. *heads come forth*] Geffrey Whitney, *A Choice of Emblemes* (1586, p. 94)
shows Envy with snakes coming from her mouth.

54-5.] *H&S* point to the rhyming couplet in what Envy hopes is the climax
of her speech.

57. *calm troop*] the audience; cf. *1 Ant.*, Prol. 2, 'this fair troop'.

58. *sink again*] W. J. Lawrence compares this slow descent with that of
Harpax in last act of *The Virgin Martyr*, 'first sinking a little and then
disappearing' (*Pre-Restoration Stage Studies* (1927), p. 111, quoted by *H&S*); it
supports the argument for a platform trap operated by a winch. The instruc-

This travail is all lost with my dead hopes.
If in such bosoms spite have left to dwell,                    60
Envy is not on earth, nor scarce in hell.

*The third sounding.*

[*Enter*] PROLOGUE [*in armour*].

*Prologue.* Stay, Monster! Ere thou sink, thus on thy head
Set we our bolder foot, with which we tread
Thy malice into earth: [ENVY *disappears.*] so spite should
   die,
Despised and scorned by noble industry.                       65
If any muse why I salute the stage
An armèd Prologue, know, 'tis a dangerous age,

---

61.1. *The third sounding*] F; *not in* Q.    61.2. PROLOGUE] F; PRO-
LOGVS Q, *which prints the speech in italic; As she disappears, enter PRO-
LOGUE hastily, in armour.* G.    64. S.D.] *This ed.*

---

tion in Marston's *Sophonisba* to 'close the vault when I am sunk' (Wood, II, 38)
points to a simple hinged door opening upwards, but this was probably acted
at Blackfriars late 1605–6, and 'may have been taken over from Paul's'
(Chambers, *ES*, III, 433), so does not provide reliable evidence.

   60. *have left*] has ceased.

   61.1 *The third sounding*] Smith, *Blackfriars*, suggests the trumpet was the
cue for the stagehands operating a winch to halt the descent while the Prologue
put his foot on Envy's head before pushing it below (p. 313).

   62–3. *on . . . foot*] Heroic virtue (Hercules) is represented thus with his
foot on the head of Envy in Rubens's decorative scheme for the Banqueting
House, Whitehall (1629–34; see Plate 1).

   65. *industry*] diligence, here in the sense of continual vigilance: not in *OED*
in this sense, but perhaps suggested by Latin *industrius*: cf. Cicero, 'homines
vigilantii . . . industrii' (*Cael.* XXXI, 74) and Juvenal VIII, 52 'armis industrius'; in both cases the adjective means simply 'diligent', but is associated
with vigilance or arms.

   67. *armèd Prologue*] The prologue normally wore a black velvet cloak: cf.
Heywood, *Four Prentises of London* (1615), Prologue, 'Enter three in blacke
clokes, at three dores. 1. *What meane you, my maisters . . . Doe you not know that
I am the Prologue? Do you not see this long blacke velvet cloke upon my backe?*'
(cited by Whalley, note to *CR*, Ind. 9). *1 Ant.* ends with an 'armed Epilogue'
which refers to J.'s Epilogue to *CR* (since *CR* was acted in late 1600 to early
1601, either Marston must have added the epilogue to *1 Ant.* after its original
performances, or the accepted dating of the play in 1599 to early 1600 must be
revised): *CR*'s Epilogue concludes '*By god 'tis good, and if you like't, you may*'.
*1 Ant.* responds with 'I stand not as a peremptory challenger of desert, either
for him that composed the comedy, or for us that acted it: but a most

Wherein who writes had need present his scenes
Forty-fold proof against the conjuring means
Of base detractors and illiterate apes,                    70
That fill up rooms in fair and formal shapes.
'Gainst these have we put on this forced defence,
Whereof the allegory and hid sense
Is that a well erected confidence
Can fright their pride, and laugh their folly hence.       75
Here now put case our Author should once more
Swear that his play were good; he doth implore
You would not argue him of arrogance,
Howe'er that common spawn of ignorance,
Our fry of writers, may beslime his fame                   80
And give his action that adulterate name.
Such full-blown vanity he more doth loathe
Than base dejection: there's a mean 'twixt both,
Which with a constant firmness he pursues,
As one that knows the strength of his own Muse.            85

---

69. Forty-fold proof] *G; Fortie fold proofe Q;* Fortie fold-proofe *F.*

___

submissive suppliant for both.' Prologue answers here with 'a well erected
confidence' (l. 74 below), a phrase taken up by Shakespeare in *Troil.* (*SR* Feb.
1603, perhaps acted 1602): 'hither am I come, / A prologue armed, but not in
confidence / Of author's pen or actor's voice' (Prol. 22–4). *H&S* note later
imitations in Randolph's *Aristippus* (1630) and Burnell's *Landgartha* (1641).

68. *scenes*] plays; cf. *H5*, Prol. 5: 'And monarchs to behold the swelling
scene'.

69. *Forty-fold*] Forty was often used indefinitely to express a large
number; cf. III.ii.8. See *OED*, A. *adj.* b; this antedates *OED*'s first example
(1607).

*conjuring*] conspiring; see *OED* s.v. 'Conjure' I.1.

71. *rooms*] the boxes that stood at right angles to the Blackfriars stage: see
Bentley, VI, 6–7.

76. *put case*] suppose: *OED*, II, 12.

*once more*] as in last line of *CR*; see l. 67n. 'J. takes the first occasion to
apologize for the language [of *CR*]. His apology, however, is but awkward'
(*G*).

78. *argue*] accuse: *OED*, 2.

79–80. *spawn . . . beslime*] Cf. *WYW*, 'the muddy spawne / Of slymie
Neughtes' (Wood, II, 250).

80. *fry*] The young of creatures produced in large numbers: 'spawn' and
'beslime' suggest that J. has frogs (or Marston's newts) in mind.

82. *vanity*] self-conceit.

83. *base dejection*] self-abasement; cf. V.iii.343.

And this he hopes all free souls will allow;
Others, that take it with a rugged brow,
Their moods he rather pities than envies:
His mind it is above their injuries.          [*Exit.*]

---

86. *allow*] accept as true or valid (*OED*, 4).
87. *rugged* ] frowning.

# Act I

ACT I   SCENE i

*[Enter]* OVID.

*Ovid.* Then, when this body falls in funeral fire,
   My name shall live, and my best part aspire.
   It shall go so. [*Writes.*]

*[Enter* LUSCUS.]

*Luscus.* Young master! Master Ovid, do you hear? Gods a me!
   Away with your songs and sonnets, and on with your gown      5
   and cap quickly: here, here, your father will be a man of
   this room presently. Come, nay, nay, nay, nay, be brief.
   These verses too, [*Picking up a paper*] a poison on 'em, I

---

I.i.o.1] *Scene draws, and discovers* OVID *in his study.* G, *who continues the scene throughout the act.*   3.1.   S.D.] *This ed.; Enter* LUSCUS *with a gown and cap.* G.   8.   S.D.] *This ed.*

---

I.i.] For Swinburne's objection to the early introduction of Ovid, see p. 19.
   1–2.] The last lines of *Amores* I.xv as translated by Marlowe (see ll. 43–84n, and p. 19). Cf. also *Amores* III.ix.28 (used by J.'s 'son' Herrick on the title-page of *Hesperides*), *Tristia* I.vii, and Hor. *Odes* III.xxx.6–7.
   2. aspire] rise, mount up.
   3. *It . . . so*] Writing these lines down, Ovid does not notice Luscus' entry.
   4. *Gods a me*] shortened form of 'God save me'.
   5. *songs and sonnets*] Cf. *C is A* IV.v.1, 'Fellow *Juniper*, no more of thy songs and sonnets', *EMI* IV.iii.17, and *Wiv.* I.i.198–9: 'I had rather than forty shillings I had my Book of Songs and Sonnets here.' The title originated with Tottel's *Songes and Sonettes, written by the right honorable Lord Henry Howard, late Earle of Surrey, and other* (1557). Penniman notes Nashe 'brought it into vulgar, slangy use' (*Anatomie of Absurdities*, 1589); it was nevertheless the title under which Donne's poems were published in 1633.
   5–6. *gown and cap*] of an English, not a Roman student; Roman dress was studied by Renaissance antiquarians such as Rosinus, consulted by J. for *Sej.*, and in specialised studies such as Aldus Manutius's *Dissertatio de Toga Romanorum* (in *De qvaesitis per epistolam*, Venice, 1576). J. makes use of such anachronisms to signal the contemporaneity of his satire: see p. 9.
   6–7. *man . . . room*] i.e. in this room; see *OED* 'Man' *sb.*18.

77

cannot abide 'em, they make me ready to cast, by the
banks of Helicon. Nay look, what a rascally untoward        10
thing this poetry is; I could tear 'em now.

*Ovid.* [*Taking the paper from him*] Give me. How near's my
father?

*Luscus.* Heart a' man! Get a law book in your hand, I will not
answer you else. [*Giving him a book*] Why, so: now there's        15
some formality in you. By Jove and three or four of the
gods more, I am right of mine old master's humour for
that; this villainous poetry will undo you, by the welkin.

*Ovid.* What, hast thou buskins on, Luscus, that thou swear'st
so tragically and high?        20

*Luscus.* No, but I have boots on, sir, and so has your father too
by this time: for he called for 'em, ere I came from the
lodging.

*Ovid.* Why, was he no readier?

*Luscus.* O no; and there was the mad skeldering captain, with        25
the velvet arms, ready to lay hold on him as he comes

---

10. Helicon] *G; Helicon Q;* helicon *F.*    12. S.D.] *This ed.*    15. S.D.]
*This ed.*    24. Why,] *G;* Why? *Q, F.*

---

9. *cast*] vomit (*H&S*).

9–10. *by . . . Helicon*] an uncharacteristic oath, probably used as an appropriate blasphemy against poetry; Luscus is not reading from Ovid's
papers, since the words are not in Ovid's poem.

10. *untoward*] foolish and unlikely to prosper (cf. *OED*, 4 and 5).

14. *Heart a' man*] shortened form of 'Heart of God, man'; cf. *New Custom*
(1573) II.3 (Dodsley, *Old English Plays*, rev. W. C. Hazlitt (1874–6), III,
37): 'Heart of God, man, be the means better or worse, I pass not.' Cf.
'Heart of me!', IV.iv.25.

*Get . . . hand*] Cf. *R3* III.vii.47: 'And look you get a prayer-book in
your hand'; see also I.ii.230n.

16. *formality*] conformity to rule, propriety (*OED*, 6).

18. *welkin*] vault of heaven; an affected usage: cf. *Wiv.* I.iii.92: 'By welkin
and her star!' and esp. *Tw.N.* III.i.58, a line which parodies J.'s use of
'element' (see p. 33).

19. *buskins*] high shoes worn in classical tragedy; cf. the 'Chopins' of *S-M*,
'To the World', 1.10.

25. *skeldering*] begging, cheating, especially in guise of a wounded or
disbanded soldier; cf. I.ii.50 and III.iv.159, and *EMO*, 'Characters', 84–5:
'SHIFT', 'One that never was Souldier, yet lives upon lendings. His profession is skeldring and odling' (so *G*).

26. *velvet arms*] a sword and dagger in velvet scabbards (sheaths); cf.
III.iv.18, *EMI* II.iv.76: 'Aye, with a velvet scabbard, I think' and *WYW*,
Wood, II, 275: 'I thought twas for somthing you goe casd in your velvit

down: he that presses every man he meets with an oath to
lend him money, and cries 'Thou must do't, old boy, as
thou art a man, a man of worship.'

*Ovid.* Who? Pantilius Tucca?                                    30

*Luscus.* Ay, he: and I met little master Lupus, the tribune,
going thither too.

*Ovid.* Nay, and he be under their arrest, I may with safety
enough read over my elegy before he come.

*Luscus.* Gods a me! What'll you do? Why young master, you      35
are not Castalian mad, lunatic, frantic, desperate? Ha?

*Ovid.* What ailest thou, Luscus?

*Luscus.* God be with you, sir, I'll leave you to your poetical
fancies and furies. I'll not be guilty, I.                *Exit.*

*Ovid.* Be not, good ignorance: I'm glad th' art gone,          40
For thus alone our ear shall better judge
The hasty errors of our morning Muse.

---

28–9. 'Thou . . . worship.'] *Nicholson; Thou . . . worshippe. Q;* (Thou . . .
worship.) *F.*   33–4. with . . . enough] *In parentheses in Q, F.*   36.
Castalian] *G; Castalian Q; castalian F.*   39. S.D.] *Q.*

---

skabberd.' Mallory quotes Fynes Morison, *Itinerary* (1617) on the fashion
being common in England and France: 'In England men of mean sort use
them'; the implication is that the sword is only for show.

28. *old boy*] Cf. I.ii.134; *OED* does not record this familiar usage before
1712; J. falls back on it to replace references to knighthood in *F* in I.ii.149,
162 and 187; see App. 1, pp. 284–5.

29. *man of worship*] *OED* s.v. 'worship' (4) quotes Stowe, *Survey of
London* (1598) indicating that a 'man of worship' was specifically a gentleman
of standing, below the rank of a nobleman. It is a favourite appellation of
Tucca's: cf. I.ii.26, III.iv.164, IV.iii.100, V.iii.145.

31. *tribune*] Roman official; there were several types of tribune: Lupus is a
magistrate (see I.ii.40), and J. probably conceived him as a *tribunus plebis*
(cf. Godwyn, pp. 127–8).

33. *and*] if; *OED* C.1–4. Cf. I.ii.184, and *EMI* (Q) III.iv.68–70:
'Sblood he shakes his head like a bottle, to feele and there be any brayne in
it.'

*under . . . arrest*] figuratively, since 'under arrest' is only used in the sense
of legal restraint.

34. *elegy*] The classical elegy was predominantly a medium for love
poetry.

36. *Castalian mad*] Castalia was the spring on Parnassus sacred to the
Muses.

42. *hasty errors*] Ovid had a reputation as a quick and careless writer: that
he should be seen to revise his poetry carefully would be important to J.

*morning Muse*] i.e. his morning's writing.

[*Reads.*] *Envy, why twit'st thou me my time's spent ill,*
*And call'st my verse fruits of an idle quill?*
*Or that (unlike the line from whence I sprung)*                    45
*War's dusty honours I pursue not young?*
*Or that I study not the tedious laws*
*And prostitute my voice in every cause?*
*Thy scope is mortal; mine, eternal fame,*
*Which through the world shall ever chant my name.*                 50
*Homer will live whilst Tenedos stands, and Ide,*
*Or to the sea fleet Simois doth slide:*
*And so shall Hesiod too, while vines do bear,*
*Or crooked sickles crop the ripened ear.*
*Callimachus, though in invention low,*                             55
*Shall still be sung, since he in art doth flow.*

---

43–4.] Ouid. Lib. I. Amo. Ele. 15. *Marginal note in Q, F*    45. sprung] *F;*
sprong *Q.*

---

43–84.] Substantially the translation of *Amores* I.xv which appeared in the
third so-called 'Middleburgh' ed. of Marlowe's translations of *All Ovids
Elegies* under the heading '*The same by* B.I.'. See p. 19, n. 40. J.'s changes
from Marlowe's text (if they are his, and not those of a MS version revised by
Marlowe) are set out in *H&S*, IX, 539–40. Eighteenth-century Shake-
speareans' malice towards J. is typified by Malone's pencilled note in the
Bodleian copy of *Q*: 'Jonson's impudence in printing this translation as his
*own*, is perhaps unparalleled. It was done by Marlowe; and he has merely
altered a word here & there, generally for the worse.' G, over-reacting,
claimed that J. had written both versions. Since the Middleburgh editions
also contained epigrams by John Davies, a prominent Middle Templar, and
since they had been well advertised by being publicly burnt, the Marlowe
translations would certainly be known to some, perhaps many, of J.'s
audience, and plagiarism is very unlikely. Nor did Dekker accuse him of this
theft. It is much more likely that he expected the audience to recognise this
version as Marlowe's, but that he took the opportunity to 'improve' and
correct it.
    43. twit'st] to censure, reproach, used seriously at this date: cf. *2H6*
III.i.178: 'Hath he not twit our sovereign lady here'.
    51. Tenedos] Aegean island mentioned in the *Iliad* I, 38, and several
times in *Aeneid* II.
    Ide] Ida, mountain overlooking the plain of Troy, mentioned often in the
*Iliad* and *Aeneid.*
    52. Simois] small river near Troy.
    53. Hesiod] Greek poet, active *c.* 735 BC. The reference to vines and corn
is to his *Works and Days*; cf. V.iii.534.
    55. Callimachus] Alexandrian writer, died *c.* 240 BC, traditionally seen as
uninspired but learned: cf. I.ii.204, and V.iii.534.

No loss shall come to Sophocles' proud vein.
With sun and moon Aratus shall remain.
Whilst slaves be false, fathers hard, and bawds be whorish,
Whilst harlots flatter, shall Menander flourish.                              60
Ennius though rude, and Accius' high-reared strain
A fresh applause in every age shall gain.
Of Varro's name, what ear shall not be told?
Of Jason's Argo, and the fleece of gold?
Then shall Lucretius' lofty numbers die                                       65
When earth and seas in fire and flames shall fry.
Tityrus, Tillage, Aenee, shall be read
Whilst Rome of all the conquered world is head.
Till Cupid's fires be out, and his bow broken,
Thy verses (neat Tibullus) shall be spoken.                                   70
Our Gallus shall be known from east to west:

---

64. *Argo*] *G; Argo? Q;* ARGO? *F.*    67. *Tityrus*] *G;* Titirus *Q;* TYTIRVS
*F.*    *Aenee*] *Subst. G;* Æney *Q;* ÆNEE *F.*

---

57. Sophocles] Greek tragic dramatist and general, c. 496–406 BC.
58. Aratus] of Soli, *c.* 270 BC, wrote (in Greek) an astronomical poem
*Phaenomena* which was translated by Cicero.
60. Menander] Greek comic dramatist, 342–291 BC.
61. Ennius] 239–169 BC, regarded by Romans as the father of Latin
poetry, especially the epic; only fragments survive. See also V.iii.530n.
rude] rough, unpolished; *Amores* I.xv.19 describes him as *arte carens* (lack-
ing art) but J. (and Marlowe who wrote 'Rude *Ennius*') are also echoing
Ovid's other judgement in *Tristia* IV, 424, 'ingenio maximus, arte rudis'
('great in wit, rough in art'); Ovid may have been punning on Ennius'
birthplace, Rudiae.
Accius] Lucius Accius, Roman tragic poet, born 170 BC.
63. Varro] 116–28 BC, wrote an *Argonautica*, now lost, on Jason's mythic
quest for the Golden Fleece (l. 68).
65. Lucretius] T. Lucretius Carus, 95–52 or 51 BC, Roman philosophical
poet, author of the *De rerum natura*.
66.] Adapted (by Ovid) from *De rerum natura* V.95.
67. Tityrus . . . Aenee] References to Virgil: Tityrus is a character in the
first *Eclogue*, Tillage ('fruges', fruits of the earth, in Ovid) refers to the art of
husbandry of the *Georgics*, Aenee to the *Aeneid*; neither it nor 'Aeney' is
recorded by *OED*.
68.] Echoes *Aeneid* IX, 449.
69.] Alludes to Tibullus II.vi.15–16: 'Fierce Love, oh, if this could
be, I would see thine arms destroyed, the arrows broken and the torches
quenched.'
70. neat] 'culte' (elegant, polished) in Ovid; cf. *UV* XXVI. 52, 'Neat
Terence', and *Gent.* I.ii.10, 'a knight well-spoken, neat, and fine'.

*So shall Lycoris, whom he now loves best.*
*The suffering ploughshare or the flint may wear,*
*But heavenly poesy no death can fear.*
*Kings shall give place to it, and kingly shows,*                    75
*The banks o'er which gold-bearing Tagus flows.*
*Kneel hinds to trash: me let bright Phoebus swell,*
*With cups full-flowing from the Muses' well.*
*Frost-fearing myrtle shall impale my head,*
*And of sad lovers I'll be often read.*                              80
*Envy the living not the dead doth bite:*
*For after death all men receive their right.*
*Then, when this body falls in funeral fire,*
*My name shall live, and my best part aspire.*


ACT I  SCENE ii

[*Enter to him*] OVID SENIOR [*followed by*] LUSCUS, TUCCA,
[*and*] LUPUS.

*Ovid Senior.* Your name shall live indeed, sir, you say true!
But how infamously, how scorned and contemned in the

---

79. *Frost-fearing*] F; *The frost-drad* Q.    81–4.] *Gnomic pointing in* Q, F.
I.ii.0.1–2.] *Subst.* G, *who continues the scene.*    1. you] F; *your* Q.

---

72. Lycoris] pseudonym for Cytheris: see Persons of the Play, 25n.
76. Tagus] 'A river dividing *Spain and Portugal*, and by the consent of the
Poets styled *aurifer*' (J.'s note to *K. Ent.*, 312); its banks ('ripa benigna' in
Ovid) thus represent gold which, like kings and 'kingly shows', will 'give
place' to poetry.
77. hinds] servants, lackeys ('vulgus' in Ovid).
trash] dross; cf. *Oth.* III.iii.157, 'Who steals my purse steals trash'.
79. impale] encircle.
81–4.] J. uses inverted commas in Q and F to emphasise *sententiae*,
gnomic or aphoristic passages, especially those on themes, such as envy,
central to the play. *H&S* note that these lines are quoted by Lovelace, 'On
Sannazaro being Honoured', *Lucasta*, 1659 (ed. Wilkinson, p. 179).
I.ii] Based on Ovid's autobiographical *Tristia* IV.x, and the elder Seneca
*Controv.* II.ii.8: 'Even in those days his [Ovid's] speech could be regarded as
simply poetry put into prose. However, he was so keen a student of Latro [a
teacher of rhetoric] that he transferred many epigrams of his to his own
verse.' Ovid was destined for a legal career, but gave it up for poetry, earning
the displeasure of his father. The attack on plays echoes those made in
numerous sermons and pamphlets in the late sixteenth century; Ovid Senior

eyes and ears of the best and gravest Romans, that you
think not on; you never so much as dream of that. Are
these the fruits of all my travail and expenses? Is this the          5
scope and aim of thy studies? Are these the hopeful
courses wherewith I have so long flattered my expectation
from thee? Verses! Poetry! Ovid, whom I thought to see
the pleader, become Ovid the playmaker?

*Ovid.* No, sir.                                                      10

*Ovid Senior.* Yes, sir! I hear of a tragedy of yours coming
forth for the common players there, called *Medea*. By my
household gods, if I come to the acting of it I'll add one
tragic part more than is yet expected to it, believe me
when I promise it. What! Shall I have my son a stager             15
now? An engle for players? A gull, a rook, a shot-clog to
make suppers, and be laughed at? Publius, I will set thee
on the funeral pile first.

---

16. gull,] *G;* Gull? *Q, Subst. F.*    rook,] *G;* Rooke? *Q, Subst. F.*    shot-
clog] *G;* Shot-clog? *Q, Subst. F.*

---

is a development of the anti-poetic elder Knowell of *EMI*; both J.'s stepfather and Marston's father are thought to have opposed their sons' literary
ambitions (see III.iv.164n). Venal lawyers are a favourite target of the
verse satirists: cf. Donne, *Satire II*, and Hall, *Virgidemiarum*, II, iii.

9. *pleader . . . playmaker*] The first syllable of each word may have sounded
similar in Elizabethan pronunciation. Cf. 'pray . . . prevail', IV.iii.155; both
are examples of '*Paranomasie*, or *Agnomination*' (III.i.92n).

12. *Medea*] Ovid's only tragedy, which has not survived; cf. *Amores*
II.xviii.13–14, *Tristia* II, 553–4, and Quintilian *Inst.* X.i.98.

13. *household gods*] the Roman *lares*, ancestral spirits 'supposed to have the
keeping of men's houses' (Godwyn, p. 34).

15. *stager*] an actor (*OED*, 3), normally used contemptuously: cf.
III.iv.184, IV.viii.3, V.iii.154 and Dekker, *S-M* I.ii.356–7.

16. *engle*] catamite (*OED* 'Ingle' *sb.* 2).

*gull*] dupe.

*rook*] simpleton, dupe; cf. *EMI* I.v.88.

*shot-clog*] one tolerated only because he pays the bill, or 'shot', for the rest.
Cf. *EMO* V.ix.47, *EH* I.i.136, and *S of N* IV.i.47; all examples in *OED*
come from J. Partridge, *Slang*, records it as 'mid-C. 19–20'.

17. *Publius*] J.'s use of the *praenomen* only is correct between members of
the same family, but Tibullus' use in I.iii.46 is more dubious: normally J.
rightly makes friends use the *cognomen*, as, e.g., 'Tibullus' rather than his
*nomen* 'Albius'; see J.G.F. Powell, 'A Note on the Use of the *Praenomen*',
*CQ*, XXXIV (1984), 238–9.

18. *funeral pile*] refers to I.i.83, but also echoes Cicero *Tusc.* I.xxxv.35,
'Aliquem in rogum imponere.'

*Ovid.* Sir, I beseech you to have patience.

*Luscus.* Nay, this 'tis to have your ears dammed up to good          20
counsel. I did augur all this to him aforehand, without
poring into an ox's paunch for the matter, and yet he
would not be scrupulous.

*Tucca.* [*To Luscus*] How now, goodman slave? What, roly
poly? All rivals, rascal? [*To Ovid Senior*] Why, my knight          25
of worship, dost hear? Are these thy best projects? Is this
thy designs and thy discipline, to suffer knaves to be
competitors with commanders and gent'men? [*To Luscus*]
Are we parallels, rascal? Are we parallels?

*Ovid Senior.* [*To Luscus*] Sirrah, go get my horses ready.          30
You'll still be prating.

*Tucca.* Do, you perpetual stinkard, do, go, talk to tapsters

---

22. paunch] *Q;* panch *F.*     24–5. roly poly] *This ed.; Rowle Powle Q,*
*Subst. F.*     25. knight] *This ed.;* Knight *Q;* Master *uncorr. F;* Master, *corr.*
*F.*     28. gent'men] *H&S;* Gent-/men *Q;* gentlemen *F.*

---

22. *ox's paunch*] Augury from the entrails of a sacrificed ox was practised
by the *haruspices* in Rome. Cf. Ovid *Tristia* I.ix.50–1: 'This was told me by
no sheep's liver or thunder on my left or the note or wing of a bird I had
observed; it is an augury and inference of the future based on reason.'

23. *scrupulous*] careful, cautious; cf. *Ant.* I.iii.48: 'scrupulous faction'.

24–5. *roly poly*] *OED* gives 'a worthless fellow', but most examples from
this date refer specifically to social overturning, as here: cf. *T of T* I.ii.15:
'What? Rowlepowle? Maple face? All fellows?' (*H&S*), and Samuel Rowlands, *Hells Broke Loose* (1605), 17: 'Wee'le ayme our thoughts on high, at
Honors marke: / All rowly, powly; Tayler, Smyth, and Clarke.'

25–6. *knight of worship*] Ovid's family were of the equestrian order (*Ex
Ponto* IV.viii.17–18, and *Tristia* II, 111–14). For J's deletion of all references
to knighthood in *F*, see App. 1, pp. 283–4. Self-censorship of knighthood
references may be explained by such passages in *S-M* as V.ii.317–22, where
Horace is made to swear that 'when a knight or Sentlemen of urship, does
give you his passe-port, to travaile in and out to his Company, and gives you
money for God's sake; I trust in Sesu, you will sweare (tooth and nayle) not
to make scalde and wry-mouth jestes upon his knight-hood, will you not?
*Hor.* I never did it by Parnassus.'

29. *parallels*] equals in worth (*OED*, 2b: this antedates the first example).
Cf. III.i.91n., 'Apol. Dial.', 93, and *S-M* IV.i.204: 'I hope he and I are not
Paralels.'

31. *prating*] talking idly, blabbing, but with suggestion of misplaced
officiousness (*OED*, 1).

32. *stinkard*] one who stinks; frequently used by Tucca as a mildly abusive
epithet: cf. III.iv.132, 169, 203, etc. (all to Histrio) and IV.iii.44, 81, 90 (to
or of Albius). In V.iii.178 he seems to use it literally of himself (see note).
First *OED* example is from *Tim.*, wrongly dated 1600.

*Tucca.* Do, you perpetual stinkard, do, go, talk to tapsters
and ostlers you slave, they are i' your element, go. Here
be the emperor's captains, you ragamuffin rascal, and not
your cam'rades.                                  [*Exit* LUSCUS.]        35
*Lupus.* Indeed, Sir Marcus Ovid, these players are an idle
generation, and do much harm in a state, corrupt young
gentry very much, I know it: I have not been a tribune
thus long and observed nothing. Besides, they will rob
us, us that are magistrates, of our respect, bring us upon        40
their stages, and make us ridiculous to the plebeians.
They will play you or me, the wisest men they can come
by still. Me! Only to bring us in contempt with the
vulgar, and make us cheap.
*Tucca.* Th' art in the right, my venerable cropshin, they will        45
indeed. The tongue of the oracle never twanged truer.
Your courtier cannot kiss his mistress' slippers in quiet
for 'em, nor your white innocent gallant pawn his
revelling suit to make his punk a supper. An honest
decayed commander cannot skelder, cheat, nor be seen in        50
a bawdy house, but he shall be straight in one of their
wormwood comedies. They are grown licentious, the
rogues; libertines, flat libertines. They forget they are i'

---

35. cam'rades] *Subst. corr. F; Comrades Q; camrades uncorr. F.      S.D.] G.*
36. Sir Marcus] *Subst. Q;* MARCVS *F.*      43. Me!] *This ed.;* me: *Q, F; not
in F2, G.*      49. punk] *G; Punque Q; punke uncorr. F; punke corr. F.*

---

33. *element*] area in which one feels at home, belongs naturally (*OED, sb.*
12); cf. *Wiv.* IV.ii.176–8: 'She works by charms . . . beyond our element'.
J.'s use is ridiculed in *S-M* I.ii.134: 'hang him: tis out of his Element to
traduce me', and *Tw.N* III.i.58–9: 'out of my welkin—I might say "element," but the word is overworn' (see p. 33).
39–44. *Besides . . . cheap*] For parallels with Cobham, see pp. 42–3.
45. *cropshin*] A small herring; *H&S* cite Nashe, *Lenten Stuffe* (*Works*, ed.
McKerrow, III, 216). J. and Nashe use such puns to ridicule Cobham (see p.
43).
46. *twanged*] 'Cf. *cano* in Latin on the chanted answer of an oracle'
(*H&S*). Cf. V.iii.334 and Dent, T626, 'As good as ever twanged'.
47. *kiss . . . slippers*] Cf. *EMO* IV.ii.34, 'kissing ladies pumps' (*H&S*).
48. *white*] spotless, innocent (*OED, 7*).
49. *punk*] whore.
50. *decayed*] impoverished.
*skelder*] See I.i.25n.
52. *wormwood*] bitter, hence satirical, referring to J.'s new 'comicall
satyres'.

the statute, the rascals, they are blazoned there, there
they are tricked, they and their pedigrees; they need no     55
other heralds, iwis.

*Ovid Senior.* Me thinks if nothing else, yet this alone, the very
reading of the public edicts should fright thee from
commerce with them, and give thee distaste enough of
their actions. But this betrays what a student you are; this     60
argues your proficiency in the law.

*Ovid.* They wrong me, sir, and do abuse you more
That blow your ears with these untrue reports.
I am not known unto the open stage,
Nor do I traffic in their theatres.                          65
Indeed I do acknowledge, at request
Of some near friends and honourable Romans,
I have begun a poem of that nature.

*Ovid Senior.* You have, sir? A poem? And where is't? That's
the law you study!                                           70

---

56. iwis] *This ed.;* Iwisse *Q, F.*     69. sir? A poem] *This ed.;* sir, a Poeme?
*Q;* sir, a *poeme? F.*

---

54. *statute*] Statutes of 14 Eliz. c.5 and 39 Eliz c.4 (1572 and 1597–8)
included 'common players of interludes' other than those 'belonging to any
Baron of this realm' amongst those liable to punishment as 'rogues, vaga-
bonds or sturdy beggars'.

   *blazoned*] described in heraldic language; cf. *EMO* III.iv.66.

   55. *tricked*] the drawing in outline of a coat of arms, colours being
indicated by letters; cf. *EMO* III.iv.69. The heraldic language suggests that
J. is satirising an actor who has taken or applied for arms; Shakespeare
probably applied in 1596 on behalf of his father, and the grant included the
motto 'Non sanz droict', parodied in *EMO* by Sogliardo's 'Not without
mustard' (III.iv.86). In 1602 Brooke, the York herald, accused the Garter
King of Arms, and J.'s friend Camden, the Clarenceux King of Arms, of
granting arms to 'base persons' including Shakespeare (Folger Shakespeare
Library, MS V.a.156). J. owned Brooke's earlier published attack on
Camden (1596), and probably knew from Camden of the contention in the
Heralds' college before Brooke's 1602 accusations.

   56. *iwis*] certainly (*OED*, B).

   58. *reading . . . edicts*] Proclamations of the Roman magistrates; the
reference is to the Elizabethan statutes, but Penniman cites an edict of the
jurist Salvius Julianus classing Roman actors with criminals.

   63. *blow your ears*] Cf. *EMI* II.i.104, where the reference is also to the
'false breath' of detraction and rumour.

   64. *open*] public (as distinct from private) theatre.

   65.] Echoing Ovid *Tristia* V.vii.27: 'I have indeed composed nothing (you
yourself know this) for the theatre'.

*Ovid.* Cornelius Gallus borrowed it to read.

*Ovid Senior.* Cornelius Gallus? There's another gallant, too,
hath drunk of the same poison: and Tibullus, and Propertius. But these are gentlemen of means and revenue
now. Thou art a younger brother, and hast nothing but       75
thy bare exhibition; which I protest shall be bare indeed,
if thou forsake not these unprofitable by-courses, and that
timely too. Name me a professed poet, that his poetry did
ever afford him so much as a competency. Ay, your god
of poets there (whom all of you admire and reverence so     80
much), Homer, he whose worm-eaten statue must not be
spewed against but with hallowed lips and grovelling
adoration, what was he, what was he?

*Tucca.* Marry, I'll tell thee, old swagg'rer: he was a poor,

---

74. revenue] *Parfitt;* Reuenewes *Q;* reuennew *uncorr.* F; reuenew *corr.* F.
84. swagg'rer] *This ed.;* Swaggrer *Q, Subst.* F; swaggerer *F2.*

---

71–4.] Gallus, Tibullus and Propertius are bracketed thus with Ovid in
Quintilian *Inst.* X.i.93 (Mallory). It was probably Ovid's systematising in the
*Ars Amatoria* of the erotic precepts scattered in these three poets that most
incensed Augustus, whose policy was to strengthen the institution of marriage by the *Lex Iulia* of 18 BC (see p. 21).

74. *revenue*] unearned income from property or possessions, especially of a
substantial kind (*OED* 2, 3).

75. *younger brother*] Ovid's elder brother died at the age of twenty (*Tristia*
IV.x.17–18, 31–2).

76. *exhibition*] allowance; cf. *EMO* II.v.27.

77. *by-courses*] sidelines.

78. *timely*] quickly.

79. *competency*] a small but sufficient income.

78–95.] Greatly amplifying the words of Ovid's father in *Tristia*
IV.x.21–2, quoted in 'Apol. Dial.', 107–8: 'Often my father said, "Why
do you try a profitless pursuit? Even the Maeonian [i.e. Homer] left no
wealth."'

81. *worm-eaten*] decayed, antiquated (*OED*, c), not a wooden statue.

81–2. *statue . . . hallowed lips*] Mallory cites Juvenal I, 131: 'against
whose statue more than one kind of nuisance may be committed'. *H&S*
compare J's objection to 'Caesar did never wrong, but with just cause' (*Disc.*
664–5), but the ellipsis is rhetorically appropriate here, reflecting Ovid
senior's anger, and there is no need to adopt Penniman's suggestion of a
missing verb or participle after 'but'.

84. *Marry*] F's use of the form 'Mary' conveys the meaning of the oath;
by the sixteenth century it is usually no more than an empty interjection,
though *Rom.* IV.v.7–8 carries the original weight: 'God forgive me! / Marry
and amen!' See also II.i.66n.

*swagg'rer*] quarreller (*OED*); cf. *2H4*: 'I'll no swaggerers, I am in good
name and fame'.

blind, rhyming rascal, that lived obscurely up and down      85
in booths and taphouses, and scarce ever made a good
meal in his sleep, the whoreson hungry beggar.

*Ovid Senior.* He says well: nay, I know this nettles you now,
but answer me, is't not true? You'll tell me his name shall
live, and that now being dead, his works have eternised      90
him and made him divine. But could this divinity feed
him while he lived? Could his name feast him?

*Tucca.* Or purchase him a senator's revenue? Could it?

*Ovid Senior.* Ay, or give him place in the commonwealth,
worship, or attendants? Make him be carried in his litter?   95

*Tucca.* Thou speakest sentences, old Bias.

*Lupus.* All this the law will do, young sir, if you'll follow it.

*Ovid Senior.* If he be mine, he shall follow and observe what I

---

89. is't not true?] *Subst. F;* I'st not true? Is't not true? *Q.*      90. now being
dead] *G;* now (being deade) *Q;* (now being dead) *F.*      91. divine. But] *F;*
diuine: but *Q.*      93–5. *Tucca . . . litter?] F; not in Q.*      97–134. *Lupus . . .*
boy.] *F; not in Q.*

---

86. *booths*] ale-booths (*H&S*), specifically temporary structures at fairs
(*OED*, 2).

*taphouses*] ale-houses.

86–7. *scarce . . . sleep*] 'He never even dreamt that he ate a good meal.' Cf.
*S of N* II.i.15–16, 'A sordid Rascall, one that never made / Good meale in his
sleep' (Mallory).

91–2. *feed him*] Homer is traditionally said to have lived his last years in
poverty.

93. *senator's revenue*] 800 000 sesterces a year, raised by Augustus to
1 200 000 sesterces (Suetonius *Divus Augustus* XLI). Godwyn estimated the
former figure as worth £6000 in 1617 (p. 25); late twentieth-century equivalents are extremely suspect: based on the silver value of the denarius (four
sesterces in the early empire) this would be worth about £60 000 in modern
silver values, but an income of over £100 000 would probably give a more
realistic comparison.

94. *commonwealth*] any independent state or community (*OED*, 2).

95. *worship*] respect, honour.

*litter*] privilege only granted to persons of rank. Mallory cites Juvenal III,
239–42: 'When the rich man has a call of social duty, the mob makes way for
him as he is borne swiftly over their heads in a huge Liburnian car'.

96. *sentences*] *sententiae*, words of wisdom.

*Bias*] Bias of Priene, one of the seven sages of Greece, *c.* 570 BC; his
sentences are preserved in Diogenes Laertius, *Lives and Opinions of Eminent
Philosophers*. *G* notes 'Immortality was cheaply purchased in his days.'

will apt him to, or I profess here openly and utterly to
disclaim in him.                                                    100

*Ovid.* Sir, let me crave you will forgo these moods;
I will be anything, or study anything.
I'll prove the unfashioned body of the law
Pure elegance, and make her ruggedest strains
Run smoothly as Propertius' elegies.                                105

*Ovid Senior.* Propertius' elegies? Good!

*Lupus.* Nay, you take him too quickly, Marcus.

*Ovid Senior.* Why, he cannot speak, he cannot think out of
poetry, he is bewitched with it.

*Lupus.* Come, do not misprise him.                                 110

*Ovid Senior.* Misprise? Ay, marry, I would have him use some
such words now: they have some touch, some taste of the
law. He should make himself a style out of these, and let
his Propertius' elegies go by.

*Lupus.* Indeed young Publius, he that will now hit the mark        115
must shoot through the law, we have no other planet
reigns, and in that sphere you may sit and sing with

---

101. will forgo] *This ed.;* will, forgoe *F.*     116. through] *F2;* thorough *F.*

---

99. *apt*] direct, incline; cf. 'Apol. Dial.', 204.

100. *disclaim in him*] In formal legal usage one disclaimed 'in' the thing or
person renounced. Cf. *C is A* V.xii.68.

103 *unfashioned*] unpolished.

105. *Run . . . elegies*] Punning on 'elegies' and 'legs', reflecting contemporary pronunciation. Since Propertius is not known for the smooth running
of his verse, this suggests that J. had not read much of it at this stage; but cf.
IV.iii.4n.

110. *misprise*] misunderstand; cf. *C is A* IV.i.38, *CR* IV.iv.31, and *Patient
Grissil* (1600) II.i.103. 'Misprision' is also a portmanteau legal term covering
every substantial misdemeanour not having a name assigned by law. Ovid
Senior refers to this legal meaning in ll. 124–6.

115–6. *he . . . law*] 'He that wishes to hit the target (of wealth and status)
must shoot at it by means of the law.' *G* notes: 'These and what follow, are
probably the passages which gave offence to the professors of the law.' Cf. *S-
M* IV.iii.184–6: 'th'ast entred Actions of assault and battery, against a
companie of honourable and worshipfull Fathers of the law: you wrangling
rascall, law is one of the pillers ath land'. For the probable dropping of these
lines from Q, see App. 1, p. 281.

117–8. *sphere . . . angels*] Punning on the angels who guide the spheres (on
which in late medieval/Renaissance versions of the Ptolemaic system the
planets revolve) and on the English coin known as an angel.

angels. Why, the law makes a man happy without
respecting any other merit: a simple scholar, or none at
all, may be a lawyer.                                                           120
*Tucca.* He tells thee true, my noble neophyte, my little
grammaticaster, he does: it shall never put thee to thy
mathematics, metaphysics, philosophy, and I know not
what supposed sufficiencies. If thou canst but have the
patience to plod enough, talk, and make noise enough, be    125
impudent enough, and 'tis enough.
*Lupus.* Three books will furnish you.
*Tucca.* And the less art the better: besides when it shall be in
the power of thy cheverel conscience to do right or wrong
at thy pleasure, my pretty Alcibiades.                                         130
*Lupus.* Ay, and to have better men than himself by many
thousand degrees, to observe him, and stand bare.

---

129. cheverel] *This ed.;* cheu'rill *F.*

118. *happy*] rich, translating *beatus* (so *G*); cf. *Alc.* I.ii.119.

119. *simple*] 'dull or stupid' (Penniman).

121. *neophyte*] novice; cf. *EMO* V.iv.8.

122. *grammaticaster*] *OED* gives this as the first recorded use, meaning
'petty or inferior grammarian': for Tucca's aggressive name-calling see
Barton, p. 184.

124. *sufficiencies*] accomplishments (*OED*, 4b); cf. *CR* I.iv.39–40: 'I
feare I may doe wrong to your sufficiencies in reporting them'.

127. *Three books*] In *EMO* II.iii.166–7 the law student Fungoso mentions
'Plowden, Dyer, Brooke and Fitzherbert' as the four books he needs (so
Penniman). Sir John Davies mentions Plowden, Dyer and Brooke ('Epigram
In Publium. 43', *Poems*, ed. Krueger (Oxford, 1975), p. 148). They were
collections of case reports used as textbooks.

128. *besides when*] an ellipsis: 'besides (the times) when'.

129. *cheverel conscience*] of the quality of kid leather, hence a pliable
conscience; used commonly of lawyers: cf. *Ep.* XXXVII and LIV on a pliant
lawyer named 'Chevr'il', and *Hist.* (Wood, III, 284): 'The cheverell conscience of corrupted law'. *OED* cites Stubbes, *Anatomie of Abuses*, II.1: 'the
lawyers have such cheverel consciences'; cf. also *H8* II.iii.32.

130. *pretty*] used throughout *Poetaster* as a vague epithet of admiration
(*OED*, 3), with some pretensions to courtliness. Cf. 'sweet', I.iii.35n, and
King, pp. 181–2.

*Alcibiades*] friend of Socrates, talented general and politician, known also
for his youthful beauty (to which Tucca's antonomasia refers).

132. *observe*] take respectful notice of.

*stand bare*] bareheaded, as a mark of respect.

*Tucca.* True, and he to carry himself proud and stately, and
have the law on his side for't, old boy.

*Ovid Senior.* Well, the day grows old, gentlemen, and I must        135
leave you. Publius, if thou wilt hold my favour, abandon
these idle fruitless studies that so bewitch thee. Send
Janus home his back-face again, and look only forward to
the law. Intend that. I will allow thee what shall suit thee
in the rank of gentlemen, and maintain thy society with       140
the best: and under these conditions I leave thee. My
blessings light upon thee if thou respect them; if not,
mine eyes may drop for thee, but thine own heart will
ache for itself. And so farewell.

[*Re-enter* LUSCUS.]

What, are my horses come?                                      145

*Luscus.* Yes, sir, they are at the gate without.

*Ovid Senior.* That's well. Asinius Lupus, a word. [*To Tucca*]
Captain, I shall take my leave of you?

*Tucca.* No, my little knight errant, dispatch with cavalier
Cothurnus there: I'll attend thee, I——                        150

*Luscus.* [*Aside*] To borrow some ten drachmas, I know his
project.

---

137. bewitch] *F*; traduce *Q*.     144.1 S.D.] *This ed.*     149. knight errant]
*Subst. Q*; old Boy *uncorr. F*; old boy *corr. F*.     149–50. cavalier Cothurnus]
*Subst. Q*; COTHVRNVS *F*.     150. I——] *corr. F*; I. *Q, uncorr. F*.     151.
S.D.] *G*.

---

134. *law . . . for't*] Cf. *BF* IV.i.80 (Mallory) and *Rom.* I.i.38, 47 (*H&S*).
   138. *Janus*] All beginnings were sacred to the two-faced god; cf. Ovid
*Fasti*, I, 65–6, 117–20. Ovid senior hopes Janus will look back on Ovid's
'fruitless studies' and forward to his new career as a lawyer.
   139. *Intend that*] probably recalling Hor. *Epist.* I.ii.36, 'intendes animum
studiis' as 'direct your mind to studies'.
   143. *drop*] drop tears.
   149. *cavalier*] as a comic title, cf. *Wiv.* II.iii.77, 'Cavaliero Slender';
dropped from *F* because of its association with knighthood (see *OED*, A.1).
   150. *Cothurnus*] the buskin or high shoe worn by tragic actors to increase
their height and signify their dignity. Tucca refers to Lupus' lack of height: cf.
I.i.31, IV.iv.15, V.iii.83.
   151. *drachmas*] Greek silver coin, still current in Rome at this time. Its
weight and value varied; for contemporary discussion of the drachma and its
relationship to the Roman denarius, see Onofrius Panvinius, *Imperium
Romanum* (Paris, 1538), pp. 225–30. J. consulted Panvinius for *Sej.* Cf.

*Ovid Senior.* [*To Lupus*] Sir, you shall make me beholding to
you. [*To Tucca*] Now, Captain Tucca, what say you?

*Tucca.* Why, what should I say, or what can I say, my most    155
magnanimous mirror of knighthood? Should I say thou
art rich? Or that thou art honourable? Or wise? Or
valiant? Or learned? Or liberal? Why, thou art all these,
and thou knowest it, my noble Lucullus, thou knowest
it: come, be not ashamed of thy virtues, old stump.    160
Honour's a good brooch to wear in a man's hat at all
times. Thou art the man of war's Maecenas, knight. Why
shouldst not thou be graced then by them, as well as he is
by his poets?

[*Enter* I PYRGUS *and whispers to* TUCCA.]

How now, my carrier, what news?    165

*Luscus.* [*Aside*] The boy has stayed within for his cue this half
hour.

*Tucca.* Come, do not whisper to me, but speak it out. What!
It is no treason against the state, I hope, is't?

*Luscus.* [*Aside*] Yes, against the state of my master's purse.    170

---

153. S.D.] *Nicholson.*    156. magnanimous . . . knighthood] *Subst. Q;*
flowre o' the order *F.*    159. my . . . Lucullus] *In parentheses in Q, F.*
162. knight] *Q;* old boy *F.*    *164.1  S.D.] Subst. G.*    166. S.D.] *G.*
168. out. What!] *This ed.;* out. what, *Q.* out: what? *F.*    170. S.D.] *This
ed.; Aside, and exit. G.*

---

Caesar's will in *Caes.* III.ii.242: 'To every several man, seventy-five dra-
chmaes'.

156. *mirror of knighthood*] title of a popular Spanish romance; cf. *S-M*
III.i.108–9: '*Tuc.* Dost loue her, my finest and first part of the Mirrour of
Knighthood?'; see also *CR* III.v.28, *BF,* Ind. 143, and Marston, *Malcontent*
I.viii.30.

159. *Lucullus*] L. Licinius Lucullus, d. 56/5 BC; as consul (74 BC) defeated
Mithridates; later lived in great magnificence, was a patron of poets, and
wrote a history of the Marsic war in Greek.

160. *stump*] (applied to a person), a block head, or a man of short, stumpy
figure (*OED,* 4; this is the first citation).

161. *good brooch*] In *All's W* (1603–4) the brooch worn in the hat is out
of fashion (I.i.156–8), as it probably is in *Christmas,* 3 (1616); it may be that
Tucca is out of touch with fashion. In *S-M* Tucca says 'thou shalt wear her
glove in thy worshipful hat like to a leather brooch' (III.i.121–2).

163. *by them*] i.e. by the men of war.

[*1*] *Pyrgus.* Sir, Agrippa desires you to forbear him till the next
    week: his moils are not yet come up.

*Tucca.* His moils? Now the bots, the spavin, and the glanders,
    and some dozen diseases more, light on him and his
    moils! What, ha' they the yellows, his moils, that they     175
    come no faster? Or are they foundered, ha? His moils ha'
    the staggers belike, ha' they?

[*1*] *Pyrgus.* O no, sir. [*Aside*] Then your tongue might be
    suspected for one of his moils.

*Tucca.* He owes me almost a talent, and he thinks to bear it     180
    away with his moils, does he? Sirrah, you, nut-cracker:
    go your ways to him again, and tell him I must ha'
    money, I. I cannot eat stones and turfs, say. What, will

---

178. S.D.] *G.*

---

171. *Agrippa*] M. Vipsanius Agrippa, 63–12 BC, associate of Augustus,
naval victor of Actium, and one of the most powerful figures of his time. He
married Augustus' daughter Julia in 21 BC; Hor. addresses him in *Odes* I.vi.
'There is some pleasantry in making Agrippa, the first man in the state,
indebted to this beggarly captain' (*G*).

172. *moils*] mules (*H&S*).

173. *bots . . . spavin . . . glanders*] All diseases of horses (and therefore of
mules). Cf. the description of Petruchio's horse, *Shr.* III.ii.50–5 (Mallory).

175. *yellows*] jaundice, also used figuratively for jealousy; cf. *EMI* (Q)
V.iii.389, where the spelling is used to suggest a common etymology: 'you
have a spice of the yealous yet both of you.'

177. *staggers*] Any disease of animals of which giddiness is a symptom.

178–9. *your . . . suspected*] indicating how J. expected the part to be
played; cf. IV.v.77–8, where he 'begins to stut for anger'. That the speech of
the historical Captain Hanham is being parodied (see pp. 48–9) seems
confirmed by Dekker's references. to the 'limping tongued captain' (*S-M*
I.ii.133) and 'the yawning captain' (II.i.57); *S-M* V.ii.179 gives the stutter
in the text: 'one a thy most faithfull—fy—fy—fy—.' *Q*'s heavy pointing of
Tucca's speeches may be intended to convey his stutter (*H&S*, V, 191).

180. *talent*] The Attic talent, referred to by Hor. and Cicero, contained
60 minae, or 6000 drachmas; for a Renaissance account, see Marcus
Meibomius, *De Fabrica Trirerium Liber*, in Graevius, *Thesaurus Antiquitatum
Romanorum* (1694–9), XII, 599. Tucca is claiming that he is owed a
thousand times the amount he is about to borrow from Ovid senior.

181. *nut-cracker*] A common spectator at a theatre, hence any lackey; cf. *S
of N* 'Prologue for the Court', 7–8: 'the vulgar sort / Of nut-crackers that
only come for sight.' 'The eating of nuts was a common practice in the
Elizabethan theatre' (Penniman), though the hazelnut shells found in the
Rose Theatre excavations are now thought to have been a building material
brought on to the site from elsewhere.

he clem me and my followers? Ask him an' he will clem
me: do, go. He would have me fry my jerkin, would he?      185
Away, setter, away! Yet stay, my little tumbler; the
knight shall supply now. I will not trouble him, I cannot
be importunate, I; I cannot be impudent.

[*1*] *Pyrgus.* [*Aside*] Alas, sir, no: you are the most maidenly
blushing creature upon the earth.                          190

*Tucca.* [*To Ovid Senior*] Dost thou hear, my little six and fifty,
or thereabouts? Thou art not to learn the humours and
tricks of that old bald cheater, Time; thou hadst not this
chain for nothing. Men of worth have their chimeras,
as well as other creatures; and they do see monsters      195
sometimes: they do, they do, brave boy.

---

184. him an'] *Corr. F;* him and *Q, uncorr. F.*     186–7. the knight] *Subst.*
*Q;* this old boy *F.*        189. S.D.] *G.*     196. brave boy] *F; not in Q.*

---

184. *clem*] starve, waste with hunger; cf. intransitive use in *EMO*
III.vi.64.
   *an'*] if; cf. I.i.33n.
   185. *jerkin*] In *S-M* I.ii.133–4 Tucca has a 'poor greasy buff jerkin' and in
I.ii.402 he is 'scurvy leather captain'.
   186. *setter*] Elizabethan underworld slang, one who 'sets up' a victim to be
cheated or robbed; cf. *1H4*, I.ii.106–7 and II.ii.50–1.
   *tumbler*] One who draws a victim into the hands of a confidence trickster.
Both 'tumbler' and 'setter' derive from names of hunting dogs; Tucca
uses names which actually draw attention to the confidence trick he is
perpetrating.
   187. *I . . . him*] i.e. Agrippa.
   191–2. *six . . . thereabouts*] 'i.e. experienced but not yet an old man'
(*H&S*).
   192–3. *Thou . . . Time*] 'You do not need to be taught, already knowing.'
Time, like *Occasio*, is frequently represented as bald, with only a forelock by
which it must be grasped as it passes; cf. *WYW*, 'Would I were time then, I
thought twas for some thing that the old fornicator was bald behinde' (Wood,
II, 284).
   192. *humours*] vagaries, caprices.
   194. *chain*] one of J.'s intentional anachronisms in costume (see p. 9);
though he may have the Roman *torquis* in mind (see e.g. Cicero *Fin.* I, 23,
Suetonius *Divus Augustus* XLIII and Isidore of Seville *Etymologiarum*
XIX.xxxi.11) as an analogy, this is the chain worn by most Elizabethan
gentlemen. Cf. Tucca's removal of Maecenas' very Elizabethan 'flagon chain'
in V.iii.38, and his borrowing of Sir Quintilian's chain in *S-M* III.i.120.
   194–5. *Men . . . monsters*] 'Men of worth (such as myself) can sometimes
have nightmarish fantasies' (such as those of starvation he has just expressed). A chimera had come to mean any unfounded conception (*OED*,
3b).

[*1*] *Pyrgus.* [*Aside*] Better cheap than he shall see you, I
warrant him.

*Tucca.* Thou must let me have six, six drachmas I mean, old
boy; thou shalt do it: I tell thee, old boy, thou shalt, and       200
in private too, dost thou see? Go, walk off. There, there.
[OVID SENIOR *withdraws to one side.*] Six is the sum. Thy
son's a gallant spark, and must not be put out of a
sudden. [*To Ovid*] Come hither, Callimachus. Thy father
tells me thou art too poetical, boy, thou must not be so;         205
thou must leave them, young novice, thou must, they are
a sort of poor starved rascals, that are ever wrapped up in
foul linen, and can boast of nothing but a lean visage
peering out of a seam-rent suit; the very emblems of
beggary. No, dost hear? Turn lawyer. Thou shalt be my           210
solicitor. [OVID SENIOR *gives him money.*] 'Tis right, old
boy, is't?

*Ovid Senior.* You were best tell it, captain.

*Tucca.* No. [*To Ovid Senior*] Fare thou well, mine honest
knight, [*To Lupus*] and thou old beaver. [*To Ovid Senior*]       215
Pray thee, knight, when thou comest to town, see me at
my lodging, visit me sometimes. Thou shalt be welcome,
old boy. Do not balk me, good swaggerer. Jove keep thy

---

197. S.D.] *G.*    201. off. There] *This ed.;* off: there *Q, F.*    202. S.D.]
*This ed.*    204. Callimachus. Thy] CALLIMACHVS. Thy *Q, uncorr. F;*
CALLIMACHVS, *thy corr. F.*    205. boy] *F;* Slaue *Q.*    211. solicitor.]
*Followed by space in Q, F, to indicate pause.*    S.D.] *This ed.*    215. knight]
*Q;* horse-man *F.*    216. knight] *Q; Romane F.*    218. swaggerer.] *F;*
Swaggrer: *Q.*

---

197. *Better cheap*] 'More readily'; cf. Donne, 'H.W. in Hibernia Bel-
ligeranti': 'better cheap / I pardon death' (*Donne,* p. 53, ll. 5–6).

204. *Callimachus*] See I.i.55n.

209. *seam-rent*] torn at the seams; cf. *EMO* II.vi.66. and *S-M* 228–9:
'that broken seame-rent lye of thine, that *Demetrius* is out at Elbowes'.

*emblems*] Pictures accompanied by interpretative verse texts used to il-
lustrate an often abstract concept, such as beggary; cf. V.iii.54n and *EMI*
V.v.35.

211. *solicitor*] Used here in approximately its modern English meaning of a
lawyer who practises only in certain types of court.

213. *tell it*] count it: referring to the money, not to Tucca's last remark.

215. *beaver*] probably referring to a beaver hat worn by Lupus. They were
expensive and fashionable: cf. *WYW*, Wood, II, 241. There may be personal
satire here recognisable by J.'s audience.

chain from pawning, go thy ways; if thou lack money, I'll
lend thee some. I'll leave thee to thy horse now. Adieu.        220
*Ovid Senior.* Farewell, good captain.
*Tucca.* [*Aside to 1 Pyrgus*] Boy, you can have but half a share
    now, boy.                        *Exit* [*followed by* 1 PYRGUS.]
*Ovid Senior.* 'Tis a strange boldness that accompanies this
    fellow. [*To Lupus and Luscus*] Come.                        225
*Ovid.* I'll give attendance on you to your horse, sir, please
    you——
*Ovid Senior.* No, keep your chamber and fall to your studies.
    Do so: the gods of Rome bless thee.
                    [*Exit followed by* LUPUS *and* LUSCUS.]
*Ovid.* And give me stomach to digest this law——                230
    That should have followed sure, had I been he.
    O sacred poesy, thou spirit of arts,
    The soul of science, and the queen of souls,
    What profane violence, almost sacrilege,
    Hath here been offered thy divinities!                        235
    That thine own guiltless poverty should arm
    Prodigious ignorance to wound thee thus!
    For thence is all their force of argument
    Drawn forth against thee; or from the abuse

---

220. Adieu] *F; Adue Q.*    222. S.D. *This ed.*    223. S.D.] *Exit. Q; Exit
followed by Pyrgus. G.*    229.1 S.D.] *This ed.; Exeunt. Q; Exit with Lupus.
G.*    232. arts] *Subst. Q, corr. F; Romane artes uncorr. F.*    236. That] *F;
Hmh! that Q.*

---

222. *half a share*] Penniman suggests the reference is to the share of
receipts of the theatre, but there is no need to look beyond the simpler
meaning, that in the division of the proceeds of their skeldering the boy will
receive only half his share.

230. *digest*] punning on Justinian's *Digest*, the codified body of Roman
law. As Mallory suggests, J. is parodying the response to the Commandments
in the Prayer Book, following Ovid senior's blessing with a version of 'and
incline our hearts to keep this law'. J. may also be remembering *R3* II.ii.109,
'and make me die a good old man!'; cf. I.i.14n.

232–57.] Ovid's speech is markedly similar in substance to that of
Lorenzo junior in *EMI* (Q) V.iii.312–43.

236. *poverty*] A commonplace *topos*, but real enough to J.; cf. *Disc.* 1358:
'Poetry, in this latter age, hath proved but a mean mistress to such as have
wholly addicted themselves to her'. There are refs. to J.'s poverty in *Conv.*
and in *S-M* I.ii.281, and I.ii.309: 'like a lowsie, pediculous vermin th'ast but
one suite to thy backe'. See pp. 4, 31.

Of thy great powers in adulterate brains.                                240
When, would men learn but to distinguish spirits,
And set true difference 'twixt those jaded wits
That run a broken pace for common hire,
And the high raptures of a happy Muse,
Born on the wings of her immortal thought,                               245
That kicks at earth with a disdainful heel
And beats at heaven gates with her bright hooves,
They would not then with such distorted faces
And desp'rate censures stab at poesy.
They would admire bright knowledge and their minds     250
Should ne'er descend on so unworthy objects
As gold or titles: they would dread far more
To be thought ignorant, than be known poor.
The time was once when wit drowned wealth: but now
Your only barbarism is t' have wit, and want.                            255
No matter now in virtue who excels,
He that hath coin hath all perfection else.

---

244. Muse] *Subst. F;* soule *Q.*     249. desp'rate] *F;* dudgeon *Q.*     254–7.]
*Gnomic pointing in Q, F.*     255. barbarism is t' have] *F;* Barbarism's, to haue
*Q.*

---

240. *adulterate*] 'of base origin, or corrupted by base intermixture' (*OED*,
2).
242. *jaded*] worn out, esp. of a horse (*OED*, 1).
243.] Dekker had been 'hired' to write *S-M* for the Chamberlain's Men
(see III.iv.322–4n); the 'broken pace' is both the gait of the tired horse and
the irregular metre of the hack poet.
249. (*Q*) *dudgeon*] resentful, but as *H&S* point out, dudgeon was the
wood used to make the handles of knives, hence the metaphor of stabbing,
left slightly stranded after J.'s revision; cf. *S-M* I.ii.135, 'stabbed with his
dudgeon wit'; see App. 1, p. 284.
254. *drowned*] overwhelmed, overpowered (*OED*, 6).
254–5.] Translating Ovid *Amores* III.viii.3–4 (*G*).
255. *barbarism*] barbarous social or intellectual condition (*OED*, 2).
256–7.] Cf. Hor. *Sat.* II.iii.94–7: 'For all things—worth, repute, honour,
things divine and human—are slaves to the beauty of wealth, and he who
has made his pile will be famous, brave and just'; and Ovid *Fasti* I.217:
'Nowadays nothing but money counts: fortune brings honours, friendships;
the poor man everywhere lies low.' See also Dent, W534, 'He is wise that is
rich'. *H&S* note that these lines are quoted by Thomas May, *The Old Couple*
II.i (1658, B2v): ''Tis matterless in goodness who excells: He that hath coin
hath all perfection else.'

ACT I  SCENE iii

[*Enter*] TIBULLUS.

*Tibullus.* Ovid!
*Ovid.*                    Who's there? Come in.
*Tibullus.*                                        Good morrow, lawyer.
*Ovid.* Good morrow, dear Tibullus, welcome. Sit down.
*Tibullus.* Not I. What, so hard at it? Let's see, what's here?
                         [OVID *tries to hide a paper.*]
         Nay, I will see it——
*Ovid.*                    Pray thee away——
                 [TIBULLUS *snatches the paper and reads.*]
*Tibullus. If thrice in field a man vanquish his foe*                    5
         *'Tis after in his choice, to serve or no.*
         How now, Ovid! Law cases in verse?
*Ovid.* In troth, I know not: they run from my pen
         Unwittingly, if they be verse. What's the news abroad?
*Tibullus.* Off with this gown, I come to have thee walk.          10
*Ovid.* No, good Tibullus, I'm not now in case,
         Pray' let me alone.
*Tibullus.*                    How, not in case?

---

I.iii.1. *Tibullus.*] Tib. [*within*] G, *continuing the scene.*    2. dear Tibullus]
*In parentheses in* Q, F.    3.1. S.D.] *This ed.*    3–4. Let's . . . it——] F;
lets see, / Whats here? *Numa in Decimo nono?* Q.    4. away——] F; away.
Q.    4.1. S.D.] *This ed.*    8–9.] Q, F; *prose in* G.    12. Pray'] F; Pray
thee Q.

---

I.iii.] Ovid's friendship with Tibullus is not historical: 'Virgil I only saw,
and to Tibullus greedy fate gave no time for friendship with me' (*Tristia*
IV.x.51–2).
    4. (Q) Numa in Decima nono] refers to a supposed book of Roman law; G
suggests that J. dropped it from F because it was unhistorical, both in using
the English system of dating statute by the year of the reign and because
Numa was traditionally responsible for legislating over ceremonial, not war.
    5–6.] The elder Seneca quotes a similar example of Ovid putting the
formal rhetoric (rather than law as such) of Porcius Latro into verse; see
I.ii.n. J. quotes M. Seneca frequently in the earlier part of *Disc.*
    8–9. *they . . . verse*] Cf. Ovid *Tristia* IV.x.24–6: 'I tried to write words
freed from rhythm, yet all unbidden song would come upon befitting
numbers and whatever I tried to write was verse'; cf. I.ii.n.
    11. *in case*] in the right state of mind: Tibullus' reply puns on the legal
sense of case.

'Slight, thou'rt in too much case, by all this law.

*Ovid.* Troth, if I live, I will new dress the law
   In sprightly poesy's habiliments.                                    15

*Tibullus.* The hell thou wilt! What, turn law into verse?
   Thy father has schooled thee, I see. Here, read that same.
                            [*Handing him a letter*]
   There's subject for you; and if I mistake not,
   A *supersedeas* to your melancholy.

*Ovid.* How! Subscribed 'Julia!' O, my life, my heaven!                      20

*Tibullus.* Is the mood changed?

*Ovid.* Music of wit! Note for th' harmonious spheres!
   Celestial accents, how you ravish me!

*Tibullus.* What is it, Ovid?

*Ovid.* That I must meet my Julia, the Princess Julia.                       25

*Tibullus.* Where?

*Ovid.* Why at—heart, I have forgot; my passion so
   transports me.

*Tibullus.* I'll save your pains: it is at Albius' house,
   The jeweller's, where the fair Lycoris lies.                          30

*Ovid.* Who? Cytheris, Cornelius Gallus' love?

---

13. 'Slight] *This ed.;* S'light *Q, F.*     15. habiliments] *Subst. F;* Accoutrements *Q.*     16. wilt! What] *G;* wilt. what *Q; Subst. F.*     17.1. S.D.] *This ed.*     20. 'Julia'] *This ed.;* Iulia *Q;* IVLIA *F.*     27. Why at—heart] *Subst. F;* Why at Hart *Q.*     29–30. house, / The] *Q, corr. F; uncorr. F divides line at* iewellers, / where.

---

13. *'Slight*] abbreviation of 'God's light'.

15. *habiliments*] Parodying Marston, *Scourge*, VI, 25: 'moderne Poesies habiliments'; *JD's Ent.*, 'To furnish thee with brave Abiliaments' (Wood, III, 216), and *1 Ant.*, 'glistering habilliments of armes' (Wood, I, 29). Cf. also Dekker, *Patient Grissil* I.ii.179, 'poore abiliments'.

16. *The hell*] not in *OED* as an imprecation; Partridge, *Slang* (II), records it as colloquial only 'since ca. 1930'.

17. *father . . . thee*] anticipating J.'s remark to Drummond that 'Marston wrott his Father in Lawes preachings & his Father in Law his Comedies' (*Conv.* 206–7).

19. supersedeas] a writ commanding a stay of proceedings; cf. Cooke, *Greene's Tu quoque* (1611), C2r: 'Rash. I would my lamentable Lover had beene heere, heere had beene a Supersedeas for his melancholy' (*H&S*).

20. *Julia*] See Persons of the Play, 24n.

22. *harmonious spheres*] See I.ii.117–8n.

23. *accents*] musical phrases (*OED*, 7).

30–1. *Lycoris . . . love*] See Persons of the Play, 25n. She had previously been Antony's mistress.

*Tibullus.* Ay, he'll be there too, and my Plautia.

*Ovid.* And why not your Delia?

*Tibullus.* Yes, and your Corinna.

*Ovid.* True—but my sweet Tibullus, keep that secret.                35
    I would not, for all Rome, it should be thought
    I veil bright Julia underneath that name.
    Julia the gem and jewel of my soul,
    That takes her honours from the golden sky,
    As beauty doth all lustre, from her eye.                     40
    The air respires the pure elysian sweets
    In which she breathes, and from her looks descend
    The glories of the summer. Heaven she is,
    Praised in herself above all praise: and he
    Which hears her speak would swear the tuneful orbs           45
    Turned in his zenith only.

*Tibullus.*                              Publius, thou'lt lose thyself.

*Ovid.* O, in no labyrinth can I safelier err,
    Than when I lose myself in praising her.

---

37. veil] *G;* vaile *Q, F.*     41. elysian] *Subst. corr. F (elyzian); Elyzium Q;*
*elyzium uncorr. F.*

---

32–3. *Plautia . . . Delia*] Delia was thought to be the pseudonym for
Plautia; cf. Apuleius *Apologia* I, where Delia is linked with 'Plania', a name
so rare early editors conjectured 'Plautia'. J. owned Colvius's edition of
Apuleius, now in the Bodleian; the relevant line is marked in pencil, not
necessarily by J. (p. 311), as is much of pp. 306–12.

34. *Corinna*] pseudonym of the mistress to whom Ovid's love poetry
is addressed: see *Tristia,* IV.x.59–60, *Amores* II.xvii.29, III.i.49, and
III.xii.16. Renaissance scholars believed she was the elder Julia (see Persons
of the Play, 24n).

35. *sweet*] The commonest epithet in *Poetaster,* seen as affected except
between intimates, as here; Crispinus uses it sixteen times, usually affectedly
(e.g. II.i.7, 103) or claiming an intimacy he does not have (e.g. III.i.13, 14).
Cf. Marston, *Scourge,* VII: 'He that salutes each gallant he doth meete / With
"farewell, sweet Captaine, kind hart, adew"'. See also King, pp. 182–5.

38–46.] Penniman suggests an imitation of Daniel, *Delia* XIX, but the
similarities are probably those of a common *topos,* and the lines a parody of
late Elizabethan 'Ovidian' love poetry.

41. *respires*] breathes back.
    *elysian*] *elysium (Q, F* originally) parodied Marston, *JD's Ent.,* 'Elizeum
pleasures' (Wood, III, 215).

45. *tuneful orbs*] the spheres on which the 'fixed stars' turned and emitted
heavenly music.

46. *zenith*] the vault of the heavens.

Hence Law, and welcome, Muses! Though not rich,
Yet are you pleasing: let's be reconciled,                    50
And now made one. Henceforth I promise faith,
And all my serious hours to spend with you:
With you, whose music striketh on my heart,
And with bewitching tones steals forth my spirit
In Julia's name. Fair Julia! Julia's love                    55
Shall be a law, and that sweet law I'll study,
The law and art of sacred Julia's love.
All other objects will but abjects prove.
*Tibullus.* Come, we shall have thee as passionate as
  Propertius anon.                                           60
*Ovid.* O, how does my Sextus?
*Tibullus.* Faith, full of sorrow for his Cynthia's death.
*Ovid.* What, still?
*Tibullus.* Still, and still more; his griefs do grow upon him
  As do his hours. Never did I know                          65
  An understanding spirit so take to heart
  The common work of fate.
*Ovid.*                        O my Tibullus,
Let us not blame him, for against such chances
The heartiest strife of virtue is not proof.
We may read constancy and fortitude                          70
To other souls: but had ourselves been struck

---

51. now] *Corr. F; new Q, uncorr. F, G.*    64. griefs] *F2; grieues Q, F.*

---

49. *Hence Law*] 'We hear no more of Ovid's law; yet he was somewhat farther advanced in it than Jonson seems to admit.' *G,* quoting *Tristia* II, 93 on Ovid's experience as a lawyer.

58. *objects . . . abjects*] a common play on the words: *H&S* quote F.P., *The Case is Altered. How? Aske Dalio and Millo,* 1604, C3r, 'this ougly obiect, or rather abiect of nature', and *Hist.* (Wood, II, 293), 'Once Objects, now all Abjects to the world'. An abject is something thrown away, trash.

62. *Cynthia's*] thought (wrongly) to be Propertius' pseudonym for Hostia (see Apuleius *Apologia* I, p. 311 in J.'s copy: see I.iii.32–3n.); her ghost appears to him in *Elegy* IV.vii. The suggestion for Ovid's sympathy towards Propertius comes from *Tristia* IV.x.45–6: 'Oft-times Propertius would declaim his flaming verse by right of the comradeship that joined him to me.'

69. *strife*] strong effort, striving (*OED,* 4).

71–2. *struck . . . planet*] struck by the same malignant fate: cf. *EMI* IV.vii.141.

With the like planet, had our loves, like his,
Been ravished from us by injurious death,
And in the height and heat of our best days,
It would have cracked our sinews, shrunk our veins,            75
And made our very heart strings jar like his.
Come, let's go take him forth, and prove if mirth
Or company will but abate his passion.

*Tibullus.* Content, and I implore the gods it may.     *Exeunt.*

---

72. like his] *In parentheses in Q, F.*     79. S.D.] *Q.*

73. *injurious death*] probably recalling the 'injurious step' ('iniurioso pede')
of Fortune in Hor. *Odes* I.xxxv.13.
    76. *heart strings*] tendons or nerves supposed to brace the heart (*OED*, 1).
*jar*] (i) be out of harmony, (ii) shudder.

# Act II

*[Enter]* ALBIUS *[and]* CRISPINUS.

*Albius.* Master Crispinus, you are welcome. Pray' use a stool
 sir. Your cousin Cytheris will come down presently. We
 are so busy for the receiving of these courtiers here, that I
 can scarce be a minute with myself for thinking of them.
 Pray you sit, sir, pray you sit, sir.                                          5
*Crispinus.* I am very well, sir. Ne'er trust me, but you are most
 delicately seated here, full of sweet delight and blandish-
 ment! An excellent air, an excellent air!
*Albius.* Ay, sir, 'tis a pretty air. *[Aside]* These courtiers run in
 my mind still, I must look out. *[To Crispinus]* For Jupiter's    10
 sake, sit, sir. Or please you walk into the garden? There's a
 garden on the back side.
*Crispinus.* I am most strenuously well, I thank you, sir.

---

II.i.0.1.] *A Room in* Albius's *House.* / *Enter* ALBIUS *and* CRISPINUS. *G,
who continues the scene throughout the act.*     3. receiving] *F;* re- / cecceauing
*Q.*     9. S.D.] *Nicholson.*     11. sake, sit, sir. Or] *F;* sake sit Sir, or *Q.*
the garden?] *F;* the Garden. *Q.*     12. back side] *G;* backside *Q;* back-side
*F.*

---

II.i.1. stool] Some patrons, particularly exhibitionist 'gallants' like
Crispinus, sat on stools on the stage in the private theatres (not in the public
amphitheatres: see Gurr, p. 30) for an extra sixpence, and Crispinus is
probably here invited to sit on one side and join them; this would explain
how Albius can speak to him (as in ll. 33–7, 69–74 below) without Chloe
noticing his presence until l. 76. Cf. IV.v.41–2n. J. satirises such spectators
in *CR*, Ind. 116–46, and complains about the lack of room they leave actors
in *D* is *A*, Prol.2–25. *WYW* opens with three actors as gallants on the stage
(Wood, II, 231). See also Dekker, *Gull's Hornbook*, in Chambers, *ES*, IV,
366–8.

 7. seated] situated.
 sweet] See I.iii.35n.
 12. back side] at the rear of the house; cf. *C is A* IV.viii.1: 'How, in my
back side?'
 13. strenuously well] 'strenuous' is one of Marston's neologisms, used in *1
Ant.*, Ind. 35; see V.iii.286n and 492–3.

*Albius.* Much good do you, sir.                    *Exit* [ALBIUS.]

[*Enter* CHLOE *with two* Maids. CRISPINUS *sits to one side.*]

*Chloe.* Come, bring those perfumes forward a little, and strew     15
some roses, and violets here. Fie, here be rooms savour the
most pitifully rank that ever I felt. [*Re-enter* ALBIUS] I cry
the gods mercy, my husband's in the wind of us.

*Albius.* Why, this is good, excellent, excellent. Well said, my
sweet Chloe. Trim up your house most obsequiously.        20

*Chloe.* For Vulcan's sake, breathe somewhere else! In troth,
you overcome our perfumes exceedingly, you are too
predominant.

*Albius.* Hear but my opinion, sweet wife.

*Chloe.* A pin for your pinion! [*Hitting him*] In sincerity, if you   25
be thus fulsome to me in everything, I'll be divorced.

---

14. S.D.] *Exit Q.*   14.1. S.D.] *This ed.; Enter* CHLOE, *with two* Maids.
*G.; Enter Chloe; Crispinus retires. Parfitt.*   17. S.D.] *This ed.; sees Albius
G.*   21. Vulcan's] *F2; Vulcanes Q; VVLCANVS F.*   25. S.D.] *This ed.*

---

15–16.] Cf. *EMO* II.iv.5ff., where Deliro's boy strews flowers and burns
perfumes for Fallace. As Penniman says, Albius and Chloe are developed
from Deliro and Fallace. *S-M* opens with '*two Gentlewomen strewing of
flowers*'.

17. *felt*] smelt: see *OED*, 'Feel' *v.* 1.7, 'To perceive by smell or taste'.

19. *Well said*] well done; cf. III.iv.344, 'Apol. Dial.', 215, and *C is
A* II.vii.83. From 'assay': see *OED* 'Say' *v.* 2, 5a.

20. *obsequiously*] a neologism, coined by Marston in *Scourge*, IV,
163. Mallory rightly suggests an attempt on Albius' part at courtly language,
but satire at Marston's expense is likely to have been foremost in J.'s mind.

21. *Vulcan's sake*] Bad smells were an attribute of Vulcan; Albius the
goldsmith appropriately plays Vulcan, the cuckolded god of fire, in the
banquet in IV.v; see IV.ii.45n.

23. *predominant*] a relatively new word: 1576 is date of first citation in
*OED*. Chloe uses it pretentiously, though with a certain logic.

25. *pinion*] punning on 'pinion', an embellishment on the shoulder or
sleeve of a dress; see Stubbes, *Anatomie of Abuses*, I.73. For Marston's use,
see V.iii.513n. Partridge, *Slang*, gives 'pinion' as Cockney slang for opinion.

S.D.] Suggested by Nicholson's note: 'I suspect a pun, and that the doting
Albius would embrace his wife, but that she pushes away his arm, and hits
him on the head. Otherwise the "bumps on the head" are dragged in apropos
of nothing.'

*In sincerity*] A characteristic phrase, used by Chloe in II.i.45, II.ii.68,
IV.ii.14, 48; cf. 'in sadness', IV.i.2. It may, like 'forsooth' (see l. 84n) have
been typical of City rather than court.

26. *fulsome*] tiresome, tedious, but also foul-smelling (*OED*, 3c, 4).

God's my body! You know what you were, before I
married you; I was a gentlewoman born, I; I lost all my
friends to be a citizen's wife, because I heard indeed they
kept their wives as fine as ladies, and that we might rule            30
our husbands like ladies, and do what we listed: do you
think I would have married you else?

*Albius.* I acknowledge, sweet wife. [*To Crispinus*] She speaks
the best of any woman in Italy, and moves as mightily:
which makes me I had rather she should make bumps on          35
my head, as big as my two fingers, than I would offend
her. [*To Chloe*] But sweet wife——

*Chloe.* Yet again? Is't not grace enough for you that I call you
husband, and you call me wife, but you must still be
poking me against my will to things?                                       40

*Albius.* But you know, wife, here are the greatest ladies and
gallantest gentlemen of Rome to be entertained in our
house now; and I would fain advise thee to entertain them
in the best sort, i' faith, wife.

*Chloe.* In sincerity, did you ever hear a man talk so idly? You       45
would seem to be master? You would have your spoke in
my cart? You would advise me to entertain ladies and
gentlemen? Because you can marshal your pack-needles,

33. S.D.] *Nicholson.*     35. rather] *Corr. Q, F;* rarher *uncorr. Q.*     42.
gallantest] *F;* Gallantst *Q.*

---

27. *God's my body!*] A meaningless conflation of such oath's as 'God save
my life' ('God's my life') and 'God's (i.e. Christ's) body'.

28. *gentlewoman born*] parodied in *S-M* III.i.193, and ironically anticipating Crispinus' similarly empty claim in II.i.88.

29. *citizen's*] Here specifically a freeman of the City, and therefore in the
context of London a tradesman, not a gentleman; a similar distinction could
be made between the Roman equestrian class and the *populus.*

35. *makes*] causes that; see *OED,* 9b.

35–6.] The allusion is to the cuckold's horns, as well as to the blow that
Chloe has probably just given him. *H&S* compare *S W* IV.ii.138–41.

40. *poking*] A *double entendre,* with 'inciting' as the primary meaning; cf.
*S-M* II.i.63–5.

46–7. *spoke . . . cart*] try to give unwanted advice, punning on 'speak': cf.
Lyly, *Euphues his England* (*Works,* ed. Bond, II, 69), but again with a
secondary sexual meaning.

48. *pack-needles*] large needles for sewing up goods in cloth packages;
Albius' trade extends beyond precious metals, as did that of many gold-
smiths, and there is no reason to accept de Vocht's argument that this is an
inconsistency that would have been removed if J. had revised the copy for *F.*

horse-combs, hobby-horses and wall candlesticks in your
warehouse better than I, therefore you can tell how to          50
entertain ladies and gentlefolks better than I?
*Albius.* O my sweet wife, upbraid me not with that. Gain
savours sweetly from anything. He that respects to get
must relish all commodities alike, and admit no difference
betwixt oade and frankincense, or the most precious            55
balsamum and a tar barrel. [*He tries to embrace her.*]
*Chloe.* [*Pushing him away*] Marry faugh! You sell snuffers too,
if you be remembered, but I pray you let me buy them out
of your hand. For I tell you true, I take it highly in snuff to
learn how to entertain gentlefolks of you at these years,       60
i'faith. Alas, man, there was not a gentleman came to your
house i' your t' other wife's time, I hope? Nor a lady? Nor
music? Nor masques? Nor you nor your house were so
much as spoken of before I disbased myself from my hood

---

52. Gain] *This ed.;* 'Gain *Q, F.*    56. S.D.] *This ed.*    57. S.D.] *This ed.*
faugh!] *This ed.;* fough: *Q, F.*    62. wife's] *G;* Wiues *Q, Subst. F.*

---

52–6. *Gain . . . barrel*] Imitating Juvenal XIV, 203–5: 'Make no dis-
crimination between hides and unguents: the smell of gain is good whatever
the thing from which it comes.' Cf. also *EH* I.i.149, 'The gain of honest
pains is never base', and Erasmus *Adagia* 886F: 'Lucri bonus est odor ex re
qualibet'.
53. *respects*] expects, anticipates: see *OED* 'respect' *v.* 5.
55. *oade*] woad; cf. *Alc.* III.iv.97. 'It supplied the old English blue dye till
it was superseded by indigo' (*H&S*).
56. *balsamum*] balsam, an aromatic resin.
57–9. *Marry . . . hand*] 'Snuffers' was slang for nostrils: Chloe complains
of Albius' smell, and prefers the snuffers he sells in his shop, probably
meaning instruments for snuffing candles, though Mallory quotes J. O.
Halliwell, *Dictionary of Archaic and Provincial Words* (1847): 'small open
dishes for holding snuff, sometimes made of silver'.
57. *Marry faugh*] a common expression of disdain. 'MARY FAUGH, *an
old woman*' is a character in Marston's *Dutch Curtezan* (?1603); cf. I.ii.84n.
59. *take . . . snuff*] take offence at it, a common usage: cf. *EMI*
IV.ii.99–100: 'Nay, you, lampe of virginitie, that take in snuffe so!'
(*H&S*); *WYW*, 'they dare suffer *Snuffe* so neere the Stage?' (Wood, II, 231),
and *S–M* I.ii.228, 'take him in snuffe'.
60. *of . . . years*] to learn from you at my age.
62. *wife's*] *Q* and *F* 'Wiues' could be singular or plural.
64. *disbased*] debased.
64–6. *hood . . . bodice*] In *EH* the farthingale is associated with becoming
a lady (S.D. I.ii.0.2); cf. Dekker, *Shoemaker's Holiday* III.ii.32–4: 'Art thou

and my farthingale to these bumrolls and your whalebone      65
bodice.

*Albius.* [*Putting his finger to his lips*] Look here, my sweet wife; I
am mum, my dear mummia, my balsamum, my sper-
maceti, and my very city of — [*To Crispinus*] She has the
most best, true, feminine wit in Rome!                       70

*Crispinus.* I have heard so, sir, and do most vehemently desire
to participate the knowledge of her fair features.

*Albius.* Ah, peace, you shall hear more anon. Be not seen yet, I
pray you; not yet; observe.                              *Exit.*

---

65. farthingale] *This ed.;* Fartingall *Q, Subst. F.*   65–6. whalebone
bodice] *G;* Whale-bone Bodies *Q;* whale-bone-bodies *F.*    67. S.D.] *This
ed.*   68. mummia] *F; Mumma Q.*   68–9. spermaceti] *G; Sperma Cete
Q; sperma cete F.*   69. of—] *F; dash followed by space in Q to indicate an
omission or pause.*   73. yet, I] *F;* yet; I *Q.*   74. S.D.] *Q.*

---

acquainted with neuer a fardingale-maker, nor a French-hoode maker, I must
enlarge my bumme, ha, ha, how shall I looke in a hoode I wonder?' (so
Mallory). J. deliberately chooses the unusual spelling 'fartingall'. The
bumroll was a bustle worn to accentuate the bottom and hips: cf. Samuel
Rowlands, *The letting of humour's blood in the head-vaine* (1600), F2r: 'A
Boulster for their buttocks.' The bodice (literally 'a pair of bodies') were
corsets made of whalebone and quilted padding.

67. S.D.] That Albius points to his lips to indicate silence is confirmed by
the similar words in IV.iii.159–60 ('Captain, look here: mum') and IV.v.57–8
('hereafter, I'll be here mum'), where 'here' must be his mouth. Cf. also
II.i.118, II.ii.210, IV.iii.67. *OED* first records 'mum' as an adjective in
1521. For the gesture, see Ovid *Met.* IX, 692.

68. *mummia*] a medicinal liquid or gum made from mummified bodies:
*OED*, s.v. 'Mummy' 1, quotes Hakluyt, *Voyages* (1599), II.i.201, 'And these
dead bodies are the Mummie which the Phisitians and Apothecaries doe
against our willes make us to swallow'. First of a sequence of *paronomasies*
(see III.i.92n) by Albius, following his use of 'mum' in l. 68.

*balsamum*] aromatic oil or ointment, especially one used for embalming;
continuing the play on 'mum'.

68–9. *spermaceti*] fatty substance from the head of the sperm-whale, used
as an ointment, and for candles.

*spermaceti . . . city of——*] The spacing in *Q* emphasises Albius' pun,
which was probably made more obvious in performance; in *F* the space
between 'sperma' and 'cete' is less clear.

70. *most best*] Cf. *Engl. Gr.* II.iv.25–36, where J. describes the usage as 'a
certaine kind of English Atticisme' giving extra emphasis.

71–2. *vehemently . . . participate*] parodying Marston, *WYW* (Wood, II,
231), 'I am vehemently fearefull' and 246, 'I am most vehemently enamor'd'.

74. *observe*] See p. 33, and II.i.157, 161–2n.

*Chloe.* 'Sbody, give husbands the head a little more, and they'll      75
   be nothing but head shortly [*Indicating Crispinus*] What's
   he there?

*1 Maid.* I know not forsooth.

*2 Maid.* [*To Crispinus*] Who would you speak with, sir?

*Crispinus.* I would speak with my cousin Cytheris.      80

[*2*] *Maid.* [*To Chloe*] He is one forsooth would speak with his
   cousin Cytheris.

*Chloe.* Is she your cousin, sir?

*Crispinus.* Yes in truth, forsooth, for fault of a better.

*Chloe.* She is a gentlewoman!      85

*Crispinus.* Or else she should not be my cousin, I assure you.

*Chloe.* Are you a gentleman born?

*Crispinus.* That I am, lady; you shall see mine arms if 't please
   you.

*Chloe.* No, your legs do sufficiently show you are a gentleman      90
   born, sir: for a man born upon little legs is always a
   gentleman born.

*Crispinus.* Yet, I pray you, vouchsafe the sight of my arms,

---

84. truth, forsooth] *F*; truth for sooth *Q*.      85. gentlewoman!] *This ed.;*
gentlewoman? *Q, F*; gentlewoman. *G*.

---

75. *'Sbody*] God's or Christ's body; cf. II.i.27n.

76. *nothing but head*] 'Head' is the hunting term for antlers: hence,
nothing but a cuckold.

84. *in truth, forsooth*] 'forsooth' is otiose, since it means 'in truth'. J. sees
the word as a city affectation: cf. IV.i.34–5; *E. Highgate* 246, 'you sip so like
a forsooth of the city'; *CR* IV.i.30, and *EMO* II.ii.14 (so *H&S*).

*for . . . better*] perhaps anglicising 'faute de mieux.' The polite formula
is misused, and emerges as an unintended insult; cf. II.ii.10, IV.iii.31.

87. *gentleman born*] Marston was described as a gentleman's son when he
matriculated at Brasenose. J. (who had more slender claims to gentility: see
p. 35, n. 71) gives ironic emphasis to Marston's status throughout, partly at
the expense of Dekker: cf. III.i.26, III.iv.64, 163–4, and V.iii.115–6.

91. *little legs*] Cf. Dekker *Gull's Hornbook*, quoted p. 9, which implies
that a personal insult to Marston is involved, and *Malcontent* (ed. Hunter,
Revels, 1975) V.v.35–6: 'as fine a man as may be, having a red beard and a
pair of warped legs', where self-parody is suspected. However, small legs are
the generic sign of a gentleman usher in *EMO* III.iii.37, and elsewhere, e.g.
Francis Lenton, *Leasures* (1631), 'Character 31: A Gentleman-Usher': 'The
smallness of his legs bewrayes his profession.' The point has added
significance in a children's company.

93–8. The arms of Marston of Heyton were *sable* a fesse dancettée *ermine*
(the bloody toe?) between three fleurs de lis *argent* (the three thorns *pungent*?),

Mistress; for I bear them about me, to have 'em seen.
[*Showing Chloe a paper*] My name is Crispinus, or      95
Cri-spinas indeed; which is well expressed in my arms, a
face crying *in chief*, and beneath it a bloody toe, between
three thorns *pungent*.

*Chloe.* Then you are welcome, sir. Now you are a gentleman
born, I can find in my heart to welcome you: for I am a      100
gentlewoman born too, and will bear my head high enough,
though 'twere my fortune to marry a tradesman.

*Crispinus.* No doubt of that, sweet feature, your carriage
shows it in any man's eye that is carried upon you with
judgement.      105

[*Re-enter* ALBIUS.] *He is still going in and out.*

---

95. S.D.] *This ed.*  96–8. a face . . . *pungent*] *Q; in parentheses in F.*
102. tradesman] *F;* Flat-cappe *Q.*  103–5.] *F; not in Q.*  105.1 He . . .
out.] *F in margin; not in Q.*

---

differenced by a crescent of the last (the face crying *in chief*?). Nason, pp.
99–104 argues that the Marston arms described bear little resemblance to
those of Crispinus, and agrees with Fleay (*Shakespeare Manual* (1878), p.
312) that J. is punning on Mars-toen = red toe, but there is enough correspondence to suggest that parody of the Marston arms is also intended. *G*'s
vague note ('there is probably some personal allusion here') shows that at this
stage he had not identified Crispinus with Marston.
    96. *Cri-spinas*] a Latin pun on *spina*, thorn (see l. 98), and the usual
English one on ass/arse (cf. V.iii.211); Dekker takes up the English pun in *S-
M* II.ii.38: 'as for *Crispinus*, that Crispin-asse'.
    97. in chief] in heraldry, occupying the upper and principal part of the
shield.
    98. pungent] Latin *pungens*, pricking, but also troublesome and strong
smelling; parodying heraldic terms like 'rampant'. Cf. *BF* Ind. 124–7 for
similar mock heraldic language.
    102. (*Q*) *Flat-cappe*] associated with city tradesmen; cf. *EMI* II.i.110,
and *EH* I.i.101. See also Harrison, *Description*: 'Apprentices [and] Journey-
men . . . whom the pages of the Court in derision called "Flat Caps" ' (quoted
in Gurr, p. 255); cf. III.i.46n, and App. 1, p. 284.
    103. *feature*] form, meaning here the whole body: *OED, sb.* 1.c cites this
passage, but J. is parodying Marston's earlier use in *Pigmalion*, stanza 2: 'So
faire an Image of a Womans feature' and *WYW*, 'To those that know the
pangs of bringing forth / A perfect feature' (Wood, II, 235).
    104. *carried upon*] watches, looks on: see *OED*, 'Carry' *v.* 34, punning
on 'carriage', which in the sense of mien, demeanour, was a relatively new
word (*OED*, 13, 14, citations dated 1596 and 1590).

*Albius.* Dear wife, be not angry.

*Chloe.* God's my passion!

*Albius.* Hear me but one thing: let not your maids set cushions
in the parlour windows, nor in the dining-chamber
windows, nor upon stools, in either of them, in any case,      110
for 'tis tavern-like; but lay them one upon another in some
out-room, or corner of the dining-chamber.

*Chloe.* Go, go, meddle with your bed-chamber only, or rather
with your bed in your chamber, only; or rather with your
wife in your bed only; or on my faith I'll not be pleased      115
with you only.

*Albius.* Look here, my dear wife, entertain that gentleman
kindly, I prithee; — mum.                          *Exit.*

*Chloe.* Go, I need your instructions indeed; anger me no more,
I advise you. City-sin, quoth'a! She's a wise gentlewoman      120
i' faith, will marry herself to the sin of the city.

[*Re-enter* ALBIUS.]

*Albius.* But this time, and no more, by heaven, wife: hang no
pictures in the hall, nor in the dining-chamber, in any
case, but in the gallery only, for 'tis not courtly else, o' my
word, wife.                                                    125

---

118. prithee] *G;* pre' thee *Q, F.*      S.D.] *Q.*      121.1. S.D.] *Subst. G.*
122 by heaven] *In parentheses in Q, F.*      124. o'] *F;* on *Q.*

107. *God's my passion*] Cf. II.i.27; a confusion of 'God's passion' (i.e.
suffering) and such oaths as 'God save my life'; *H&S* compare *AWW*
V.ii.39, 'Cox my passion!'

108–9. *cushions ... windows*] Cf. Middleton, *A Chaste Maid in Cheapside,*
ed. Brissenden (1968), V.i.171–2, where a house in the Strand may be
'simply stocked with cloth of tissue cushions, / To furnish out bay windows',
and *How a Man May Choose a Good Wife from a Bad* (1602) III.iii: 'Come
spread the Table; Is the hall well rubd, / The cushions in the windowes
neatly laid?' (*H&S*).

115. *pleased*] satisfied (sexually).

120. *City-sin*] Penniman quotes Dekker, *Lanthorne and Candlelight* (1608):
'The citizen is sued here (i.e. in Hell) and condemned for the city-sins'
(Temple Classics ed. (1904), p. 191). Chloe's pun bears out Hoskyns' (and
J.'s) assertion that such word-play is 'a toy' best avoided (see III.i.92n).

*qouth'a*] 'The phrase said he?, used with contemptuous or sarcastic force in
repeating a word or phrase used by another' (*OED*).

124. *in the gallery*] The display of family portraits in the long gallery of the
Elizabethan house was a relatively new fashion; this suggests it had come, on
a reduced scale, to large city houses.

*Chloe.* 'Sprecious, never have done! [*She makes a threatening gesture.*]

*Albius.* Wife——                                          *Exit.*

*Chloe.* Do I not bear a reasonable corrigible hand over him, Crispinus?

*Crispinus.* By this hand, lady, you hold a most sweet hand over    130
him.

[*Re-enter* ALBIUS.]

*Albius.* And then for the great gilt andirons—?

*Chloe.* Again! Would the andirons were in your great guts, for me.

*Albius.* I do vanish, wife.                              *Exit.*    135

*Chloe.* How shall I do, Master Crispinus? Here will be all the bravest ladies in court presently, to see your cousin Cytheris: O the gods! How might I behave myself now, as to entertain them most courtly?

*Crispinus.* Marry, lady, if you will entertain them most courtly,   140
you must do thus: as soon as ever your maid or your man brings you word they are come, you must say 'A pox on 'em, what do they here?' And yet when they come, speak them as fair and give them the kindest welcome in words that can be.                                               145

*Chloe.* Is that the fashion of courtiers, Crispinus?

*Crispinus.* I assure you it is, lady, I have observed it.

*Chloe.* For your pox, sir, it is easily hit on; but, 'tis not so easy to speak fair after, methinks?

[*Re-enter* ALBIUS.]

126. S.D.] *This ed.*     127. Wife——] *F;* Wife. *Q.*     S.D.] *Q.*     131.1.
S.D.] *Subst. G.*     135. S.D.] *Q.*     142–3. say 'A pox . . . here?'] *Nichol-
son;* say, A poxe . . . here? *Q;* say (A poxe . . . here?) *F.*     148. on] vpon
*Q.*     easy] *Q;* easily *F.*     149.1. S.D.] *Subst. G.*

---

126. *'Sprecious*] a contraction of 'God's precious blood'. Cf. *BF* I.v.11.
S.D.] Cf. Nicholson's note: 'She makes some sudden sign of anger'.

128. *corrigible*] corrective; an affected word, despite Iago's use in *Oth.*
I.iii.325.

132. *gilt andirons*] firedogs; the front uprights were gilded on the more
expensive varieties.

148–9. *'tis . . . after*] because of facial disfigurement, and because of
'melancholy': cf. Burton, *Anatomy,* I, 376 on mental disorder following 'the
French pox', or syphilis.

*Albius.* O wife, the coaches are come, on my word, a number of    150
coaches and courtiers.

*Chloe.* A pox on them, what do they here?

*Albius.* How now, wife! Would'st thou not have 'em come?

*Chloe.* Come? Come, you are a fool, you. [*To Crispinus*] He
knows not the trick on't. [*To Albius*] Call Cytheris, I pray    155
you. [*Exit* ALBIUS.] And good Master Crispinus, you can
observe you say; let me entreat you for all the ladies'
behaviours, jewels, jests, and attires, that you marking as
well as I, we may put both our marks together when they
are gone, and confer of them.                                     160

*Crispinus.* I warrant you, sweet lady; let me alone to observe,
till I turn myself to nothing but observation.

[*Re-enter* ALBIUS *with* CYTHERIS.]

Good morrow, cousin Cytheris.

*Cytheris.* Welcome, kind cousin. What? Are they come?

*Albius.* Ay, your friend Cornelius Gallus, Ovid, Tibullus, Pro-    165
pertius, with Julia the emperor's daughter, and the lady
Plautia, are lighted at the door; and with them Hermogenes
Tigellius, the excellent musician.

*Cytheris.* Come, let us go meet them, Chloe.

---

152. *Italicised in* Q.    154. S.D.] *Nicholson.*    156. S.D.] *This ed.* 162.1
S.D.] *This ed.; Enter* CYTHERIS. G    163. Good morrow, cousin] *F;*
God morrow cosen Q; *begins new line in* Q, F.

---

150. *coaches*] associated more with court than city. Cf. Stow, *Annales*
(1631), p. 867: 'In the yeare 1564 Guilliam Boonen, a Dutchman, became the
Queene's Coachman, and was the first that brought the use of coaches into
England . . . by little and little, they grew usual among the nobility and
others of sort . . . Lastly, even at this time, 1605, began the ordinary use of
Coaches.' Cf. IV.ii.14–18, where riding in a coach is still a novelty for Chloe,
and *S-M* III.i.221–2, where Tucca promises Miniver she will be 'Coacht'.
The wives and daughters of citizens use them in *EH* III.ii.27–39, and *BF*
IV.v.94–103. In late 1601 (when *Poetaster* was probably on the stage) a bill
was unsuccessfully introduced to restrain their 'excessive use'.

157. *entreat*] an affected, courtly word here, used by Chloe and Crispinus
(II.ii.127–32, III.i.61) and by Julia (II.ii.134), Cytheris (IV.i.19) and Gallus
(IV.ii.28). Marston uses it frequently, often in this affected way, e.g. 'Entreat
soft rest' (*1 Ant.* II.i.253), 'my Grand-mother intreates you to come to dinner
to morrow morning' (*WYW*, Wood, II, 255). Cf. King, pp. 76–7 for
occurrence in J. and Marston.

161–2. *observe . . . observation*] J.'s use of the word is ridiculed in *JD's
Ent.* (Wood, III, 209); see p. 33.

*Chloe.* Observe, Crispinus.                                    170
*Crispinus.* At a hair's breadth, lady, I warrant you.

### ACT II   SCENE ii

[*Enter to them*] GALLUS, OVID, TIBULLUS, PROPERTIUS,
HERMOGENES, JULIA [*and*] PLAUTIA.

*Gallus.* Health to the lovely Chloe. [*To Cytheris*] You must
pardon me, Mistress, that I prefer this fair gentlewoman.
*Cytheris.* I pardon and praise you for it, sir. [*To Julia*] And I
beseech your excellence, receive her beauties into your
knowledge and favour.                                            5
*Julia.* Cytheris, she hath favour and behaviour that commands
as much of me; and sweet Chloe, know I do exceedingly
love you, and that I will approve in any grace my father the
emperor may show you. Is this your husband?
*Albius.* For fault of a better, if it please your highness.     10
*Chloe.* [*Aside to Cytheris*] God's my life! How he shames me!
*Cytheris.* Not a whit, Chloe, they all think you politic and
witty; wise women choose not husbands for the eye, merit,
or birth, but wealth and sovereignty.
*Ovid.* Sir, we all come to gratulate for the good report of you.   15
*Tibullus.* And would be glad to deserve your love, sir.
*Albius.* My wife will answer you all, gentlemen; I'll come to
you again presently.                                   *Exit.*
*Plautia.* You have chosen you a most fair companion here,
Cytheris, and a very fair house.                                 20
*Cytheris.* To both which, you and all my friends are very
welcome, Plautia.
*Chloe.* With all my heart, I assure your ladyship.
*Plautia.* Thanks, sweet Mistress Chloe.

---

II.ii.0.1–2.] *As they are going out, enter* CORNELIUS GALLUS . . .
PLAUTIA. *G, continuing the scene.*   3. S.D.] *Nicholson.*   11. S.D.]
*Nicholson.*   18. S.D.] *Q.*

---

171. *At . . . breadth*] minutely, with utmost exactness; not in *OED*, but
similar to 'To a hair', s.v. 'Hair' 8c, and 'Hairbreadth' 1.
  II.ii.2. *prefer*] give precedence to.
  6. *behaviour*] good manners, elegance (*OED*, 1e).
  10. *For . . . better*] Cf. II.i.84n.
  15. *gratulate*] offer congratulations, felicitate; Latin *gratulor*.

*Julia.* You must needs come to court, lady, i' faith, and there          25
be sure your welcome shall be as great to us.

*Ovid.* She will well deserve it, Madam. I see, even in her looks,
gentry and general worthiness.

*Tibullus.* I have not seen a more certain character of an excellent
disposition.                                                               30

*[Re-enter* ALBIUS.]

*Albius.* Wife.

*Chloe.* *[Aside to Albius]* O, they do so commend me here, the
courtiers! What's the matter now?

*Albius.* For the banquet, sweet wife.

*Chloe.* Yes; and I must needs come to court, and be welcome,          35
the princess says.                         *Exit [with* ALBIUS].

*Gallus.* Ovid and Tibullus, you may be bold to welcome your
mistresses here.

*Ovid.* We find it so, sir.

*Tibullus.* And thank Cornelius Gallus.                                   40

*Ovid.* Nay, my sweet Sextus, in faith thou art not sociable.

*Propertius.* In faith, I am not, Publius, nor I cannot.
Sick minds are like sick men that burn with fevers,
Who when they drink please but a present taste,
And after bear a more impatient fit.                                      45
Pray let me leave you; I offend you all,
And myself most.

*Gallus.*                    Stay, sweet Propertius.

*Tibullus.* You yield too much unto your griefs and fate,
Which never hurts, but when we say it hurts us.

*Propertius.* O peace, Tibullus; your philosophy                          50
Lends you too rough a hand to search my wounds.

---

30.1. S.D.] *Subst. G.*    36. S.D.] *Exit. Q; Exit with ALBIUS. G.*
40. Gallus] *Gallsn Q.*    41. in faith] *F; infaith Q.*    42. In faith] *G;*
Infaith *Q, F.*    44. present] *F;* lingring *Q.*    48. griefs] *F2;* grieues *Q, F.*

---

26. *to us*] i.e. by us.

29–30. *I . . . disposition*] For the face as a not altogether reliable indicator
of moral disposition, cf. *Tw.N* I.ii.48–51 and *Mac.* I.iv.11–12.

43–5.] Echoing Cicero *Cat.* I, 31: 'Men who are seriously ill often toss to
and fro with the heat of their fever and, if they drink cold water, seem to get
relief at first, but then are much more seriously and acutely distressed.'

49.] Imitating Plutarch, 'On Exile', *Moralia* 599, 1 (so *H&S*); in fact
Plutarch is quoting a line of Menander, *Epitrepontes*, frag. 9.

Speak they of griefs that know to sigh and grieve;
The free and unconstrainèd spirit feels
No weight of my oppression.                    *Exit.*
*Ovid.*                              Worthy Roman!
Methinks I taste his misery, and could                    55
Sit down and chide at his malignant stars.
*Julia.* Methinks I love him, that he loves so truly.
*Cytheris.* This is the perfect'st love, lives after death.
*Gallus.* Such is the constant ground of virtue still.
*Plautia.* It puts on an inseparable face.                    60

[*Re-enter* CHLOE.]

*Chloe.* [*Aside to Crispinus*] Have you marked everything,
Crispinus?
*Crispinus.* Everything, I warrant you.
*Chloe.* What gentlemen are these? Do you know them?
*Crispinus.* Ay, they are poets, lady.                    65
*Chloe.* Poets? They did not talk of me since I went, did they?
*Crispinus.* O yes, and extolled your perfections to the heavens.
*Chloe.* Now in sincerity, they be the finest kind of men that
ever I knew. Poets! Could not one get the emperor to make
my husband a poet, think you?                    70
*Crispinus.* No, lady, 'tis love and beauty make poets: and since
you like poets so well, your love and beauties shall make
me a poet.
*Chloe.* What, shall they? And such a one as these?
*Crispinus.* Ay, and a better than these: I would be sorry else.    75

---

54. S.D.] *Q.*    60.1. S.D.] *G.; Enter Chloe and Albius. Parfitt.*    61.
S.D.] *This ed.*    69. Poets!] *G*; Poets? *Q, F.*

52–4.] 'Let those who have suffered and know what it is like to sigh and
grieve speak of griefs: the spirit unconstrained by grief feels no weight like
that which oppresses me.'
58. *love, lives*] an ellipsis: 'love, [that] lives'.
59. *ground*] reason, motive (*OED*, 5c).
60.] 'It takes up a determined attitude of inseparability' (see *OED*, s.v
'face' *sb.* 2g).
71. *love . . . poets*] Cf. Plato, *Symposium*, 196 (trans. Jowett) where Love is
'the source of poesy in others . . . at the touch of him every one becomes a
poet'.

*Chloe.* And shall your looks change, and your hair change, and all, like these?

*Crispinus.* Why, a man may be a poet and yet not change his hair, lady.

*Chloe.* Well, we shall see your cunning: yet if you can change      80
your hair, I pray, do.

[*Re-enter* ALBIUS.]

*Albius.* Ladies and lordings, there's a slight banquet stays within for you, please you draw near and accost it.

*Julia.* We thank you, good Albius: but when shall we see those excellent jewels you are commended to have?      85

*Albius.* At your ladyship's service. [*Aside*] I got that speech by seeing a play last day, and it did me some grace now; I see 'tis good to collect sometimes. I'll frequent these plays more than I have done, now I come to be familiar with courtiers.      90

*Gallus.* Why, how now Hermogenes, what ailest thou, trow?

*Hermogenes.* A little melancholy, let me alone, pray thee.

*Gallus.* Melancholy! How so?

---

82.1. S.D.] *G.*    86. At . . . service.] *Italicised in Q.*    S.D.] *G (after 90).*

76. *hair change*] See p. 9 for Marston's presumed red hair, though Mallory points to ridicule of red beards in *1 Ant.* III.ii.73, 'I ha' not a red beard, take not tobacco much', *Malcontent* V.v.35–6, 'as fine a man as may be, having a red beard and a pair of warped legs', and *WYW* (Wood, II, 274–5): 'his beard is derectly brick collour, and perfectly fashion'd like the husk of a cheessnut'. The very frequency of these allusions, however, suggests self-mockery by Marston; cf. II.i.91n.

82–3.] *H&S* quote *Tim.* I.ii.155–6: 'Ladies, there is an idle banquet attends you, / Please you to dispose yourselves.' *Tim.* was not published until 1623, and probably not acted until 1761, but it is such courtly language that Albius is imitating; cf. the 'trifling foolish banquet' of *Rom.* I.v.122.

82. *lordings*] commonly used as a form of address, meaning 'Gentlemen'.

83. *accost*] address, assail: cf. *Tw.N* I.iii.49–59.

85. *commended to have*] Cf. *Tw.N* II.v.153 'remember who commended thy yellow stockings'. An affected usage, as Mallory points out; it may reflect fashionable court jargon. Such misuse of language is a serious matter for J., and helps place his attitude to Julia. Albius' reply points up the affectation involved.

86–7. *At . . . day*] For a possible allusion to *Tw.N*, see p. 37. *Q*'s italics probably signify a quotation.

91. *trow*] here simply an expletive; cf. *EMI* (Q) IV.ii.67.

*Hermogenes.* With riding: a plague on all coaches for me.

*Chloe.* [*Aside to Cytheris*] Is that hard-favoured gentleman a          95
poet too, Cytheris?

*Cytheris.* No this is Hermogenes, as humorous as a poet,
though: he is a musician.

*Chloe.* A musician? Then he can sing.

*Cytheris.* That he can excellently; did you never hear him?          100

*Chloe.* O no, will he be entreated, think you?

*Cytheris.* I know not. [*To Gallus*] Friend, Mistress Chloe would
fain hear Hermogenes sing; are you interested in him?

*Gallus.* No doubt his own humanity will command him so far,
to the satisfaction of so fair a beauty; but rather than fail,          105
we'll all be suitors to him.

*Hermogenes.* 'Cannot sing.

*Gallus.* Pray thee, Hermogenes.

*Hermogenes.* 'Cannot sing.

*Gallus.* For honour of this gentlewoman, to whose house I          110
know thou mayst be ever welcome.

*Chloe.* That he shall in truth, sir, if he can sing.

*Ovid.* What's that?

*Gallus.* This gentlewoman is wooing Hermogenes for a song.

*Ovid.* A song? Come, he shall not deny her. Hermogenes?          115

*Hermogenes.* 'Cannot sing.

*Gallus.* No, the ladies must do it, he stays but to have their
thanks acknowledged as a debt to his cunning.

*Julia.* That shall not want; ourself will be the first shall pro-

---

95. S.D.] *This ed.*

95. *hard-favoured*] usually   ugly,   but   here   possibly   referring   to
Hermogenes' surliness.

103. *interested in him*] i.e. do you have influence with him?

104. *humanity*] civility; cf. Evelyn, *Diary*, 21 July 1664: 'his lordship used
me with singular humanity.'

107–89.] The source for Hermogenes' behaviour in this scene is Hor.
*Sat.* I.iii.1–8: 'All singers have this fault: if asked to sing among their friends
they are never so inclined; if unasked, they never leave off . . . [Hermogenes]
Tigellius was of this sort. If Caesar, who might have forced him to comply,
should beg him by his father's friendship and his own, he could make no
headway. If the man took the fancy, then from the egg-course to the fruit he
would keep chanting "Io Bacche!"' '

118. *cunning*] skill.

mise to pay him more than thanks, upon a favour so          120
worthily vouchsafed.

*Hermogenes.* Thank you Madam, but 'will not sing.

*Tibullus.* Tut, the only way to win him, is to abstain from
entreating him.

*Crispinus.* [*Aside to Chloe*] Do you love singing, lady?          125

*Chloe.* O, passingly.

*Crispinus.* Entreat the ladies to entreat me to sing then, I
beseech you.

*Chloe.* I beseech your grace, entreat this gentleman to sing.

*Julia.* That we will, Chloe; can he sing excellently?          130

*Chloe.* I think so, Madam: for he entreated me to entreat you to
entreat him to sing.

*Crispinus.* Heaven and earth! Would you tell that?

*Julia.* Good sir, let's entreat you to use your voice.

*Crispinus.* Alas, Madam, I cannot in truth.          135

*Plautia.* The gentleman is modest; I warrant you he sings
excellently.

*Ovid.* Hermogenes, clear your throat; I see by him here's a
gentleman will worthily challenge you.

*Crispinus.* Not I, sir, I'll challenge no man.          140

*Tibullus.* That's your modesty, sir; but we, out of an assurance
of your excellency, challenge him in your behalf.

*Crispinus.* I thank you gentlemen, I'll do my best.

*Hermogenes.* Let that best be good, sir, you were best.

*Gallus.* O, this contention is excellent. What is't you sing, sir?          145

*Crispinus.* *If I freely may discover*, etc. Sir, I'll sing that.

*Ovid.* One of your own compositions, Hermogenes. He offers
you vantage enough.

*Crispinus.* Nay truly, gentlemen, I'll challenge no man:—
[*Pauses*] I can sing but one staff of the ditty neither.          150

---

125. S.D.] *This ed.*     136. gentleman] *F;* Gentlemans *Q.*     146. etc.]
*Parfitt; &c. Q, F.*     147–8.] *G; verse in Q, F, line divided at* Hermogenes. /
He.     149. man:—] *Nicholson;* man—: *Q, F; space after dash in Q indicating*
*pause.*

---

120. *pay . . . thanks*] reward him with something more tangible than words
of thanks.

126. *passingly*] exceedingly.

150. *staff*] stanza.

*neither*] strengthening a preceding negative ('Nay . . . no man'); *OED*, 3b.

*Gallus.* The better: Hermogenes himself will be entreated to
    sing the other.

[*Music.* CRISPINUS *sings.*]

> *If I freely may discover*
> *What would please me in my lover,*
> *    I would have her fair and witty,*
> *    Savouring more of court than city;*                              155
> *A little proud, but full of pity;*
> *Light, and humorous in her toying;*
> *Oft building hopes, and soon destroying;*
> *    Long, but sweet in the enjoying;*                                160
> *Neither too easy, nor too hard;*
> *All extremes I would have barred.*

*Gallus.* Believe me, sir, you sing most excellently.

*Ovid.* If there were a praise above excellence, the gentleman
    highly deserves it.                                                 165

*Hermogenes.* Sir, all this doth not yet make me envy you, for I
    know I sing better than you.

*Tibullus.* Attend Hermogenes now.

[*Music.* HERMOGENES *sings.*]

---

152.1 S.D.] *This ed.;* CANTVS. *Q;* SONG. *F;* CRISPINUS *sings. G.*
153. *may*] *Q, F; can F2.*    168.1. S.D.] *This ed.;* HERMOGENES,
*accompanied. G; verse headed 2. in Q, F.*

---

153–62, 169–78.] a considerably expanded imitation of Martial I.lvii: 'Do
you ask, Flaccus, what sort of girl I like or dislike? I dislike one too yielding,
and one too coy. That middle type between the two I approve: I like not that
which racks me, nor like I that which cloys.' It is the only song in *Poetaster*
for which there is a contemporary setting, probably that used in the play: see
Chan, pp. 64–9, who gives a modernised score based on BL MS Add.
24665, ff. 59v–60; there is a later setting by Henry Lawes (BL MS Add.
53723, f. 7). Beal, *Index*, I, 292–3 records twenty-four MS versions, mainly
in mid-seventeenth-century collections.
    158. Light] Light-hearted, cheerful, rather than 'fickle'.
    humorous] 'Full of humours or fancies' (*OED*, 3).
    159.] The 'humorous toying' will often build up the lover's hopes, and
then destroy them.
    163–5.] It is likely that the boy playing Crispinus performed the song
seriously, rather than giving a comically poor rendition to mock
Crispinus/Marston's abilities. Thus Gallus' praise is straightforward, though
Ovid's hyperbolic language is that of the flattering courtier.

She should be allowed her passions,
So they were but used as fashions:                                    170
   Sometimes froward, and then frowning;
   Sometimes sickish, and then swowning;
   Every fit with change still crowning.
   Purely jealous I would have her,
   Then only constant when I crave her;                      175
   'Tis a virtue should not save her.
Thus, nor her delicates would cloy me,
Neither her peevishness annoy me.

*Julia.* Nay, Hermogenes, your merit hath long since been both
   known and admired of us.                                 180

*Hermogenes.* You shall hear me sing another; now will I begin.

*Gallus.* We shall do this gentleman's banquet too much wrong,
   that stays for us, ladies.

*Julia.* 'Tis true, and well thought on, Cornelius Gallus.

*Hermogenes.* Why 'tis but a short air, 'twill be done presently,    185
   pray' stay; strike music.

*Ovid.* No, good Hermogenes: we'll end this difference within.

*Julia.* 'Tis the common disease of all your musicians that they
   know no mean to be entreated, either to begin or end.

*Albius.* Please you lead the way, gentles?                          190

*All.* Thanks, good Albius.     *Exeunt [all but* ALBIUS].

*Albius.* O, what a charm of thanks was here put upon me! O
   Jove, what a setting forth it is to a man, to have many
   courtiers come to his house! sweetly was it said of a good
   old housekeeper, 'I had rather want meat, than want          195

---

169. *allowed*] Q, F; *allow'd* G.   191. *All.*] F; *Omnes.* Q.   S.D.] *Exeunt*
Q; *Exeunt all but Albius.* G.; *Exit all but Albius and Crispinus. Parfitt.*   193.
*many*] F; *may* Q.

---

   171. *froward*] perverse, hard to please (*OED*, A.1).
   172. *swowning*] swooning.
   174. *Purely jealous*] chastely vigilant, suspicious.
   177. *delicates*] delights.
   178. *peevishness*] obstinacy, perversity.
   188–9.] Cf. Hor. *Sat.* I.iii.1–3, quoted above II.ii.107–89n.
   192–3. *charm . . . setting forth*] Albius uses jeweller's vocabulary: the
'charm' is both a blended collection of voices and an amulet. The 'setting
forth' is both a means to advancement and a way of displaying a jewel to best
advantage.
   195–6. *'I had . . . guests'*] Dent, M822 gives this as the only example in
drama; *H&S* quote Sir H. Cock, writing to Lord Burleigh on 29 April 1602

guests', specially if they be courtly guests. For never trust
me if one of their good legs made in a house be not worth
all the good cheer a man can make them. He that would
have fine guests, let him have a fine wife; he that would
have a fine wife, let him come to me.                          200

[*Re-enter* CRISPINUS.]

*Crispinus.* By your kind leave, Master Albius.
*Albius.* What, you are not gone, Master Crispinus?
*Crispinus.* Yes faith, I have a design draws me hence; pray', sir,
fashion me an excuse to the ladies.
*Albius.* Will you not stay and see the jewels, sir? I pray you    205
stay.
*Crispinus.* Not for a million, sir, now. Let it suffice, I must
relinquish; and so in a word, please you to expiate this
compliment.
*Albius.* [*Pointing to his lips*] Mum.                *Exit.*    210
*Crispinus.* I'll presently go and engle some broker for a poet's
gown, and bespeak a garland: and then, jeweller, look to
your best jewel i' faith.                              *Exit.*

---

200.1 S.D.]  *G.*    202. Crispinus] *Subst. F; Crispine Q.*    205. pray] *Q;*
*pay F.*    210. *Pointing . . . lips*] *This ed.    Exit*] *Q.*    213. S.D.] *Q.*

---

about entertaining King James at Broxbourn: 'as for the shortnes of ye tyme
I shal be able, which I hope your honor will take in good parte, remembring,
under your good favor, ye olde sayinge, Better to lacke meate than good
companie.'
   197. *good legs*] bows, obeisances; cf. *CR* III.iv.29 (*H&S*), and *T of T*
IV.i.59.
   203. *design*] plan.
   208. *relinquish*] a pretentious substitute for 'leave'. J. uses it in a similar
intransitive sense in *CR* IV.i.127 (the only example of this sense in *OED*, 5);
It is also mocked in Wilson's parody inkhorn letter (see p. 27).
   *expiate*] a recently coined verb in 1601. Earliest examples in various senses
in *OED* date from between 1594 and 1665. It makes no sense here: Crispinus
is misusing a fashionable neologism.
   209. *compliment*] See p. 33.
   211. *engle*] as verb, to scrounge, with overtones of homosexuality derived
from the noun (see I.ii.16n).
   *broker*] pawnbroker.
   211–12. *poet's gown . . . garland*] There was no specific gown or toga for
poets, and the poet's garland of laurel ('bays') was awarded, not 'bespoken'.
Crispinus has a confused notion of a poet's accoutrements.

# Act III

ACT III   SCENE i

*[Enter]* HORACE, CRISPINUS *[following]*.

*Horace.* Hmh? Yes, I will begin an ode so, and it shall be to
Maecenas.

*Crispinus.* *[Aside]* 'Slid, yonder's Horace! They say he's an
excellent poet. Maecenas loves him. I'll fall into his acquaintance if I can; I think he be composing as he goes i'     5
the street. Ha! Tis a good humour, and he be: I'll compose too.

*Horace.* Swell me a bowl with lusty wine,

---

III.i.0.1.] *The Via Sacra, (or Holy Street.)* / *Enter* HORACE, CRISPINUS
*following. G.*    1–2.] Hor.Lib.I. / Sat.9. *Marginal note in Q;* Hot.li.I. / Sat.
9 *F; F2 as Q, but places note in margin at* 10–11, *referring it to Horace's
ode.*    3. S.D.] *This ed.*    4. Mæcenas] *Parfitt; Mecænas Q;* MECŒNAS
*F; (H&S wrongly say Mecænas Q originally.)*

---

III.i. A considerably expanded version (continued into III.iii) of the
seventy-eight lines of Hor. *Sat.* I.ix, which Donne had also imitated during
the 1590s in *Satires I* and *IV*. Hor. locates it in the Via Sacra (I.ix.1), leading
into the Forum; his boor is unnamed.

2. *Maecenas*] See Persons of the Play 2n.

3. *'Slid*] abbreviation of 'God's lid' (i.e. eyelid).

5. *composing*] Constructing in words; this is the first example in *OED* of
its use in this absolute sense (5b); cf. l. 46. J. mocks it as an affected
Latinism (from *componere*) for which there are good English alternatives.

6. *humour*] state of mind, mood.

*and*] if; cf. I.i.33n.

8–12.] This fragment was apparently important to J.; it was one of the
poems he recited to Drummond (*Conv.* 96), and was parodied by Dekker, *S-
M* I.ii.1–20. It is similar to, but not a translation of, the many apostrophes to
wine in Hor., esp. *Odes* III.xxi and *Epodes* IX, 33–8: 'Bring hither, lad,
more generous bowls, and Chian wine or Lesbian, or pour out for us
Caecuban, to check our rising qualms. 'Tis sweet to banish anxious fear for
Caesar's fortunes with Bacchus' mellow gift.' Mallory notes the intriguing
similarity to *AR* V.iv.20–3: 'Fill red-cheek'd Bacchus, let Lyaeus float / In
burnished goblets. Force the plump-lipped god / Skip light lavoltas in your
full-sapped veins. / 'Tis well, brim full.' Chapman imitated the latter in *May
Day* (?1609).

*Till I may see the plump Lyaeus swim*
    *Above the brim:*                                                    10
    *I drink as I would write,*
*In flowing measure, filled with flame and sprite.*

*Crispinus.* Sweet Horace, Minerva and the Muses stand
    auspicious to thy designs. How farest thou, sweet man?
    Frolic? Rich? Gallant? Ha?                                          15

*Horace.* Not greatly gallant, sir; like my fortunes, well. I'm
    bold to take my leave sir. You'd naught else, sir, would
    you?

*Crispinus.* Troth, no, but I could wish thou didst know us,
    Horace. We are a scholar, I assure thee.                           20

*Horace.* A scholar, sir? I shall be covetous of your fair
    knowledge.

*Crispinus.* Gramercy, good Horace. Nay, we are new turned
    poet too, which is more; and a satirist too, which is more
    than that; I write just in thy vein, I. I am for your odes or      25
    your sermons, or anything indeed. We are a gentleman

---

16–18.] *G; verse in Q, F, line divided at* well. / I'm (I am *F2*).

---

9. plump Lyaeus] Bacchus; cf. *Faerie Queene* III.i.51, 'Lyaeus fat' and *Ant.* II.vii.112, 'Plumpy Bacchus' (so *H&S*).

13. *Minerva*] goddess of wisdom and the arts.

14. *sweet*] See I.iii.35n.

15. *Frolic . . . Gallant*] parodying *WYW* (Wood, II, 245): 'faire, gallant, rich'.

*Frolic*] mirthful, carefree.

*Gallant*] here probably as a general epithet meaning splendid, excellent (*OED*, 4), but with overtones of chivalry (*OED*, 5) and fashionableness (*OED*, 3).

16. *Not . . . gallant*] Horace rejects the idea of showiness (*OED*, 1).

19–20. *know . . . scholar*] J. retains Hor.'s first person plural: 'noris nos' and 'docti sumus' (*Sat.* I.ix.7).

21–2. *covetous . . . knowledge*] meaning both covetous of what he knows and of knowing him.

23. *Gramercy*] Thanks.

23–4. *we . . . satirist*] referring to Crispinus' 'design' to become a poet (II.ii.71–3 and 203–13), but also to Marston's recent emergence as a satirical poet with *Pigmalion* and *Scourge* (both 1598). Henslowe calls him 'mr. maxton the new poete' in September 1599: see p. 31.

25–8. *I write . . . too*] As a professedly learned satirist with pretensions to gentle birth and stoicism, Marston was an obvious rival to J. None of these attributes is mentioned in Hor. I.ix.

26. *sermons*] The normal Latin title of Hor.'s *Satires* is *Sermones*.

besides: our name is Rufus Laberius Crispinus. We are a
pretty stoic too.
*Horace.* To the proportion of your beard, I think it, sir.
*Crispinus.* By Phoebus, here's a most neat fine street, is't          30
not? I protest to thee, I am enamoured of this street now,
more than of half the streets of Rome again; 'tis so polite
and terse! There's the front of a building now. I study
architecture too: if ever I should build, I'd have a house
just of that prospective.          35
*Horace.* [*Aside*] Doubtless this gallant's tongue has a good
turn when he sleeps.

---

36. S.D.] G (*so also 44, 57, 60, 84, 102*)

---

28. *stoic*] By J.'s time the word had come to mean anyone who lived an
austere life cultivating indifference to pleasure or pain; J. would have known
that many Romans were stoics in a more precise philosophical sense, Cato,
Brutus, Cicero, Seneca and Marcus Aurelius among them. Their belief in the
pursuit of virtue and wisdom and acceptance of fate is patently not shared or
understood by Crispinus.

29. *proportion . . . beard*] In Sat. II.iii.35 Hor. speaks of a stoic being told
'to grow a wise man's beard', a phrase based on the Greek saying that 'his
wisdom is in his beard'. The boy playing Crispinus was probably wearing a
red beard in imitation of Marston's (cf. p. 9 and II.ii.76n): red would
suggest a choleric, not a stoic, disposition.

30. *Phoebus*] Phoebus Apollo, god of poetry and music.

31. *protest*] a courtly affectation, used by Crispinus (III.i.161, 234,
III.iv.365) and Histrio (III.iv.134, 247). Marston's uses are discussed by
King, esp. pp. 180–1. In *WYW* Lampatho's overuse is condemned by
Quadratus: 'protest, protest! / *Catzo!* I dread these hotte protests that presse,
/ Come on so fast' (Wood, II, 247). Shakespeare may glance at J.'s use in
giving it to Malvolio in *Tw.N* I.v.88.

32. *again*] at the end of a phrase for emphasis; cf. III.iv.166, IV.v.55.

*polite and terse*] Latin *politus* (polished) and *tersus* (smooth) (*H&S*), but
highly affected language for a street; not in Hor.

33–5. *I . . . prospective*] probably referring to the new trend for accomplished gentlemen to know something of architecture, rather than to any
specific activity by Marston as a designer for the theatre. For gentlemen
architects in the seventeenth century, see T.G.S. Cain, 'The Visual Arts and
Architecture in Britain, 1625–1700', in *'Into Another Mould': Change and
Continuity in English Culture, 1625–1700*, ed. T.G.S. Cain and Ken Robinson
(1992), pp. 117–34, 144–9.

35. *prospective*] perspective.

36–7.] Cf. *C is A* I.viii.25–6 (Mallory).

*Crispinus.* I do make verses, when I come in such a street as
this. O your city ladies, you shall ha' 'em sit in every shop
like the Muses—[*Pauses.*] offering you the Castalian dews    40
and the Thespian liquors, to as many as have but the
sweet grace and audacity to—[*Pauses.*] sip of their lips.
Did you never hear any of my verses?

*Horace.* No, sir. [*Aside*] But I am in some fear, I must now.

*Crispinus.* I'll tell thee some, if I can but recover 'em, I    45
composed e'en now of a dressing I saw a jeweller's wife
wear, who indeed was a jewel herself. I prefer that kind
of tire now; what's thy opinion, Horace?

*Horace.* With your silver bodkin, it does well, sir.

*Crispinus.* I cannot tell, but it stirs me more than all your    50
court curls, or your spangles, or your tricks. I affect
not these high gable-ends, these Tuscan tops, nor your
coronets, nor your arches, nor your pyramids; give me a

---

40. Muses—] *Subst. F; Muses,—Q; dash followed by space in Q indicating
pause or omission.*    42. to—] *F; dash followed by space in Q indicating pause
or omission.*    44. No . . . But] *This ed.;* No Sir; but *Q;* No, sir (but *F.*
now.] *Q;* now.) *F.*    45. if . . . 'em] *In parentheses in Q, F.*    46. dressing]
*F;* veluet cap *Q.*

---

40. *Castalian*] See I.i.36n.; cf. *EMO*, Ind.335.

*Thespian*] refers to Thespis, traditionally the father of Greek tragedy; cf.
*EMO* Ind.70: both predate *OED*'s earliest citation (1675).

46. (Q) *cap*] Cf. *EMI* III.iii.36, 'these little caps' and *BF* III.ii.56, 'your
fine velvet caps'. J. may have changed *F* here and elsewhere to avoid
anachronism (Roman citizens' wives did not wear velvet caps), but he exploits such anachronisms elsewhere (e.g. III.i.67–9). The use in *BF* (1614)
suggests it was not due to a change in fashion by 1615–16; the revision
should be considered alongside that of 'Flat-cappe' (II.i.102). See also
App. 1, p. 284.

48. *tire*] head-dress; subsequent speeches show that it is a simple braided
cap held with a pin or brooch.

49. *bodkin*] 'Sneered at by Gertrude in *EH* I.ii.23 as a common ornament
of a city dame. Cf. *The Honest Man's Fortune*, IV.i (Beaumont and Fletcher
folio, 1679, p. 525): "They come to steal [your] Napkins and your Spoons; /
Look to your Silver-Bodkin, (Gentlewoman)"' (*H&S*).

51. *spangles*] glittering metallic fragments, decking the hair.

*tricks*] fashionable styles.

52–3. *gable-ends . . . pyramids*] elaborate fashionable head-dresses of the
period.

fine sweet—[*Pauses.*] little delicate dressing, with a
bodkin, as you say, and a mushroom for all your other          55
ornatures.

*Horace.* [*Aside*] Is't not possible to make an escape from him?

*Crispinus.* I have remitted my verses all this while, I think I
ha' forgot 'em.

*Horace.* [*Aside*] Here's he could wish you had else.          60

*Crispinus.* Pray Jove I can entreat 'em of my memory.

*Horace.* You put your memory to too much trouble, sir.

*Crispinus.* No, sweet Horace, we must not ha' thee think so.

*Horace.* I cry you mercy. [*Aside*] Then, they are my ears
That must be tortured; well, you must have patience, ears.          65

*Crispinus.* Pray thee, Horace, observe.

*Horace.* Yes, sir. [*Looking closely at him*] Your satin sleeve
begins to fret at the rug that is underneath it, I do
observe, and your ample velvet bases are not without

---

54. sweet—] *F; Q has space after dash indicating pause.*          delicate dressing]
*F;* veluet Cap *Q.*          64. S.D.] *Nicholson.*          67. S.D.] *This ed.*          69.
bases] *F;* hose *Q.*

---

54. *delicate*] 'dainty to behold' (*OED*, 1d); cf. II.i.7. Used frequently by
Marston, e.g. *Hist.*, Wood, III, 252, 266; *JD's Ent.*, Wood, III, 236, 239;
*AR*, Prol.6 (see King, p. 39).

55. *mushroom*] In this sense of 'something worthless' (cf. 'a fig for') not in
*OED*; J. uses it to mean 'upstart' in *EMO* I.ii.162.

56. *ornatures*] embellishments.

58. *remitted*] postponed, put off (*OED*, 12); this antedates first example
(1635).

61. *entreat*] Cf. II.i.157n.

67–9.] Dekker responds to this passage and to III.iv.320 in *S-M*
I.ii.322–6: 'Thou wrongst heere a good honest rascall *Crispinus*, and poore
varlet, *Demetrius Fannius* (bretheren in thine owne trade of Poetry) thou sayst
*Crispinus* Sattin dublet is Reavel'd out heere, and that this penurious sneaker
is out at elboes, goe too my good full mouth'd ban-dog, Ile ha thee friends
with both'. Donne had similarly satirised the worn velvet of the 'thing' in
*Satire IV*, ll. 30–4.

68. *rug*] a coarse woollen material, here worn instead of the expensive
lining of fashionable doublets (see *EMO* IV.vi.101–6 for the latter).

69. *bases*] *Q*'s 'hose' supports *G*'s suggestion that here it means 'bre-
eches,' the garment also called 'hose' which was attached to the doublet by
'points' or laces. Satin and velvet were both forbidden to the lower orders in
England under sumptuary legislation, and hence were the signs of a courtier.
Cf. Marston, *Malcontent* I.viii.9–10.

evident stains of a hot disposition, naturally.                          70
*Crispinus.* O—[*Pauses.*] I'll dye them into another colour at
pleasure. How many yards of velvet dost thou think they
contain?
*Horace.* [*Aside*] Heart! I have put him now in a fresh way
To vex me more. [*To him*] Faith, sir, your mercer's book       75
Will tell you with more patience than I can.
[*Aside*] For I am crossed, and so's not that, I think.
*Crispinus.* 'Slight, these verses have lost me again: I shall not
invite 'em to mind now.
*Horace.* Rack not your thoughts, good sir; rather defer it       80
To a new time. I'll meet you at your lodging,
Or where you please: till then, Jove keep you, sir.
*Crispinus.* Nay, gentle Horace, stay. I have it now.
*Horace.* Yes, sir. [*Aside*] Apollo, Hermes, Jupiter,
Look down upon me!                                                85
*Crispinus.* *Rich was thy hap, sweet dainty cap,*
            *There to be placed:*
        *Where thy smooth black, sleek white may smack,*
            *And both be graced.*
'White' is there usurped for her brow, her forehead, and          90

---

74. S.D.] *Nicholson.*    Heart] *Subst. F;* 'Hart *Q; not in F2.*    77. S.D.]
*This ed.*    For . . . think] *In parentheses in F.*    78. 'Slight] *Q;* S'light *F.*
84–5.] *G; prose in Q, F.*    86. sweet dainty] *F;* Sweete Veluet *Q.*    90.
'White'] *Nicholson; White Q, subst. F.*

---

70. *hot*] lustful, cf. *Oth.* III.iii.403, 'as hot as monkeys', but also referring
to the anger of Marston's satire.
   *naturally*] as a natural consequence of Crispinus' 'natural' sexual indul-
gences (*OED*, 5c, antedating the first example).
   74. *Heart!*] An abbreviation of 'God's heart!'; cf. III.i.152, III.ii.6,
IV.vii.6.
   75. *mercer's book*] 'proverbial in the Elizabethan period with reference to
the debts of a gallant' (*OED*, b); a mercer was a trader in textiles.
   77. *crossed . . . think*] The account book would be crossed after payment;
Dekker replies in *S-M* IV.iii.238–9. Cf. *Tim.* I.ii.157: 'When all's spent,
he'ld be crossed then, an he could.'
   79. *invite*] A Latinism substituted pretentiously for 'call'; not in *OED* in
this sense.
   86. *hap*] luck, chance.
   90. *usurped for*] employed in place of (*OED*, 4c).

then 'sleek' as the parallel to 'smooth', that went before. A
kind of *Paranomasie*, or *Agnomination:* do you conceive, sir?
*Horace.* Excellent. Troth, sir, I must be abrupt and leave you.
*Crispinus.* Why, what haste hast thou? Pray thee stay a little;
thou shalt not go yet, by Phoebus!                              95
*Horace.* I shall not? [*Aside*] What remedy? Fie, how I sweat
with suffering!
*Crispinus.* And then——
*Horace.* Pray, sir, give me leave to wipe my face a little.
*Crispinus.* Yes do, good Horace.                              100
*Horace.* Thank you, sir.
        [*Aside*] Death! I must crave his leave to piss anon,
        Or that I may go hence with half my teeth,

---

91. 'sleek'] *Nicholson; sleeke Q, F.*     'smooth'] *Nicholson; smooth Q, F.*
102. I] *F; not in Q.*

91. *parallel*] Though J. uses it seriously in a similar figurative sense in
'Apol. Dial.', 93, he seems to have regarded this less precise use, meaning
'counterpart', as affected. Cf. I.ii.29, where it is also loosely used to mean
'equals'.
92. Paranomasie, *or* Agnomination] here referring to the alliteration of
'smooth' and 'sleek': '*Paranomasia* is a pleasant touch of the same letter
Sillable, or word, wyth a different meaning . . . Sr. *Phillip Sidney* in *Astrophel
& Stella calls* [it] the *Dictionary* method, & the verses soe made rymes
running in ratling rowes, wch is an example of it' (*Hoskyns*, p. 129). It
covered similarity of sound beyond alliteration, including puns, and is
synonymous with Agnomination, which Hoskyns illustrates by such examples
as 'our Paradice is a pair of dice'. J. makes Ovid senior, Albius, Chloe and
Crispinus use the figure in I.ii.9, II.i.68–9, II.i.120 and IV.iii.155 respectively, but warns against it in *Disc.* 1954: 'Marry, we must not play, or
riot too much with them [i.e. words], as in *paranomasies*'. Hoskyns is similarly cautious, seeing it as 'prettie to play wth amonge gentlewomen', and as
an overused and easy device which 'best become the tuff taffata Orator. if the
Tymes gives itselfe too much to any one florish, it makes it a toy & barrs a
learned mans writings from it, least it seeme to come more of the generall
humor then the private Judgment' (p. 130).
    *conceive*] understand (*OED*, 9d); cf. *EMO* IV.iii.14, *CR* IV.iii.415; in all
these cases J. sees the absolute use as pretentious (cf. King, p. 30). He is
probably parodying Marston, *Scourge*, 'In Lectores', 65: 'So you will nere
conceive, and yet dispraise / That which you nere conceiv'd'.
    93. *abrupt*] playing on the rhetorical term 'abrupt', defined in *Disc.*
1975–6: 'The abrupt stile, which hath many breaches, and doth not seem to
end, but fall.'
    102. *Death!*] Abbreviation of 'God's death!', 'Christ's death!' etc.
    103.] imported into Hor.'s poem from the post-Augustan Juvenal III,
300–1: 'he begs and prays to be allowed to return home with a few teeth in
his head!'.

I am in some such fear. This tyranny
Is strange, to take mine ears up by commission,                   105
Whether I will or no, and make them stalls
To his lewd solecisms and worded trash.
Happy thou, bold Bolanus, now I say,
Whose freedom and impatience of this fellow
Would long ere this have called him fool, and fool,               110
And rank and tedious fool, and have slung jests
As hard as stones, till thou hadst pelted him
Out of the place; whilst my tame modesty
Suffers my wit be made a solemn ass
To bear his fopperies——                                           115
*Crispinus.* Horace, thou art miserably affected to be gone, I
see. But—[*Pauses.*] pray thee, let's prove to enjoy thee
awhile. Thou hast no business, I assure me. Whither is
thy journey directed? Ha?
*Horace.* Sir, I am going to visit a friend that's sick.          120
*Crispinus.* A friend? What's he? Do not I know him?
*Horace.* No, sir, you do not know him. [*Aside*] And 'tis not the
worse for him.

---

106. Whether . . . no] *In parentheses in Q, F.*     108. thou, bold] *F;* the
bold *Q.*     109. Whose . . . fellow] *F; Romes* Common Buffon: His free
Impudence *Q.*     110. called him fool, and fool,] *F;* cald this fellow, Foole;
*Q.*     112. thou hadst] *F;* he had *Q.*     117. But—] *F; Q has space after
dash, indicating pause.*     122. S.D.] *This ed.*

---

105. *by commission*] seizure by legal warrant.

106. *stalls*] stables; this is the only example of a figurative use in *OED* (3).

107. *solecisms*] Here, both irregularity of speech or diction (*OED*, 1) and a
violation of good manners (*OED*, 2). Cf. Dekker, *S-M* IV.ii.70–2, where
Horace apologises to Tucca: 'Hence forth Ile rather breath out *Soloecismes* /
(To doe which Ide as soone speake blasphemie) / Than with my tongue or
pen to wound your worth.'

108. *Bolanus*] 'O te Bolane, cerebri / felicem' (Hor. *Sat.* I.ix.11); the
historical Bolanus was a quick-tempered friend of Cicero. *Q*'s reading suggests that J. originally had Carlo Buffone of *EMO* in mind, and corrected
when he learnt more of Bolanus. Bond also misinterprets the passage as
meaning that Bolanus was placid (a valid reading without the biographical
information).

116. *affected*] disposed.

117. *prove*] strive, attempt (*OED*, 4), not 'make trial' as *H&S*, following
*G*, suggest.

120–43.] J. had already imitated this passage (Hor. *Sat.* I.ix.16–19) in
*EMO* II.vi.91–9 (so Mallory).

*Crispinus.* What's his name? Where's he lodged?

*Horace.* Where I shall be fearful to draw you out of your way,     125
  sir, a great way hence. Pray', sir, let's part.

*Crispinus.* Nay, but where is't? I pray thee, say.

*Horace.* On the far side of all Tiber yonder, by Caesar's
  gardens.

*Crispinus.* O, that's my course directly; I am for you. Come,     130
  go. Why stand'st thou?

*Horace.* Yes, sir. Marry, the plague is in that part of the city; I
  had almost forgot to tell you, sir.

*Crispinus.* Faugh! It's no matter, I fear no pestilence, I ha' not
  offended Phoebus.                                                135

*Horace.* [*Aside*] I have, it seems, or else this heavy scourge
  Could ne'er have lighted on me——

*Crispinus.* Come along.

*Horace.* I am to go down some half mile this way, sir, first, to
  speak with his physician: and from thence to his apothe-        140
  cary, where I shall stay the mixing of divers drugs——

*Crispinus.* Why, it's all one. I have nothing to do, and I love
  not to be idle, I'll bear thee company. How callest thou
  the 'pothecary?

*Horace.* [*Aside*] O, that I knew a name would fright him now.    145
  [*To him*] Sir, Rhadamanthus! Rhadamanthus, sir.

---

126. Pray'] *F;* Pray *Q.*    134. Faugh!] *Parfitt;* Fow: *Q, F;* Foh! *G.*
136. S.D.] *Nicholson.*    145. S.D.] *Nicholson.*    145–6.] *G; prose in Q,*
*F.*    Sir, Rhadamanthus] *F; not in Q.*

---

128–9. *Caesar's gardens*] Pleasure-grounds on the north-west bank of the
Tiber bequeathed by Julius Caesar to the people of Rome, and a long way
from the Via Sacra. Shakespeare, following North, wrongly places them 'on
this side Tiber': *Caes.* III.ii.247–51.

130. *directly*] exactly (*OED*, 4).

134–7. *I . . . me*] Phoebus Apollo, in his role as the god who punishes,
was responsible for sudden deaths; Horace's reply refers to his role as the god
of poetry.

146.] Rhadamanthus, like his brother Minos, was a judge in the underworld. The name suggests itself because the apothecary's name is Minos; no
such figure appears in *Sat.* I.ix, where the plaintiff is anonymous, but in J.'s
'The Famous Voyage' up the Fleet river, Rhadamanthus is a soap maker and
'little MINOS / An ancient pur-blind fletcher, with a high nose' (*Ep.*
CXXXIII, 187–90). That the Inns of Court revels also referred to tradesmen
in this way is suggested by Rudyerd's account in *Prince d'Amour*: 'What said
*Silas Titus*, the Sope-maker of Holborn-bridge?' (p. 38).

There's one so called, is a just judge in hell,
And doth inflict strange vengeance on all those
That here on earth torment poor patient spirits.

*Crispinus.* He dwells at the Three Furies, by Janus' temple?    150
*Horace.* Your 'pothecary does, sir.

*Crispinus.* Heart! I owe him money for sweetmeats, and he has
laid to arrest me I hear: but——

*Horace.* Sir, I have made a most solemn vow: I will never bail
any man.                                                        155

*Crispinus.* Well then, I'll swear and speak him fair, if the worst
come. But his name is Minos, not Rhadamanthus,
Horace.

*Horace.* That may be, sir: I but guessed at his name by his
sign. But your Minos is a judge too, sir!                       160

*Crispinus.* I protest to thee, Horace, do but taste me once, if I
do know myself and mine own virtues truly, thou wilt not

---

149. here on earth] *In parentheses in* Q, F.    161. do . . . once] *In parentheses in* Q, F.

---

150. *Three Furies*] possibly a London allusion, identifying a particular
apothecary: cf. 'The Famous Voyage': 'Behold where CERBERUS, rear'd on
the wall / Of *Hol'borne* ([the] three sergeants heads) looks ore' (176-7),
referring to the serjeants-at-law of the Holborn Inns.

*Janus' temple*] on the other side of the Forum, near the Circus Maximus; if
Minos was identifiable as a contemporary, it may equate with a London
church.

153. *laid to*] G suggests 'plotted to', but here probably in the sense of
laying a complaint against (cf. *OED* 'Lay' *v.* IV.26). In Roman law a plaintiff
could compel the defendant in a civil action to appear in court (hence Horace
can 'arrest' Crispinus and Demetrius in V.iii.168).

157. *Minos*] Cf. III.i.146n; he was supreme judge of the dead in Hades
(*Odyssey* XI, 568-71).

161-79.] Based on Hor. *Sat.* I.ix.22-5: 'If I do not deceive myself, you
will not think more of Viscus or of Varius as a friend than of me: for who can
write more verses or write more quickly than I? Who can dance more
daintily? Even Hermogenes might envy my singing.' J. adds attributes ('kiss
her hand . . . or her dog') which make Crispinus sound more like an Inns of
Court gallant. For Hor.'s contempt for those who write fast, see *Sat.*
I.iv.13-21, where Crispinus challenges him to see who can write fastest; cf.
*Poetaster* IV.iii.100-03.

161. *taste*] put to the proof (*OED*, *v.* 2); cf. *Tw.N.* III.i.78-81, where
Toby's use in this sense is questioned; here it has ridiculous associations with
*OED*, 3b, 'To have carnal knowledge of' (cf. King, p. 49).

make that esteem of Varius, or Virgil, or Tibullus, or any
of 'em indeed, as now in thy ignorance thou dost; which I
am content to forgive. I would fain see which of these          165
could pen more verses in a day, or with more facility than
I, or that could court his mistress, kiss her hand, make
better sport with her fan, or her dog——

*Horace.* I cannot bail you yet, sir.

*Crispinus.* Or that could move his body more gracefully,          170
or dance better: you should see me, were it not i' the
street——

*Horace.* Nor yet.

*Crispinus.* Why, I have been a reveller, and at my cloth of
silver suit and my long stocking in my time, and will be
again——          175

*Horace.* If you may be trusted, sir.

*Crispinus.* And then for my singing, Hermogenes himself
envies me, that is your only master of music you have in
Rome.

*Horace.* Is your mother living, sir?          180

*Crispinus.* Au! Convert thy thoughts to somewhat else, I pray
thee.

---

168. dog——] *F;* Dogge? *Q.*    172. street——] *F;* street. *Q.*

---

163. *Varius*] L. Rufus Varius, friend of Hor. and Virgil, tragic and epic
poet; he was Virgil's executor and edited the *Aeneid* after Virgil's death.

171–2. *dance . . . street*] Dancing in public was seen as degraded by the
Romans; cf. III.v.43–5.

173–5.] Referring to the revels of the Inns of Court; Marston probably
participated in the Middle Temple revels recorded by Rudyerd in *Prince
d'Amour*: see Finkelpearl, p. 86.

173–4. *cloth . . . suit*] made of a cloth woven in part with silver thread, or
with both gold and silver thread, for masqueing and dancing. Cf. Laverdure's
'Silver hose', *WYW*, Wood, II, 247.

174. *long stocking*] for dancing; cf. *EMO* III.ix.53–4: 'Or if you had but
your long stockings on, to be dancing a galliard, as she comes by'.

176. *trusted*] by his tailor (Nicholson).

178. *your .. you*] 'Your' and 'you' are commonly used indefinitely at this
time (see 'your' *OED*, 5b, 'you' *OED*, 6), expressing familiarity or con-
descension towards the object.

180–6.] J. adapts Hor. ll. 26–8 ('"Have you a mother or kindred who
are dependent upon your welfare?" "Not one; I have laid them all to rest"')
to suit Marston's circumstances. Marston's father had died in 1599, but his
mother, Maria Guarsi, lived till 1621.

*Horace.* You have much of the mother in you, sir. Your father
    is dead?

*Crispinus.* Ay, I thank Jove, and my grandfather too, and all   185
    my kinsfolk, and well composed in their urns.

*Horace.* [*Aside*] The more their happiness, that rest in peace,
    Free from th' abundant torture of thy tongue;
    Would I were with them too.

*Crispinus.*                What's that, Horace?

*Horace.* I now remember me, sir, of a sad fate   190
    A cunning woman, one Sabella, sung
    When in her urn she cast my destiny,
    I being but a child.

*Crispinus.*             What was't I pray thee?

*Horace.* She told me, I should surely never perish
    By famine, poison, or the enemy's sword;
    The hectic fever, cough, or pleurisy,   195
    Should never hurt me, nor the tardy gout:
    But in my time I should be once surprised
    By a strong tedious talker, that should vex
    And almost bring me to consumption.   200
    Therefore, if I were wise, she warned me shun

---

186. urns] *F*; Graues *Q*.   187. S.D.] *Nicholson.*   191. one] on *Q*.
201. if . . . wise] *In parentheses in Q, F.*

---

183. *much . . . mother*] a propensity towards hysteria, and hence talking
nonsense; cf. *Lr* II.iv.56: 'O how this mother swells up toward my heart.' See
Edward Jorden, *A Briefe Discourse of a Disease Called the Suffocation of the
Mother* (1603), *passim*.

186. *composed*] Hor. I.ix.28, 'Omnes composui', 'I have laid them all to
rest'. The first example in this semse in *OED* (15b) is 1677. Though
translating Hor., J. probably regarded this Latinism as pretentious.

*urns*] In ancient Rome, the dead were cremated and 'Anon after the
body had been burned, his nearest friends did gather up the ashes & bones,
which being washed with milk & wine, were put into certain pitchers called
*vrnae*' (Godwyn, p. 94).

191. *cunning woman*] wise woman, fortune teller.

*Sabella*] Hor. refers to the inhabitants of Venusia, where he was born,
rather than to a person, but Bond annotates Sabella as 'An old soothsayer,
perhaps Horace's nurse' ('Anus sortilega, fortasse Horatii nutrix') a reading
J. evidently accepted.

192. *urn . . . destiny*] Like the lots 'tossed' in the urn of Fate (*Odes* II.3.26),
the lot of the child Horace was taken from the shaken urn by the soothsayer,
who then 'cast' (calculated, foretold) his future.

196. *hectic fever*] An addition to Hor.: it was associated with consumption.

All such long-winded monsters as my bane.
For if I could but 'scape that one discourser,
I might no doubt prove an old aged man.
By your leave, sir?                                                      205
*Crispinus.* Tut, tut, abandon this idle humour, 'tis nothing
but melancholy. 'Fore Jove, now I think on't, I am to
appear in court here to answer to one that has me in suit.
Sweet Horace, go with me, this is my hour. If I neglect it,
the law proceeds against me. Thou art familiar with these    210
things, pray thee, if thou lov'st me, go.
*Horace.* Now let me die, sir, if I know your laws,
Or have the power to stand still half so long
In their loud courts, as while a case is argued.
Besides, you know, sir, where I am to go,                           215
And the necessity——
*Crispinus.* [*Hesitating*] 'Tis true——
*Horace.* [*Aside*] I hope the hour of my release be come. He will
upon this consideration discharge me, sure.
*Crispinus.* Troth, I am doubtful what I may best do; whether    220
to leave thee, or my affairs, Horace?
*Horace.* O Jupiter, me, sir! Me by any means. I beseech you,
me, sir.
*Crispinus.* No faith, I'll venture those now: thou shalt see I
love thee. Come, Horace.                                              225
*Horace.* Nay then, I am desperate. I follow you, sir. 'Tis hard
contending with a man that overcomes thus.
*Crispinus.* And how deals Maecenas with thee? Liberally, ha?
Is he open-handed? Bountiful?

---

204–5.] *F; one line in Q.*    213. still] *F; not in Q.*    214. their loud
courts] *F;* their ( ) Courts *Q.*    215–16.] *F; one line in Q.*    217. S.D.]
*This ed.;* He meditates. *Nicholson.*    218. S.D.] *This ed.*    219. upon . . .
consideration] *In parentheses in Q, F.*

202. *bane*] that which threatens life (*OED,* 2).
204. *prove*] become (*OED,* 9).
206–80.] Based on Hor. *Sat.* I.ix.35–60.
208. *one . . . suit*] one that is suing me.
210–11. *Thou . . . things*] An addition of J.'s to emphasise Horace's subsequent denial of any contact with so corrupt a profession as the law.
224. *venture those*] i.e. risk his affairs.
226. *desperate*] without hope (*OED,* 1).
228. *ha?*] King suggests this is the ancestor of 'eh?' (p. 153).

*Horace.* He's still himself, sir.                                    230

*Crispinus.* Troth, Horace, thou art exceeding happy in thy
  friends and acquaintance; they are all most choice spirits,
  and of the first rank of Romans. I do not know that poet,
  I protest, has used his fortune more prosperously than
  thou hast. If thou wouldst bring me known to Maecenas,    235
  I should second thy desert well. Thou shouldst find a
  good sure assistant of me, one that would speak all good
  of thee in thy absence, and be content with the next
  place, not envying thy reputation with thy patron. Let me
  not live, but I think thou and I, in a small time, should    240
  lift them all out of favour, both Virgil, Varius, and the
  best of them: and enjoy him wholly to ourselves.

*Horace.* [*Aside*] Gods, you do know it, I can hold no longer;
  This brize hath pricked my patience. [*To him*] Sir, your
    silkness

Clearly mistakes Maecenas, and his house,                             245
To think there breathes a spirit beneath his roof
Subject unto those poor affections
Of undermining envy and detraction,
Moods only proper to base, grovelling minds;
That place is not in Rome, I dare affirm,                             250
More pure, or free from such low, common evils.
There's no man grieved, that this is thought more rich,

---

234. has] *G;* ha's *Q, F.*     237. assistant] *F;* Assistance *Q.*     240. in . . .
time] *In parentheses in Q, F.*     243. S.D.] *Nicholson.*     244. silkness] *G;*
Silkenesse *Q, Subst. F.*

---

231–5.] Dekker replies to such boasting on J.'s part in *S-M*
IV.iii.208–23.

234. *used . . . prosperously*] capitalised on his good luck more successfully.

236. *second thy desert*] support your merit (*OED*, s.v. 'desert' *sb.* 1.1b).

244. *brize*] gadfly (modern form 'breeze'); cf. *Troil.* I.iii.48, *Ant.* III.x.14.
*pricked*] stung, as by the gadfly, into abandoning his patience.

*silkness*] *OED* thinks the text may be corrupt here, but the mock title
merely alludes to what in *CR* III.ii.32 J. calls 'the silken disposition of
courtiers'.

247. *affections*] mental states (*OED*, 2).

248. *envy and detraction*] charges against Crispinus and Demetrius emphasised throughout: the play opens with Envy, and closes with the word
*invidia.* Dekker denies envy in *S-M* IV.iii.217 and 221, and accuses J. of
detraction in V.ii.238. See also pp. 23–4.

252. *There's*] 'There' is an adverb, 'referring to the household of
Maecenas' (Mallory).

Or this more learned; each man hath his place,
And to his merit, his reward of grace,
Which with a mutual love they all embrace.                           255
*Crispinus.* You report a wonder! 'Tis scarce credible, this.
*Horace.* I am no torturer, to enforce you to believe it, but
'tis so.
*Crispinus.* Why, this inflames me with a more ardent desire to
be his than before: but I doubt I shall find the entrance to        260
his familiarity somewhat more than difficult, Horace.
*Horace.* Tut! You'll conquer him, as you have done me;
there's no standing out against you, sir, I see that. Either
your importunity, or the intimation of your good parts,
or——                                                                265
*Crispinus.* Nay, I'll bribe his porter, and the grooms of his
chamber; make his doors open to me that way first, and
then I'll observe my times. Say he should extrude me his
house today; shall I therefore desist, or let fall my suit
tomorrow? No, I'll attend him, follow him, meet him i'          270
the street, the highways, run by his coach, never leave
him. What! Man hath nothing given him in this life,
without much labour.
*Horace.* [*Aside*] And impudence.
Archer of heaven, Phoebus, take thy bow,                            275
And with a full-drawn shaft nail to the earth
This Python, that I may yet run hence and live.
Or brawny Hercules, do thou come down,
And, though thou mak'st it up thy thirteenth labour,
Rescue me from this Hydra of discourse here.                        280

---

257. torturer] *Subst. Q;* torture *F.*      264. importunity] *Subst. F;* Importunacy *Q.*      272. Man] *F;* 'Man *Q.*        nacy *Q.*      274. S.D.] *Nicholson.*      279. though
. . . labour] *In parentheses in Q, F.*

254. *of grace*] as a matter of favour, not of right or on demand.
261. *familiarity*] circle of intimates (*OED*, 4c).
268. *extrude*] throw out; Latin, *extrudere.*
275–80.] In Greek myth, the Python was a huge serpent which was killed
by Phoebus Apollo. The second labour of Hercules was to kill the nine-
headed Lernean Hydra, whose middle head was immortal, and who sprouted
two heads for every one that Hercules knocked off. Neither myth is referred
to by Hor., but both are appropriate to Horace's predicament here. Cf. the
equally apposite simile of Alcides' shirt, III.ii.6–7.

### ACT III  SCENE ii

*[Enter to them]* FUSCUS ARISTIUS.

*Aristius.* Horace, well met!

*Horace.* *[Aside to Aristius]* O welcome, my reliever.
Aristius, as thou lov'st me, ransom me.

*Aristius.* What ail'st thou, man?

*Horace.*                          'Death! I am seized on here
By a land-remora. I cannot stir,
Not move, but as he please.

*Crispinus.*                   Wilt thou go, Horace?                    5

*Horace.* 'Heart! He cleaves to me like Alcides' shirt,
Tearing my flesh and sinews. O, I ha' been vexed
And tortured with him beyond forty fevers.
For Jove's sake, find some means to take me from him.

*Aristius.* *[Aside to Horace]* Yes, I will. But I'll go first and tell     10
Maecenas.

*Crispinus.* Come, shall we go?

*Aristius.* *[Aside to Horace]* The jest will make his eyes run, i'
faith. *[He begins to leave them.]*

*Horace.* Nay, Aristius?

*Aristius.* Farewell, Horace.                                          15

*Horace.* 'Death! Will a' leave me? *[Calling after him]* Fuscus

---

III.ii.0.1.] *Enter* FUSCUS ARISTIUS. *G,* continuing the scene.   1.
S.D.] *This ed.*   *reliever] Subst. F; Redeemer Q.*   8. beyond] *F; worse*
then *Q.*   10. S.D.] *Subst. G.*   13. S.D.] *Subst. G.*   14. S.D.] *This
ed.*   17. S.D.] *This ed.*

---

III.ii] based on Hor. *Sat.* I.ix.60–74. Aristius was a friend of Horace, who
addressed *Odes* I.xxii and *Epist.* I.x to him (*H&S*); Bond describes him as a
'renowned grammarian' ('Grammaticus illo tempore nobilis'), following the
scholiasts.

3. *'Death!*] See III.i.102n.

4. *remora*] a sucking fish, supposed to have the power to hold back a ship;
cf. Montaigne, *Essayes* II.xii (trans. Florio, Everyman ed., II, 162): 'in the
last and famous sea-fight, which *Antonie* lost against *Augustus*, his Admirall-
gally was in her course staid by that little fish the Latins call *Remora*, and the
English a Suck-stone, whose property is, to stop any ship he can fasten
himself unto.' Part quoted in *H&S*, who add *EH* IV.ii.14, *ML* II.ii.25–30.

6. *Alcides' shirt*] The poisoned shirt of the centaur Nessus, given inno-
cently to Hercules (Alcides) by his wife; it stuck to his skin, and poisoned his
blood, leading to his death and apotheosis: see Ovid *Met.* IX, 107–210.

8. *forty*] See Ind. 69n.

Aristius, do you hear? Gods of Rome! [ARISTIUS *turns*
*back*.] You said you had somewhat to say to me in private.
*Aristius.* Ay, but I see you are now employed with that gentle-          20
man. 'Twere offence to trouble you. I'll take some fitter
opportunity. Farewell.                                          *Exit.*
*Horace.* Mischief and torment! O my soul and heart,
How are you cramped with anguish! Death itself
Brings not the like convulsions. O this day,                    25
That ever I should view thy tedious face——
*Crispinus.* Horace, what passion, what humour is this?
*Horace.* Away good prodigy, afflict me not.
A friend, and mock me thus! Never was man
So left under the axe—how now?                                  30


ACT III   SCENE iii

*[Enter]* MINOS *[and two]* Lictors.

*Minos.* [*Pointing to Crispinus*] That's he, in the embroidered
hat there, with the ash coloured feather. His name is
Laberius Crispinus.
*[1] Lictor.* [*Seizing Crispinus by the arm*] Laberius Crispinus, I
arrest you in the emperor's name.                               5
*Crispinus.* Me, sir? Do you arrest me?
*[1] Lictor.* Ay, sir, at the suit of Master Minos, the 'pothecary.

18–19. S.D.] *This   ed.*    21. offence] *F;*   sinne   *Q.*    22. Farewell] *F;*
adue *Q.*   S.D.] *Q.*   25. convulsions] *F;* Conuulsion *Q.*   26. face——]
*F;* face? *Q.*   27. humour is] *F;* Humours *Q.*   29. A . . . thus] *Q; in
parentheses in F.*   30. now?] *F2, G (continuing the scene);* now. *Q, F.*
III.iii.1. embroidered] *G;* imbrodered *Q, F.*   3, 4. Laberius] *Subst. F;*
Liberius *Q.*   4. S.D.] *This ed.*

20–2.] In Hor. Aristius claims he should not transact business on the
Jewish sabbath; *H&S* suggest that the Jewish reference might have been
dangerous for J. to reproduce, quoting his remark to Drummond that Savile
could not translate the last book of his version of Tacitus (*The Ende of Nero
and the Beginning of Galba*) 'for ye evill it containes of ye Iewes'. But there is
no 'evil' in Hor., and it is more likely that J. altered Hor. because the Jewish
sabbath was seen as closely related to the Christian sabbath.
   III.iii.0.1.] Hor. I.ix ends with the arrival of the plaintiff, who asks
Horace to witness the arrest.
   1–2.] See p. 9 for boy actors wearing parodic versions of the clothes of
satirised characters.

*Horace.* [*Aside*] Thanks great Apollo, I will not slip thy favour
   offered me in my escape, for my fortunes.              *Exit.*
*Crispinus.* Master Minos? I know no Master Minos. [*Looking*      10
   *around*] Where's Horace? Horace! Horace!
*Minos.* Sir, do not you know me?
*Crispinus.* O yes, I know you, Master Minos, 'cry you mercy.
   But Horace? God's me, is he gone?
*Minos.* Ay, and so would you too, if you knew how. Officer,       15
   look to him.
*Crispinus.* Do you hear, Master Minos? Pray', let's be used
   like a man of our own fashion. By Janus and Jupiter, I
   meant to have paid you next week, every drachma. Seek
   not to eclipse my reputation thus vulgarly.                    20
*Minos.* Sir, your oaths cannot serve you; you know I have
   forborne you long.
*Crispinus.* I am conscious of it sir. [*The* Lictors *begin to pull
   him away.*] Nay, I beseech you, gentlemen, do not exhale
   me thus. Remember 'tis but for sweetmeats——                   25
[*1*] *Lictor.* Sweet meat must have sour sauce, sir. Come along.
*Crispinus.* Sweet Master Minos, I am forfeited to eternal dis-

---

8. S.D.] *This ed.*    9. S.D.] *Q.*    14. God's me] *Nicholson;* Gods me *F;*
Gods 'Slid *Q.*    23–4. S.D.] *This ed.*

---

8. *slip*] overlook (*OED, v.* 7a).
9. *for my fortunes*] [not] for my fortunes, as in 'not for my life'.
13. *'cry*] omitting 'I'.
14. *God's me*] shortened form of 'God save me'.
18. *Janus and Jupiter*] A classical rather than contemporary oath.
19. *drachma*] See I.ii.151n; later (III.iv.59) the debt is said to be eighty
sesterces.
20. *eclipse*] Used figuratively thus by Marston, *JD's Ent.* (Wood, III,
218): 'when will true valour be at the full? Oh theres an opposition tis
eclipsed'.
*vulgarly*] publicly; this is the first example given in *OED* (3), but since
J. is ridiculing it as a pretentious Latinism he is not likely to have coined it.
Not found in Marston; Shakespeare uses it seriously in the same sense in
*Meas.* (1604), V.i.160.
23. *conscious*] A Marstonism, vomited in V.iii.497: see V.iii.282n.
24. *exhale*] drag away, absurdly englishing Latin *exhaurio.*
26. *Sweet . . . sauce*] proverbial; Dent, M839; cf. Florio, *Second Frutes*
(1591), p. 169 (*H&S*) and *Rom.* II.iv.79–80.
27. *forfeited*] Not found in Marston, but clearly a courtly word. Not in
*OED* in this sense, but King notes *All's W* (?1602–3) II.iii.267: 'Undone,
and forfeited to cares for ever!'

grace if you do not commiserate. [*To 1 Lictor as he is dragged across stage*] Good officer, be not so officious.


ACT III   SCENE iv

[*Enter to them*] TUCCA [*and*] PYRGI.

*Tucca.* Why, how now my good brace of bloodhounds, whither do you drag the gent'man? You mongrels, you curs, you bandogs! We are Captain Tucca that talk to you, you inhuman pilchers.
                                              [*Lictors pause.*]
*Minos.* Sir, he is their prisoner.                              5
*Tucca.* Their pestilence! What are you, sir?
*Minos.* A citizen of Rome, sir.
*Tucca.* Then you are not far distant from a fool, sir.
*Minos.* A 'pothecary, sir.
*Tucca.* [*Sniffing at Minos*] I knew thou wast not a physician.   10
Faugh! Out of my nostrils, thou stinkst of lotium and the syringe. Away, quack-salver! [*To 1 Pyrgus*] Follower, my sword!
[*1*] *Pyrgus.* Here noble leader. [*Aside*] You'll do no harm with it, I'll trust you.                              15

---

28–9. S.D.] *This ed.*   III.iv.0.1.] *Subst. G, continuing the scene.*   4.1.
S.D.] *This ed.*   10. S.D.] *This ed.*   thou wast] *F;* that was *Q.*   11.
Faugh!] *This ed.;* fough: *Q, F.*   14. [1] *Pyrgus] Subst. G; Pyr. Q;* PYRG.
*F (also at 22, 28, 74, 91, 124).*   S.D.] *G.*

28. *commiserate*] A Latinism, from *commiserari*, to pity; this antedates first *OED* example (1606).
III.iv.3. *bandogs*] chained, and hence fierce, dogs.
4. *pilchers*] A common term of abuse at the time; the origin is not clear, but it is probably from 'pilch', to steal, rather than from the 'pilch', a leather jerkin, as *G* suggests.
7. *citizen*] Tucca takes the term to mean that Minos is a tradesman rather than a courtier. J. plays on Tucca's ignorance of the dignity ideally associated with the concept of Roman citizenship.
11. *lotium*] stale urine, used by barbers as a hair lotion; cf. *SW* III.v.90 (*H&S*).
12. *quack-salver*] the original form, shortened later to 'quack'; cf. *Volp.* II.ii.5: 'quack-salvers, / Fellowes, that live by venting oyles, and drugs'.

*Tucca.* [*To 1 Lictor*] Do you hear, you goodman slave? Hook,
ram, rogue, catchpole, loose the gent'man, or by my
velvet arms——
      *The Officer strikes up his heels* [*and takes his sword*].
[*1*] *Lictor.* What will you do, sir?
*Tucca.* [*Rising*] Kiss thy hand, my honourable active varlet,      20
and embrace thee, thus.
[*1*] *Pyrgus.* [*Aside*] O patient metamorphosis!
*Tucca.* [*To 1 Lictor*] My sword, my tall rascal.
[*1*] *Lictor.* Nay, soft, sir. Some wiser than some.
*Tucca.* What? And a wit too! By Pluto, thou must be cherished,      25
slave. [*Giving him money*] Here's three drachmas for thee:
hold.
[*1*] *Pyrgus.* [*Aside*] There's half his lendings gone.
*Tucca.* Give me.

---

17. loose] *Q;* lose *F.*   18.1. *The . . . heels*] *F in margin; not in Q; and . . .
sword. Subst. G.*   22. S.D.] *Subst. Nicholson.*   25. too!] *F2;* to? *Q;* to!
*F.*   26. S.D.] *This ed.*   28. S.D.] *Nicholson.*

---

16. *goodman slave*] 'Goodman' usually prefixed a designation of occupation;
*H&S* note its ironic use in *BF* III.iv.113, 'good-man angry-man' and *Lr*
II.ii.45.
   *Hook*] usually 'unhappy hook' as a term of disdain, but it may have
been slang for a constable: Mistress Quickly calls the Beadle 'Nuthook' (*2H4*
V.iv.7), and other terms used there refer contemptuously to officers of the
law.
   17. *ram*] perhaps alluding to the lictor's virility, perhaps short for battering
ram; the context suggests slang for a legal officer, but there is no record of
such a usage.
   *catchpole*] originally used to translate Latin *lictor*, but by 1600 an abusive
term for any petty legal officer, especially a debt-collector.
   18. *velvet arms*] See I.i.26n.
   18.1. S.D. *strikes . . . heels*] throws him flat on the ground: cf. Marston, *1
Ant.* I.i.215–16: 'Now gusty flaws struck up the very heels / Of our
mainmast'.
   24. *Some . . . some*] proverbial: *H&S* cite Field (who acted in *Poetaster*), *A
Woman is a Weathercock* (1609–10): '*Stra.* Give me thy sword, or I will kill
thee. *Capt.* Some wiser than some. I love my reputation well, yet I am not so
valiant an ass, but I love my life better, there's my sword' (*Plays*, ed. Austin
(1950), IV.ii.112–15); cf. also ? Chapman, *Sir Giles Goosecap* V.ii.330 (*Comedies*, ed. Parrott, II, 668).
   25. *By Pluto*] another name for Hades, god of the dead; cf. III.iv.202n,
and *Troil.* IV.iv.127, 'by the dreadful Pluto'.
   28. *half his lendings*] half of what he has borrowed from Ovid senior
(I.ii.199).

[*1*] *Lictor*. No, sir, your first word shall stand; I'll hold all.     30
*Tucca*. Nay, but rogue——
[*1*] *Lictor*. You would make a rescue of our prisoner, sir, you?
*Tucca*. I, a rescue? Away, inhuman varlet. Come, come, I
    never relish above one jest at most; do not disgust me:
    sirrah, do not. Rogue, I tell thee, rogue, do not.     35
[*1*] *Lictor*. How, sir, rogue?
*Tucca*. Ay, why! Thou art not angry, rascal, art thou?
[*1*] *Lictor*. I cannot tell, sir; I am little better upon these
    terms.
*Tucca*. Ha! Gods and fiends! Why, dost hear? Rogue, thou,     40
    give me thy hand. I say unto thee, thy hand, rogue.
    What? Dost not thou know me? Not me, rogue? Not
    Captain Tucca, rogue?
*Minos*. Come, pra' surrender the gentleman his sword, officer;
    we'll have no fighting here.     45
*Tucca*. What's thy name?
*Minos*. Minos, an't please you.
*Tucca*. Minos? Come hither, Minos; thou art a wise fellow, it
    seems. Let me talk with thee.
*Crispinus*. Was ever wretch so wretched as unfortunate I?     50
*Tucca* [*Aside to Minos*] Thou art one of the *centum viri*, old
    boy, art not?
*Minos*. No indeed, master captain.
*Tucca*. Go to, thou shalt be then: I'll ha' thee one Minos.
    Take my sword from those rascals, [*Indicating Lictors*]     55
    dost thou see? Go, do it: I cannot attempt with patience.
    [*Raising his voice*] What does this gentleman owe thee,
    little Minos?

---

34. disgust] *F;* disgeste *Q.*     51. S.D.] *This ed.*

---

34. *disgust*] transitive, meaning to excite distaste or nausea, first recorded
in this sense in *OED* in 1659; cf. III.iv.316.
44. *pra'*] shortening 'pray'; J. often writes *pray'*, indicating an abbreviation of 'pray thee' (e.g. II.i.1), or *'pray*, indicating ommission of 'I'
(III.iv.263), but this abbreviation is peculiar to Minos.
51. centum viri] A bench of commissioners out of whom were chosen
those who tried civil cases, 'that is, touching equity and uprightness of any
act, or the restitution of any money or goods unlawfully detained from the
right owner' (Godwyn, p. 163); cf. Rosinus VII.xxx and IX.xiv. Ovid served
as one (*Tristia* II, 93–6).

*Minos.* Fourscore sesterces, sir.

*Tucca.* What, no more? Come, thou shalt release him, Minos.        60
What, I'll be his bail, thou shalt take my word, old boy,
and cashier these furies. Thou shalt do't I say, thou shalt,
little Minos, thou shalt.

*Crispinus.* Yes, and as I am a gentleman and a reveller, I'll
make a piece of poetry, and absolve all within these five        65
days.

*Tucca.* Come, Minos is not to learn how to use a gent'man of
quality, I know. [*Aside to Minos*] My sword. [*Raising his
voice*] If he pay thee not, I will, and I must, old boy.
Thou shalt be my 'pothecary too; hast good eringoes,         70
Minos?

*Minos.* The best in Rome, sir.

*Tucca.* Go to then—[*To Pyrgi*] Vermin, know the house.

[*1*] *Pyrgus.* I warrant you, colonel.

*Tucca.* [*Indicating Crispinus*] For this gentleman, Minos?        75

*Minos.* I'll take your word captain.

*Tucca.* Thou hast it. My sword——

*Minos.* Yes, sir. But you must discharge the arrest, Master
Crispinus.

*Tucca.* How, Minos? Look in the gentleman's face, and but        80
read his silence. Pay, pay: 'tis honour, Minos.

[MINOS *pays* 1 Lictor. 2 Lictor *releases* CRISPINUS.]

---

68. S.D.] *This ed.*    68–9. S.D.] *This ed.*    69. must,] *Q omits the comma*
*in the catchword of E4r.*    73. to then—] *Subst. F;* too, then *Q.*    77. it.
My] *F2;* it, my *Q, F.*    81.1. S.D.] *This ed.*

---

59. *Fourscore sesterces*] Godwyn estimated the sestertius at 'three half
pence farthing' in 1614; if this was J.'s valuation, Crispinus' debt was
equivalent to 11s. 8d, or about 58p.

64. *gentleman . . . reveller*] See III.i.173–5n.

65. *absolve*] discharge, a pretentious Latinism from *absolvere*, not in *OED*.

70. *eringoes*] a sea-holly, whose candied root was regarded as an aphrodisiac. Francis Lenton specifies it as part of the diet of an Inns of Court man:
'His oysters, lobsters, caviare, and crabs, / With which he feasted his con-
tagious drabs; / Oringoes, hartichokes, potato pies / Provocatives unto their
luxuries.' *The Young Gallant's Whirligig: Or Youth's Reakes* (1629), p. 16. Cf.
also Marston, *Malcontent* II.iv.12–13.

73. *know*] make a mental note of.

74. *colonel*] used ironically; it already implied superior military rank by
the late sixteenth century (*OED*, 1).

78. *discharge*] pay the costs of.

*Crispinus.* By Jove, sweet captain, you do most infinitely
endear and oblige me to you.

*Tucca.* Tut! I cannot compliment, by Mars; but Jupiter love
me, as I love good words and good clothes, and there's an          85
end. Thou shalt give my boy that girdle and hangers,
when thou hast worn them a little more——

*Crispinus.* O Jupiter! Captain, he shall have them now,
presently. [*To 1 Pyrgus*] Please you to be acceptive, young
gentleman.                                                         90

[*1*] *Pyrgus.* Yes, sir, fear not, I shall accept. [*Aside*] I have a
pretty, foolish humour of taking, if you knew all.

*Tucca.* Not now, you shall not take, boy.

*Crispinus.* By my truth and earnest, but he shall, captain, by
your leave.                                                        95

*Tucca.* Nay, and a' swear by his truth and earnest, take it,
boy. Do not make a gent'man forsworn.

                    [MINOS *speaks to* Lictors *aside.*]

[*1*] *Lictor.* [*To Tucca*] Well, sir, there is your sword; but thank
Master Minos: you had not carried it as you do else.

                    [Lictors *begin to leave.*]

*Tucca.* Minos is just, and you are knaves and——                  100

[*1*] *Lictor.* [*Turning back*] What say you, sir?

*Tucca.* Pass on, my good scoundrel, pass on, I honour thee.

[Lictors *again begin to leave.*] But that I hate to have action

---

88. shall] *This ed.;* 'shall *Q, F.*   91. S.D.] *G.*   94. he shall] *Subst. F;* a'
shal *Q.*   96. and earnest] *F; not in Q.*   97. gent'man] *F;* Gentleman
*Q.*   97.1. S.D.] *This ed.*   99.1. S.D.] *This ed.*   101. S.D.] *This ed.*
103. S.D.] *This ed.;* Lictors *move off. Nicholson.*

---

84. *compliment*] See p. 33.

86. *girdle . . . hangers*] belt and loops from which the sword hung; cf. *EMI*
I.v.8. (*H&S*) and *Ham.* V.ii.150–60.

89. *presently*] at once.

*acceptive*] ready to accept, receptive, an affected usage: cf. *C is A* II.vii.62
(*H&S*); J. is probably parodying *1 Ant.* V.ii.79–80, 'your brightest beams /
Of sunny favor and acceptive grace'.

92. *taking*] stealing.

94. *By . . . earnest*] mocked as a weak oath in *AYL* IV.i.188–90: 'By my
troth, and in good earnest . . . and by all pretty oaths that are not dangerous'.
Marston ridicules it in *1 Ant.* II.i.67, 99, so J. is being disingenuous in giving
it to Crispinus.

*earnest*] sincerity.

99. *carried it*] won the contest (*OED*, 15b).

with such base rogues as these, you should ha' seen me
unrip their noses now, and have sent 'em to the next     105
barber's to stitching; for, do you see—[Lictors *again turn
back*.] I am a man of humour, and I do love the varlets,
the honest varlets; they have wit, and valour; and are
indeed good profitable—[*Exeunt* Lictors.] errant rogues,
as any live in an empire. [*Aside to Crispinus*] Dost thou    110
hear, poetaster? Second me. [*To Minos*] Stand up, Minos,
close, gather, [*Draws them together*.] yet, so. Sir, [*Aside to
Crispinus*] thou shalt have a quarter share, be resolute.
[*Raising his voice*] You shall at my request take Minos by
the hand; here, little Minos [*Putting their hands together*] I    115
will have it so. All friends and a health; be not inexorable.
       [MINOS *shakes hands reluctantly with* CRISPINUS.]
And thou shalt impart the wine, old boy, thou shalt do't,
little Minos, thou shalt. Make us pay it in our physic.
What? We must live, and honour the gods sometimes:
now Bacchus, now Comus, now Priapus. Every god a    120
little.

                    [*Enter* HISTRIO.]

---

106. see—] *F*; see? *Q*.    106–7. S.D.] *This ed.; Overhearing in part, they
return. Nicholson.*    109. S.D.] *Nicholson.*    errant] *F; Arrant Q*.    110.
S.D.] *Subst. G*.    111. up Minos] *This ed.; vp; Minos; Q; vp* (MINOS)
*F*.    112. S.D.] *This ed.*    112–13. S.D.] *This ed.; Aside to 1st.* PY-
RGUS. *Nicholson*.    113. thou . . . resolute] *In parentheses in Q, F*.    114.
S.D.] *This ed.*    115. S.D.] *This ed.*    116.1. S.D.] *This ed.*    121.1.
S.D.] *G, who puts the entry at l. 127;* HISTRIO *passes by. Nicholson.*

---

106. *barber's . . . stitching*] Though the Company of Barber-Surgeons was
separated into distinct professions, barbers performed dental and other minor
operations well into the eighteenth century; cf. 'Apol. Dial.', 151–4n and
*EMO* IV.iii.100–1.
  109. *profitable*] valuable, beneficial (*OED*, 1).
  *errant*] arrant; J.'s etymologically correct form recalls the root meaning of
wandering or vagrant.
  111. *poetaster*] See title-page, 1n.
  116. *inexorable*] recalling his namesake's role as judge.
  117. *impart*] provide; cf. III.iv.368.
  118. *Make . . . physic*] add it to our bills.
  120. *Bacchus . . . Priapus*] presiding over wine, revelry and procreation
respectively.

What's he that stalks by there? Boy, Pyrgus, you were
best let him pass, sirrah; do, ferret, let him pass, do.
[*I*] *Pyrgus.* 'Tis a player, sir.
*Tucca.* A player? Call him! Call the lousy slave hither. What,          125
will he sail by, and not once strike or vail to a man of
war? Ha! Do you hear? You, player, rogue, stalker, come
back here. No respect to men of worship, you slave?
What, you are proud you rascal, are you proud, ha? You
grow rich do you, and purchase, you twopenny tear-              130
mouth? You have fortune and the good year on your side,
you stinkard? You have? You have?

---

123. do, ferret] do Leueret *Q.*     125–6. What, will] *Subst. F;* what'l *Q.*
126–7. man of war] *This ed.; Man of warre Q, F.*     129. are proud] *F;* are
ptoude *Q.*     130. purchase,] *F;* purchase? *Q.*     130–1. you . . . tear-
mouth?] *Subst. F; not in Q.*

---

123. *ferret*] the change from *Q* emphasises the boy's quick wit and role
in seeking out prey for Tucca. Mallory quotes *NI*, 'Persons': 'FERRET, . . .
Lovel's servant, a fellow of a quick, nimble wit, knows the manners and
affections of people, and can make profitable and timely discoveries of them'
(ed. Hattaway, Revels, 1984), ll. 15–18.
   126. *strike*] to lower a sail as a salute or sign of submission; cf. Rudyerd,
*Prince D'Amour*, p. 27: 'He shall suffer no ship to come near him, but shall
make her strike and come under his lee.'
   *vail*] similar nautical use to 'strike', but here with secondary meaning of
removing a hat, or making other sign of deference, to another.
   126–7. *man of war*] Tucca is a 'man of war'; his pun on a warship
demanding submission from a merchant vessel is emphasised by the italics of
*Q* and *F.*
   127. *stalker*] See l. 165n.
   130. *rich . . . purchase*] refers to the increasing claims to social status of the
players, particularly of those like Shakespeare who were shareholders by
'purchase'. 'Purchase' was also used for robbery (cf. *BF* II.v.174), and stolen
goods: cf. *Alc.* IV.vii.122–3: 'Doe you two pack up all the goods, and
purchase, / That we can carry i'thee two trunkes.'
   130–1. *twopenny tear-mouth*] a ranting actor who aims at the 'twopenny
rooms', the cheapest galleries in the public amphitheatres. Cf. V.iii.577,
*S-M*, Epilogue, 15, and *EMO*, Ind. 312. *H&S* quote C.B., *The Hospital of
Incurable Fools* (1600), Epistle Ded.: 'I beg it with as forced a look as a player
that is speaking an epilogue, makes love to the two penny room for a
plaudit.'
   131. *fortune*] a pun on Alleyn's Fortune Theatre, the contract for building
which was signed in January 1600.
   *good year*] a malign spirit, perhaps the devil; cf. Kenneth Muir's note to *Lr*
V.iii.24 (Arden, 1972 ed.): 'According to Morwenstow (*NQ*, V, 607, 1852)
the Goujere is the old Cornish name of the Fiend.'

*Histrio.* Nay, sweet captain, be confined to some reason. I
  protest, I saw you not, sir.

*Tucca.* You did not? Where was your sight, Oedipus? You    135
  walk with hare's eyes do you? I'll ha' 'em glazed, rogue:
  and you say the word, they shall be glazed for you. Come,
  we must have you turn fiddler again, slave, get a bass
  violin at your back, and march in a tawny coat with one
  sleeve to Goose Fair, and then you'll know us, you'll see    140
  us then; you will, gulch, you will! Then [*Mimicking a
  player*] 'Will't please your worship to have any music,
  captain?'

*Histrio.* [*Laughing*] Nay, good captain.

138. get] *F2;* 'get *Q, F.*       bass] *This ed.;* Base *Q, Subst. F.*    141–2.
S.D.] *This ed.*    142–3. 'Will't . . . captain?'] *This ed.;* wil't . . . Captaine?
*Q, F.*    144. S.D.] *This ed.*

135. *Where . . . Oedipus*] referring to the myth of Oedipus, king of Thebes,
who in Sophocles' version (*Oedipus Rex*) blinded himself on discovering he
had unknowingly killed his father and married his own mother, thus bringing
a plague on the city.

136. *walk . . . eyes*] sleepwalk: cf. *C is A* V.xi.15 (*H&S*). The hare was
thought to sleep with its eyes open; see Chapman, *An Epicede* (1612),
marginal note to l. 388: 'Out of the property of the Hare that never shuts her
eyes sleeping' (*Poems*, ed. Bartlett (1941), 262).

*glazed*] with tears; cf. *R2* II.ii.16, 'sorrow's eyes, glazed with blinding
tears.'

138–9. *bass violin*] The cello, as distinct from the bass viol. The four-
stringed violin family, to which the cello belongs, was at this date still
associated with itinerant musicians and actors, unlike the more respectable
viol family: see Hayes, pp. 189–98, 206–8. Old cellos have a button for a
carrying-strap. A print from *Scarron's Comical Romance of a Company of
Stage Players* (1676, reproduced in *The Riverside Shakespeare*, Plate 14),
shows a French touring company, including an actor with a large bass viol on
his back.

139. *tawny coat*] worn by itinerant musicians; *G* quotes Deloney, *The
Pleasant History of John Winchcomb* (1630), B4: 'They had not sitten long,
but in comes a noise of musicians in tawny coats'.

139–40. *one sleeve*] This seems to refer to a specific feature of the itinerant
musician's costume, rather than to a torn coat: it may be that the bowing arm
was kept free.

140. *Goose Fair*] 'Green goose fair', still held in *G*'s time at Bow, near
Stratford, Essex, on Whit Monday. Young ('green') geese were eaten there.
It attracted itinerant players and musicians.

141. *gulch*] glutton; cf. Cotgrave, *Dictionary* (1611): '*Engorgeur*, a ravener,
glutton, gulch, ingorger'. It is also the name of an actor satirised in *Hist*.

*Tucca.* What, do you laugh, Owlglass? Death, you per-      145
stemptuous varlet, I am none of your fellows! I have
commanded a hundred and fifty such rogues, I.
*1 Pyrgus.* [*Aside*] Ay, and most of that hundred and fifty
have been leaders of a legion.
*Histrio.* If I have exhibited wrong, I'll tender satisfaction,      150
captain.
*Tucca.* Say'st thou so, honest vermin? Give me thy hand, thou
shalt make us a supper one of these nights.
*Histrio.* When you please, by Jove, captain, most willingly.
*Tucca.* Dost thou swear? Tomorrow then. Say and hold,      155
slave. There are some of you players honest gent'man-like
scoundrels and suspected to ha' some wit, as well as your
poets; both at drinking and breaking of jests, and are
companions for gallants. A man may skelder ye now and
then of half a dozen shillings or so. [*Indicating Crispinus*]      160

---

145 Owlglass? Death] *Parfitt; Howleglass?* 'death *Q; Owleglas?* death *F.*
148. S.D.] *G.*      155. swear] *Subst. Q;* 'sweare *F* (*compositor misreading a
space mark in Q*).      157–9. and . . . gallants] *F; not in Q.*      160. S.D.] *This
ed.*

---

145. *Owlglass*] English version of Eulenspiegel, comic hero of a medieval
German jest book; Mallory, *H&S*, cite 'Howle-glasse' (*FI* 232, 349, 350),
'Owle-spiegle' (*SS* II.iii.9) and 'Vlen-spiegle' (*FI* 237 and *Alc.* II.iii.32).
145–6. *perstemptuous*] a malapropism for 'presumptuous'.
147. *hundred and fifty*] equating the *centuria* with the size of an English
infantry company; Rosinus and other historians available to J. give the
Roman *centuria* as a hundred men (Rosinus X.v.), though in fact they varied
in size. Cf. *1H4*, IV.ii.13–14: 'I have got, in exchange of a hundred and fifty
soldiers, three hundred and odd pounds'.
149. *leaders of a legion*] of lice, a common joke, used by Falstaff, *2H4*
III.ii.165–7 (so *H&S*).
150. *exhibited*] 'done', 'offered', a pretentious Latinism from *exhibere*, to
present.
*tender*] 'offer', again pretentious because normally used in more serious
contexts, and originally a legal term (*OED*, 1 and 2).
155. *Say and hold*] a common phrase, meaning 'make your promise
and hold to it'; cf. King, p. 148.
159. *skelder*] swindle, cheat; cf. I.i.25n.
160. *or so*] though not wholly redundant here, it is an affected colloquial-
ism, used also by Chloe (IV.ii.52), Tibullus (IV.iii.151) and Tucca (V.iii.432);
its use by the would-be courtiers Amorphus (*CR* III.i.55) and Emulo
(Dekker, *Patient Grissil*, III.ii.22) confirms that King is right to classify it as
'Courtly colloquial' (p. 149).

Dost thou not know that Pantolabus there?

*Histrio.* No, I assure you, captain.

*Tucca.* Go and be acquainted with him then; he is a gent'man parcel-poet, you slave. His father was a man of worship, I tell thee. Go, he pens high, lofty, in a new stalking strain, 165 bigger than half the rhymers i' the town again. He was born to fill thy mouth, Minotaurus, he was: he will teach thee to tear and rant, rascal: to him, cherish his Muse, go! Thou hast forty—forty shillings I mean, stinkard—

161. Pantolabus] *G; Caprichio Q;* PANTALABVS *F (cf. III.v.39).* 168. rant] *This ed.;* rand *Q, F.* 169. forty—forty shillings] *G;* fortie, fortie; shillings *Q;* fortie, fortie, shillings *F.*

161. *Pantolabus*] 'one that takes all' is a parasitical character in Hor. *Sat.* I.vii.11 and II.i.22; the compositor misread J.'s revision of *Q*'s Caprichio (a freak); contemporary editions of Hor. all have 'Pantolabus', and J. spells it thus in III.v.39. As *G* points out, the name is more appropriate to Tucca than Crispinus. *G*'s note on this name was the occasion on which he 'let loose [his] opinion' 'that the CRISPINUS of Jonson is MARSTON, to whom every word of this directly points. This will derange much confident criticism; but I shall be found eventually in the right. Decker I take to be the Demetrius of the present play.'

164. *parcel-poet*] part-poet: Crispinus describes himself thus in IV.vi.28, and Tucca pronounces him and Demetrius 'parcel guilty' in V.iii.413. *H&S* compare *BF* II.ii.16, *S of N* 'The Persons', 20 ('Lickfinger, master-cook and parcel-poet'), *D is A* II.iii.15 and *Alc.* IV.vi.33 ('parcel-broker and whole bawd'). See also *Meas.* II.i.63, 'A tapster, sir; parcel-bawd'.

*father . . . worship*] Marston's father, a Reader of the Middle Temple, had died in 1599, apparently disappointed at Marston's failure to follow him in the law: leaving him his law books, he says 'I hoped [he] would have profited by them in the study of the law but man proposeth and God disposeth'. For 'worship' see I.i.29n.

165. *stalking strain*] grandiloquent, but also suggesting a style suited to histrionics in the theatre, as exemplified in *1 Ant.* and *AR*; cf. *The Puritan, or the Widow of Watling Street* (anon., 1607) III.v.84: 'Have you never seen a stalking-stamping player?' It is close in meaning to the 'scenical strutting' which J. and others objected to in Marlowe as acted by Alleyn (*Disc.* 775–9).

167. *Minotaurus*] monster, half man and half bull, which devoured seven maidens and seven youths a year in the labyrinth at Crete. Tucca uses the name to suggest that Histrio bellows like a bull.

168. *rant*] *Q* and *F* 'rand' is an obsolete form.

169–70. *forty shillings . . . earnest*] An obvious and conscious anachronism, uneasily sandwiched between references to Roman currency (ll. 59, 185); all J.'s references to the theatre are to that of contemporary London. This is Henslowe's normal 'earnest', or advance: he records several such payments in his *Diary*, J., Marston and Dekker among the recipients (see p. 31).

give him in earnest, do, he shall write for thee, slave. If    170
he pen for thee once, thou shalt not need to travel with
thy pumps full of gravel any more after a blind jade and a
hamper, and stalk upon boards and barrel heads to an old
cracked trumpet——
*Histrio.* Troth, I think I ha' not so much about me captain.    175
*Tucca.* It's no matter, give him what thou hast, stiff-toe, I'll
give my word for the rest: though it lack a shilling or two,
it skills not. Go, thou art an honest shifter, I'll ha' the
statute repealed for thee. Minos, I must tell thee, Minos,
[*Indicating Crispinus*] thou hast dejected yon gent'man's    180
spirit exceedingly: dost observe, dost note, little Minos?
*Minos.* Yes, sir.

---

171. travel] *Subst. Q, F;* travaile *F2.*    173–4. and stalk . . . trumpet——]
*Subst. F; not in Q.*    176. stiff-toe] *Subst. F; Paunch Q.*    178. shifter,] *F;*
*Twentie i' the hundred; Q.*    179. thee. Minos] *F; thee, Minos Q.*    I] *Q;*
*appears only as part of catchword in F.*    180. S.D.] *This ed.*

---

171–2. *travel . . . gravel*] from *Hist.* (Wood, III, 264): '*Besides we that*
*travell, with pumps full of gravell,* / *Made all of such running leather:* / *That once*
*in a weeke, new maisters wee seeke,* / *And never can hold together.*' The
description (*pace H&S*) fits the Chamberlain's Men, whom Histrio represents: they may have 'travelled' just after the Essex rising (February 1601),
and were, according to *Ham.* II.ii.329–44 also forced to tour (perhaps at the
same time) by the success of the children's companies. Touring in summer
was, in any case, common: see G.E. Bentley, *The Profession of Player in*
*Shakespeare's Time, 1590–1642* (Princeton, N.J., 1984), pp. 177–205.
    172. *pumps*] light, low-heeled shoes, particularly associated with dancers
and acrobats (*OED*, *sb.* 2) and therefore with itinerant players.
    *jade*] a worn out or otherwise worthless horse.
    173. *hamper*] the horse pulled a cart containing a hamper for the costumes
and props; see the print from *Scarron's Comical Romance*, cited above ll.
138–9n.
    *boards . . . heads*] an accurate description of the construction of touring
stages, versions of which can be seen in contemporary engravings.
    176. *stiff-toe*] *H&S* suggest a slang term for an actor; cf. III.iv.305.
    178. *skills not*] matters not.
    *shifter*] money lender; *Q*'s reading confirms J. had this meaning in mind
('Twentie i' the hundred' was twice the legal rate of interest).
    179. *statute*] either the 1572 statute listing actors amongst vagabonds (see
I.ii.54n.), or the statute of 1571 which limited interest to ten per cent.
    183. *raise; recover*] omitting 'him': 'Tucca's commonest verb-trick is using
transitives absolutely' (King, p. 115). It is a significant element in his el-
liptical, repetitive style (cf. next line: 'a player, a rogue, a stager', all meaning
'an actor'), creating 'an edgy, asyndetic verbal manner that gives the effect of
crackling high tension' (Barish, p. 123).

*Tucca.* Go to then, raise; recover, do. Suffer him not to droop
in prospect of a player, a rogue, a stager. Put twenty into
his hand, twenty sesterces I mean, and let nobody see.     185
Go, do it, the work shall commend itself: be Minos, I'll
pay.

*Minos.* Yes forsooth, captain.

[MINOS *and* CRISPINUS *talk apart.*]

2 *Pyrgus.* [*Aside to* 1 *Pyrgus*] Do not we serve a notable
shark?                                                      190

*Tucca.* And what new matters have you now afoot, sirrah, ha?
I would fain come with my cockatrice one day and see a
play, if I knew when there were a good bawdy one: but
they say you ha' nothing but humours, revels and satires
that gird and fart at the time, you slave.                 195

*Histrio.* No, I assure you, captain, not we. They are on the
other side of Tiber. We have as much ribaldry in our
plays as can be, as you would wish, captain. All the
sinners i' the suburbs come and applaud our action daily.

---

185. sesterces] *F; Drachmes Q.*    188.1. S.D.] *This ed.*    189. S.D.] *Subst.*
G.    191. matters] *F; Playes Q.*    you] *Q, F;* wee *F2.*    194. humours
. . . satires] *Parfitt; Humours, Reuels,* and *Satyres Q, Subst. F.*

---

185. *sesterces*] a quarter of the debt Crispinus owes Minos: see III.iv.59. J.
probably thought of this as equivalent to about three shillings.

186. *be Minos*] i.e. Minos the judge: 'be just and merciful.'

190. *shark*] cheat, parasite (not derived from the fish at this date); cf.
V.iii.149, *SW* IV.iv.217–18, and *EMO*, Character of the Persons, 83–4:
'SHIFT. A Thred-bare Sharke'; the latter is the first use cited by *OED*.

192. *cockatrice*] whore; cf. IV.iii.64, IV.v.53, 109 and IV.vii.5, and *CR*
II.ii.101: 'his *cockatrice,* or *punquetto*'.

194. *humours . . . satires*] J.'s own plays, *EMI* (1598), *EMO* (1599), and
*CR* (1600), esp. the two latter.

195. *gird*] sneer, jibe.

197. *other . . . Tiber*] The men's companies played largely on the South
Bank of the Thames at the Theatre, Rose, Swan, and (from 1599) the Globe,
and further south at Newington Butts. The Chamberlain's Men performed at
the Curtain, north of the river in Shoreditch, between 1597 and 1599, and
the Admiral's Men moved into the Fortune in the north-west suburbs in
1600. Otherwise north of the river was the preserve of the children's companies, whose theatres, though physically within the City, were legally outside its jurisdiction (see p. 38).

199. *daily*] probably here drawing attention to the fact that while the
men's companies acted daily, the children performed only once or twice a
week. A Privy Council order of 22 June 1600 had limited the number of
public (i.e. adult) playhouses to two (the Fortune and the Globe), and had

*Tucca.* I hear you'll bring me o' the stage there: you'll play      200
me, they say. I shall be presented by a sort of copper-
laced scoundrels of you. Life of Pluto! And you stage me,
stinkard, your mansions shall sweat for't, your tabernacles, varlets, your Globes and your Triumphs!

*Histrio.* Not we by Phoebus, Captain, do not do us imputation      205
without desert.

*Tucca.* I wu' not, my good twopenny rascal. Reach me thy
neuf. [*Shaking his hand*] Dost hear? What wilt thou give
me a week for my brace of beagles here, my little point

---

202. Life] *Subst. F;* Death *Q.*      204. Globes] *G; Globes Q, F.*      Triumphs]
*G; Tryumphes Q; Triumphs F.*

---

limited performances to twice a week by each company, but a letter from the
Privy Council to the magistrates of Middlesex and Surrey (31 December
1601) shows that this was 'farr from takinge dew effect' and that 'no daie
passeth over without many stage plaies in one place or other' (in Chambers,
*ES,* IV, 329–31, 332–3).

200. *bring . . . stage*] Tucca was brought on the stage by Dekker in *S-M,*
performed at the Globe by the Chamberlain's Men shortly after *Poetaster.*

201–2. *copper-laced*] worn by actors in imitation of gold lace (hence also
meaning spurious); Henslowe, *Diary,* mentions it on several occasions (e.g.
pp. 49, 85).

202. *Life of Pluto*] See III.iv.25n; the change from *Q*'s 'Death' is probably
explained by the fact that he was the immortal judge of the dead in the
underworld (cf. III.iv.260–1).

*And*] If.

203–4. *mansions . . . Triumphs*] 'mansions' and 'tabernacles' are used in
the New Testament to mean the body of man (2 Cor. v.1, 2 Peter i.13–14),
and thus bodily punishment is threatened; but Tucca is also referring to the
theatres. 'Tabernacles' were also ornate structures used in pageants or
'Triumphs', however, and 'mansions' may also refer in a general way to such
elaborate, ephemeral structures. No theatre is known to have been called the
Triumph, though it may have been an inn where plays were performed.

207. *wu'*] abbreviating 'would'; cf. Tucca's much more frequent 'ha'' for
'have'.

*twopenny rascal*] See III.iv.130–1n.

208. *neuf*] fist; *H&S* quote *MND* IV.i.19, 'Give me your neaf, Monsieur
Mustardseed'; King (p. 165) suggests it is Cockney.

208–9. *What . . . week*] Child actors were sometimes hired out by the
week; see J., *Christmas:* 'I could ha' had money enough for him . . . and ha'
let him out by the weeke to the King's Players: Master *Burbadge* has been
about and about with me, and so has old Mr. *Hemings* too, they ha' need of
him' (133–7).

209. *beagles*] normally 'spies' (*OED,* 2), but here probably merely like a
pair of small hounds who follow him around. In *S-M* II.ii.15 Asinius proudly

trussers? You shall ha' them act among ye. [*To 1 Pyrgus*]     210
Sirrah, you, pronounce. Thou shalt hear him speak in
King Darius' doleful strain.
*1 Pyrgus. O doleful days! O direful deadly dump!*
*O wicked world! And worldly wickedness!*
*How can I hold my fist from crying thump*     215
*In rue of this right rascal wretchedness!*
Tucca. In an amorous vein now sirrah: peace.
*1 Pyrgus. O, she is wilder, and more hard withal*
*Than beast or bird or tree or stony wall.*
*Yet might she love me to uprear her state:*     220
*Ay, but perhaps she hopes some nobler mate.*
*Yet might she love me to content her sire:*
*Ay, but her reason masters her desire.*
*Yet might she love me as her beauty's thrall:*
*Ay, but I fear she cannot love at all.*     225
Tucca. Now the horrible fierce soldier, you, sirrah.
*2 Pyrgus. What? Will I brave thee? Ay, and beard thee too.*

---

222. sire] *Q, F;* Fire *F3, Whalley, G.*     226. horrible] *F;* orrible *Q.*     227.
2 Pyrgus] *Subst. G;* 1 Pyr. *Q, Subst. F.*

---

claims 'one calls me *Horaces* Ape, another *Horaces* Beagle', again meaning a
diminutive follower. Cf. *Gull's Hornbook*, 'bee thou a beagle to them all, and
never lin snuffing till you have scented them' (in Chambers, *ES*, IV, 367).
  209–10. *point trussers*] Points were laces which fastened hose to doublet;
Tucca's pages helped to tie them. Cf. *EMI* I.iii.34, and Marvell, 'On Mr.
Milton's *Paradise Lost*', 49–50.
  212–16. *Darius . . . wretchedness*] Darius, king of Persia, 521–486 BC,
figures in the anonymous *Pretie new Enterlude . . . of the Story of Kyng Daryus*
of 1565. These lines are not from it, but are probably J.'s parody of its crude
'doleful strain'. *D is A* I.i.44–75 also parodies this type of drama. Penniman
notes that Alexander's *Tragedie of Darius* (Edinburgh, 1603) is also similar in
tone; but a then-unpublished Scottish closet drama is not a likely subject for
parody on the Blackfriars stage. Cf. *1H4* II.iv.386–7, where Falstaff says 'I
must speak in passion, and I will do it in King Cambyses' vein.'
  218–25.] From Balthazar's speech in Kyd's *Spanish Tragedy*, II.i.9–10,
25–6, 21–2, 27–8; J. slightly misquotes and reorders the lines. He was paid
by Henslowe for 'additions' to the play on 25 September 1601 and 24 June
1602 (*Diary*, pp. 182 and 203). Field later parodied the same passage in *A
Woman is a Weathercock*, I.ii (*H&S*; cf. III.iv.24n). In *Return From Parnassus
II, The Spanish Tragedy* is used in a similar 'audition' (*Parnassus Plays*,
p. 341, ll. 1802–7).
  227–9.] source unidentified, probably a lost Roman play, but possibly
parody by J. as in ll. 213–16.

A *Roman spirit scorns to bear a brain*
*So full of base pusillanimity.*

*Histrio.* Excellent!                                                    230

*Tucca.* Nay, thou shalt see that shall ravish thee anon: prick
up thine ears, stinkard! The ghost, boys.

*1 Pyrgus. Vindicta!*

*2 Pyrgus. Timoria!*

*1 Pyrgus. Vindicta!*                                                    235

*2 Pyrgus. Timoria!*

*1 Pyrgus. Veni!*

*2 Pyrgus. Veni!*

*Tucca.* [*To 2 Pyrgus*] Now thunder, sirrah, you, the rumbling
player.                                                                  240

*2 Pyrgus.* Ay, but somebody must cry 'Murder!' then in a
small voice.

230. *Histrio*] Subst. *G; Demet. Histrio. Q;* DEMET. HIST. *F (also 247).*
241. *2 Pyrgus*] Subst. *G; 1 Pyr. Q, Subst. F.*      cry 'Murder!'] *Nicholson;* cry
*murder, Q;* crie (*murder*) *F.*

---

228. *bear a brain*] 'a quibble on the sense "be cautious". Skelton,
*Magnyficence,* 1526, l. 1422, "I counsel you, bere a brayne"' (*H&S*).

230. *Histrio*] *Q* and *F*'s *Demet. Histrio* is clearly a mistake, probably
deriving from a misreading of, or confusion in, the copy for *Q.*

233–8.] unidentified, but Senecan in style. J. is probably parodying the
terse exchange in *AR* V.iii.1–4: '*Ant. Vindicta! / Alb. Mellida! / Ant. Alberto!*
*/ Alb. Antonio!*'; cf. also *AR* V.iii.40: 'O, now, *Vindicta!* that's the word we
have'. '*Vindicta mihi*' is used in *The Spanish Tragedy* III.xiii.1 by Hieronimo,
not a ghost, but Dekker in *Seven Deadly Sins* (1606) speaks of the 'Ghost in
Ieronimo crying "Revenge"', and J. may still have Kyd in mind also. The
word occurs in many ghost scenes, echoing both the biblical 'Vengeance is
mine' (Rom. xii.19; 'vindicta' in the Vulgate) and such classical uses as the
pseudo-Senecan *Octavia,* 849: 'vindicta debetur mihi', and Juvenal XIII,
180: 'O! but vengeance ['vindicta'] is good, sweeter than life itself.' See e.g.
Peele, *Battle of Alcazar* (acted 1588–9) II.i.Prol.: '*Three ghosts crying* Vindicta'
(ed. Yoklavich in *Dramatic Works,* ed. Prouty, II, 306); 'W.S.', *Locrine* (acted
1591–5) III.vi, and the opening lines of the anonymous *True Tragedy of
Richard III* (acted 1588–94). *A Warning for Fair Women* (? T. Heywood,
1599) parodies the cliché: 'a filthy whining ghost / . . . Comes screaming like a
piggie half sticked, / And cries *Vindicta,* revenge, revenge.' ?Fletcher, *Fair
Maid of the Inn* (*Works,* ed. Dyce, X, 47) makes the clown cry '*Vindicta,*
*Vindicta*', for a broken pate (most examples cited by *G*). 'Timoria' (from
Greek meaning 'terror', not classical Latin) and 'veni' (either imperative,
'come' or past, 'I have come') have not been traced in English plays.

239. *rumbling*] possibly indicating that the boy's voice was breaking, but
probably referring to a drum (see III.iv.248n).

242. *small*] gentle, low (*OED,* 13), perhaps indicating an unbroken voice.

*Tucca.* Your fellow sharer there shall do't. *[To 1 Pyrgus]* Cry, sirrah, cry!

*1 Pyrgus. Murder, murder!*

*2 Pyrgus. Who calls out murder? Lady, was it you?*                      245

*Histrio.* O admirable good, I protest.

*Tucca. [To 2 Pyrgus]* Sirrah, boy, brace your drum a little straighter and do the t'other fellow there, he in the— what sha' call him—and 'yet stay' too.                                  250

*2 Pyrgus. Nay, and thou dalliest, then I am thy foe,*
*And fear shall force what friendship cannot win;*
*Thy death shall bury what thy life conceals:*
*Villain! Thou diest for more respecting her——*

*1 Pyrgus. O stay my lord!*

*2 Pyrgus. —than me.*                                                  255

*Yet speak the truth, and I will guerdon thee:*

---

249. the—] *F; space after dash in Q.*       250. him—] *F; space after dash in Q.* 'yet stay'] *Subst. Nicholson;* yet, stay *Q, F.*       254. her——] *F;* her, than me *Q.*       255. O . . . lord] *Subst. F; roman in Q.*

---

243. *sharer*] a leading actor who paid part of the expenses of the company and shared in the profits, as opposed to a waged 'journeyman' actor: cf. IV.iv.9. Chambers, *ES,* II, 199, gives 'ten original sharers' in the Chamberlain's Men, while the lease for the Globe was originally shared between the Burbage brothers (who had half the interest), and Shakespeare, Heminges, Phillips, Pope and Kempe (*ES,* II, 203).

245–6.] From Chapman's *Blind Beggar of Alexandria* (1596; ed. Berry, in *Plays: The Comedies,* ed. Holaday, p. 30): 'Murder, Murder of good prince Doricles. / *Enter* Euribates. / Who calls out murther 'Lady was it you', a passage also quoted in *EH* (of which Chapman was part-author) II.i.110. *The Spanish Tragedy* II.iv.62 is again echoed.

248. *brace . . . drum*] Mallory suggests 'brace your chest' or voice, but probably a real drum: see *Christmas,* 140–1, 'Are you readie, Boyes? strike up, nothing will drown this noise but a Drum', and *The Spanish Tragedy* I.v.S.D.: 'Enter Hieronimo with a drum.' Cf. also *EMI,* Prol. 19–20, where no 'tempestuous drum / Rumbles'.

249. *t'other fellow*] Lorenzo (as opposed to Hieronimo) in *The Spanish Tragedy.*

250. *and . . . too*] punctuation suggested by Nicholson, who argues 'This "yet stay" appears to me to be his attempt to remember the passage. We have it in "O stay", and close to it "Yet speak"'.

251–8.] *The Spanish Tragedy* II.i.67–75.

255.] All editions of *The Spanish Tragedy* place Horatio's plea for mercy after Lorenzo has completed his sentence, as does *Q.* J.'s alteration in *F* must reflect his view of how this passage should be, and probably was, performed.

257. guerdon] reward.

*But if thou dally once again, thou diest.*
*Tucca.* Enough of this, boy.
*2 Pyrgus.* Why then, *lament therefore: damned be thy guts*                    260
*Unto King Pluto's hell and princely Erebus,*
*For sparrows must have food.*
*Histrio.* 'Pray sweet captain, let one of them do a little of a
lady.
*Tucca.* [*Indicating 1 Pyrgus*] O, he will make thee eternally                    265
enamoured of him there. Do, sirrah, do, 'twill allay your
fellow's fury a little.
*1 Pyrgus.* *Master mock on: the scorn thou givest me*
*Pray Jove some lady may return on thee.*
*2 Pyrgus.* No, you shall see me do the Moor. [*To Tucca*]                    270
Master, lend me your scarf a little.
*Tucca.* Here, 'tis at thy service, boy.
*2 Pyrgus.* You, Master Minos, hark hither a little.
                    *They [2 PYRGUS and MINOS]*
                    *withdraw to make themselves ready.*
*Tucca.* How dost like him? Art not rapt, art not tickled now?
Dost not applaud, rascal, dost not applaud?                    275
*Histrio.* Yes. What will you ask for 'em a week, captain?
*Tucca.* No, you mangonising slave, I will not part from 'em.
You'll sell 'em for engles, you. Let's ha' good cheer

---

261–2.] *G; prose in Q, F.*   265. S.D.] *This ed.*   273. little.] *F;* little.
*Exeunt. Q.*   273.1–2. S.D.] *F in margin; not in Q.*

260–2.] parodying Peele, *Battle of Alcazar* IV.2, part of which is quoted
by Pistol in *2H4* V.iii.108 and (again Pistol) *Wiv.* I.iii.35.
    261. Erebus] son of Chaos, and a personification of darkness; used in
Elizabethan times to signify a place of darkness through which the dead
passed on their way to Hades, or the underworld itself: cf. Pistol's 'to Pluto's
damned lake . . . to th' infernal deep, with Erebus and tortures vile' (*2H4*
II.iv.156–8).
    268–9.] unidentified.
    270. *the Moor*] Muly Mahomet, from *The Battle of Alcazar.*
    271. *scarf*] badge of an English (not a Roman) officer, worn as a sash: cf.
·*Ado* II.i.190: 'under your arm, like a lieutenant's scarf.'
    276. *What . . . week*] See III.iv.208–9n.
    277. *mangonising*] originally trafficking in slaves (from Latin, *mango*), but
here with suggestion of prostitution. Cf. *Dutch Courtesan*, Wood, II, 73: 'The
common bosome of a money Creature, / One that sells humane flesh: a
Mangonist.'
    278. *engles*] catamites, boy prostitutes.

tomorrow night at supper, stalker, and then we'll talk.
Good capon and plover, do you hear, sirrah? And do not   280
bring your eating player with you there. I cannot away
with him, he will eat a leg of mutton while I am in my
porridge, the lean Poluphagus; his belly is like Barathrum,
he looks like a midwife in man's apparel, the slave. Nor
the villainous-out-of-tune fiddler Aenobarbus, bring not   285
him. [*Seeing Histrio count his money*] What hast thou
there, six and thirty, ha?

*Histrio.* No, [*Giving him money*] here's all I have captain, some

---

286. S.D.] *This ed.*   288. S.D.] *This ed.*   captain] *In parentheses in Q, F.*

---

280. *capon*] castrated and fattened cockerel.

280–307. *And . . . so*] J. acknowledges personal lampooning of actors in
'Apol. Dial.', 141–3. G, keen to prove J. was not an enemy of Shakespeare,
argued that the actors involved were the Admiral's Men, based at the
Fortune, mentioned above, III.iv.131; Fleay, *Biographical Chronicle* I, 368–
9, agrees, but identification with the Chamberlain's company is more convincing: see Thomas Davies, *Dramatic Misc.* (1783) ii, 81–2; Small, p. 57;
Penniman *The War of the Theatres*, p. 116; T. W. Baldwin, *The Organisation
and Personnel of the Shakespearean Company* (1924), 232–4; H. D. Gray,
*MLR*, XLII (1947), 173–9; P. Simpson, *MLR*, XLIII (1948), 403–5; and
Gray, *MLR*, XLV, 148–51. See also *H&S* IX, 558–9 and Mallory, pp.
lxxiv–lxxix. Identifications are too conjectural to be of much value, but may
be summarised thus: Histrio: Augustine Phillips, business manager of
the Chamberlain's Men; Poluphagus: Burbage, Armin or Sincklo; Aesop:
Heminges or Shakespeare; Frisker: Sly, Kempe or Armin; the 'fat fool':
Pope or Lowin; Aenobarbus: Cowley. The argument for the Chamberlain's
Men is based on Demetrius having been hired by Histrio's company to attack
Horace; Dekker's *S-M* was commissioned by the Chamberlain's Men (see
III.iv.322–4n). Against this, the three identifiable plays from which the
Pyrgi recite were all in the recent repertoire of the Admiral's Men, led by
Alleyn, described by Joseph Hall as a 'stalking' actor (*Virgidemiarum* I.iii.16,
*Poems*, p. 14). Given the circumstances of Dekker's commission, the
Chamberlain's Men must have been J.'s main target, but it is highly likely
that he wished to embrace all the adult actors in his attack.

283. *porridge*] at this date a 'soup made by stewing vegetables, herbs, or
meat' (*OED*, 1).

*Poluphagus*] Greek, 'one who eats much'; used by Aristophanes (fragment
520).

*Barathrum*] a yawning gulf, probably suggested by Hor. *Epist.* I.xv.31,
where Maenius is described as 'pernicies et tempestas barathrumque
macelli'—'the market's ruin, a cyclone and abyss' (so *H&S*).

285. *Aenobarbus*] Latin, 'bronze-bearded'.

287. *six and thirty*] shillings, as also in l. 289.

five and twenty. Pray, sir, will you present and accommodate it unto the gentleman? For mine own part, I    290
am a mere stranger to his humour; besides, I have some
business invites me hence with Master Asinius Lupus,
the tribune.
*Tucca.* Well, go thy ways, pursue thy projects, let me alone
with this design. My poetaster shall make thee a play, and   295
thou shalt be a man of good parts in it. But stay, let me
see. Do not bring your Aesop, your politician, unless you
can ram up his mouth with cloves: the slave smells ranker
than some sixteen dung hills, and is seventeen times more
rotten. Marry, you may bring Frisker, my zany; he's a     300
good skipping swaggerer. And your fat fool there, my
Mango, bring him too, but let him not beg rapiers nor
scarfs in his over-familiar playing face, nor roar out his

297. Aesop] *Subst. F;* Father *Æsope Q.*     300. Frisker] *Subst. F; Friskin Q.*

289–90. *accommodate*] present, furnish; cf. *EMI* I.iv.126; condemned as a
'perfumed term' by Hoskyns (p. 121), in a passage J. copied into *Disc.*,
changing 'accommodate' to '*Accommodation*' (2275); cf. King, pp. 68, 167.
292. *invites*] an affected usage: cf. *CR* I.iii.44, I.iv.165; Marston, *Pigmalion* 214 (King, p. 168).
295. *design*] the plan for Crispinus to write a play.
296. *of good parts*] of high abilities, as in *EMI* (Q) III.iv.191–2, 'a gentleman . . . of very excellent good partes', but punning on the actor's 'good
part'.
297. *Aesop*] the greatest Roman tragic actor, contemporary of Roscius;
both were friends of Cicero (*Q. Fr.* I.2). J. praises him in *Ep.* LXXXIX, 'To
Edward Allen.'
*your politician*] not in the modern sense, but as *H&S* suggest a 'factotum,
who represented the company and managed their outside business'.
300. *my zany*] technically a clown's stooge, but sometimes used vaguely to
mean a buffoon; there is no reason to suppose, as *H&S* do, that Tucca is
claiming that Frisker is copying him as the master clown. 'My' is used
patronisingly as it is in 'my Mango' (ll. 301–2).
302. *Mango*] See note to 'mangonising', l. 277; the 'fat fool' sells his own
flesh, but there is also the suggestion of pimping.
302–7. *but . . . so*] Cf. *Ham.* III.ii.38–45, and the ten lines on 'the fool'
added to the 'bad' *Hamlet* quarto of 1603 (quoted in Arden *Ham.* ed.
Jenkins, p. 499). For the relationship betweem *Ham.* and *Poetaster*, see p.
36, n. 74.
302–3. *rapiers . . . scarfs*] both were associated with military officers (see
III.iv.271n); this may have been a successful role, or 'Mango' may have
parodied a 'captain' as a party-piece.
303–5. *nor . . . dry*] For the suggestion of a possible echo of *Tw.N*, see p.
38.

barren bold jests with a tormenting laughter, between
drunk and dry. Do you hear, stiff-toe? Give him warning,    305
admonition, to forsake his saucy, glavering grace and his
goggle eye; it does not become him, sirrah, tell him so. I
have stood up and defended you, I, to gent'men, when
you have been said to prey upon puisnes and honest
citizens for socks or buskins, or when they ha' called you    310
usurers or brokers, or said you were able to help to a
piece of flesh—I have sworn I did not think so. Nor that
you were the common retreats for punks decayed i' their
practice. I cannot believe it of you——

*Histrio.* 'Thank you, captain; Jupiter and the rest of the gods    315
confine your modern delights, without disgust!

> [*He makes as if to leave.*]

*Tucca.* Stay, thou shalt see the Moor ere thou goest——

> [*Enter* DEMETRIUS.]

What's he with the half arms there that salutes us out of
his cloak like a motion, ha?

*Histrio.* O sir, his doublet's a little decayed; he is otherwise a    320

---

305. stiff-toe] *Subst. F;* Rascall *Q.*     307–14. I have . . . you——] *F; not in*
*Q.*     309. puisnes] *G;* pu'nees *F.*     315. 'Thank you] *F;* Yes *Q.*     316.1.
S.D.] *This ed.*     317.1. S.D.] *Subst. G.*     320. otherwise] *Q, F;* other-
wayes *F2.*

---

305. *stiff-toe*] See III.iv.176n.
306. *glavering*] deceitful, flattering. *H&S* note Marston's use in *Scourge* I,
137, and *WYW* (Wood, II, 259).
309. *puisnes*] novices, particularly in the legal profession; cf. Hall, *The
Kings Prophecy* (*Poems*, p. 112): 'my puis-nè Muse'.
311–12. *able . . . flesh*] i.e. act as procurers.
316. *confine . . . disgust*] perhaps parodying *Tw.N* I.iii.8–9: 'you must
confine yourself within the modest limits of order.' See p. 37. Here it seems
to mean 'restrict your modish (?sexual) pleasures without vexation'.
318. *half arms*] with short sleeves (*OED* s.v. 'half' II n), perhaps as
Dekker interprets it in *S-M* I.ii.325 meaning 'out at elboes'.
319. *motion*] puppet, used contemptuously of a person (*OED*, 13b). Here
the more apposite since Demetrius' cloak makes his salute seem puppet-like.
320. *his . . . decayed*] Cf. *S-M* I.ii.322–6, quoted above III.i.67–9n.
*doublet's*] The doublet was a tight-fitting, jacket-like garment, which
varied considerably through the period; it was worn over a shirt, and was
attached to the upper hose by laces (points). A cloak (l. 319 above) or jerkin
was usually worn over it.

very simple, honest fellow, sir, one Demetrius, a dresser
of plays about the town here. We have hired him to abuse
Horace, and bring him in in a play with all his gallants, as
Tibullus, Maecenas, Cornelius Gallus and the rest.

*Tucca.* And why so, stinkard?                                                    325

*Histrio.* O, it will get us a huge deal of money, captain, and
we have need on't, for this winter has made us all poorer
than so many starved snakes. Nobody comes at us, not a
gentleman nor a——

*Tucca.* But you know nothing by him, do you, to make a        330
play of?

*Histrio.* Faith, not much, captain: but our author will devise
that, that shall serve in some sort.

*Tucca.* Why, my Parnassus here shall help him, if thou wilt.
Can thy author do it impudently enough?                                           335

---

326. captain] *In parentheses in Q, F.*      333. that . . . sort.] *F;* inough: *Q*
*with space perhaps indicating an omission.*

321. *dresser*] puns on 'decker'; Dekker was a prolific collaborator: in 1600,
he had been part or sole author of seven plays for the Admiral's Men. He was
also occasionally paid by Henslowe to alter old plays: see e.g. *Diary*, p. 187.
Cf. V.iii.212.

322–4. *We . . . rest*] though most of Dekker's work was for the Admiral's
Men, he was a freelance; the title-page of *S-M* says it was played by both
the Chamberlain's Men and 'the Children of Paules', the order probably
indicating that the Chamberlain's men had priority. J. had evidently heard
that Dekker had been commissioned by the Chamberlain's Men, and claims
(Ind. 14–15) that he wrote *Poetaster* in fifteen weeks to anticipate the attack.
This description shows he knew at this stage that he was to be 'brought in' as
Horace, but did not know the rest of Dekker's plot, which he clearly
expected (not unreasonably) to be set in Rome. In fact 'all his gallants' never
appear in *S-M*. See also IV.vii.27–8n, V.iii.296n.

326–9.] See p. 28. Cf. 'Apol. Dial.' 135–6, and *Ham.* II.ii.329–44.

330. *by*] about; cf. *All's W* V.ii.237: 'By him and by this woman here
what know you?' and *Ado* V.i.316.

334. *Parnassus*] meaning 'poet', an example of Tucca's antonomasia; cf.
III.iv.376, and 'Callimachus' (I.ii.204).

334–5.] If Marston did help Dekker with *S-M* his part must have been
small: it is attributed solely to Dekker on the title-page, and 'I' governs all of
the address 'To the World'. J., however, refers to 'the untrussers' in 'Apol.
Dial.', l. 141 as if holding both responsible for the play, and in IV.vii.29–30
makes Crispinus quibble about 'innocence' as if he had some hand in it.
Marston may have been a 'producer' or adaptor for the Paul's performances
rather than co-author.

*Histrio.* O I warrant you, captain, and spitefully enough too.
He has one of the most overflowing, rank wits in Rome.
He will slander any man that breathes if he disgust him.
*Tucca.* I'll know the poor, egregious, nitty rascal; and he have
these commendable qualities, I'll cherish him.                    340
                            [DEMETRIUS *approaches.*]
Stay, here comes the tartar. I'll make a gathering for him,
I, a purse, and put the poor slave in fresh rags. Tell him
so to comfort him.
        *The boy comes in on* MINOS' *shoulders, who stalks,*
                                            *as he acts.*
    Well said, boy.
2 *Pyrgus. Where art thou, boy? Where is Calipolis?*              345
    *Fight, earthquakes, in the entrails of the earth,*
    *And eastern whirlwinds in the hellish shades;*
    *Some foul contagion of th' infected heavens*
    *Blast all the trees, and in their cursèd tops*
    *The dismal night-raven and tragic owl*                       350
    *Breed and become forerunners of my fall.*
*Tucca.* [*To Histrio*] Well, now fare thee well, my honest
    penny-biter. Commend me to seven shares and a half,

---

337. rank] *F;* villanous *Q.*      340. these] *F;* such *Q.*      340.1. S.D.] *This
ed.; Demetrius comes forward. G, after 343.*      341. Stay . . . tartar] *This ed.;*
stay; here comes the *Tartar Q;* (stay, here comes the *Tartar) F.*      343.1–2.
S.D.] *F in margin; not in Q.*

---

337–8. *He . . . him*] anticipating *S-M,* rather than any surviving work of
Dekker's up to that point.
338. *disgust*] dislike, used transitively, as in III.iv.34.
339. *egregious*] outstanding, used ironically: hence gross, outrageous.
*and*] if.
341. *tartar*] cant word for a thief or beggar.
*gathering*] collection.
344. *well said*] well done; cf. II.i.19n (so also l. 371 below).
345–51.] from *The Battle of Alcazar,* II.3.468–78, omitting 469–71 (ed.
Yoklavich, *Dramatic Works,* II, 313).
345. Calipolis] wife of Muly Mahomet, 'the Moor' of ll. 270, 317 above.
353. *penny-biter*] 'one who bites a (silver) penny to test if it is genuine'
(*H&S*), here when collecting the gate at the theatre.
*seven . . . half*] possibly Burbage, who was the largest shareholder in the
Chamberlain's Men, with two and a half shares. The phrase is repeated
by ?Joseph Beaumont in the Preface to Crashaw's *Steps to the Temple* (1646);
see *Poems,* ed. L.C. Martin (Oxford, 2nd ed., 1957), p. 75. Mallory, and

and remember tomorrow. If you lack a service, you shall
play in my name, rascals, but you shall buy your own          355
cloth, and I'll ha' two shares for my countenance. Let thy
author stay with me.

                                      [*Exit* HISTRIO.]

*Demetrius.* Yes, sir.

*Tucca.* 'Twas well done, little Minos, thou didst stalk well.
Forgive me that I said thou stunk'st, Minos; 'twas the          360
savour of a poet I met sweating in the street hangs yet in
my nostrils.

*Crispinus.* Who, Horace?

*Tucca.* Ay, he, dost thou know him?

*Crispinus.* O he forsook me most barbarously, I protest.          365

*Tucca.* Hang him, fusty satyr, he smells all goat; he carries a
ram under his arm-holes, the slave. I am the worse when
I see him. [*Aside to Crispinus*] Did not Minos impart?

*Crispinus.* [*Aside to Tucca*] Yes, here are twenty drachmas he
did convey.          370

*Tucca.* [*Aside to Crispinus*] Well said; keep 'em, we'll share
anon. [*To Minos*] Come, little Minos.

---

354. tomorrow.] *This ed.;* to / morrow: *Q;* to morrow—*F.*     357.1. S.D.]
*G.*     366. satyr] *G; Satyre Q, F Subst.*     368. S.D.] *G.*     369. here are]
*F;* here's *Q.*

---

Chambers (*ES*, I, 353), note the similar phrase in *Ratseis Ghost*, 'Sir Simon
Two Shares and a Halfe'; cf. Honigmann, *Shakespeare's Impact*, pp. 287–8.

    354–5. *service . . . name*] Actors had to have a noble patron to avoid the
charge of vagabondage (see I.ii.54n).

    356. *cloth*] possibly livery of their patron, but more likely costume,
bought by the company, not the patron.

    *countenance*] patronage.

    359. *stalk*] See above, 343.1 S.D.

    366. *fusty . . . goat*] Cf. Hor. *Sat.* I.ii.27, 'Gargonius [smells like] a goat'.
The spelling *satyr* emphasises the supposed origins of satire in the Greek satyr
plays; see e.g. Scaliger, *Poetices* (1561), p. 19; just after *Poetaster*, Isaac
Casaubon traced the true etymology to *satura* (a mixture, a mixed dish) in *De
satyrica graecorum poesi et romanorum satira libri duo* (Paris, 1605), but this was
not immediately accepted by any means. See also App. 1, pp. 287–8.

    366–7. *carries . . . arm-holes*] Cf. Catullus LXIX, 5–6: 'what hurts you is a
slander that says you have the rank goat under your armpits' and Plautus
*Pseudolus*: 'goaty, by the smell of his armpits' (*Pot of Gold and Other Plays*),
trans. E. F. Watling (Harmondsworth, 1965), p. 246.

    369. *drachmas*] Tucca had asked for twenty sesterces in III.iv.184–5,
where Q had drachmas; J. failed to revise this second passage.

*Crispinus.* Faith, captain, I'll be bold to show you a mistress
    of mine, a jeweller's wife, a gallant, as we go along.
*Tucca.* There spoke my genius. Minos, some of thy eringoes,    375
    little Minos, send. [*To Crispinus*] Come hither, Parnassus;
    I must ha' thee familiar with my little locust here, 'tis
    a good vermin they say. See, here's Horace and old
    Trebatius, the great lawyer, in his company. Let's avoid
    him now, he is too well seconded.         [*Exeunt.*]    380


                    ACT III   SCENE V

            [*Enter*] HORACE [*and*] TREBATIUS.

*Horace.* There are, to whom I seem excessive sour,
    And past a satire's law t' extend my power:
    Others that think whatever I have writ
    Wants pith and matter to eternise it,
    And that they could in one day's light disclose          5
    A thousand verses such as I compose.


---

378.] *After* say. *Exeunt.* / *Finis Actus tertij. Q*    378–80. See . . .
seconded.] *F; not in Q.*    380. S.D.] *G.*    III.v.] *F; not in Q; G as an
appendix with title* HORACE *and* TREBATIUS. A Dialogue.    1.]
Hor.Sat.I.li.2. *Marginal note in F.*    2. satire's] *G; satyres F.*

---

374. *gallant*] a fashionable beauty (*OED*, 1b).
375. *genius*] tutelary spirit, but also appetite (*OED*, 1 and 3; the modern
meaning of exalted original powers of mind had not yet developed). It is a
favourite word of Marston's: see V.iii.269n.
376. *Parnassus*] poet: cf. III.iv.334n.
III.v. A very literary scene, inserted in *F*, and probably not intended for
the stage (see App. 1, p. 287). J. makes two significant expansions in what is
otherwise a free translation of Hor. *Sat.* II.i; in l. 100, the simple 'scribam'
becomes 'I will write satires still', and the last four lines of Hor. become ten
(130–40), emphasising the probity and privilege of the Horatian satirist.
1. *There . . . whom*] a literal version of Hor.'s blunt opening, 'Sunt quibus',
'there are [those] to whom'.
2. *satire's*] See III.iv.366n; here, referring to the genre. Hor. does not call
himself a satyr, though Renaissance texts retained the spelling *Satyra* here.
4. *pith*] vigour, energy (*OED*, 5b).
5–6.] J. probably welcomed accusations of slowness of composition
(belied by *Poetaster's* fifteen weeks and *Volp.*'s five weeks) because such
accusations were also made against Hor., who condemns those who are 'too
lazy to put up with the trouble of writing—of writing correctly, I mean; for
as to quantity, I let that pass. See, Crispinus challenges me at long odds:

What shall I do, Trebatius? Say.
*Trebatius.*                                    Surcease.
*Horace.* And shall my Muse admit no more increase?
*Trebatius.* So I advise.
*Horace.*                    An ill death let me die
    If 'twere not best; but sleep avoids mine eye,          10
    And I use these lest nights should tedious seem.
*Trebatius.* Rather contend to sleep, and live like them
    That holding golden sleep in special price,
    Rubbed with sweet oils, swim silver Tiber thrice,
    And every e'en with neat wine steepèd be.               15
    Or, if such love of writing ravish thee,
    Then dare to sing unconquered Caesar's deeds,
    Who cheers such actions with abundant meeds.
*Horace.* That, father, I desire; but when I try
    I feel defects in every faculty;                         20
    Nor is't a labour fit for every pen
    To paint the horrid troops of armèd men,
    The lances burst in Gallia's slaughtered forces,
    Or wounded Parthians tumbled from their horses:
    Great Caesar's wars cannot be fought with words.        25
*Trebatius.* Yet what his virtue in his peace affords,

---

15. e'en] *This ed.;* eu'en *F.*

"Take your tablets, please . . . let us see which can write the most." The gods
be praised for fashioning me of meagre wit and lowly spirit, of rare and
scanty speech!' (*Sat.* I.iv.12–18).
    11. *these*] verses; this line is not in Hor., who simply says he cannot sleep
('verum nequeo dormire', l. 7).
    13–14. *golden . . . silver*] *H&S* reasonably object to the awkward juxta-
position of the two epithets as simply 'an Elizabethan mannerism'. Neither is
in Hor.
    14. *thrice*] inadvisable, since the swimmer finishes on the side opposite
that on which he left his toga; Hor. may have used it as a sacred number.
    15. *e'en*] *F*'s 'eu'en' is an example of J.'s 'metrical apostrophe', indicating
that the word is stressed as if one syllable; cf. 'The'attentive' (*F*), l. 33
below.
    18. *meeds*] rewards.
    23–4.] Augustus had campaigned in Gaul (Gallia) at various times be-
tween 39 and 31 BC, but he never had to fight any battles against the
Parthians, who asked him for protection.
    23. *burst*] broken.

His fortitude and justice, thou canst show,
As wise Lucilius honoured Scipio.
*Horace.* Of that my powers shall suffer no neglect,
When such slight labours may aspire respect;                    30
But if I watch not a most chosen time,
The humble words of Flaccus cannot climb
Th' attentive ear of Caesar. Nor must I
With less observance shun gross flattery,
For he, reposèd safe in his own merit,                          35
Spurns back the glozes of a fawning spirit.
*Trebatius.* But how much better would such accents sound,
Than with a sad and serious verse to wound
Pantolabus, railing in his saucy jests,
Or Nomentanus, spent in riotous feasts?                         40
In satires each man, though untouched, complains
As he were hurt, and hates such biting strains.
*Horace.* What shall I do? Milonius shakes his heels
In ceaseless dances when his brain once feels
The stirring fervour of the wine ascend,                        45
And that his eyes false number apprehend.
Castor his horse, Pollux loves handy-fights:
A thousand heads, a thousand choice delights.

33. Th'] *G;* The' *F.*     41–2.] *Gnomic pointing in F.*     41. satires] *G;*
satyres *F.*     though untouched] *In parentheses in F.*     48. A thousand] *G;*
Thousand *F.*

---

28. *Lucilius*] Gaius Lucilius, seen by Hor. as the father of Roman satire:
see *Sat.* I.iv.6–13, I.x.50–71, and II.i.28–34, 62–74. His work survives only
in fragments, but Book VI was addressed to his patron, Scipio Aemilianus,
the younger Scipio Africanus.

32. *Flaccus*] The *cognomen* of Hor.

33. *Th' attentive*] See above, l. 15n.

36. *glozes*] flatteries.

39. *Pantolabus*] See III.iv.161n.

40. *Nomentanus*] a prodigal spender, coupled with Pantolabus in *Sat.*
I.i.101–2 and I.viii.11. 'Spent' is ambiguous, combining 'exhausted' with
translation of Hor.'s 'nepotem', prodigal.

41–2.] Hor.'s line 23, quoted in *Volp.* Epistle, l. 79.

43–5.] See III.i.171–2n. Milonius is unidentifed.

46. *his . . . apprehend*] the wine makes him see double; in Hor. 'the lights
begin to seem double' ('accessit numerus lucernis').

47.] Based on *Iliad* III, 237: 'Kastor, breaker of horses, and the strong
boxer, Polydeukes [Pollux]'.

*handy-fights*] hand to hand fights (*OED*, 5).

My pleasure is in feet my words to close,
As, both our better, old Lucilius does:            50
He, as his trusty friends, his books did trust
With all his secrets; nor in things unjust,
Or actions lawful, ran to other men.
So that the old man's life described was seen
As in a votive table in his lines:            55
And to his steps my genius inclines,
Lucanian or Apulian, I not whether,
For the Venusian colony ploughs either,
Sent thither when the Sabines were forced thence
(As old fame sings) to give the place defence            60
'Gainst such as, seeing it empty, might make road
Upon the empire, or there fix abode:
Whether the Apulian borderer it were,
Or the Lucanian violence they fear.
But this my style no living man shall touch,            65
If first I be not forced by base reproach;
But like a sheathèd sword it shall defend
My innocent life. For why should I contend
To draw it out, when no malicious thief

---

65. style] *G;* stile *F.*

49. *in feet*] of poetry, translating 'pedibus'.
52. *in things unjust*] not necessarily translating 'si male gesserat', 'if he conducted [matters] badly', as *H&S* suggest; the accepted reading is 'si male cesserat', 'if things had gone badly'. Contemporary editions offered both (Bond has 'cesserat', Heinsius 'gesserat'), and J.'s phrase, perhaps intentionally, is loose enough to cover either.
55. *votive table*] Bond annotates: 'a painted tablet (*tabula*) hung in the temple by shipwrecked sailors (*naufragis*) as a votive offering'. Cf. Hor. *Odes* I.v.12; Virgil *Aeneid* XII, 768.
56. *genius*] particular talent or inclination.
56–64.] Hor. was born in Venusia, on the borders of Lucania and Apulia, a town colonised by the Romans as a stronghold in the Samnite (Sabine) Wars of 449 BC or 290 BC. His point is that he is naturally a defender, not an aggressor.
57. *not*] know not (from 'ne wot').
61. *road*] inroad, attack: *H&S* cite *H5* I.ii.138, 'the Scot, who will make road upon us'.
65. *style*] Latin *stilus*, both a dagger and a pen; cf. 'Apol. Dial.', l. 84 (so *H&S*).
68. *contend*] struggle.

Robs my good name, the treasure of my life?                    70
O Jupiter, let it with rust be eaten
Before it touch, or insolently threaten
The life of any with the least disease,
So much I love and woo a general peace.
But he that wrongs me, better, I proclaim,                      75
He never had assayed to touch my fame,
For he shall weep, and walk with every tongue
Throughout the city, infamously sung.
Servius the praetor threats the laws and urn
If any at his deeds repine or spurn.                            80
The witch Canidia, that Albucius got,
Denounceth witchcraft where she loveth not.
Thurius the judge doth thunder worlds of ill

75–6. better . . . fame] *F2; in parentheses in* F.     78. sung] *F2;* song *F.*
81. Albucius] *Subst.* F; ALBVTIVS *F2.*

---

70. *my . . . life*] proverbial, not in Hor.; cf. Dent, N22, 'a good name is
better than riches'. *H&S* say J. 'anticipates' *Oth.* III.iii.155–6, but this scene
may have been written after *Oth.*, which is usually dated around 1604.

73. *disease*] uneasiness.

76. *assayed*] ventured (*OED, v.* 17c).

77–8.] Hor. simply says that his name will be sung through the whole city
('tota cantabitur urbe').

79. *Servius*] Heinsius, and modern editors, read 'Cervius', Bond, perhaps
following Lambinus, 'Servius', an informer mentioned by Cicero (*Q. Fr.*
ii.13). J. makes him a *praetor* (not in Hor.) because of the reference to the
law. Bond notes: 'Quaesitor vel accusator', meaning a judicial examiner.

*threats*] threatens.

*urn*] the urn into which the *iudices* put their tablets in criminal trials (as in
V.iii.336).

80. *spurn*] kick at, object strongly to (*OED,* 3); cf. *R3* I.iv.197–8: 'Will
you then / Spurn at his edict, and fulfil a man's?'

81–2.] The usual interpretation is that Canidia threatens to use poison
('venenum') against her enemies, but J. translates 'venenum' by the rare
figurative meaning of 'evil, virulence', hence 'witchcraft', perhaps because it
is used thus by Hor. in *Sat.* I.vii.1. See Lewis and Short, s.v. 'venenum'
II.A.1b.

81. *Canidia*] mentioned several times by Hor., said by the scholiasts to be
Gratidia, a perfume seller, but always in Hor. a witch.

*Albucius*] not identified, except as a poisoner; J.'s reading that Canidia was
his daughter is a possible one adopted by Renaissance editors (Bond glosses
the passage thus), but Hor. probably meant that the poison, not Canidia,
belonged to Albucius.

83. *Thurius*] Bond says 'A corrupt and venal judge' ('Iudex nummarius &
venalis'), but not clearly identified.

To such as strive with his judicial will.
All men affright their foes in what they may,                    85
Nature commands it, and men must obey.
Observe with me: the wolf his tooth doth use,
The bull his horn, and who doth this infuse
But nature? There's luxurious Scaeva: trust
His long-lived mother with him, his so just                      90
And scrupulous right hand no mischief will;
No more than with his heel a wolf will kill,
Or ox with jaw. Marry, let him alone
With tempered poison to remove the crone.
    But briefly: if to age I destined be,                        95
Or that quick death's black wings environ me,
If rich or poor, at Rome, or fate command
I shall be banished to some other land
What hue soever my whole state shall bear,
I will write satires still, in spite of fear.                    100
*Trebatius.* Horace, I fear thou draw'st no lasting breath,
    And that some great man's friend will be thy death.
*Horace.* What! When the man that first did satirise
    Durst pull the skin over the ears of vice,

---

85–6.] *Gnomic pointing in* F.   87. the] *This ed.;* 'The F.   88–9.]
*Gnomic pointing in* F.   100. satires] *G; satyres* F.   103. satirise] *Subst. G;
satyrise* F.

---

89. *Scaeva*] unknown; 'scaeva' meant left-handed, and therefore sinister,
unfavourable.
    90–1. *just . . . hand*] translating Hor.'s 'pia dextera' (*Sat.* II.i.54); the
right hand (set by Hor. against the implications of 'Scaeva') stood for fidelity,
courage or good fortune, as in Hor. *Epist.* I.vii.94. J.'s own first name had
similar connotations in Hebrew: see *Ep.* XLV.1, where his son, also
Benjamin, is 'child of my right hand, and joy'.
    99. *hue . . . state*] translating 'vitae . . . color', where *color* means 'outward
appearance' or 'state' as well as 'hue' (Lewis and Short, II.A).
    102. *will . . . death*] Hor. says 'frigore te feriat', 'will strike [or kill] you
with a frost', which Bond glosses 'will cause your death'.
    103. *man . . . satirise*] i.e. Lucilius.
    104. *pull . . . vice*] In Hor., to expose any particular vice by stripping off
its outer skin of respectability, but *H&S* note that in 1601 J.'s phrase implied
dismissal from a job; cf. *C is A* I.vii.48 and Dekker, *S-M* III.i.28–39:
'tesirous to have his blew coate pul'd over his eares', and V.ii.227–9: 'rather
then thus to be netled, Ile ha my Satyres coate pull'd over mine eares, and be
turn'd out a the nine Muses Service.' See Dent, C474.

And make who stood in outward fashion clear                    105
Give place, as foul within, shall I forbear?
Did Laelius, or the man so great with fame
That from sacked Carthage fetched his worthy name,
Storm, that Lucilius did Metellus pierce,
Or bury Lupus quick in famous verse?                    110
Rulers and subjects by whole tribes he checked,
But virtue and her friends did still protect;
And when from sight, or from the judgement seat,
The virtuous Scipio and wise Laelius met
Unbraced, with him in all light sports they shared,                    115
Till their most frugal suppers were prepared.
Whate'er I am, though both for wealth and wit
Beneath Lucilius I am pleased to sit,
Yet envy (spite of her empoisoned breast)
Shall say I lived in grace here with the best,                    120

---

105. *make who*] 'make [those] who'.

107. *Laelius*] close friend of Scipio Aemilianus, and central figure in Cicero's *Amic.*

107–8. *man . . . name*] Scipio Aemilianus Africanus took Carthage in 146 BC.

109. *Metellus*] Q. Caecilius Metellus Macedonicus, a political opponent of Scipio Aemilianus, but not a personal enemy, or these lines would have no point.

*pierce*] pronounced 'perse' (*H&S*).

110. *Lupus*] possibly L. Cornelius Lentulus Lupus, consul in 156 BC. *quick*] alive.

*famous*] 'famosis' in Hor. probably means 'defamatory' (Lewis and Short, II, B); cf. *Epist.* I.xix.31, 'famoso carmine'.

111. *by . . . tribes*] translating 'populumque tributim', people throughout all tribes (classes); J. uses 'tribes' to mean the Roman *tribus* in *Cat.* II.i.97: 'unto all the *tribes*'.

113. *judgement seat*] translating 'scena', 'the public stage', glossed by Bond as 'a populi conspectu', 'away from the gaze of the people'. J. probably interpreted it as a court since one that was both a stage for the formal, public appearances of such men, and a 'stage' for rhetoric.

115. *Unbraced*] Latin 'discincti', literally 'in loose garments', hence unrestrained, relaxed.

116. *frugal suppers*] Hor. has 'holus', vegetables.

117–18. *though . . . sit*] 'though I am happy to acknowledge that I am inferior to Lucilius both in wealth and ability.'

119. *spite of*] (in) spite of.

And seeking in weak trash to make her wound,
Shall find me solid, and her teeth unsound,
'Less learn'd Trebatius' censure disagree.
*Trebatius.*  No, Horace, I of force must yield to thee;
Only take heed as being advised by me,                    125
Lest thou incur some danger: better pause
Than rue thy ignorance of the sacred laws.
There's justice, and great action may be sued
'Gainst such as wrong men's fames with verses lewd.
*Horace.*  Ay, with lewd verses, such as libels be,        130
And aimed at persons of good quality.
I reverence and adore that just decree;
But if they shall be sharp yet modest rhymes,
That spare men's persons and but tax their crimes,
Such shall in open court find current pass,               135
Were Caesar judge, and with the maker's grace.
*Trebatius.*  Nay, I'll add more: if thou thyself, being clear,
Shalt tax in person a man fit to bear
Shame and reproach, his suit shall quickly be
Dissolved in laughter, and thou thence set free. [*Exeunt.*]  140

140. set] *G;* sit *F.*

---

121. *trash*] apparently in the sense of soft flesh, but not in *OED* unless under 1d, an example from 1550 for which no definition can be given.

124. *of force*] under compulsion; cf. 'perforce'.

127. *sacred laws*] the Roman Twelve Tables prescribed capital punishment for writing which intended to bring infamy on another: later the so-called *lex Remmia* prescribed branding: see V.iii.168n, 209.

129. *verses lewd*] translating 'mala . . . carmina', which Bond glosses 'Carmina maledica', slanderous or abusive verses.

130–40.] A significant expansion of the original, which reads: 'To be sure, in case of ill verses. But what if a man compose good verses, and Caesar's judgement approve? If he has barked at someone who deserves abuse, himself all blameless? The case will be dismissed with a laugh. You will get off scot-free' (ll. 83–6). See also pp. 18–19.

134.] Martial X.xxxiii.10: 'to spare the person, to denounce the vice', also quoted in 'Apol. Dial.', l. 72, and *SW*, 2nd Prol. 4.

# Act IV

ACT IV  SCENE i

*[Enter]* CHLOE, CYTHERIS *[and* Maids].

*Chloe.* But, sweet lady, say, am I well enough attired for the court, in sadness?

*Cytheris.* Well enough? Excellent well, sweet Mistress Chloe; this straight bodied city attire, I can tell you, will stir a courtier's blood more than the finest loose sacks the ladies use to be put in. And then you are as well jewelled as any of them, your ruff and linen about you is much more pure than theirs, and for your beauty, I can tell you there's many of them would defy the painter if they could change with you. Marry, the worst is you must look to be envied, and endure a few court frumps for it.

*Chloe.* O Jove, madam, I shall buy them too cheap! *[To Maids]* Give me my muff, and my dog there. *[To Cytheris]* And will the ladies be anything familiar with me, think you?

*Cytheris.* O Juno! Why, you shall see 'em flock about you with

5

10

15

IV.i.0.1.] *A Room in Albius's House. Enter* CHLOE, CYTHERIS, *and Attendants.* G.    4. I . . . you] *In parentheses in Q, F.*    12. Jove,] *Subst. F;* God! *Q.*    cheap!] *F;* cheape: *Q*    16. Juno] *Subst. F; Hercules Q.*

IV.i.1. *sweet*] Chloe's first use of the affected epithet; cf. I.iii.35n.
2. *in sadness*] in earnest (*OED*, 2b); cf. III.iv.94n, II.i.25n, *CR* IV.ii.36 and *Rom.* I.i.199–204.
4. *straight . . . attire*] Cf. II.i.64–6n.
5. *loose sacks*] Court dress for women was often loose above the waist, especially in masqueing costumes; *H&S* note *Shr.* IV.iii.134–44: 'a loose-bodied gown . . . sleeves curiously cut', but the real significance of this comparison may be that both uses of 'loose' point to sexual looseness as well as to fashion: cf. Marston, *Scourge*, VII, 172–3: 'Her mask, her vizard, her loose-hanging gown / For her loose-lying body'.
9. *defy the painter*] by allowing themselves to be painted as they are.
11. *frumps*] sneers, snubs.
13. *muff*] In *CR* Moria 'always wears a muff' (II.ii.46–7).
*dog*] a fashionable lapdog.
16. *Juno*] changed from *Q* as more appropriate for a woman.

171

their puff wings, and ask you where you bought your
lawn, and what you paid for it, who starches you, and
entreat you to help 'em to some pure laundresses out of
the city.                                                                                     20

*Chloe.* O Cupid! [*To Maids*] Give me my fan, and my mask
too. [*To Cytheris*] And will the lords and the poets there
use one well too, lady?

*Cytheris.* Doubt not of that: you shall have kisses from them
go pit-pat, pit-pat, pit-pat upon your lips as thick as          25
stones out of slings at the assault of a city. And then your
ears will be so furred with the breath of their compli-
ments that you cannot catch cold of your head, if you
would, in three winters after.

*Chloe.* Thank you, sweet lady. O heaven! And how must one     30
behave herself amongst 'em? You know all.

*Cytheris.* Faith, impudently enough, Mistress Chloe, and well
enough. Carry not too much under thought betwixt
yourself and them; nor your city mannerly word
'forsooth', use it not too often in any case, but plain 'Ay,   35
madam' and 'No, madam'. Nor never say 'Your lordship'
nor 'Your honour', but 'You' and 'You, my lord' and 'My
lady'. The other they count too simple and minsitive.
And though they desire to kiss heaven with their titles,
yet they will count them fools that give them too humbly.       40

---

19. laundresses] *G;* Landresses *Q, F Subst.*     28–9. if . . . would] *In paren-*
*theses  in  Q,  F.*     35. 'forsooth'] *Nicholson;  (forsooth) Q;  Subst.*
*F.*     35–6. 'Ay, madam'] *Nicholson; I, Madam Q; not italicised in F: so also*
*Subst. 36–8:* 'No, madam'; 'Your lordship'; 'Your honour'; 'You' and 'You;*
*my lord' and 'My lady'.*

---

17. *puff wings*] stiffened lawn or other material worn on the shoulders and
sleeves, but the flocking about suggests harpies.

18. *lawn*] fine linen.

19. *pure laundresses*] *H&S* note 'the pure linen of the city wives was
famous'; see *EH* I.ii.20. *G* suggests 'a hit at the Puritans, many of whom
followed the business of tire-women, clear-starchers, feather-makers, &c.'.

21. *fan . . . mask*] appurtenances of a lady; *H&S* cite *S-M* II.i.16, *BF*
V.iv.44, *S of N* 1st Intermean, 56.

25–6. *thick . . . city*] echoing Ovid *Tristia* I.ii.47–8: 'no lighter blow falls
upon her planks from the billows than the heavy pounding of the balista
upon a wall.'

33. *under thought*] sense of inferiority.

34–5. *city . . . 'forsooth'*] See II.i.84n.

38. *minsitive*] probably mincing, affected: see *OED* s.v. minceative.

*Chloe.* O, intolerable, Jupiter! By my troth, lady, I would not
for a world, but you had lain in my house; and i' faith
you shall not pay a farthing for your board, nor your
chambers.

*Cytheris.* O sweet Mistress Chloe!                                   45

*Chloe.* I' faith you shall not, lady; nay, good lady, do not offer
it.

## Act IV  Scene ii

[*Enter to them*] CORNELIUS GALLUS [*and*] TIBULLUS.

*Gallus.* Come, where be these ladies? By your leave bright
stars, this gentleman and I are come to man you to court,
where your late kind entertainment is now to be requited
with a heavenly banquet.

*Cytheris.* A heavenly banquet, Gallus?                                5

*Gallus.* No less, my dear Cytheris.

*Tibullus.* That were not strange lady, if the epithet were only
given for the company invited thither, yourself and this
fair gentlewoman.

*Chloe.* Are we invited to court, sir?                                 10

*Tibullus.* You are, lady, by the great princess Julia, who longs
to greet you with any favours that may worthily make you
an often courtier.

*Chloe.* In sincerity, I thank her, sir. You have a coach, ha' you
not?                                                                   15

*Tibullus.* The princess hath sent her own, lady.

*Chloe.* O Venus, that's well! I do long to ride in a coach most
vehemently.

---

42. lain] *G;* lyen *Q, F.*    IV.ii.0.1.] *Enter* GALLUS *and* TIBULLUS. *G,
continuing the scene.*    1. *Gallus.] This ed.; Cor. Gallus. Q; no s.p. in F, but
follows Q in printing* COR. GALL. *subsequently throughout this scene.*    17.
O . . . well!] *This ed.; O Venus! that's well: Q, F Subst.*

---

41. *intolerable*] misused by Chloe, who does not disapprove.

41–2. *I . . . house*] i.e. she is glad that she has lodged in her house.

42. *lain*] lodged; 'lyen' is used as past participle by J. in *SW* V.ii.76, *Alc.*
IV.i.46, and (spelt 'lien') in *Volp.* IV.v.81, *BF* V.iv.239–40 (so *H&S*).

IV.ii.1–2. *bright stars*] because they are going to the 'heavenly banquet'.

2. *man*] escort (*OED, v.* 5).

13. *often*] commonly used as an adjective in the seventeenth century.

17. *long . . . coach*] See II.i.150n.

18. *vehemently*] learnt from Crispinus: see II.i.71n.

*Cytheris.* But sweet Gallus pray you resolve me why you give
    that heavenly praise to this earthly banquet?                    20
*Gallus.* Because, Cytheris, it must be celebrated by the
    heavenly powers. All the gods and goddesses will be there,
    to two of which you two must be exalted.
*Chloe.* A pretty fiction in truth.
*Cytheris.* A fiction indeed, Chloe, and fit for the fit of a poet.    25
*Gallus.* Why Cytheris, may not poets, from whose divine
    spirits all the honours of the gods have been deduced,
    entreat so much honour of the gods, to have their divine
    presence at a poetical banquet?
*Cytheris.* Suppose that no fiction: yet where are your abilities to    30
    make us two goddesses at your feast?
*Gallus.* Who knows not, Cytheris, that the sacred breath of a
    true poet can blow any virtuous humanity up to deity?
*Tibullus.* To tell you the female truth, which is the simple
    truth, ladies, and to show that poets, in spite of the world,    35
    are able to deify themselves: at this banquet to which you
    are invited, we intend to assume the figures of the gods,
    and to give our several loves the forms of goddesses. Ovid
    will be Jupiter, the Princess Julia, Juno; Gallus here,
    Apollo; you Cytheris, Pallas; I will be Bacchus, and my    40
    love Plautia, Ceres; and to install you and your husband,

---

21. Cytheris] *In parentheses in Q, F (so also 32).*    26–7. from . . . deduced]
*In parentheses in F.*    30. abilities] *This ed.;* Habilities *Q, F Subst.*    34–5.
which . . . truth] *In parentheses in Q, F.*    35. in . . . world] *In parentheses in
Q, F.*

---

19. *resolve me*] explain to me.

25. *fit . . . poet*] song or canto of a poet; cf. Puttenham, *English Poesie*
I.xxvi: 'This Epithalamie was devided by breaches into three partes to serve
for three severall fittes'.

27. *deduced*] drawn down to earth: poets have been interpreters of the
gods, hence are entitled to represent them at the banquet. Gallus' argument
here and in ll.35–6 conflates the high seriousness of poetry with the flippancy
of the banquet.

30–1.] Cytheris' questions reflect an uneasiness about the poet's relationship to the divine inspirers of poetry that anticipates Caesar's condemnation
in IV.vi.33–7 (see pp. 20–2).

34. *female . . . simple*] This is the only example in *OED*.

35. *in . . . world*] even though the world does not value them highly.

36–43. *at . . . god*] See p. 16; Augustus himself was the organiser of the
historical banquet, and he, not Gallus, played Apollo.

fair Chloe, in honours equal with ours, you shall be a
goddess and your husband a god.

*Chloe.* A god? O my God!

*Tibullus.* A god, but a lame god, lady: for he shall be Vulcan,          45
and you Venus. And this will make our banquet no less
than heavenly.

*Chloe.* In sincerity, it will be sugared. Good Jove, what a
pretty, foolish thing it is to be a poet! [*Aside to Cytheris*]
But hark you, sweet Cytheris, could they not possibly         50
leave out my husband? Methinks a body's husband does
not so well at court. A body's friend or so—but husband,
'tis like your clog to your marmoset for all the world, and
the heavens.

*Cytheris.* Tut, never fear, Chloe, your husband will be left          55

---

44. A god?] *This ed.; A God? Q, Subst. F.*       my God!] *Q;* my god! *F.*       45.
A god,] *G;* A God; *Q;* A God, *uncorr. F;* A God; *corr. F.*       49. S.D.] *This
ed.*       52. court.] *G;* Court; *Q; corr. F;* Court: *uncorr. F.*       so—] *F;* so: *Q.*

---

45. *lame . . . Vulcan*] appropriate to the goldsmith Albius because
Vulcan (Hephaestus), the god of fire, was patron of smiths, and was an
outsider, thrown from heaven by Jupiter (the cause of his lameness). He was
married to Venus, hence also a cuckold.

48. *sugared*] full of sweetness, alluring (*OED*, 2b); cf. *Tim.* IV.iii.259:
'The sug'red game'.

48–9. *what . . . poet*] echoing Marlowe, *Tamburlaine, Part I* (ed.
Cunningham, Revels, Manchester, 1981) II.ii.54: 'And 'tis a pretty toy to be
a poet.'

53. *clog*] block tied to the neck or leg of the marmoset to impede movement. *H&S* quote Selden, *Table Talk*, ed. Reynolds, p. 194: 'You shall see a
monkey sometime that has been playing up and down the garden, at length
leap up to the top of the wall, but his clog hangs a great way below on this
side: the bishop's wife is like that monkey's clog, himself is got up very high,
takes place of temporal barons, but his wife comes a great way behind.'

*marmoset*] at this date, any small monkey; for monkeys as pets, cf. *CR*
II.i.41–2, IV.i.156.

55–7. *husband . . . lady*] Cf. *CR* V.iii.46: 'Husbands are not allow'd here';
Chapman, *Conspiracy of Charles Duke of Byron*, ed. Margeson (1988) II.i.1–4:
'*Henry.* Was he so courted? *Rois.* As a Cittie Dame, / Brought by her jealous
husband to the Court, / Some elder Courtiers entertaining him, / While
others snatch a favour from his wife'; Sir Edward Peyton, *The Divine
Catastrophe of the Stuarts* (1652), p. 47: 'The Masks and Playes at Whitehal
were used only for Incentives to lust: therefore the Courtiers invited the
Citizens wives to these shews, on purpose to defile them in such sort.'

without in the lobby or the great chamber when you shall
be put in i' the closet by this lord and by that lady.
*Chloe.* Nay, then I am certified: he shall go.


ACT IV   SCENE iii

[*Enter to them*] HORACE.

*Gallus.* Horace! Welcome.
*Horace.* Gentlemen, hear you the news?
*Tibullus.* What news, my Quintus?
*Horace.* Our melancholic friend Propertius
    Hath closed himself up in his Cynthia's tomb,                    5
    And will by no entreaties be drawn thence.

[*Enter* ALBIUS *and* CRISPINUS, *followed by* TUCCA *and* DEMETRIUS.]

*Albius.* Nay, good master Crispinus, pray you bring near the
    gentleman.
*Horace.* Crispinus? Hide me, good Gallus. Tibullus, shelter
    me.                                                             10
*Crispinus.* [*To Tucca*] Make your approach, sweet captain.
*Tibullus.* What means this, Horace?
*Horace.* I am surprised again! Farewell.
*Gallus.*                              Stay, Horace.
*Horace.* What, and be tired on by yond vulture! No,
    Phoebus defend me.                              *Exit.*

---

IV.iii.0.1.] *Subst.* G, *continuing the scene.*   6.1. S.D.] *Subst. G.*   12.
*Tibullus*] F; *Tihullus Q.*   15. S.D.] *Q.*

57. *closet*] at Court, a private apartment of the monarch as opposed to the
more public 'great chamber'.
58. *certified*] reassured; cf. *1H6* II.iii.32, 'I go to certify her Talbot's
here'.
    IV.iii.4–5.] See I.iii.61n.
4. *friend*] in fact Hor. probably disliked Propertius intensely. *Epist.*
II.ii.90ff. is thought to refer to his vanity, though this is not the view of
Renaissance commentators like Bond or Heinsius (1612 ed., *Notae*, pp.
63–4), and is not likely to be J's. *H&S* say J. does not show a very close
knowledge of Propertius at this stage (cf. I.ii.105n), but criticism of his lack
of stoicism in I.iii.64–6 and ll. 17–18 of this scene suggests some familiarity.
11. *sweet captain*] See I.iii.35n; cf. l. 156 below.
14. *tired on*] as a hawk tears flesh: G suggests the allusion is to 'the story
of Prometheus, or rather, perhaps, of Tityus' (see *Odyssey* XI, 576–81), but

*Tibullus.*                    'Slight! I hold my life,                    15
This same is he met him in Holy Street.
*Gallus.* Troth, 'tis like enough. This act of Propertius'
relisheth very strange with me.
*Tucca.* [*To Crispinus*] By thy leave my neat scoundrel. What,
[*Indicating Albius*] is this the mad boy you talked on?         20
*Crispinus.* Ay, this is Master Albius, captain.
*Tucca.* [*To Albius*] Give me thy hand, Agamemnon. We hear
abroad thou art the Hector of citizens. What sayest thou,
are we welcome to thee, noble Neoptolemus?
*Albius.* Welcome, captain? By Jove and all the gods i' the         25
Capitol——
*Tucca.* No more, we conceive thee. Which of these is thy
wedlock, Menelaus, thy Helen, thy Lucrece, that we may
do her honour, mad boy?
*Crispinus.* She i' the little fine dressing, sir, is my mistress.         30
*Albius.* For fault of a better, sir.

---

16. Holy Street] *Subst. F; Via Sacra Q.*   20. S.D.] *This ed.*   24.
Neoptolemus] *Subst. F; Pyrrhus Q.*   30. fine dressing, sir,] *F;* veluet Cap,
Sir; *Q.*

---

J. is probably recalling *Hist.*, Wood, III, 288: 'Chri. O, how this vulture,
(vile Ambition,) / Tyers on the heart of greatnesse' (Mallory).

15. *Phoebus*] as god of poetry; Dekker ridicules this in *S-M* II.i.108: 'his
being *Phoebus* priest cannot save him'.

16. *Holy Street*] Via Sacra: see III.i.n.

18. *relisheth*] tastes (*OED*, 5b).

20. *talked on*] See III.iv.373–4.

22–4.] The absurdly inflated names are all of Homeric heroes: Agamemnon, king of Mycenae; Hector, the leading Trojan warrior; Neoptolemus, son
of Achilles. For Tucca's nicknames, see Barton, pp. 183–4.

27. *conceive*] understand.

28. *wedlock*] wife; cf. *EH* III.i.19, 'How now my coy wedlock!'

*Menelaus*] younger brother of Agamemnon and cuckolded husband of
Helen of Troy.

*Lucrece*] her rape by Sextus, son of Tarquinius, last king of Rome, led
to the downfall of the monarchy. Tucca has thus just suggested both adultery
with and rape of Chloe to her husband.

30. *dressing*] See III.i.46n. *G*'s explanation that Chloe has changed from
the citizen's cap because of Cytheris' recent tuition in court fashion fails to
account for the earlier change, while Mallory's suggestion that J. wanted to
'placate the citizens' is absurd both in regard to J.'s character, and in that the
references are not themselves offensive.

*Tucca.* A better, profane rascal! I cry thee mercy, my good
scroyle, was't thou?

*Albius.* No harm, captain.

*Tucca.* She is a Venus, a Vesta, a Melpomene! [*To Chloe*]      35
Come hither, Penelope. [*Kisses her.*] What's thy name,
Iris?

*Chloe.* My name is Chloe, sir; I am a gentlewoman.

*Tucca.* Thou art in merit to be an empress, Chloe, for an eye
and a lip. Thou hast an emperor's nose. Kiss me again:      40
[*They kiss.*] 'tis a virtuous punk. [*Kisses her again.*] So!
Before Jove, the gods were a sort of goslings when they
suffered so sweet a breath to perfume the bed of a
stinkard. Thou hadst ill fortune, Thisbe; the fates were
infatuate; they were, punk, they were.                     45

*Chloe.* That's sure, sir. Let me crave your name, I pray you,
sir.

*Tucca.* I am known by the name of Captain Tucca, punk; the
noble Roman, punk; a gent'man and a commander,
punk.                                                       50

[CHLOE *walks aside.*]

*Chloe.* In good time! A gentleman and a commander? That's
as good as a poet, methinks.

---

32–3. my . . . scroyle] *In parentheses in Q, F.*    36. S.D.] *This ed.*    39.
Chloe] *In parentheses in Q, F.*    41. S.Ds.] *This ed.*    50.1. S.D.] *Subst.*
G.    52. poet, methinks.] *F; Poet? Q.*

---

32–4. *I . . . captain*] perhaps referring to some stage business involving
physical contact; Tucca is not likely to apologise for 'profane rascal', which
ranks so low in his list of insulting epithets as to be almost a compliment.

33. *scroyle*] scoundrel (*OED*).

35–7.] Vesta was the Roman hearth-goddess, served by the Vestal Virgins;
Melpomene, the Muse of Tragedy; Penelope, wife of Odysseus; Iris, goddess
of the rainbow.

40. *emperor's nose*] i.e. a large one.

41. *punk*] whore.

42. *goslings*] fools; cf. *Cor.* V.iii.35.

44. *Thisbe*] heroine of tragic love story in Ovid *Met.* IV, 55ff.

45. *infatuate*] made foolish (*OED*), punning on 'fate'.

48–50.] An extreme example of Tucca's repetitive style; cf. King, pp.
133–4.

51. *In good time*] An expression of pleased surprise, like 'To be sure!'
(*OED* s.v. 'Time' 42.c.[d]); cf. *Tp.* II.i.96.

*Crispinus.* [*Taking up a viol*] A pretty instrument! It's my
   cousin Cytheris' viol this, is't not?

*Cytheris.* Nay, play, cousin, it wants but such a voice and      55
   hand to grace it as yours is.

*Crispinus.* Alas, cousin, you are merrily inspired.

*Cytheris.* 'Pray you play, if you love me.

*Crispinus.* Yes, cousin. You know I do not hate you.

*Tibullus.* [*Aside*] A most subtle wench! How she hath baited    60
   him with a viol yonder, for a song.

*Crispinus.* Cousin, 'pray you call Mistress Chloe: she shall
   hear an essay of my poetry.

*Tucca.* I'll call her. [*To Chloe*] Come hither, cockatrice: here's
   one will set thee up, my sweet punk, set thee up.              65

*Chloe.* [*To Crispinus*] Are you a puet so soon, sir?

*Albius.* [*Putting his finger to his lips*] Wife, mum.

[CRISPINUS *plays and sings.*]

   *Love is blind, and a wanton;*
   *In the whole world there is scant-*
      *One such another,*                                          70
      *No, not his mother.*

---

53. S.D.] *This ed.*   60. S.D.] *This ed.*   67. S.D.] *This ed.*   67.1.
S.D.] *G;* CANTVS. *Q;* SONG. *F.*   69–70. *scant- / One*] *Q, F; scant one G.*

---

53. S.D. viol] family of instruments similar to the violin family (see
III.iv.138–9n) but with six strings, and frets on the finger board. There were
treble, alto, tenor, bass and double-bass viols (Hayes, pp. 7–19). The
accompaniment transcribed by Chan to Crispinus' earlier song (see
II.ii.153–62, 169–78n) suggests this one was a bass-viol, similar in range to
the cello.
   63. *essay*] sample (*OED*, 2, first example 1614); a new and pretentious
word (cf. King, p. 10).
   64. *cockatrice*] whore; cf. III.iv.192n; cf. *S-M* IV.iii.194–6: 'thou cryest
ptrooh at worshipfull Cittizens, and cal'st them Flat-caps, Cuckolds, and
banckrupts, and modest and vertuous wives punckes and cockatrices'.
   65. *set . . . up*] make you vain, elated (*OED* s.v. 'set' 154k).
   66. *puet*] 'a peewit, Jonson's sneering pun' (Nicholson); it was a common
seventeenth-century variant for the lapwing.
   69–70.] the awkward metre and loss of end-ryhme emphasise Crispinus'
defects as a poet: though plagiarising Horace (see ll. 96–7 below), he still
fails to get it right. I have not followed *G* in restoring 'one' to the second line
because J.'s point is that rhyme and scansion have become disengaged.
   71. *mother*] Venus.

*He hath plucked her doves and sparrows*
*To feather his sharp arrows,*
*And alone prevaileth,*
*Whilst sick Venus waileth.*                                    75
*But if Cypris once recover*
*The wag, it shall behove her*
*To look better to him*
*Or she will undo him.*

*Albius.* O most odoriferous music!                             80

*Tucca.* [*To Albius*] Aha, stinkard! Another Orpheus, you
    slave, another Orpheus! An Arion riding on the back of a
    dolphin, rascal.

*Gallus.* Have you a copy of this ditty, sir?

*Crispinus.* Master Albius has.                                 85

*Albius.* Ay, but in truth they are my wife's verses, I must not
    show 'em.

*Tucca.* [*Snatching the verses and giving them to Gallus*] Show
    'em, bankrupt, show 'em; they have salt in 'em, and will
    brook the air, stinkard.                                    90

*Gallus.* [*Reading*] How! *To his bright mistress Canidia?*

*Crispinus.* Ay, sir; that's but a borrowed name, as Ovid's
    Corinna, or Propertius his Cynthia, or your Nemesis, or
    Delia, Tibullus.

*Gallus.* It's the name of Horace his witch as I remember.      95

---

81. Aha, stinkard] *G;* A, ha; Stinkard *Q;* A, ha! stinkard *F.*    88. S.D.]
*This ed.*    91. To . . . *mistress*] *G; roman in Q, F.*

---

76. Cypris] Venus.

80. *odoriferous*] an affected word mockingly defined by J. in *CR*
IV.iii.109–11: 'that which containes most varietie of savour, and smell, we
say is most odoriferous'.

81. *Orpheus*] mythic singer, said by Aeschylus and Euripides to have
moved (figuratively and literally) trees, animals and even stones by his
singing.

82. *Arion*] Greek lyric poet and singer of *c.* 625 BC, thrown off a ship but
saved from drowning by music-loving dolphins.

89. *salt*] Cf. Hor. *Ars P* 271, where Plautus' wit is 'sales'; see also *Epist.*
II.ii.60, *Sat.* I.x.3.; cf. 'Apol. Dial.', l. 63.

90. *brook*] tolerate.

93. *Nemesis*] succeeded 'Delia' (see Persons of the Play, 26n) as mistress
of Tibullus: cf. Ovid *Amores* III.ix.30–1.

95.] See III.v.81n.

*Tibullus*. [*Reading*] Why! The ditty's all borrowed! 'Tis
  Horace's; hang him, plagiary!

*Tucca*. How? He borrow of Horace? He shall pawn himself to
  ten brokers first! Do you hear, poetasters? I know you to
  be knights and men of worship—He shall write with          100
  Horace for a talent, and let Maecenas and his whole
  College of Critics take his part. [*To Crispinus*] Thou shalt
  do't, young Phoebus, thou shalt, Phaethon, thou shalt.

*Demetrius*. Alas sir, Horace! He is a mere sponge, nothing but
  humours and observation; he goes up and down sucking       105
  from every society, and when he comes home squeezes
  himself dry again. I know him, I.

*Tucca*. Thou sayest true, my poor poetical Fury, he will pen

---

96. ditty's] *This ed.*; Ditt' is *Q, Subst. F.*     100. knights and men] *Subst. Q;*
men *F.*     102. S.D.] *This ed.*     105. humours] *F; Humours Q.*

96–7.] The song bears no resemblance to anything by Hor., and little to
any by J., though Hedon's song in *CR* IV.iii.242–53 offers some metrical
parallels. *Hadd. M.* 85–156, 'Beauties, have ye seen this toy', an imitation of
Moschus, *Idyl.* I, treats a similar subject with much more poise.

97. *plagiary*] one who plagiarises; this is first example in *OED* (2).

100. *worship*] See I.i.29n.

101. *talent*] See I.ii.180n; here simply meaning 'for a very large sum'. The
competition proposed echoes that in Hor. *Sat.* I.iv.12–18; see III.v.5–6n.

102. *College of Critics*] Cf. Webster 'Nay, truly, I am no great censurer,
and yet I might have been one of the College of Critics once' (*Malcontent*,
Ind. 98–9), and Dekker, *Gull's Horn Book* (1609, ed. Grosart, p. 202): 'the
new-found College of Critics'; these references depend on common recognition of such an entity, but none is known.

103. *Phaethon*] son of Helios, the sun-god. *H&S* note that Dekker was
paid for a play of this name in 1598; it was performed at court at Christmas
1600.

104–7.] See p. 33. Jasper Mayne rebuts the charge 'that when thou in
company wert met, / Thy *meate* tooke *notes*, and *thy discourse was net*' (*To the
Memory of* BEN IOHNSON', ll. 113–14, *H&S*, XI, 454). Penniman quotes
William Winstanley, *Lives of the Most Famous English Poets* (1687), p. 124:
'His [Jonson's] constant humour was to sit silent in learned company, and
suck in (besides wine) their several humours into his observation; what was
ore in others he was able to refine unto himself.' Cf. also Oldham's praise of
J.'s 'strict Observation' ('Upon the WORKS of *BEN. JOHNSON*', *H&S*,
XI, 541, l. 149).

108. *poetical Fury*] personifying in Crispinus the *furor poeticus* on which
true poetry depends: cf. *EMO*, Ind. 147

all he knows. A sharp, thorny-toothed satirical rascal, fly
him; he carries hay in his horn. He will sooner lose his　　110
best friend than his least jest. What he once drops upon
paper against a man lives eternally to upbraid him in the
mouth of every slave tankard-bearer or water-man; not a
bawd or a boy that comes from the bake-house but shall
point at him. 'Tis all dog and scorpion: he carries poison　　115
in his teeth and a sting in his tail. Fough! Body of Jove!
I'll have the slave whipped one of these days for his satires
and his humours, by one cashiered clerk or another.

*Crispinus.* We'll undertake him, captain.

---

109. *thorny-toothed*] King (p. 110) suggests an echo of the *'spinosorum dentium'* of the hidden serpent carried by Dialectica in Martianus Capella *De nuptiis* IV.328; Hor. is 'mordax', 'biting, snarling', in *Sat.* I.iv.93.

109–15. *fly . . . him*] imitating Hor. *Sat.* I.iv.34–8: '"He carries hay on his horns, give him a wide berth. Provided he can raise a laugh for himself, he will spare not a single friend, and whatever he has once scribbled on his sheets he will rejoice to have all know, all the slaves and old dames as they come home from bakehouse and pond."' J. may have quoted this to Drummond of himself, for Drummond records 'He is a great lover and praiser of himself, a contemner and Scorner of others, given rather to losse a friend, than a Jest' (*Conv.* 680–1).

110. *hay . . . horn*] a vicious animal was so labelled by Roman law; H&S note the echo in Herrick, 'Oberon's Palace', ll. 13–14 (*Poetical Works* ed. L.C. Martin (Oxford, 1958), p. 165). The horns here are those of the satyr; in *S-M* Dekker has Horace and Bubo *'pul'd in by th'hornes bound, both like Satyres'* (V.ii.158.2). Hor. describes himself as having 'ready horns' in *Epode* VI, 11–12.

115–6. *dog . . . tail*] Cf. 'Apol. Dial.', l. 63 for a similar pairing; the dog and scorpion were traditionally associated with satire for obvious reasons; Callimachus says that Archilochus 'drank the bitter wrath of the dog and the sharp sting of the wasp; from both of these comes the poison of his mouth' (Frag. 37a in *Callimachus and Lycophron*, trans. A. W. Mair (1921), quoted in Elliott, *Satire*, p. 11).

117–29.] anticipating Dekker's attack in *S-M*. For the whipping, see *S-M* V.ii.241–5. For the succession of books referring to satire as whipping, see p. 28, n. 54.

117–8. *I'll . . . another*] Perhaps referring specifically to Weever's *Whipping of the Satire*: see p. 28.

118. *cashiered*] sacked.

119. *undertake*] deal with; cf. *Tw. N* I.iii.58.

*Demetrius.* Ay, and tickle him i' faith for his arrogancy and his       120
    impudence in commending his own things, and for his
    translating. I can trace him i' faith. O, he is the most
    open fellow living; I had as lief as a new suit I were at it.
*Tucca.* Say no more then, but do it: 'tis the only way to get
    thee a new suit. Sting him, my little newts: I'll give you       125
    instructions, I'll be your intelligencer, we'll all join and
    hang upon him like so many horse-leeches, the players
    and all. We shall sup together soon, and then we'll
    conspire i' faith.
*Gallus.* [*Aside to Tibullus*] O that Horace had stayed still here.     130
*Tibullus.* [*Aside to Gallus*] So would not I: for both these
    would have turned Pythagoreans then.
*Gallus.* [*Aside to Tibullus*] What, mute?
*Tibullus.* [*Aside to Gallus*] Ay, as fishes i' faith. [*To Cytheris
    and Chloe*] Come, ladies, shall we go?                           135
*Cytheris.* We await you, sir. But Mistress Chloe asks if you
    have not a god to spare for this gentleman?
*Gallus.* Who, Captain Tucca?
*Cytheris.* Ay, he.
*Gallus.* Yes, if we can invite him along, he shall be Mars.         140
*Chloe.* Has Mars anything to do with Venus?
*Tibullus.* O, most of all lady.

---

124. but do it] *Subst. F; italics in Q.*        125. newts] *Nicholson; Neufts Q,
Subst. F.*

120. *tickle*] for this ironic use, 'to beat, chastise' (*OED*, 6b) cf. IV.iv.37,
V.iii.32, 69, and *Tw. N* V.i.193.
120-2. *arrogancy ... translating*] Cf. V.iii. 224-5, 304-7, and the attack
on Crites in *CR* III.ii.60-4.
122. *translating*] pejoratively, with a meaning close to plagiarism: Demetrius fails to understand the humanist strategy of imitation of classical
authors. See pp. 7-14.
*trace*] follow the traces of, as in hunting (*OED* 5).
123. *had ... suit*] 'I would enjoy it as much as getting a new suit.'
127. *horse-leeches*] large leeches, supposed (erroneously) to suck blood
insatiably; cf. *BF* II.iii.13. *OED* quotes figurative use in Sylvester's trans. of
Du Bartas (1608): 'Thou life of strife, thou Horse-leach sent from hell'.
132-4. *Pythagoreans ... fishes*] Pythagoras' religious order imposed silence
on novitiates: see E. R. Dodds, *The Greeks and the Irrational* (1963), pp. 154,
175. *H&S* cite *SW* II.ii.3, 'Fishes! Pythagoreans all!' and *NW*, 199,
'Pythagoreans, all dumb as fishes.'
141-2. *Mars ... lady*] in classical mythology, Mars is Venus' lover.

*Chloe.* Nay then, I pray' let him be invited. And what shall
    Crispinus be?
*Tibullus.* Mercury, Mistress Chloe.                                        145
*Chloe.* Mercury? That's a poet, is't?
*Gallus.* No, lady, but somewhat inclining that way: he is a
    herald at arms.
*Chloe.* A herald at arms? Good! And Mercury? Pretty! He has
    to do with Venus too?                                                    150
*Tibullus.* A little with her face, lady, or so.
*Chloe.* 'Tis very well. Pray' let's go, I long to be at it.
*Cytheris.* [*To Crispinus and Tucca*] Gentlemen, shall we pray
    your companies along?
*Crispinus.* You shall not only pray but prevail, lady. Come,     155
    sweet captain.
*Tucca.* Yes, I follow. [*Aside to Albius*] But thou must not talk
    of this now, my little bankrupt.
*Albius.* [*Aside to Tucca*] Captain, look here: [*Pointing to his
    lips*] mum.                                                             160
*Demetrius.* I'll go write, sir.
*Tucca.* Do, do: stay, there's a drachma to purchase ginger-
    bread for thy Muse.                                *Exeunt.*

ACT IV    SCENE iv

[*Enter*] LUPUS, HISTRIO, [*and*] Lictors.

*Lupus.* Come, let us talk here; here we may be private. Shut
    the door, lictor. [*To Histrio*] You are a player, you say?
*Histrio.* Ay, and't please your worship.
*Lupus.* Good: and how are you able to give this intelligence?

157. S.D.] *This ed.*    159–60. S.D.] *This ed.*    163. S.D.] *Q.* V.iv.0.1.]
*A Room in Lupus's House. / Enter* LUPUS . . . Lictors. *G.* Lictors] *Subst. F2;*
Lictor *Q, Subst. F.*

147–8. *somewhat . . . arms*] genealogies approved by the College of Arms
were often fictions; cf. I.ii.61n.
    151. *face*] mercury was an ingredient of many cosmetics.
    155. *pray . . . prevail*] perhaps playing on a similar pronunciation in con-
temporary speech.
    IV.iv.] For the contemporary relevance of this scene see p. 42. J.
presents Lupus as living in an atmosphere of paranoia and intrigue (cf. ll.
1–2, 7, and esp. 26–31) which reflects his experience, as a Catholic and a
satirist, of late Elizabethan England.

*Histrio.* Marry, sir, they directed a letter to me and my fellow     5
sharers.

*Lupus.* Speak lower, you are not now i' your theatre, stager.
[*To 1 Lictor*] My sword, knave. [*To Histrio*] They directed
a letter to you and your fellow sharers: forward.

*Histrio.* Yes, sir, to hire some of our properties, as a sceptre     10
and a crown for Jove, and a *caduceus* for Mercury, and a
*petasus*——

*Lupus.* *Caduceus* and *petasus*? Let me see your letter. [*Reads.*]
This is a conjuration! A conspiracy, this! [*To 1 Lictor*]
Quickly, on with my buskins: I'll act a tragedy i' faith.     15
Will nothing but our gods serve these poets to profane?
[*To 1 Lictor*] Dispatch! [*To Histrio*] Player, I thank thee;
the emperor shall take knowledge of thy good service. [*A
knocking within*] Who's there now? [*To 1 Lictor*] Look,
knave.                                    [*Exit 1 Lictor.*]     20
A crown and a sceptre! This is good. Rebellion now!

[*Re-enter 1 Lictor.*]

[*1*] *Lictor.* 'Tis your 'pothecary, sir, Master Minos.

*Lupus.* What tell'st thou me of 'pothecaries, knave? Tell him I
have affairs of state in hand; I can talk to no 'pothecaries
now. [*Pauses.*] Heart of me! Stay the 'pothecary there.     25
                                        [*Exit 1 Lictor.*]
You shall see, I have fished out a cunning piece of plot

---

7. theatre] *G; Theater Q; theater F.*     18–19. S.D.] *G.*     20. S.D.] *Subst.*
*G.*     21.1. S.D.] *Subst. G.*     23. him] *Parfitt;* him; *Q;* him; *Q catchword,*
*F.*     24. state] *G;* state, *Q, Subst. F.*     25. S.D.] *This ed.; pause indicated*
*by space in Q, F;* Muses for a moment or two. *Nicholson.*     25.1. S.D.] *This*
*ed.;* Walks in a musing posture. *G.*     26. You] *Q, F start new para. here.*

---

6. *sharers*] See III.iv.243n.

11. caduceus] Mercury's staff, winged and with two snakes twined around
its head; Henslowe lists one among the props of the Admiral's Men (*Diary*, p.
320).

12. petasus] winged cap of Mercury.

14. *conjuration*] meaning both a conspiracy and an invocation of the devil:
Lupus takes *caduceus* and *petasus* to be part of a spell, but 'conjure' also
meant to conspire (*OED, v.* 1 and 2).

15. *buskins*] See I.i.19n.

17. *Dispatch*] Hurry.

21.] See p. 42.

26. *piece of*] individual instance of (*OED*, 8b).

now. They have had some intelligence that their project is
discovered, and now have they dealt with my 'pothecary
to poison me. 'Tis so: knowing that I meant to take
physic today. As sure as death, 'tis there. Jupiter I thank          30
thee that thou hast yet made me so much of a politician.

[*Re-enter* 1 Lictor *with* MINOS.]

You are welcome, sir. [*To 1 Lictor*] Take the potion from
him there. [*To Minos*] I have an antidote more than you
wot of, sir. [*To 1 Lictor*] Throw it on the ground there:
so! Now fetch in the dog. And yet we cannot tarry to try          35
experiments now: arrest him. [*To Minos*] You shall go
with me, sir. I'll tickle you, 'pothecary, I'll give you a
glister i' faith. Have I the letter? Ay, 'tis here. Come,
your *fasces*, lictors: the half-pikes and the halberds, take
them down from the *lares* there. [*To Histrio*] Player, assist          40
me.

[*As they are going out, enter* MAECENAS *and* HORACE.]

*Maecenas.* Whither now, Asinius Lupus, with this armoury?
*Lupus.* I cannot talk now. I charge you, assist me: treason,
treason!

31.1. S.D.] *This ed.; Enter* MINOS *G.*     41.1. S.D.] *G.*     42. Whither]
*F;* Whether *Q.*

---

28. *dealt*] made a deal.
31. *politician*] J. is playing on the two senses, of 'statesman' (*OED*, 2),
which is Lupus' meaning, and of 'schemer, intriguer' (*OED*, 1) which
describes him more accurately.
34. *wot*] know.
37. *tickle*] See IV.iii.120n.
38. *glister*] a clyster, or enema.
39. fasces . . . *halberds*] Roman lictors carried *fasces*, 'certain bundles of
birchen-rods, with an axe wrapped up in the middest of them' (Godwyn, p.
111); J. equates them with the weapons of the English under-sheriff or
constable: the half-pike was a small staff with a sharp steel tip, said by *OED*
to be carried by infantry officers, and the halberd a combined spear and axe
(*OED*, 1).
40. lares] here used to mean the *lararium*, a shrine to the *lares*, or
household gods, in which the weapons which defended the household (and
the state) were also kept.

*Horace.* How? Treason!

*Lupus.* Ay; if you love the emperor and the state, follow    45
me.                                                 *Exeunt.*

### ACT IV  SCENE v

[*Enter*] OVID, JULIA, [CORNELIUS] GALLUS, CYTHERIS,
TIBULLUS, PLAUTIA, ALBIUS, CHLOE, TUCCA, CRISPINUS,
HERMOGENES [*and* 1] PYRGUS.

*Ovid.* Gods and goddesses, take your several seats. Now
Mercury, move your *caduceus* and in Jupiter's name
command silence.

*Crispinus.* In the name of Jupiter, silence.

*Hermogenes.* The crier of the court hath too clarified a voice.    5

*Gallus.* Peace, Momus.

*Ovid.* O, he is the god of reprehension, let him alone; 'tis his

---

47. S.D.] *Q.*    IV.v.0.1–3.] SCENE III. / *An Apartment in the Palace.* /
*Enter* OVID, . . . Pyrgus, *characteristically habited, as gods and goddesses. G.*

IV.v.] The scene is suggested by Suetonius' description of a banquet
organised by Augustus himself (*Divus Augustus* LXX; see pp. 16–17, 20–1)
and by the account of the gods in *Iliad* I, 533–604. It may owe something also
to the heavenly marriage feast of Philology and Mercury in Martianus Capella
*De nuptiis*; see *Martianus Capella and the Seven Liberal Arts, II, The Marriage
of Philology and Mercury* (trans. W. H. Stahl, Richard Johnson, E. L. Burge,
New York, 1977). J. frequently associates disguise with sexual licence or
excitement: see p. 13, *Volp.* III.vii.220–38, *Alc.* IV.i.166–9, *EMO* II.i.138–
80 and II.ii *passim*, *D is A* IV.iii.ff., *NI* IV.ii.52–IV.iv.104 and *Ep.* XXV,
'On Sir Voluptuous Beast'. His attitude to the banquet is likely to have been
influenced most by Cicero *Tusc.* I.xxvi.65: 'I do not think the gods delight in
ambrosia or nectar or Hebe filling the cups, and I do not listen to Horace
who says that Ganymede was carried off by the gods for his beauty to serve as
cup-bearer to Zeus . . .Homer imagined these things and attributed human
feelings to the gods; I had rather he had attributed divine feelings to us.' See
also the passage from Seneca, quoted below ll. 12–13n. Minerva, goddess of
wisdom, and Diana, goddess of chastity, are significant absentees.

5. *clarified*] clear, but probably in this case too thin; the boy's high pitch
may also be glanced at.

6–7. *Momus . . . reprehension*] Momos was the personification of fault-
finding, used as a narrator by Lucian, the only Greek writer of whom J.
shows close knowledge (see pp. 13, 26 and V.iii.385–549n). *H&S* rightly say
that J.'s 'tone and treatment in this scene are Lucianic', but there is no
source in Lucian, other than the *Deorum concilium* in which Momus takes
part. Lodge's *Fig for Momus* (1595) pioneered the vogue for verse satire.

office. Mercury go forward, and proclaim after Phoebus
our high pleasure to all the deities that shall partake this
high banquet.                                                          10
*Crispinus.* Yes, sir.

> [*As* GALLUS *proclaims,* CRISPINUS *repeats loudly*
> *after him at each break.*]

*Gallus.* The great god Jupiter——
  Of his licentious goodness——
  Willing to make this feast no fast——
  From any manner of pleasure——                                         15
  Nor to bind any god or goddess——
  To be anything the more god or goddess
  for their names——
  He gives them all free licence——
  To speak no wiser than persons of baser titles——                      20
  And to be nothing better than common men or women——
  And therefore no god——
  Shall need to keep himself more strictly
  to his goddess——
  Than any man does to his wife——                                        25
  Nor any goddess——
  Shall need to keep herself more strictly to her god——
  Than any woman does to her husband——
  But since it is no part of wisdom——
  In these days to come into bonds——                                     30
  It shall be lawful for every lover——
  To break loving oaths——

---

11.1–2. S.D.] *This ed.; Q, F print beginning of Crispinus's echo of each of lines*
*12–36 thus:* GALL. The great God, IVPITER, CRIS. The great, &c.; *Q omits*
&c. *after these l. 30.*

---

9. *our . . . pleasure*] in the sense of divine will.

12–13. *Jupiter . . . goodness*] Cf. Seneca *De brevitate* vitae xvi.5, on 'the
madness of poets in fostering human frailties by the tales in which they
represent that Jupiter under the enticement of the pleasures of a lover
doubled the length of the night. For what is it but to inflame our vices to
inscribe the name of the gods as their sponsors, and to present the excused
indulgence of divinity as an example to our own weakness?'

17–18.] The cramped syntax is probably intended to mean they do not
need to behave like gods or goddesses because they have been given their
names (cf. 'baser titles', l. 20).

31–2. *It . . . oaths*] in direct contradiction of Augustus' criminalising of
adultery in the *Lex Iulia*: see p. 21.

To change their lovers and make love to others——
As the heat of everyone's blood——
And the spirit of our nectar shall inspire——         35
And Jupiter save Jupiter!——
*Tibullus.* So now we may play the fools by authority.
*Hermogenes.* To play the fool by authority is wisdom.
*Julia.* Away with your mattery sentences, Momus; they are
too grave and wise for this meeting.                  40
*Ovid.* [*To Crispinus*] Mercury, give our jester a stool, let him
sit by, and reach him of our cates.
*Tucca.* Dost hear, mad Jupiter? We'll have it enacted: he that
speaks the first wise word shall be made cuckold. What
sayst thou? Is't not a good motion?                   45
*Ovid.* Deities, are you all agreed?
*All.* Agreed, great Jupiter.
*Albius.* I have read in a book that to play the fool wisely is
high wisdom.
*Gallus.* How now, Vulcan, will you be the first wizard?    50
*Ovid.* [*To Tucca*] Take his wife, Mars, and make him cuckold
quickly.
*Tucca.* [*To Chloe*] Come, cockatrice.
*Chloe.* No, let me alone with him, Jupiter. [*To Albius*] I'll

---

47. *All.*] Subst. *F; Omnes. Q.*

35. *nectar*] the 'sweet nectar' of *Iliad* I, 598.
37-8.] Cf. 48-9 below.
39. *mattery*] full of 'matter', or wisdom; cf. 'material Horace', V.i.128.
41. *jester*] Momus, one of whose roles was as jester to the gods.
*stool . . . by*] probably placing him amongst the spectators seated on
the stage, as Crispinus may have been placed earlier: see II.i.1n. From this
position Hermogenes comments like a member of the audience on Tucca's
acting: see ll. 79, 147-8 below.
42. *reach him*] hand him.
*cates*] delicacies.
48-9. *read . . . wisdom*] Mallory cites Guazzo's *Civil Conversation*, trans.
G. Pettie, 1586, and *H&S* more plausibly Erasmus, *Praise of Folly*, chapter
52, where it is said to be 'a common verse among schoolboys'. It derives from
an aphorism of Dionysius Cato, 'It is the highest wisdom to feign stupidity in
the right place.' The most interesting comparison is with *Tw. N* III.i.60,
'This fellow is wise enough to play the fool'; Albius could not have read *Tw.
N* in 1601, but he seems to have seen it on stage (see p. 37).
50. *wizard*] wise man (*H&S*).
53. *cockatrice*] See III.iv.192n.

make you take heed, sir, while you live again, if there be      55
twelve in a company, that you be not the wisest of 'em.

*Albius.* No more I will not, indeed wife; hereafter, I'll be here
[*Pointing to his lips*] mum.

*Ovid.* [*To 1 Pyrgus*] Fill us a bowl of nectar, Ganymede; we
will drink to our daughter Venus.                               60

*Gallus.* [*To Albius*] Look to your wife, Vulcan, Jupiter begins
to court her.

*Tibullus.* Nay, let Mars look to it; Vulcan must do as Venus
does—bear.

*Tucca.* [*To 1 Pyrgus*] Sirrah, boy; catamite! Look you play     65
Ganymede well now, you slave. Do not spill your nectar;
carry your cup even: so. You should have rubbed your
face with whites of eggs, you rascal, till your brows had
shone like our sooty brother's here [*Indicating Albius*] as
sleek as a horn book, or ha' steeped your lips in wine, till    70
you made 'em so plump that Juno might have been
jealous of 'em. [*To Chloe*] Punk, kiss me punk!

*Ovid.* [*To Chloe*] Here, daughter Venus, I drink to thee.

*Chloe.* 'Thank you, good father Jupiter.

[OVID *embraces* CHLOE.]

---

58. S.D.] *This ed.*      74.1. S.D.] *This ed.*

---

56. *twelve ... company*] There were twelve Olympian gods, though not
precisely the twelve represented here (for the absence of Minerva and Diana,
see IV.v.n); presumably Chloe is unaware of this, and refers simply to the
number present.

59. *Ganymede*] page to the gods, here 1 Pyrgus.

60. *daughter*] Homer makes Aphrodite (Venus) daughter of Zeus (Jupiter)
and Dione (*Iliad* V, 370–1).

64. *bear*] i.e. bear her lover Mars on top of her.

65–72.] Although these lines may indicate that Tucca is making drunken
advances to 1 Pyrgus, it is highly unlikely that he would call him 'Punk'
(l. 72), a word specifically used of women, and the epithet Tucca has already
used for Chloe (see IV.iii.41, 48–50).

65. *catamite*] boy kept for homosexual purposes.

68. *whites of eggs*] used to make a cosmetic gel; cf. *D is A* IV.iv.21.

69. *sooty*] because he is the god of fire, and a smith; see IV.ii.45n.

70. *horn book*] 'Originally a leaf of paper containing the alphabet and a few
simple words, generally the Lord's Prayer, all covered with a thin covering of
[transparent] horn to preserve it. It was usually mounted on a small board
with a handle and was the primer for children' (Penniman).

*steeped ... wine*] Cf. Hor. *Odes* III.iii.11–12 where Augustus 'shall sip
nectar with ruddy lips' amongst the gods.

*Tucca.* [*To Julia*] Why, mother Juno, gods and fiends! What,      75
wilt thou suffer this ocular temptation?

*Tibullus.* Mars is enraged: he looks big, and begins to stut for
anger.

*Hermogenes.* Well played, Captain Mars.

*Tucca.* Well said, minstrel Momus. I must put you in, must      80
I? When will you be in good fooling of yourself, fiddler?
Never?

*Hermogenes.* O, 'tis our fashion to be silent when there is a
better fool in place, ever.

*Tucca.* 'Thank you, rascal.                                    85

*Ovid.* [*To 1 Pyrgus*] Fill to our daughter Venus, Ganymede,
who fills her father with affection.

> [OVID *embraces* CHLOE *again.*]

*Julia.* [*To Ovid*] Wilt thou be ranging, Jupiter, before my face?

*Ovid.* Why not, Juno? Why should Jupiter stand in awe of
thy face, Juno?                                                 90

*Julia.* Because it is thy wife's face, Jupiter.

*Ovid.* What, shall a husband be afraid of his wife's face? Will
she paint it so horribly? We are a king, cotquean, and we
will reign in our pleasures: and we will cudgel thee to
death if thou find fault with us.                               95

*Julia.* I will find fault with thee, King Cuckold-Maker! What,
shall the king of gods turn the king of good fellows, and
have no fellow in wickedness? This makes our poets, that
know our profaneness, live as profane as we. By my
godhead, Jupiter, I will join with all the other gods here,     100
bind thee hand and foot, throw thee down into earth, and
make a poor poet of thee, if thou abuse me thus.

*Gallus.* A good smart-tongued goddess, a right Juno!

---

87.1. S.D.] *This ed.*

---

77. *stut*] stammer; cf. I.ii.178–9n, and pp. 26 and 40.

80–2. *I . . . Never*] Tucca's complaint is that he is the source of the
humour, rather than Hermogenes' wit.

88–139.] based loosely on *Iliad* I, 536–611.

88. *ranging*] being unfaithful; cf. *Shr.* III.i.91–2.

93. *cotquean*] a nagging woman; Hera (Juno) is described as 'nagging' in
*Iliad* I, 539.

98–9. *poets . . . profane*] Cf. above, ll. 12–13n.

100–1. *I . . . foot*] Cf. *Iliad* I, 399–400, where Athena, Hera and Poseidon
want to bind Zeus.

*Ovid.* Juno, we will cudgel thee, Juno: we told thee so
    yesterday, when thou wert jealous of us for Thetis.          105
[*1*] *Pyrgus.* Nay, today she had me in inquisition too.
*Tucca.* Well said, my fine Phrygian fry: inform, inform. [*To
    Crispinus*] Give me some wine, king of heralds, I may
    drink to my cockatrice.
*Ovid.* [*To 1 Pyrgus*] No more, Ganymede. [*To Julia*] We will          110
    cudgel thee, Juno, by Styx, we will.
*Julia.* Ay, 'tis well; gods may grow impudent in iniquity, and
    they must not be told of it——
*Ovid.* Yea, we will knock our chin against our breast, and
    shake thee out of Olympus into an oyster boat for thy          115
    scolding.
*Julia.* Your nose is not long enough to do it, Jupiter, if all thy
    strumpets thou hast among the stars took thy part. And
    there is never a star in thy forehead but shall be a horn, if
    thou persist to abuse me.          120
*Crispinus.* A good jest, i' faith.
*Ovid.* We tell thee thou angerst us, cotquean, and we will
    thunder thee in pieces for thy cotqueanity. We will lay
    this city desolate and flat as this hand for thy offences.
    These two fingers are the walls of it; these within, the          125
    people, which people shall all be thrown down thus, and
    nothing left standing in this city but these walls.

---

112. Ay, 'tis well;] *Subst. F;* I'ts well; *Q.*     113. it——] *F;* it. *Q.*     123–7.
We . . . walls.] *Q; not in F.*

---

104–5.] Cf. *Iliad* I, 555–67, for Hera's jealousy of Thetis, the mother of
Achilles, and Zeus' angry reply.
    107. *Phrygian fry*] Ganymede's father was Tros, king of Phrygia: *Iliad*
XX, 230–5.
    111. *cudgel . . . Styx*] punning on 'sticks'.
    114–5. *knock . . . Olympus*] parodying *Iliad* I, 528–30: 'He spoke, the son
of Kronos, and nodded his head with the dark brows, / and the immortally
anointed hair of the great god / swept from his divine head, and all Olympos
was shaken.'
    115. *oyster boat*] normally a boat used in the cultivation of oysters, but
here used for selling them; oyster-wives, like fishwives, were proverbial
scolds.
    117. *nose . . . enough*] alluding to Ovid's name, Publius Ovidius Naso; *naso*
meant large-nosed.
    119. *horn*] of a cuckold.
    123–7. *We . . . walls*] accompanied by a series of hand gestures: first a flat
hand; then all four fingers raised (the outer two 'the walls', the inner 'the

*Crispinus.* Another good jest.

*Albius.* O my hammers and my Cyclops! This boy fills not
wine enough to make us kind enough to one another.          130

*Tucca.* [*To Albius*] Nor thou hast not collied thy face enough,
stinkard.

*Albius.* I'll ply the table with nectar, and make them friends.

*Hermogenes.* Heaven is like to have but a lame skinker, then.

*Albius.* Wine and good livers make true lovers. I'll sentence   135
them together. [*Gives them wine.*] Here father, here
mother, for shame, drink yourselves drunk, and forget
this dissension. You two should cling together before our
faces, and give us example of unity.

*Gallus.* O excellently spoken, Vulcan, on the sudden.          140

*Tibullus.* Jupiter may do well to prefer his tongue to some
office for his eloquence.

*Tucca.* His tongue shall be gent'man usher to his wit, and still
go before it.

*Albius.* An excellent fit office!                              145

*Crispinus.* Ay, and an excellent good jest besides.

*Hermogenes.* [*To Tucca*] What, have you hired Mercury to cry
your jests you make?

---

135. Wine] *G;* 'Wine, *Q, F.*    136. S.D.] *This ed.*

---

people'); then only the first and fourth fingers left in the cuckold's salute as
the middle fingers are 'all . . . thrown down'. *H&S* unconvincingly suggest a
puppet play. Omitted from *F* because of its non-literary nature.

129. *Cyclops*] The Cyclopes often appear as the assistants of Hephaestus
(Vulcan); cf. *Merc. Vind.* 2–4.

131. *collied*] blackened.

133–9.] Cf. *Iliad* I, 571–600, where Hephaestus reconciles Zeus and
Hera, and serves wine to all the gods.

134. *skinker*] server of liquor.

135. *Wine . . . lovers*] proverbial, probably classical: the liver was seen by
the Romans as the seat of passion. *H&S* cite J.'s 'terrible translation' of Hor.
*Odes* IV.i.12 by 'If a fit livor thou dost seek to toast'.

135–6. *sentence . . . together*] either 'bind them together by my sentence'
(*sententia*, aphorism, wise words) or simply 'pass judgement on them
together'.

138–9. *You . . . unity*] Cf. *Iliad* I, 573–5: 'This will be a disastrous matter
and not endurable / if you two are to quarrel thus for the sake of mortals /
and bring brawling among the gods.'

141. *prefer*] promote.

143–4. *His . . . it*] Cf. Dent, T412; *H&S* quote Ray, *Proverbs* (1678), p.
273: 'Your tongue runs before your wit', where it is traced back to Isocrates.
The gentleman usher went before a person of rank.

147. *cry*] advertise, recommend.

*Ovid.* [*To Hermogenes*] Momus, you are envious.

*Tucca.* [*To Hermogenes*] Why, you whoreson blockhead, 'tis    150
your only block of wit in fashion nowadays, to applaud
other folks' jests.

*Hermogenes.* True, with those that are not artificers
themselves.

[ALBIUS *begins to fall asleep.*]
Vulcan, you nod, and the mirth of the feast droops.    155

[*1*] *Pyrgus.* He has filled nectar so long, till his brain swims
in it.

*Gallus.* What, do we nod, fellow gods? Sound music, and let
us startle our spirits with a song.

*Tucca.* [*To Gallus*] Do Apollo, thou art a good musician.    160

*Gallus.* What says Jupiter?

*Ovid.* [*Drowsily*] Ha? Ha?

*Gallus.* A song.

*Ovid.* Why do, do, sing.

*Plautia.* [*To Tibullus*] Bacchus, what say you?    165

*Tibullus.* [*Drowsily*] Ceres?

*Plautia.* But, to this song?

*Tibullus.* Sing, for my part.

*Julia.* Your belly weighs down your head, Bacchus: here's a
song toward.    170

*Tibullus.* Begin, Vulcan——

*Albius.* [*Waking*] What else, what else?

*Tucca.* Say, Jupiter——

*Ovid.* Mercury——

*Crispinus.* Ay, say, say——[*Music. He sings.*]    175

---

150. Why, you] *Q, F;* Why, ay, you *G.*    151. nowadays] *Parfitt;* (now
adaies) *Q, F.*    154.1. S.D.] *This ed.*    155. feast] *Q;* iest *F* (*a misreading due to 146, 148, 152*).    162. S.D.] *This ed.*    166. S.D.] *This ed.*
171. Vulcan——] *Subst. F;* Vulcan. *Q.*    172. S.D.] *This ed.*    173.
Jupiter——] *Subst. F; Iupiter. Q.*    174. Mercury——] *Subst. F; Mercury.
Q.*    175. say——] *Subst. F; say. Q.*    S.D.] *This ed.;* CANTVS *Q;*
SONG *F; Music. G.* (*so also 187.1*).

---

151. *block*] a mould, especially for a hat; cf. Dekker, *S-M* I.ii.120–1, 'of
what fashion is this knights wit, of what blocke?'

156. *so . . . till*] so long that (Mallory).

160. *Apollo . . . musician*] Cf. *Iliad* I, 603, 'the beautifully wrought lyre
in the hands of Apollo'.

170. *toward*] impending.

*Wake, our mirth begins to die,*
*Quicken it with tunes and wine:*
*Raise your notes, you're out, fie! fie!*
*This drowsiness is an ill sign.*
   *We banish him the choir of gods*       180
     *That droops again:*
     *Then all are men,*
     *For here's not one but nods.*

*Ovid.* I like not this sudden and general heaviness amongst
our godheads, 'tis somewhat ominous. Apollo, command   185
us louder music, and let Mercury and Momus contend to
please, and revive our senses.

    [*Music.* HERMOGENES *and* CRISPINUS *sing.*]

*Hermogenes.*  *Then in a free and lofty strain*
        *Our broken tunes we thus repair;*
*Crispinus.*    *And we answer them again,*      190
        *Running division on the panting air,*
*Both.*        *To celebrate this feast of sense,*
        *As free from scandal as offence.*
*Hermogenes.*    *Here is beauty for the eye;*
*Crispinus.*     *For the ear, sweet melody;*      195
*Hermogenes.*  *Ambrosiac odours for the smell;*
*Crispinus.*     *Delicious nectar for the taste;*
*Both.*       *For the touch, a lady's waist,*
        *Which doth all the rest excel!*

*Ovid.* Ay, this hath waked us. [*To Crispinus*] Mercury, our  200

---

176. *Wake,*] F; *WAKE;* Q; Alb. *Wake!* G (*giving the song to Albius because
of 171*).   179. *drowsiness*] G; *Drouzinesse* Q; *drouzinesse* F; *H&S wrongly
note drouzinesse, as corr. in* F.   180. *choir*] Parfitt; *Queere* Q, *Subst.* F; *Quire*
F2.   192. *Both*] Nicholson; *Ambo* Q, *Subst.* F; *so also 198.*

---

186–7. *let . . . please*] The duet between Crispinus and Hermogenes
parodies the 'antiphonal sweet sound of the muses singing', *Iliad* I, 604.

191. *division*] here probably descant, though it also meant the division of
one long note into a series of shorter ones; cf. V.iii.187, and *EMO* III.ix.135,
*CR* I.ii.68 and *SS* III.iv.15.

192. *feast . . . sense*] recalling Chapman's title, Ovid's *Banquet of Sence*,
1595 (Mallory).

194–9.] itemising the senses in what should be descending order:
sight is the highest and nearest to the spiritual, touch the lowest, but here
significantly it excels the rest.

herald, go from ourself, the great god Jupiter, to the great
emperor, Augustus Caesar, and command him from us
(of whose bounty he hath received his surname Augustus)
that for a thank-offering to our beneficence he presently
sacrifice as a dish to this banquet his beautiful and          205
wanton daughter, Julia. She's a cursed quean, tell him,
and plays the scold behind his back. Therefore, let her be
sacrificed. Command him this Mercury, in our high name
of Jupiter Altitonans.

*Julia.* Stay, feather-footed Mercury, and tell Augustus from     210
us, the great Juno Saturnia, if he think it hard to do as
Jupiter hath commanded him and sacrifice his daughter,
that he had better to do so ten times than suffer her to
love the well-nosed poet Ovid, whom he shall do well to
whip, or cause to be whipped, about the Capitol, for          215
soothing her in her follies.


### ACT IV   SCENE vi

[*Enter to them*] CAESAR, MAECENAS, HORACE, LUPUS, HISTRIO,
MINOS [*and*] Lictors.

*Caesar.* What sight is this? Maecenas, Horace, say,
Have we our senses? Do we hear and see?
Or are these but imaginary objects

---

IV.vi.o.1–2.] *Enter* AUGUSTUS CÆSAR . . . Lictors. *G, continuing the
scene.* 1. Maecenas . . . say,] *Subst. Parfitt; Mecœnas, Horace, say; Q;*
MECŒNAS! HORACE! say! *F.*

---

203. *of . . . Augustus*] Octavian was given the *cognomen* 'Augustus'
by the Senate in 27 BC: 'some were of minde that he should be called
*Romulus* . . . But it was at length decreed by the advise of *Manutius Plancus*,
that he should be styled by the name of *Augustus*: which we may English
*Soveraigne*' (Godwyn, p. 120). 'Majesty' is the usual translation, but the
Latin *augustus*, 'originally belonging to the language of religion' (Lewis and
Short), retained also the sense of holiness.
209. *Altitonans*] 'high-thundering'; cf. *Iliad* I, 528–30.
210. *feather-footed*] from his winged feet: cf. *CR* I.i.22, 'feather-heeled'.
211. *Juno Saturnia*] Juno/Hera was daughter of Saturn/Kronos.
215. *Capitol*] the *Capitolium*, the temple of Jupiter, built on the Capitoline
hill.
216. *soothing*] encouraging (*OED*, 4).

Drawn by our fantasy? Why speak you not?
Let us do sacrifice! Are they the gods?                            5
Reverence, amaze and fury fight in me.

[OVID *and the rest kneel.*]
What! Do they kneel? Nay, then I see 'tis true
I thought impossible. O impious sight!
Let me divert mine eyes; the very thought
Everts my soul with passion. Look not man!                        10
There is a panther whose unnatural eyes
Will strike thee dead. Turn then    *He offers to kill*
    and die on her                 *his daughter.*
With her own death.

[MAECENAS *and* HORACE *stand in his way.*]
*Maecenas, Horace.*      What means imperial Caesar?
*Caesar.* What, would you have me let the strumpet live,
That for this pageant earns so many deaths?                       15

---

5. Let . . . sacrifice!] *Nicholson; Let . . . Sacrifice? Q, Subst. F.*      6.1. S.D.]
*G.*    12. S.D.] *F in margin; not in Q.*      13. With . . . Caesar] *This ed.; Q,
F, print as two lines.*    S.D.] *This ed.*

---

IV.vi.4. *fantasy*] delusive imagination (*OED*, 4) as in *Ham.* I.i.54, 'Is not
this something more than fantasy?'

5. *Let . . . sacrifice!*] An ironic command, rather than a question, as the
punctuation of *Q* and *F* can make it seem (so *G*). Whalley sees it as a
question to the attendants.

6. *amaze*] wonder, amazement.

8. *impious sight*] because blasphemous, libertine and a betrayal of the
poet's god-given responsibility; even so, Caesar overreacts in attempting to
kill Julia (see p. 21).

10. *Everts*] overturns.

*man*] addressing himself: *H&S* cite *EMI* III.vi.22.

11–12. *panther . . . dead*] Cf. Pliny, *Natural History*, trans. Holland (1601)
VIII.xvii: 'It is said, that all four-footed beasts are wonderfully delighted and
enticed by the smell of Panthers; but their hideous looke and crabbed
countenance which they bewray so soone as they shew their heads, skareth
them as much againe'; see also Edward Topsell, *The History of Foure-footed
Beasts* (1607), pp. 450–1. For the panther's breath, cf. *CR* V.iv.433 and
*Volp.* III.vii.214. Julia is the 'panther' here.

12–13. *Turn . . . death*] Having averted his gaze, Caesar now turns to look
at Julia, and expects to die while killing her; for 'die on' meaning to die while
killing one's enemy, cf. *Gent.* II.iv.114, 'I'll die on him that says so but
yourself'.

12. S.D. offers] attempts (*OED*, 5).

13. *imperial*] The epithet draws attention to Caesar's special responsibilities, which must come before the 'passion' of the man.

*Tucca.* [*Aside to 1 Pyrgus*] Boy, slink, boy.

[*1*] *Pyrgus.* 'Pray Jupiter we be not followed by the scent,
    master.          [*Exeunt* TUCCA *and* 1 PYRGUS *unnoticed.*]

*Caesar.* [*To Albius*] Say, sir, what are you?

*Albius.* I play Vulcan, sir.                                                    20

*Caesar.* But what are you, sir?

*Albius.* Your citizen and jeweller, sir.

*Caesar.* [*To Chloe*] And what are you, dame?

*Chloe.* I play Venus, forsooth.

*Caesar.* I ask not what you play, but what you are!          25

*Chloe.* Your citizen and jeweller's wife, sir.

*Caesar.* [*To Crispinus*] And you, good sir?

*Crispinus.* Your gentleman parcel-poet, sir.

*Caesar.* O that profanèd name!

[*To Julia*] And are these seemly company for thee,          30
Degenerate monster? All the rest I know,
And hate all knowledge for their hateful sakes.

[*To Ovid, Gallus and Tibullus*] Are you, that first the
    deities inspired
With skill of their high natures and their powers,
The first abusers of their useful light,                                    35
Profaning thus their dignities in their forms,
And making them, like you, but counterfeits?
O who shall follow virtue and embrace her,
When her false bosom is found naught but air?
And yet of those embraces centaurs spring,          40
That war with human peace and poison men.

---

16. S.D.] *This ed.*          18. S.D.] *Subst. G.*          28. sir.] sir. *Exit. G.*          30.
S.D.] *G.*

25.] On the significance of this statement for J.'s attitude to the theatre,
see Womack, pp. 109–11.

28. *parcel-poet*] See III.iv.164n.

33. *first*] poetry is seen here as both the oldest and the pre-eminent art
form; cf. *Disc.* 2291 and 2382–5.

*inspired*] for J.'s view of divine inspiration, see *Disc.*, 2411–34, Ovid
himself being quoted: 'There is a god within us; his stirring heats us; from
heavenly places comes our inspiration.' Cf. *Fasti* VI.5 and *Ars amatoria* III,
549–50.

34. *skill*] knowledge, understanding.

38–41.] In some versions the centaurs were born of Ixion 'embracing' a
cloud of air shaped like Hera; they were associated by the Greeks with lust,
wine and barbarism.

Who shall with greater comforts comprehend
Her unseen being and her excellence
When you that teach and should eternise her
Live as she were no law unto your lives,                    45
Nor lived herself, but with your idle breaths?
If you think gods but feigned and virtue painted,
Know we sustain an actual residence,
And with the title of an emperor
Retain his spirit and imperial power;                    50
By which, in imposition too remiss,
Licentious Naso, for thy violent wrong
In soothing the declined affections
Of our base daughter, we exile thy feet
From all approach to our imperial court                    55
On pain of death; and thy misgotten love
Commit to patronage of iron doors,
Since her soft-hearted sire cannot contain her.
*Maecenas.* O good my lord, forgive: be like the gods.
*Horace.* Let royal bounty, Caesar, mediate.                    60
*Caesar.* There is no bounty to be showed to such
       As have no real goodness. Bounty is

---

51–4. in . . . daughter] *In parentheses in Q, F.*     54. our] *F;* my *Q.*     we]
*F;* I *Q.*     60. Caesar] *In parentheses in Q, F.*

---

42–6.] Cf. *Volp.* Epistle, 19–29, and *Disc.* 2388–96, for the relationship
between virtue and poetry, and the need for the good poet to be first a good
man; J.'s ideas are based on Hor. *Epist.* II.i.126–31 (addressed to Augustus),
Cicero *Arch.* VII.16, and Renaissance theorists such as Minturno *De Poeta*
(Venice, 1559), p. 8.
   42. *comforts*] encouragements, support (*OED*, 1).
   46. *idle*] worthless, trifling (*OED*, 2).
   51. *imposition*] penalty (*OED* s.v. 'impose' 4d).
   53. *declined*] in Latin sense of having turned away from a proper course.
   53–6.] For belief in Julia's part in Ovid's banishment, see Persons of the
Play, 8n and 24n.
   57. *patronage*] guardianship, tutelary care (*OED*, 2).
   *iron doors*] J. would have known that the elder Julia was exiled in 2 BC to
the island of Pandateria, where she remained five years under harsh conditions (Suetonius *Divus Augustus* LXV). Though she was allowed to return
to the mainland, Tiberius, her former husband, increased her privations and
she died, probably of malnutrition, in AD 14.
   59. *be . . . gods*] proverbial, but referring ironically to the cause of Caesar's
anger.
   62. *real*] punning on Horace's appeal to 'royal' bounty, l. 60; 'royal' was

A spice of virtue, and what virtuous act
Can take effect on them that have no power
Of equal habitude to apprehend it,                                              65
But live in worship of that idol, vice,
As if there were no virtue, but in shade
Of strong imagination, merely enforced?
This shows their knowledge is mere ignorance,
Their far-fetched dignity of soul a fancy,                                      70
And all their square pretext of gravity
A mere vainglory. Hence, away with 'em.
I will prefer for knowledge none but such
As rule their lives by it, and can becalm
All sea of humour with the marble trident                                      75
Of their strong spirits. Others fight below
With gnats and shadows, others nothing know.    *Exeunt.*

ACT IV   SCENE vii

[*Enter*] TUCCA, CRISPINUS, [*and* 1] PYRGUS.

*Tucca.* What's become of my little punk, Venus, and the
poltfoot stinkard her husband, ha?

---

77. S.D.] *Q.*   IV.vii.o.1.] *A Street before the Palace. / Enter* TUCCA,
CRISPINUS, *and* Pyrgus. *G.*

---

often spelt 'real', and *OED* first records 'real' in its common modern sense in
1601.
    62–3. *Bounty . . . virtue*] *H&S* note the echo of Seneca *Ben.* I.xv.3: 'Since
no effort of the mind is praiseworthy, even if it springs from right desire,
unless moderation turns it into some virtue, I protest against the squandering
of liberality. The benefit that it is a delight to have received, yea, with
outstretched hands, is the one that reason delivers to those who are worthy,
not the one that chance and irrational impulse carry no matter where.'
    63. *a spice of*] a kind of (*OED*, 3b, quoting this passage).
    65. *habitude*] moral disposition (*OED*, 1).
    67–8. *but . . . enforced*] except that merely imposed form which can only
exist in the protective shade of strong imagination. J. may have Chapman in
particular in mind: see *The Shadow of Night* (1594) and *Ovid's Banquet of
Sence* (1595).
    69. *knowledge*] understanding, apprehension of truth (cf. *OED*, 9).
    71. *square*] solid, reliable.
    73. *prefer*] favour, advance.
    IV.vii.2. *poltfoot*] clubfooted, because Vulcan (not Albius) was lame;
Mallory cites *Merc. Vind.* 37, where Vulcan is 'this polt-footed Philosopher'.

*Crispinus.* O, they are rid home i' the coach as fast as the wheels can run.

*Tucca.* God Jupiter is banished, I hear, and his cockatrice Juno    5
locked up. 'Heart, and all the poetry in Parnassus get me
to be a player again, I'll sell 'em my share for a sesterce.
But this is Humours Horace, that goat-footed envious
slave. He's turned fawn now, an informer, the rogue; 'tis
he has betrayed us all. Did you not see him with the    10
emperor, crouching?

*Crispinus.* Yes.

*Tucca.* Well, follow me. Thou shalt libel, and I'll cudgel the
rascal. [*To 1 Pyrgus*] Boy, provide me a truncheon.
Revenge shall gratulate him, *tam Marti, quam Mercurio.*    15

[*1*] *Pyrgus.* Ay, but master, take heed how you give this
out; Horace is a man of the sword.

*Crispinus.* 'Tis true, in troth; they say he's valiant.

*Tucca.* Valiant? So is mine arse! Gods and fiends! I'll blow
him into air when I meet him next. He dares not fight    20
with a puck-fist.

[*1*] *Pyrgus.* Master, here he comes.

---

6. and] *Parfitt;* and and *Q, F;* an *G.*     7. a sesterce] *F;* six pence *Q.*     8.
Humours] *This ed.; Humours; Q;* humours, *uncorr. F;* humours, *corr. F;*
*humorous F2.*     15. quam] *Q; quàm F.*

---

6. *'Heart*] See III.i.74n.

7. *player*] as he has just been in the banquet.

8. *Humours Horace*] referring to J.'s theory of 'humours'; see esp. *EMO*
Ind. 88–109. This is the most explicit identification J. makes between
himself and Horace; he had been addressed as 'Monsieur Humorist' by 'W.I.'
(John Weever) in *The Whipping of the Satyre* (see p. 28 and IV.iii.117–8)
and the term was so clearly identified with J. that Dekker's stage-title for *S-
M* was *The Untrussing of the Humorous Poet.*

9. *fawn*] one who fawns: cf. V.i.95. *H&S* note that Faunus was identified with the goat-footed Pan, and thus with satyrs. J. may also still be
thinking of Weever, whose *Faunus and Melliflora* appeared in 1600.

15. *gratulate*] both greet (as in II.ii.15) and reward.

tam Marti, quam Mercurio] both with the cudgel (Mars) and the libel
(Mercury) (so Nicholson). It had been Gascoigne's motto: see *The Steel Glas*
(1576), title-page.

17. *Horace . . . sword*] a boast ridiculed in *S-M* IV.ii.50–1: 'Holde Capten,
tis knowne that Horace is valliant, and a man of the sword.' Hor. and J. had
both been soldiers: see p. 10.

21. *puck-fist*] the puff-ball mushroom; cf. *Alc.* I.ii.62–3: 'I'ld choake, ere
I would change / An article of breath, with such a puck-fist'.

HORACE *passes by.*

*Tucca.* Where? [*To Horace*] Jupiter save thee, my good
poet, my noble prophet, my little fat Horace. I scorn to
beat the rogue i' the court, and I saluted him thus fair,        25
because he should suspect nothing, the rascal. Come,
we'll go see how forward our journeyman is toward the
untrussing of him.

*Crispinus.* Do you hear, captain? I'll write nothing in it but
innocence, because I may swear I am innocent.    *Exeunt.*      30


[ACT IV   SCENE viii]

[*Enter* HORACE, MAECENAS, LUPUS, HISTRIO *and* Lictors.]

*Horace.* Nay, why pursue you not the emperor
For your reward now, Lupus?

---

22.1 S.D.] *F in margin; not in Q.*     24. noble] *F; not in Q.*     little fat]
*noble Q.*     30. S.D.] *Q.*     ACT IV. SCENE viii] *Subst.G., who starts a
new scene* SCENE VI. / *Enter* HORACE ... Lictors. *Q and F continue the
scene to l. 31 below.*     1–2. Nay ... Lupus] *G; prose in Q, F.*

---

22.1. S.D.] Allardyce Nicoll plausibly suggests that such stage directions
as 'passes by' meant the actor walked across in front of the stage: see 'Passing
Over the Stage', *Sh.S*, XII (1959), 47–53; cf. Chambers, *ES*, III, pp. 29 and
40.

24. *prophet*] as in Latin *vates*, the poet as teller of inspired truth.

*little fat*] Suetonius describes Hor. as 'short and fat'. Cf. Dekker, *S-M*
V.ii.261–2: '*Horace* was a goodly Corpulent Gentleman'.

26. *because*] so that (*OED*, 2).

27–8. *journeyman ... him*] either Dekker took this phrase for his title or
(much more likely) J. knew at this stage of the title of Dekker's projected
play. Cf. also V.iii.296 and notes to III.iv.322–4, 334–5. It is probable
that during the earliest performances of *Poetaster* the 'journeyman' Dekker
actually was hard at work on *The Untrussing of the Humorous Poet*, the
stage-title of *S-M*, but that for most of the winter season of 1601–2 the
two plays ran simultaneously: see pp. 28–9.

27. *journeyman*] hireling (*OED*, 2).

28. *untrussing*] exposing: see V.iii.296n.

30. *innocence ... innocent*] See III.iv.334–5n, and cf. V.iii.287n.

IV.viii.] Nicholson, evidently transcribing *G*, wrongly notes that J. 'has a
new scene here in the folios, against his own rule'. It is not a new scene in the
folios, but it is 'against his own rule' to continue the scene with the entrance
of six new characters and the exit of Tucca, Crispinus and the Pyrgi.

*Maecenas.*                                Stay Asinius;
    You and your stager, and your band of Lictors,
    I hope your service merits more respect
    Than thus without a thanks to be sent hence?                    5
*Lupus.* Well, well; jest on, jest on.
*Horace.* Thou base, unworthy groom.
*Lupus.*                                Ay, ay, 'tis good.
*Horace.* Was this the treason, this the dangerous plot,
    Thy clamorous tongue so bellowed through the court?
    Hadst thou no other project to increase                        10
    Thy grace with Caesar, but this wolfish train,
    To prey upon the life of innocent mirth
    And harmless pleasures, bred of noble wit?
    Away! I loathe thy presence. Such as thou,
    They are the moths and scarabs of a state,                     15
    The bane of empires, and the dregs of courts,
    Who, to endear themselves to any employment,
    Care not whose fame they blast, whose life they endanger;
    And under a disguised and cobweb mask
    Of love unto their sovereign, vomit forth                      20
    Their own prodigious malice; and pretending
    To be the props and columns of his safety,
    The guards unto his person and his peace,

---

2-3. Stay ... Lictors] *Corr. F; one line in Q, uncorr. F.*    6. *Lupus*]
*This ed.; Histrio Q; HIST F.*    7. *Lupus.* Ay, ay,] *Subst. G; (Lupus) I
Q; LVPV. I, I, F.*    8. *Horace.*] *F; not in Q, owing to its confusion
in l. 7.*    16. empires] *F; Kingdomes Q.*    17. to ... any employment]
*Nicholson;* (to ... any'mploiment) *Q;*    (to ... any 'employment) *F;* to ...
an employment *G.*

---

    6. Lupus.] *Q* and *F* both give this reply to Histrio, but he would not
speak thus to Horace and, especially, Maecenas; Horace and Maecenas have
addressed Lupus, who would be expected to reply, and the dialogue is
continued by him (l. 7) in exactly the same style of speech.
    11. *wolfish*] alluding to Lupus' name.
    14-24.] Cf. Ind. 35-40; V.iii.132-9, and *Volp.* Epistle, 64-6, 'these
invading interpreters . . . who . . . utter their own virulent malice under other
men's simplest meanings.' For the role of informers, see pp. 41-2.
    15. *scarabs*] at this time a dung beetle, hence a term of general abuse
(*OED,* 1b, quoting this example); cf. *Alc.* I.i.59.
    17. *any employment*] *F*'s 'any' employment' is an example of J.'s metrical
apostrophe, indicating elision of a syllable; cf. III.v.15n. It is not used in *Q.*
    19. *cobweb*] both treacherous and flimsy.

Disturb it most with their false lapwing cries.

*Lupus.* Good! Caesar shall know of this, believe it.                    25

               *Exeunt* [LUPUS, HISTRIO *and* Lictors].

*Maecenas.* Caesar doth know it, wolf, and to his knowledge,

    He will, I hope, reward your base endeavours.

    Princes that will but hear, or give access

    To such officious spies, can ne'er be safe:

    They take in poison with an open ear,                    30

    And, free from danger, become slaves to fear.   *Exeunt.*

### [ACT IV   SCENE ix]

#### [*Enter*] OVID.

*Ovid.* Banished the court? Let me be banished life,

    Since the chief end of life is there concluded:

    Within the court is all the kingdom bounded,

    And as her sacred sphere doth comprehend

    Ten thousand times so much, as so much place                    5

    In any part of all the empire else;

    So every body moving in her sphere

    Contains ten thousand times as much in him

---

25.1. *Exeunt*] Q.     26. wolf] *In parentheses in* Q, F.     27. I hope] *In parentheses in* Q, F.     28–31. *Gnomic pointing in* Q, F.     31. S.D.] Q. IV.ix.0.] SCENA OCTAVA. Q; Act IIII. Scene VIII. F; SCENE VII / *An open Space before the Palace.* / *Enter* OVID. G.

---

24. *lapwing*] Cf. Dent, L68: 'The lapwing cries most when farthest from her nest.' See *Sej.* V.568, and *Err.* IV.ii.27: 'Far from her nest the lapwing cries away; / My heart prays for him though my tongue do curse.'

IV.ix.] See pp. 22–3; *H&S* say that, together with IV.x, this is the 'only passage in J. in which his conception of a love-scene is elaborately worked out. Usually he disposes of such episodes and characters rather summarily.' *G* differs: 'I am afraid that this ridiculous love scene will not strike the reader as much in the manner of Ovid: there is neither pathos, nor passion, nor interest in it, but a kind of metaphysical hurly-burly, of which it is not easy to discover the purport or end.' The end is that of serious parody (see p. 22). The echoes of *Rom.* have often been noted, but not those of Ovid's description of his farewell to his wife in *Tristia* I.iii, and his memories of her in *Tristia* IV.iii, nor of Chapman's Ovid in *Ovid's Banquet of Sence.*

2. *concluded*] encompassed, confined (Latin, *concludo*).

4. *sphere*] in early astronomy, a transparent globe surrounding the earth and carrying heavenly bodies (l. 7) on it. The astronomical imagery continues to l. 9.

*comprehend*] take in, encompass.

As any other her choice orb excludes.
As in a circle a magician then                                    10
Is safe against the spirit he excites,
But out of it is subject to his rage
And loseth all the virtue of his art,
So I exiled the circle of the court
Lose all the good gifts that in it I 'joyed.                      15
No virtue current is, but with her stamp,
And no vice vicious, blanched with her white hand.
The court's the abstract of all Rome's desert,
And my dear Julia th' abstract of the court.
Methinks now I come near her I respire                            20
Some air of that late comfort I received;
And while the evening with her modest veil
Gives leave to such poor shadows as myself
To steal abroad, I, like a heartless ghost
Without the living body of my love,                               25
Will here walk and attend her. For I know
Not far from hence she is imprisonèd,
And hopes of her strict guardian to bribe
So much admittance as to speak to me,
And cheer my fainting spirits with her breath.                    30

[ACT IV   SCENE x]

[*Enter to him*] JULIA. *She appeareth above, as at her chamber window.*

*Julia.*  Ovid? My love?
*Ovid.*                    Here, heavenly Julia.

---

15. 'joyed] *Subst. F2;* ioy'd *Q, F.*    16–17.] *Gnomic pointing in Q, F.*
17. And] *F; Nor Q.*    IV.x.0.] SCENA NONA. *Q;* Act IIII. Scene IX.
*F; G. continues the scene.*    0.1. *She . . . window.*] *F in margin; not in Q.*

---

11. *excites*] calls up (Latin, *excito*).
13. *virtue*] power.
15. *'joyed*] enjoyed.
17. *blanched*] literally 'made white', hence pure.
18. *abstract*] compendium, microcosm.
20. *respire*] breathe, but with suggestion of 'recover hope' (*OED*, 3).
24–5. *like . . . love*] emphasising the sensual, physical quality of Ovid's love: cf. IV.x.31–41, 108–9.
26. *attend*] wait for.
29. *admittance*] consent.

*Julia.* Here and not here? O how that word doth play
    With both our fortunes, differing like ourselves:
    Both one, and yet divided, as opposed!
    I high, thou low! O this our plight of place          5
    Doubly presents the two lets of our love,
    Local and ceremonial height and lowness;
    Both ways I am too high, and thou too low.
    Our minds are even yet; O why should our bodies,
    That are their slaves, be so without their rule?          10
    I'll cast myself down to thee. If I die
    I'll ever live with thee; no height of birth,
    Of place, of duty, or of cruel power
    Shall keep me from thee. Should my father lock
    This body up within a tomb of brass          15
    Yet I'll be with thee. If the forms I hold
    Now in my soul be made one substance with it,
    That soul immortal, and the same 'tis now,
    Death cannot raze th' affects she now retaineth;
    And then may she be anywhere she will.          20
    The souls of parents rule not children's souls
    When death sets both in their dissolved estates;
    Then is no child, nor father; then eternity
    Frees all from any temporal respect.
    I come, my Ovid, take me in thine arms,          25
    And let me breathe my soul into thy breast.
*Ovid.* O stay, my love! The hopes thou dost conceive
    Of thy quick death and of thy future life

---

IV.x.6. *lets*] obstacles.
    7. *Local*] of physical place.
*ceremonial*] of the ceremony of social hierarchy.
    9. *even*] equal in rank (*OED*, 13); cf. *Ovid's Banquet of Sence*, st. 90.
    15. *tomb of brass*] J. may be recalling Hor.'s 'monument more lasting than bronze', *Odes* III.xxx.1.
    16–17. *If . . . it*] The form/substance duality is loosely Aristotelian, and one that J. uses in *Hym.* Here, the insubstantial 'forms' of love are to be fused after death with the shaping principle of the soul to form one substance. Cf. *Ovid's Banquet of Sence*, st. 93: 'and t'is thy substance must my longings ease.'
    19. *affects*] affections.
*she*] the soul.
    28. *quick*] speedy, but also living, in that Julia's view of fulfilled love after death is conceived as if she were to be still alive, as Ovid points out.

Are not authentical. Thou choosest death
So thou mightst 'joy thy love in th' other life.                    30
But know, my princely love, when thou art dead,
Thou only must survive in perfect soul,
And in the soul are no affections.
We pour out our affections with our blood,
And with our blood's affections fade our loves.                     35
No life hath love in such sweet state as this;
No essence is so dear to moody sense
As flesh and blood, whose quintessence is sense.
Beauty composed of blood and flesh moves more,
And is more plausible to blood and flesh                            40
Than spiritual beauty can be to the spirit.
Such apprehension as we have in dreams
(When sleep, the bond of senses, locks them up)
Such shall we have when death destroys them quite.
If love be then thy object, change not life:                        45
Live high, and happy still. I still below,
Close with my fortunes, in thy height shall joy.

---

29. authentical] *F2; autenticall Q, F Subst.*    30. 'joy] *G;* ioy *Q, F* (cf.
IV.ix.15).    31. my . . . love] *In parentheses in Q, F.*    36–41.] *Gnomic
pointing in Q, F.*

---

29. *authentical*] authentic; this form is favoured by J.; cf. *EMO* IV.iii.24,
'autenticall physicians', and *SW* III.ii.28, 'shee is the onely authenticall
courtier'. Cf. *Ovid's Banquet of Sence*, st. 79: 'let autentique Reason be our
guide'.

36–41.] The pointing may indicate an unidentified quotation, but is more
probably gnomic. *H&S* quote Donne, 'Extasy', but neither there nor in 'Air
and Angels' does Donne separate 'spiritual beauty' from the physical as
absolutely as Ovid does here. In this respect he is still the 'banquet of sense'
spokesman, not a neoplatonist.

37. *moody*] subject to varying emotions.

38. *flesh . . . sense*] echoing or anticipating Donne, 'Valediction Forbidding
Mourning', 13–14: 'Dull sublunary lovers' love / (Whose soul is sense)'; cf.
also *NI* III.ii.130–1: 'They are the earthly, lower form of lovers / Are only
taken with what strikes the senses'.

40. *plausible*] gratifying (*OED*, 2), a meaning of crucial importance in
understanding Ovid's speech. It does not have the common modern sense of
'specious' (*OED*, 3). Ovid is in effect saying that physical, earthly love is
preferable to spiritual.

42. *apprehension*] sensual perception (*OED*, 5); cf. *MND* III.ii.177–8:
'Dark night, that from the eye his function takes, / The ear more quick of
apprehension makes.'

47. *close*] secretive, with a suggestion of stoic acceptance.

*Julia.* Ay me, that virtue, whose brave eagle's wings
     With every stroke blow stars in burning heaven,
     Should like a swallow, preying towards storms,                    50
     Fly close to earth, and with an eager plume
     Pursue those objects which none else can see
     But seem to all the world the empty air.
     Thus thou, poor Ovid, and all virtuous men,
     Must prey like swallows on invisible food,                    55
     Pursuing flies, or nothing; and thus love,
     And every worldly fancy, is transposed
     By worldly tyranny to what plight it list.
     O father, since thou gav'st me not my mind,
     Strive not to rule it; take but what thou gav'st                    60
     To thy disposure. Thy affections
     Rule not in me; I must bear all my griefs,
     Let me use all my pleasures. Virtuous love
     Was never scandal to a goddess' state.
     But he's inflexible! And, my dear love,                    65
     Thy life may chance be shortened by the length
     Of my unwilling speeches to depart.
     Farewell sweet life: though thou be yet exiled
     Th' officious court, enjoy me amply still;
     My soul in this my breath enters thine ears,                    70
     And on this turret's floor will I lie dead
     Till we may meet again. In this proud height
     I kneel beneath thee in my prostrate love,

---

50. preying . . . storms] *In parentheses in Q, F.*   54. poor Ovid] *In parentheses in Q, F.*   63. Virtuous] 'Vertuous *Q (which should therefore have
printed* 'Was *in* 64).

---

48. *virtue*] moral goodness; cf. l. 54, and Caesar's statement in V.i.66–7,
which effectively denies to Ovid the virtue that Julia is claiming for him here.
   49. *blow*] in sense of hit, rather than blossom.
   50–1. *like . . . earth*] *H&S* quote *The Faithful Friends* III.iii (*Beaumont
and Fletcher*, ed. Dyce, IV, 264): 'My father was a soldier, and that blood / I
took from him which flows within this breast, / Not, swallow-like, foreseeing
of a storm, / Flags to the ground, but soars up higher still.'
   57. *fancy*] both a mental construct, product of the imagination (*OED*, 4b,
earliest example 1663) and amorous inclination (*OED*, 8b).
   61. *disposure*] power to dispose.
   *affections*] both feelings and state of mind.
   71.] Cf. *Tristia* I.iii.92, where Ovid's wife 'fell half dead in the midst of
our home'.

And kiss the happy sands that kiss thy feet.
Great Jove submits a sceptre to a cell,                          75
And lovers ere they part will meet in hell.

*Ovid.* Farewell all company, and, if I could,
  All light with thee: hell's shade should hide my brows
  Till thy dear beauty's beams redeemed my vows.
              [OVID *turns to leave.] She calls him back.*

*Julia.* Ovid my love, alas, may we not stay                      80
  A little longer, think'st thou, undiscerned?

*Ovid.* For thine own good fair goddess, do not stay.
  Who would engage a firmament of fires
  Shining in thee, for me, a falling star?
  Begone sweet life-blood; if I should discern                 85
  Thyself but touched for my sake I should die.

*Julia.* I will be gone then, and not heaven itself
  Shall draw me back.
              *[She turns to leave.] He calls her back.*

*Ovid.*            Yet Julia, if thou wilt,
  A little longer stay.

*Julia.*              I am content.

*Ovid.* O mighty Ovid! What the sway of heaven                    90
  Could not retire, my breath hath turnèd back.

*Julia.* Who shall go first, my love? My passionate eyes
  Will not endure to see thee turn from me.

*Ovid.* If thou go first, my soul will follow thee.

*Julia.* Then we must stay.

*Ovid.*             Ay me, there is no stay            95
  In amorous pleasures; if both stay, both die.

---

75–6.] *Gnomic pointing in Q, F.*   79.1. *Ovid . . . leave] This ed.*   *She . . .
back.] Corr. F in margin; not in Q, uncorr. F.*   81. think'st thou] *In parentheses in Q, F.*   88. *She . . . leave] This ed.*   *He . . . back.] Corr. F in
margin; not in Q, uncorr. F.*

---

75. *submits]* changes, reduces: Latin, *submitto.*

76. *ere . . . part]* i.e. rather than part.

80–9.] Cf. *Tristia* I.iii.47–60 for the indecision about leaving, esp. 55–6:
'Thrice I touched the threshold, thrice did something call me back'.

83. *engage]* expose to danger.

91. *retire]* bring back (*OED*, 9); cf. *EMI* (Q) I.i.9–11: 'How happy
would I estimate my selfe, / Could I . . . retyre my sonne, / From one vayne
course of study he affects?'

95–6. *no stay . . . die]* A complex pun on 'stay' (noun) as both 'physical
restraint' (*OED, sb.* 3. 2) and 'emotional support' (*OED, sb.* 2. 1b, c) and

I hear thy father! Hence my deity.            *Exit* JULIA.
Fear forgeth sounds in my deluded ears:
I did not hear him. I am mad with love.
There is no spirit under heaven that works              100
With such illusion; yet such witchcraft kill me
Ere a sound mind without it save my life.     [*Kneeling*]
Here on my knees I worship the blest place
That held my goddess, and the loving air
That closed her body in his silken arms.                105
Vain Ovid! Kneel not to the place, nor air.    [*Rising*]
She's in thy heart: rise then, and worship there.
The truest wisdom silly men can have
Is dotage on the follies of their flesh.            *Exit.*

---

97. S.D.] Q.    102. S.D.] *This   ed.*    106. S.D.] *This    ed.*    108–9.]
*Gnomic pointing in* Q, F.    109. S.D.] Q.

---

(as verb), 'remain in the same place' (*OED*, *v.* 1. 4) and 'appease the
[sexual] appetite' (*OED*, *v.* 1. 29), and on 'die' in the literal sense and the
common figurative one meaning 'orgasm'.
    108–9.] echoing *Ovid's Banquet of Sence*, st. 12: 'Nature, our fate, our
wisdom, folly.'

# Act V

[*Enter*] CAESAR, MAECENAS, [CORNELIUS] GALLUS, TIBULLUS
[*and*] HORACE.

*Caesar.* We that have conquered still to save the conquered,
  And loved to make inflictions feared, not felt,
  Grieved to reprove, and joyful to reward,
  More proud of reconcilement than revenge,
  Resume into the late state of our love                                    5
  Worthy Cornelius Gallus and Tibullus.
  You both are knights; and you, Cornelius,
  A soldier of renown, and the first provost
  That ever let our Roman eagles fly
  On swarthy Egypt, quarried with her spoils.                              10

---

V.i.0.1. GALLUS] *F; Pallus Q. An Apartment in the Palace. / Enter*
CÆSAR, . . . Equites Romani. *G.*   7. knights; and you] *Q;* gentlemen,
you *F;* gentlemen, and you *G.*

---

V.i.1–4.] Distantly based on Virgil *Aeneid* VI, 851–3: 'remember thou, O
Roman, to rule the nations with thy sway—these shall be thine arts—to
crown Peace with Law, to spare the humbled, and tame in war the proud',
and Augustus' Triumph as portrayed on Aeneas' shield (*Aeneid* VIII,
714–31). Cf. also Suetonius *Divus Augustus* LXVII: 'As patron and master he
was no less strict than gracious and merciful'.
  1. *still*] always, ever.
  5. *Resume*] Take back (*OED*, 4a).
  7. *knights*] Gallus rose to equestrian rank, Tibullus was probably born to
it. Tibullus was not part of the circle close to Augustus.
  8–10.] Gallus was sent to Egypt by Octavius in 31 BC, helped to defeat
Antony, and after Cleopatra's death became first *praefectus* ('provost') of
Egypt. He set up statues to himself, and had boastful inscriptions carved on
the pyramids, thought to be the reason why he was renounced by Augustus,
and committed suicide before charges were brought against him.
  10. *quarried*] describing a hawk being taught to hunt prey (*OED, v.* 1a):
Egypt has supplied spoils to teach the Roman eagles.

Yet, not to bear cold forms, nor men's out-terms
Without the inward fires and lives of men,
You both have virtues shining through your shapes
To show your titles are not writ on posts
Or hollow statues, which the best men are,                    15
Without Promethean stuffings reached from heaven.
Sweet poesy's sacred garlands crown your knighthoods,
Which is, of all the faculties on earth,
The most abstract and perfect, if she be
True born and nursed with all the sciences.                    20
She can so mould Rome and her monuments
Within the liquid marble of her lines
That they shall stand fresh and miraculous,
Even when they mix with innovating dust.
In her sweet streams shall our brave Roman spirits          25
Chase and swim after death with their choice deeds
Shining on their white shoulders; and therein

---

11–12. not . . . men] *In parentheses in* Q, F.      17. knighthoods] Q; gentrie
F.

11. *out-terms*] external, bodily forms; the only recorded use in *OED*, but
*H&S* cite *Ep.* CXIV, 3–4: 'For Cupid, who at first took vain delight / In
mere out-forms, until he lost his sight'.
12.] i.e. both have the inner life and fire necessary to make them complete
men.
14–15.] Perhaps an ironic echo of Gallus' fondness for inscribing his deeds
at large; posts were set up outside the houses of Elizabethan sheriffs and
magistrates: see *Tw.N* I.v.147–8: 'He'll stand at your door like a sheriff's
post.'
16. *Promethean stuffings*] the life-infusing fire with which Prometheus
animated the man he made out of clay (cf. Hor. *Odes* I.xvi.13–16).
17–20.] Cf. *EMI* (Q) V.iii.342–3: 'a true Poet: then which reverend
name, / Nothing can more adorn humanitie'; also *Disc.* 1873–6 and 2386–96,
and *Volp.* Epistle, 15–29 and 121–6.
19–20. *if . . . sciences*] Such largeness of moral and intellectual achievement is what Ovid in particular lacks: later Horace points to such moral
'knowledge' as the source of his freedom from envy (l. 88).
19. *abstract*] pure, withdrawn from contaminating material considerations
(*OED*, 4).
22. *liquid marble*] based on Virgil's 'Others . . . shall from marble draw
forth the features of life' ('vivos ducent de marmore vultus'), *Aeneid* VI, 848.
24. *innovating*] bringing innovations, often at this time with the sense of
revolution (*OED* s.v. 'innovation' 1b).

Shall Tiber and our famous rivers fall
With such attraction, that th' ambitious line
Of the round world shall to her centre shrink          30
To hear their music. And for these high parts
Caesar shall reverence the Pierian arts.

*Maecenas.* Your majesty's high grace to poesy
Shall stand 'gainst all the dull detractions
Of leaden souls, who, for the vain assumings          35
Of some, quite worthless of her sovereign wreaths,
Contain her worthiest prophets in contempt.

*Gallus.* Happy is Rome of all earth's other states
To have so true and great a president
For her inferior spirits to imitate                    40
As Caesar is, who addeth to the sun
Influence and lustre, in increasing thus
His inspirations, kindling fire in us.

*Horace.* Phoebus himself shall kneel at Caesar's shrine
And deck it with bay garlands dewed with wine          45

---

35–6. for . . . wreaths] *In parentheses in Q, F.*

---

28–31. *Tiber . . . music*] Cf. *Caes.* I.i.44–7: 'Have you not made an universal shout, / That Tiber trembled underneath her banks / To hear the replication of your sounds / Made in her concave shores?'; and 58–60: 'Draw them to Tiber banks, and weep your tears / Into the channel, till the lowest stream / Do kiss the most exalted shores of all.'

28. *fall*] discharge (into the 'sweet streams' of poetry).

29. *attraction*] drawing power; cf. *Tim.* IV.iii.436–7: 'The sun's a thief, and with his great attraction / Robs the vast sea'.

*ambitious*] encompassing, going around, from Latin *ambitiosus*, as in Hor. *Odes* I.xxxvi.20; this meaning is not in *OED*. J. also uses it to mean rising, as if aspiring, in *Volp.* I.ii.111–13: 'Hood an ass with reverend purple, / So you can hide his two ambitious ears, / And he shall pass for a cathedral doctor.'

*line*] not the equator but the circumference in general.

32. *Pierian*] the Muses came from Pieria, near Mount Olympus.

33–7.] Cf. I.ii.232–40, and *Volp.* Epistle, 10–18.

35–6. *for . . . some*] because of the bad poetry written by some.

37. *Contain*] to hold (in contempt); the only example in *OED* (9).

39. *president*] probably here a conflation of 'precedent' (commonly spelt thus) and 'governor'.

41–3. *who . . . us*] Phoebus Apollo was god both of poetry and of the sun: here, the sun's heat is associated with poetic heat. Augustus was specially devoted to Apollo, erecting a great temple to him on the Palatine.

To quit the worship Caesar does to him,
Where other princes, hoisted to their thrones
By fortune's passionate and disordered power,
Sit in their height like clouds before the sun,
Hind'ring his comforts, and by their excess          50
Of cold in virtue, and cross heat in vice,
Thunder and tempest on those learned heads
Whom Caesar with such honour doth advance.
*Tibullus.* All human business fortune doth command
Without all order, and with her blind hand          55
She, blind, bestows blind gifts, that still have nursed
They see not who, nor how, but still the worst.
*Caesar.* Caesar, for his rule, and for so much stuff
As fortune puts in his hand, shall dispose it,
As if his hand had eyes and soul in it,              60
With worth and judgement. Hands that part with gifts,
Or will restrain their use, without desert,
Or with a misery, numbed to virtue's right,
Work as they had no soul to govern them,
And quite reject her, severing their estates          65
From human order. Whosoever can
And will not cherish virtue is no man.

---

46. quit] *F2;* quite *Q, F.*        50–1. by . . . vice] *In parentheses in Q, F.*
60. As . . . it] *In parentheses in Q, F.*        61. Hands] *G;* 'Hands *Q, F.*
62–7.] *Gnomic pointing in Q, F.*

---

46. *quit*] repay.
47–53.] Playing on the image of Apollo as sun god: other princes, whose virtue is untempered by warmth and whose vice is conversely overheated, act like clouds, hiding the sun and bringing storms onto the heads of poets, rather than encouraging the sun to shine on them. The obscurity of the passage may be related to its implied criticism of Elizabeth. Since Augustus had been hoisted to his throne in just this way, it must also be taken as either courtly tact (i.e. flattery) on Horace's part or gross falsification of history on J.'s.
52. *tempest*] used as a verb; *G* compares *Paradise Lost* VII, 412, 'Tempests the ocean'.
56. *blind gifts*] random, fortuitous gifts: (*OED*, 3b, first example 1873).
58. *for*] with respect to (*OED*, 26).
*stuff*] goods.
63. *misery*] miserliness (*OED*, 4).
65. *her*] i.e. virtue, like 'merit' a key word in the play.
66–7. *Whosoever . . . man*] answering the accusation made by Julia (IV.x.48–58) that virtue in men like Ovid goes unrewarded in the Augustan order.

[*Enter one of the* Equites Romani.]

[*1*] *Eques.* Virgil is now at hand, imperial Caesar.
*Caesar.* Rome's honour is at hand then. Fetch a chair
    And set it on our right hand, where 'tis fit                  70
    Rome's honour, and our own, should ever sit.
                        [*1* Eques *sets the chair and exit.*]
    Now he is come out of Campania,
    I doubt not he hath finished all his *Aeneids*,
    Which, like another soul, I long t' enjoy.
    [*To Maecenas, Gallus and Tibullus*] What think you three
        of Virgil, gentlemen,                                     75
    That are of his profession, though ranked higher,
    Or Horace, what sayest thou, that are the poorest,
    And likeliest to envy or to detract?
*Horace.* Caesar speaks after common men in this,
    To make a difference of me for my poorness,                   80
    As if the filth of poverty sunk as deep
    Into a knowing spirit as the bane
    Of riches doth into an ignorant soul.
    No Caesar, they be pathless, moorish minds
    That being once made rotten with the dung                     85

---

67.1. S.D.] *Subst. G (Enter some of the Equestrian order).*    71.1. S.D.] *This
ed.*    75. you] *Q;* *you *with marginal note* *Viz. Mecœnas, Gallus, Tibullus
F.*    76.] *In parentheses in Q, F.*

70–1.] echoing Col. iii.1: 'where Christ sitteth at the right hand of God',
and the Apostles' Creed.
    72. *Campania*] area to south of Rome, including the Bay of Naples, where
Virgil had a house.
    73–4.] See p. 15.
    76. *ranked higher*] socially: Virgil's father was believed, probably wrongly,
to be of humble origin.
    78. *envy or detract*] It is important for J. to give Horace the occasion for
rejecting the vices of Crispinus and Demetrius.
    81–3.] Cf. Hor. *Odes* III.xxix.49–56: 'Fortune, exulting in her cruel
work, and stubborn to pursue her wanton sport, shifts her fickle favours,
kind now to me, now to some other. I praise her while she stays; but if she
shake her wings for flight, I renounce her gifts, enwrap me in my virtue, and
woo honest Poverty, undowered though she be.'
    82. *bane*] poison (*OED*, 2b).
    84. *moorish*] swampy.
    85–7.] The image of ground made into a rotten quagmire by the addition
of dung is clearly that of a city-dweller.

Of damnèd riches ever after sink
Beneath the steps of any villainy.
But knowledge is the nectar that keeps sweet
A perfect soul even in this grave of sin;
And for my soul, it is as free as Caesar's,                    90
For what I know is due, I'll give to all.
He that detracts or envies virtuous merit
Is still the covetous and the ignorant spirit.
*Caesar.* Thanks, Horace, for thy free and wholesome sharpness,
Which pleaseth Caesar more than servile fawns.                    95
A flattered prince soon turns the prince of fools,
And for thy sake we'll put no difference more
'Twixt knights and knightly spirits, for being poor;
Say then, loved Horace, thy true thought of Virgil.
*Horace.* I judge him of a rectified spirit,                    100
By many revolutions of discourse
In his bright reason's influence refined
From all the tartarous moods of common men,

---

92–3.] *Gnomic pointing in Q, F.*    96.] *Gnomic pointing in Q, F.*    98.
'Twixt . . . spirits] *Q;* Betweene the great and good *F.*    102. In . . .
influence] *In parentheses in Q, F.*    reason's] *Subst. Q;* reason *F.*

---

88. *knowledge*] See IV.vi.69n and ll. 19–20n above.
*nectar*] See *Iliad* XIX, 38–9, where Thetis distils red nectar 'through the
nostrils of Patroklos . . . so that his flesh might not spoil'.
92–3.] given gnomic pointing by J. because central to his argument.
94–6.] Cf. IV.viii.28–31, and *Conv.* 330–2, quoted p. 17. Lamb comments on 'The economical liberality by which greatness, seeming to waive
some part of its prerogative, takes care to lose none of the materials; the
prudential liberties of an inferior which flatter by commanded boldness and
soothe with complimental sincerity' (*Specimens of English Dramatic Poets*,
quoted in *H&S*). Cf. *Disc.* 1110–15 for a similarly cynical analysis of 'fain'd
familiarity in great ones'.
100. *rectified*] purified.
101. *revolutions*] in sense of planetary orbits, as well as revolving thoughts.
*discourse*] thought: *OED* quotes J.'s friend Clement Edmonds, *Observations* (1604): 'The soule of man is imbued with a power of discourse, whereby
it concludeth either according to the certainetie of reason or the learning of
experience' (J. wrote two poems, *Ep.* CX and CXI, for the 1609 ed. of
*Observations*). Horace is stressing the higher faculty of reason: his own poetry
belongs to 'the learning of experience'.
102. *bright . . . influence*] his reason is the sun around which his thought
revolves and becomes purified.
103. *tartarous*] unrefined, sour.

Bearing the nature and similitude
Of a right heavenly body; most severe                                    105
In fashion and collection of himself,
And then as clear and confident as Jove.
*Gallus.* And yet so chaste and tender is his ear
In suffering any syllable to pass
That he thinks may become the honoured name                              110
Of issue to his so examined self,
That all the lasting fruits of his full merit
In his own poems he doth still distaste,
As if his mind's piece, which he strove to paint,
Could not with fleshly pencils have her right.                           115
*Tibullus.* But to approve his works of sovereign worth
This observation, methinks, more than serves
And is not vulgar: that which he hath writ
Is with such judgement laboured and distilled
Through all the needful uses of our lives                                120
That could a man remember but his lines
He should not touch at any serious point,
But he might breathe his spirit out of him.

---

109. any] *F;* in any *Q.*      117. methinks] *G;* (me thinkes) *Q, F.*

---

105. *heavenly body*] godlike or angelic, but also continuing the astrological imagery of the preceding lines.
106. *fashion . . . collection*] forming and controlling.
108. *chaste*] from Latin *castus*, used figuratively of literary style to mean free from barbarisms, pure (Lewis and Short, 1.II.A.b, citing Aulus Gellius XIX.viii.3); not recorded in *OED* in this sense before 1753. J. may be recalling Cicero's 'castus animus purusque' (*Div.* I.liii.121).
*tender*] sensitive (*OED*, IV, 10).
113. *distaste*] regard with dissatisfaction.
114. *piece*] picture.
115. *pencils*] paint brushes.
*her*] i.e. 'his mind's piece'.
118–23. *that . . . him*] a commonplace about Virgil: cf. Bacon, *Advancement of Learning*, I.vii.21, 'certain critics are used to say hyperbolically, That if all sciences were lost, they might be found in Virgil'. (*H&S*) There are also echoes of the *sortes Virgilianae*, in which the *Aeneid* was opened at random, and a random line read and interpreted as oracular. *G* took this passage to refer to Shakespeare, with whom he thus identified the Virgil of the play, but there is no evidence to suggest J. had any but the historical Virgil in mind. The care described in ll. 108–15 is inappropriate for a description of Shakespeare by J.

*Caesar.* You mean he might repeat part of his works
　　As fit for any conference he can use?　　　　　　　　125
*Tibullus.* True, royal Caesar.
*Caesar.* 　　　　　　　　　Worthily observed,
　　And a most worthy virtue in his works.
　　What thinks material Horace of his learning?
*Horace.* His learning labours not the school-like gloss
　　That most consists in echoing words and terms,　　130
　　And soonest wins a man an empty name,
　　Nor any long or far-fetched circumstance
　　Wrapped in the curious generalties of arts,
　　But a direct and analytic sum
　　Of all the worth and first effects of arts.　　　　135
　　And, for his poesy, 'tis so rammed with life
　　That it shall gather strength of life with being,
　　And live hereafter more admired than now.
*Caesar.* This one consent in all your dooms of him,
　　And mutual loves of all your several merits,　　　140
　　Argues a truth of merit in you all.

ACT V   SCENE ii

[*Enter to them*] VIRGIL [*and*] Equites Ro[mani].

*Caesar.* See, here comes Virgil; we will rise and greet him.
　　Welcome to Caesar, Virgil. Caesar and Virgil
　　Shall differ but in sound; to Caesar, Virgil

126. Worthily] *F;* 'Tis worthily *Q.*　　129. labours] *Q, F;* savours *F2.*
133. generalties] *F;* General'ties *Q.*　　V.ii.0.1.] *Enter* VIRGIL *G, con-*
*tinuing the scene.*

125. *conference*] conversation, discourse.
128. *material*] See IV.v.39n.
129. *school-like gloss*] superficial and arcane learning of the 'schools', i.e.
the learned institutions generally, but here particularly the 'schools' in which
Greek and Roman philosophers and their medieval counterparts taught.
131–3.] J. may be thinking of Marston's rise to fame on 'echoing words
and terms': cf. V.iii.537–42.
133. *generalties*] general propositions (*OED*, 2, citing this passage).
*arts*] learning, scholarship (as also in l. 135).
138. *admired*] wondered at.
139. *dooms*] personal judgements (*OED*, 3).
V.ii.] based on the reading described in Aelius Donatus' *Life* of Virgil: see
p. 15.

Of his expressed greatness shall be made
A second surname, and to Virgil, Caesar.
Where are thy famous *Aeneids*? Do us grace                          5
To let us see, and surfeit on their sight.
*Virgil.* Worthless they are of Caesar's gracious eyes
　If they were perfect; much more with their wants,
　Which yet are more than my time could supply.                      10
　And could great Caesar's expectation
　Be satisfied with any other service
　I would not show them.
*Caesar.*                        Virgil is too modest,
　Or seeks in vain to make our longings more.
　Show them, sweet Virgil.
*Virgil.*                        Then in such due fear                15
　As fits presenters of great works to Caesar,
　I humbly show them. [*He gives a manuscript to* CAESAR.]
*Caesar.*                        Let us now behold
　A human soul made visible in life,
　And more refulgent in a senseless paper
　Than in the sensual complement of kings.                           20
　Read, read thyself dear Virgil, let not me
　Profane one accent with an untuned tongue.
　　　　　　[*He returns the manuscript to* VIRGIL.]
　Best matter badly shown shows worse than bad.
　See then this chair, of purpose set for thee
　To read thy poem in: refuse it not.                                25
　Virtue without presumption place may take

---

4. Of . . . greatness] *In parentheses in Q, F.*   5. surname] *Subst. F;* Sir-
name *Q.*   17. S.D.] *This ed.*   22.1. S.D.] *This ed.*   23, 26–7.]
*Gnomic pointing in Q, F.*

---

5. *second surname*] the *cognomen*, an extra personal name sometimes
adopted by Roman men.
　6–13.] dramatising the request and denial recorded by Donatus: see p. 15.
　9–10. *wants . . . supply*] Virgil continually revised the *Aeneid*, but still left
it unfinished at his death, instructing his executors, Varius and Plotius
Tucca, to destroy it; Augustus countermanded the will, ordering Varius to
edit the poem.
　19. *refulgent*] radiant.
　*senseless*] incapable of sensation: cf. *Ham.* II.ii.474: 'senseless Ilium'.
　20. *complement*] ceremony, formality (*OED*, 8).

Above best kings, whom only she should make.
*Virgil.* It will be thought a thing ridiculous
    To present eyes, and to all future times
    A gross untruth that any poet, void                    30
    Of birth or wealth or temporal dignity,
    Should with decorum transcend Caesar's chair.
    Poor virtue raised, high birth and wealth set under,
    Crosseth heaven's courses and makes worldlings wonder.
*Caesar.* The course of heaven and fate itself in this       35
    Will Caesar cross, much more all worldly custom.
*Horace.* Custom in course of honour ever errs,
    And they are best whom fortune least prefers.
*Caesar.* Horace hath (but more strictly) spoke our thoughts.
    The vast rude swing of general confluence               40
    Is, in particular ends, exempt from sense;
    And therefore reason, which in right should be
    The special rector of all harmony,
    Shall show we are a man, distinct by it
    From those whom custom rapteth in her press.            45

---

30–1. void . . . dignity] *In parentheses in Q, F.*   33–4.] *Gnomic pointing in*
*Q, F.*   34. heaven's] *Subst. Q;* heau'ns *F.*   37–8.] *Gnomic pointing in Q,*
*F.*   42–3. which . . . harmony] *In parentheses in Q, F.*   45. those whom]
*F;* those that *Q.*

---

27. *Above . . . kings*] See p. 16.

*whom . . . make*] Apparently saying that only virtue should make kings, a
sentiment fraught with radical implications in the context of English politics.

32. *transcend*] not 'ascend' as interpreted by *OED* (4b, giving this as only
example), but 'rise beyond' (*OED*, 3): Virgil is placed not in Caesar's chair
but next to it (V.i.69–71) and apparently above it (V.ii.24–7).

34. *heaven's courses*] that which is (or seems) ordained by heaven.

*worldlings*] the worldly.

37–8.] Cf. Hor. *Odes* III.xxix.49–56, quoted V.i.81–3n.

37. *in course*] following the scent of.

39. *strictly*] concisely.

40–1.] 'The undiscriminating operation of custom renders society unable
to distinguish the particular case, or pursue a particular purpose.'

40. *confluence*] 'flowing together' (Latin *confluentia*) of events, fate: not in
*OED* in this sense.

43. *rector*] director, in this case especially leader of a choir (*OED*, 2b).

45. *rapteth*] carries away; this form was briefly popular in the period
1570–1620.

*press*] urgency of business (*OED*, 4).

Ascend then, Virgil, and where first by chance
We here have turned thy book, do thou first read.
*Virgil.* Great Caesar hath his will: I will ascend.
      'Twere simple injury to his free hand
      That sweeps the cobwebs from unusèd virtue,                    50
      And makes her shine proportioned to her worth,
      To be more nice to entertain his grace
      Than he is choice and liberal to afford it.
*Caesar.* [*To Equites Romani*] Gentlemen of our chamber, guard
      the doors
      And let none enter; peace. Begin, good Virgil.                 55
*Virgil.* [*Reads*] *Meanwhile the skies 'gan thunder, and in tail*
      *Of that fell pouring storms of sleet and hail.*
      *The Tyrian lords and Trojan youth, each where*
      *With Venus' Dardan nephew, now in fear*
      *Seek out for several shelter through the plain,*              60
      *Whilst floods come rolling from the hills amain.*
      *Dido a cave, the Trojan prince the same*

---

56.] Virg.lib.4. / Æneid. *Marginal note in* Q, F.      59. *Dardan*] *This ed.*;
Dardane\* *with marginal note* \*Iulus. Q, F.      62. *Trojan*] G; Troian\* *with
marginal note* \*Æneas. Q, F.

---

46–7. *where . . . book*] for the *sortes Virgilianae* see V.i.118–23n.
52. *nice to entertain*] reluctant, fastidious, to receive.
53. *choice*] carefully selective (*OED*, 3),
*afford*] proffer.
56–97.] from *Aeneid* IV, 160–88; G notes 'the ancient notion of what
translation should be . . . It was not a general view of an author's sense,
which contented the writers of those times: they aspired to give his precise
words, without addition or diminution; and unfortunately attempted to do it
within the compass of the original. It is to Jonson's praise, perhaps, that he
moves in his awkward trammels with more facility than his rivals; still,
however, there is little grace in his steps, and he more frequently excites
wonder than communicates pleasure.' The translation is not always literal,
but it is laboriously close. Cf. J.'s dismissal of Duperron's 'free' translations
of Virgil as 'naught' (see p. 17).
56. *in tail*] following.
58. *Tyrian*] of Tyre; hence Carthaginian.
*each where*] Latin *passim*, 'in various places.'
59. *Venus' . . . nephew*] Ascanius, also called Julus, son of Aeneas, hence
grandson (Latin *nepos*) of Venus, and a descendant of Dardanus, son of Zeus.
60. *several shelter*] Latin 'diversa . . . tecta', meaning that both paths to
and places of shelter varied.
62. *Trojan prince*] Aeneas.

Lighted upon. There Earth, and heaven's great dame,
That hath the charge of marriage, first gave sign
Unto this contract. Fire and Air did shine                    65
As guilty of the match; and from the hill
The nymphs with shriekings do the region fill.
Here first began their bane: this day was ground
Of all their ills. For now nor rumour's sound
Nor nice respect of state moves Dido aught.                    70
Her love no longer now by stealth is sought:
She calls this wedlock, and with that fair name
Covers her fault. Forthwith the bruit and fame
Through all the greatest Lybian towns is gone.
Fame, a fleet evil, than which is swifter none;               75
That moving grows, and flying gathers strength;
Little at first and fearful, but at length
She dares attempt the skies, and stalking proud
With feet on ground, her head doth pierce a cloud!
This child our parent, Earth, stirred up with spite           80
Of all the gods, brought forth; and, as some write,
She was last sister of that giant race
That thought to scale Jove's court: right swift of pace,
And swifter far of wing, a monster vast

---

63. _Earth_] _Subst. Q; earth F._     _dame_] _This ed.;_ *dame _with marginal note_
*Iuno. Q, F._     65. _Air_] _Subst. Q; aire F._     80. _Earth_] _Subst. Q; earth_
_F._     82. _giant_] _G;_ Giant* _with marginal note_ *Cœus,Enceladus,&c. Q,
_Subst. F._

---

63. Earth] personified as a deity, as are Fire and Air (l. 65): with Juno,
'heaven's great dame' and goddess of marriage, they are witnesses to the
union of Dido and Aeneas.
   64–5. gave . . . contract] translating 'dant signum', interpreting the ambiguous phrase as approving or authenticating the union.
   68. bane] ruin, fatal mischief (_OED_, 5); only strictly applicable to Dido,
who in the _Aeneid_ kills herself after Aeneas' departure for Italy.
   ground] source, foundation.
   72–3. calls . . . fault] See p. 25.
   73. bruit] rumour, report (_OED_, _sb._ 2).
   75. Fame] malicious rumour, the 'Blatant Beast' which accompanies Envy
and Detraction in _The Faerie Queene_ V.xii, a 'Monster bred of hellishe race'
(VI.i.7).
   78. attempt] attack (_OED_, 9, first example 1605).
   82–3. giant race . . . court] children of Ge (Earth) who in Greek mythology tried to dethrone the gods: see p. 25.

And dreadful. Look, how many plumes are placed                85
On her huge corpse, so many waking eyes
Stick underneath; and (which may stranger rise
In the report) as many tongues she bears,
As many mouths, as many listening ears.
Nightly in midst of all the heaven she flies,                 90
And through the earth's dark shadow shrieking cries;
Nor do her eyes once bend to taste sweet sleep.
By day on tops of houses she doth keep,
Or on high towers, and doth thence affright
Cities and towns of most conspicuous site.                    95
As covetous she is of tales and lies,
As prodigal of truth. This monster——
          [*He is interrupted by shouting off-stage.*]

### ACT V   SCENE iii

[*Enter downstage and invisible to* CAESAR, LUPUS, TUCCA *and* Lictors,
          *held back by Equites Romani.*]

*Lupus.* Come follow me, assist me, second me! Where's the
    emperor?

*1 Eques.* Sir, you must pardon us.

*2 Eques.* Caesar is private now, you may not enter.

*Tucca.* Not enter? Charge 'em upon their allegiance, cropshin.    5

86. *corpse*] This ed.; *Corps Q, Subst. F.*    97. *monster*——] *G; Monster &c
Q, Subst. F.*    V.iii.0.1–2.] *This ed.; G. continues the scene, marking the
speeches of Lupus, Tucca and the Equites to 26 'within'.*

---

85. *plumes*] feathers.

86. *corpse*] body.

95. *conspicuous site*] introduced awkwardly for the rhyme. Virgil simply
has 'great cities' ('magnas urbes'; *Aeneid* IV, 187).

V.iii.0.1.] The numbers involved in this scene suggest that Augustus'
court was on the open stage, perhaps in an atrium of the palace; Lupus and
his followers may at first have been behind one of the tiring-house doors, but
the duration of the dialogue that would have to be carried on off-stage
suggests that they were in a position to be more audible (if not visible) to the
audience, either on the fringes of the stage or pushing through an open
tiring-house door. Nicholson suggests that the stage was divided by a curtain,
which is possible.

1. *second*] support, encourage (*OED*, 1); cf. *Caes.* III.i.29.

3. *private*] secluded (*OED*, 13).

4. *cropshin*] See I.ii.45n.

*1 Eques.* We have a charge to the contrary, sir.

*Lupus.* I pronounce you all traitors, horrible traitors. What, do
you know my affairs? I have matter of danger and state to
impart to Caesar.

*Caesar.* What noise is there? Who's that names Caesar?        10

*Lupus.* A friend to Caesar. One that for Caesar's good would
speak with Caesar.

*Caesar.* [*To Gallus*] Who is't? Look, Cornelius.

*1 Eques.* [*To Caesar*] Asinius Lupus.

*Caesar.* O, bid the turbulent informer hence.        15
We have no vacant ear now to receive
The unseasoned fruits of his officious tongue.

*Maecenas.* [*To 1 Eques*] You must avoid him there.

*Lupus.* I conjure thee, as thou art Caesar, or respect'st thine
own safety, or the safety of the state, Caesar, hear me,        20
speak with me, Caesar; 'tis no common business I come
about, but such as being neglected may concern the life of
Caesar.

*Caesar.* The life of Caesar? Let him enter. Virgil, keep thy
seat.        25

*Equites.* Bear back there! Whither will you? Keep back!

                    [LUPUS, TUCCA and Lictors *approach.*]

*Tucca.* [*To 1 Eques*] By thy leave goodman usher; mend thy
peruke, so.

*Lupus.* Lay hold on Horace there, and on Maecenas, Lictors.

                    [Lictors *seize them.*]

Romans, offer no rescue, upon your allegiance.        30

---

7–9.] *Subst. G; verse in Q, F, divided at* traitors / What . . . affairs? / I.
26.1 S.D.] *This ed.; Enter Lupus, Tucca, and Lictors. G.*        28. peruke]
*Subst. F;* Periwig *Q.*        29.1. S.D.] *This ed.*

---

18. *avoid him*] send him away (*OED*, 5).

27–8. *mend . . . peruke*] straighten your wig: Tucca has knocked it in
pushing in. Wigs were part of the 'uniform' of a gentleman usher: cf.
Massinger, *Maid of Honour* II.i: 'he has been all this morning in practice /
With a peruked gentleman-usher' (ed. Symons, 1887, I, 314). Aubrey noted
'Peruques not commonly worne till 1660' (*Brief Lives*, ed. Andrew Clarke
(Oxford, 1898), I, 274), but they seem to have been more common than is
usually assumed: Hall devotes a whole satire to them (III.v, *Poems*, p. 39),
and part of the duty of the 'gallant's page' in *WYW* is to 'curle his perriwig'
(Wood, II, 271).

[*Giving Caesar a paper*] Read, royal Caesar. [*To Horace*] I'll
tickle you, satyr.

*Tucca.* [*To Horace*] He will, Humours, he will. He will squeeze
you, poet puck-fist.

*Lupus.* I'll lop you off for an unprofitable branch, you satirical     35
varlet.

*Tucca.* Ay, and [*Indicating Maecenas*] Epaminondas your
patron here, with his flagon chain. [*To Maecenas*] Come,
resign: though 'twere your great grandfather's, the law has
made it mine now sir. [*He takes the chain. To Lictors*]     40
Look to him, my party-coloured rascals, look to him.

*Caesar.* What is this, Asinius Lupus? I understand it not.

*Lupus.* Not understand it? A libel, Caesar. A dangerous,
seditious libel. A libel in picture.

*Caesar.* A libel?
                                                                         45
*Lupus.* Ay, I found it in this Horace his study, in Maecenas his
house here. I challenge the penalty of the laws against 'em.

---

31. S.D.] *Subst. G.*   32. satyr] *Subst. G; Satyre Q, F.*   33. Humours]
*G; Humors Q; humours F.*   40. S.D.] *This ed.; takes off Mecœnas' chain. G.*

---

32. *tickle*] See IV.iii.120n.

33–4. *Humours . . . puck-fist*] See IV.vii.8n and 21n; cf. also *EMO*,
Ind.145: 'Squeeze out the humour of such spongie natures.'

37. *Epaminondas*] Theban commander and statesman, traditionally seen as
noble: Tucca may simply be attracted by the sound of the name.

38. *flagon chain*] See I.ii.194n. 'Flagon' is often used to describe Elizabethan chains, but its meaning is not clear; *OED*, s.v 'flagon' 4, suggests a
chain to which a smelling-bottle could be attached.

39–40. *law . . . mine*] Under English law a traitor's property became forfeit
to the crown, and this was seen as an incentive to informing; *G* cites *JD's
Ent.*: 'I have followed Ordinaries this twelve month, onely to find a Foole
that had landes, or a fellow that would talke treason, that I might beg him'
(Wood, III, 192). See also p. 41.

41. *party-coloured*] of various colours: another indication that little if any
costume in the play was 'Roman' (see p. 9). Godwyn (p. 111) notes that
Lictors 'did somewhat resemble our Serjeants', but as *H&S* suggest this
uniform is more suited to the Yeomen of the Guard than Roman Lictors.

43. *libel*] any writing of a seditious kind (*OED*, 5, first example 1601);
both factions in the Essex affair circulated 'libels' against each other, and
Elizabeth's animosity towards Essex was believed to have been kept alive by
forged documents attributed popularly to Raleigh and, in particular,
Cobham; see p. 43.

*Tucca.* Ay, and remember to beg their land betimes, before
some of these hungry court-hounds scent it out.

*Caesar.* [*To 1 Eques*] Show it to Horace. Ask him if he know it.     50

*Lupus.* Know it? His hand is at it, Caesar.

*Caesar.* Then 'tis no libel.

*Horace.* [*Looking at the paper*] It is the imperfect body of an
emblem, Caesar, I began for Maecenas.

*Lupus.* An emblem? Right! That's Greek for a libel. Do but     55
mark how confident he is.

*Horace.* A just man cannot fear, thou foolish tribune,
Not though the malice of traducing tongues,
The open vastness of a tyrant's ear,
·     The senseless rigour of the wrested laws,     60
Or the red eyes of strained authority,
Should, in a point, meet all to take his life.
His innocence is armour 'gainst all these.

*Lupus.* Innocence? O impudence! [*Taking the paper*] Let me
see, let me see. Is not here an eagle? And is not that eagle     65

---

53. S.D.] *This ed.*     55–6.] *Subst. Q; verse in F, divided at* libel. / Do.
59. tyrant's] *G;* Tyrants *Q;* tyrannes *F.*     64. S.D.] *This ed.*

---

48. *beg . . . betimes*] Cf. above, 39–40n.

51. *hand . . . libel*] parodied in *S-M* III.i.67: 'By Sesu tis no libell, for
heere is my hand to it.'

54. *emblem*] a picture accompanied by an interpretative verse: none by J.
survive, but his first dated poem (*UV* I) is in praise of Thomas Palmer's
unpublished botanical emblem book, *The Sprite of Trees and Herbs* (1598–9).
No emblems for the Augustan period are known. Here 'imperfect body'
means it is the picture only.

57–63.] imitating Hor. *Odes* III.iii.1–8: 'The man tenacious of his purpose
in a righteous cause is not shaken from his firm resolve by the frenzy of his
fellow-citizens bidding what is wrong, not by the face of threatening tyrant,
not by Auster, stormy master of the restless Adriatic, not by the mighty hand
of thundering Jove. Were the vault of heaven to break and fall upon him, its
ruins would smite him undismayed.' The assertion of the independence of
the satirist has profound implications in 1601.

59. *open . . . ear*] *G* suggests 'some allusion to the auriform cavity of the
Syracusian dungeon', but the simple suggestion that tyrants are ready to
believe any malicious rumour seems adequate.

60. *wrested laws*] misused to stifle truth.

61. *strained*] stretching its powers beyond what is just.

62. *in . . . all*] converge in a single place, but also to a single end.

63.] Cf. *Disc.* 1330–1: 'An Innocent man needs no Eloquence'.

meant by Caesar? Ha? Does not Caesar give the eagle?
Answer me: what sayest thou?

*Tucca.* [*To Horace*] Hast thou any evasion, stinkard?

*Lupus.* Now he's turned dumb. I'll tickle you, satyr.

*Horace.* [*Waving him away*] Pish! Ha! Ha!                              70

*Lupus.* Dost thou pish me? [*To 1 Lictor*] Give me my long
sword.

*Horace.* With reverence to great Caesar: worthy Romans,
Observe but this ridiculous commenter.
The soul to my device was in this distich:                              75
*Thus oft the base and ravenous multitude*
*Survive to share the spoils of fortitude.*
Which in this body I have figured here
A vulture——

*Lupus.* A vulture! Ay, now 'tis a vulture. O, abominable!              80
Monstrous! Monstrous! Has not your vulture a beak? Has
it not legs? And talons? And wings? And feathers?

*Tucca.* [*To Lupus*] Touch him, old Buskins.

*Horace.* And therefore must it be an eagle?

---

69. satyr] *Subst. G; Satyre Q, F.*     70. S.D.] *This ed.*

---

66. *meant by*] intended to refer to (*OED*, 1e).

*give . . . eagle*] *H&S* suggest display as an armorial bearing (*OED*, 24); cf. Nason, p. 31, quoting Gerrard Legh, *The Accedens of Armory* (1562) f. 38b, on Julius Caesar's 'arms', 'Or, an Eagle displayed with ii. heddes Sable'; but see Juvenal XIV, 197–8: 'your sixtieth year may bring you the eagle that will make you rich', referring to being awarded the post of Senior Centurion, in charge of the eagle of the legion, which was also 'given' by Caesar.

69. *tickle*] the satirist tickles in the sense of goading and irritating, as well as causing laughter; Lupus is threatening physical retaliation; cf. IV.iii.120n.

71. *pish*] for use as a verb, cf. *EMI* III.i.164.

71–2. *long sword*] Cf. IV.iv.8; the size of the diminutive Lupus' sword may have been exploited in performance.

74. *commenter*] interpreter; cf. Ind.24n, and 114.

75–9. *soul . . . body*] the soul is the verse, the body the picture; the distinction is similar to the one J. makes in *Hym.* 1–10 between the physical presentation of the masque, and the text, which is its 'soul'.

75. *distich*] a couplet, usually rhyming in English verse, and syntactically complete.

79. *figured*] presented pictorially.

83. *Buskins*] emphasising Lupus' lack of height, as in I.ii.150, and IV.iv.15.

*Maecenas.* Respect him not good Horace. Say your device.    85
*Horace.* A vulture and a wolf——
*Lupus.* A wolf? Good! That's I, I am the wolf. My name's
    Lupus, I am meant by the wolf. On, on: a vulture and a
    wolf——
*Horace.* Preying upon the carcase of an ass——    90
*Lupus.* An ass? Good still! That's I too, I am the ass. You mean
    me by the ass——
*Maecenas.* 'Pray thee, leave braying then.
*Horace.* [*To Lupus*] If you will needs take it, I cannot with
    modesty give it from you.    95
*Maecenas.* But by that beast the old Egyptians
    Were wont to figure in their hieroglyphics
    Patience, frugality and fortitude,
    For none of which we can suspect you, tribune.
*Caesar.* Who was it Lupus that informed you first    100
    This should be meant by us? Or was't your comment?
*Lupus.* No, Caesar. A player gave me the first light of it,
    indeed.
*Tucca.* Ay, an honest, sycophant-like slave, and a politician
    besides.    105

---

91–2.] *Subst. Q; verse in F, divided at* ass. / You.

---

85. *Respect*] heed.
*Say*] possibly a simple imperative ('speak'), but more probably 'describe',
a meaning last recorded by *OED* in 1400 ('Say', *v.* 8).
91. *I . . . ass*] punning on his *praenomen*, Asinius: Latin for ass is
*asinus*. Cf. *Ado* IV.ii.76–8: 'But, masters, remember that I am an ass; though
it be not written down, yet forget not that I am an ass.'
95. *give . . . you*] take it away from you (cf. *OED* s.v. 'give' 6d, but with
'from' instead of 'to').
96–8.] From Claude Mignault's commentary on Alciati's *Emblems*, 1600,
p. 50 (*H&S*): 'It is not irrelevant to add that the ass was for the ancient
Egyptians a symbol of prudence, fortitude, unwearied labour and frugality'
(my trans.). J. had already punned on Maecenas' name in *C is A* I.ii.52–3:
'Why, you shal be one of my Maecen-asses'; cf. *S-M* IV.ii.63.
101. *comment*] interpretation; cf. l. 74 above.
102. *gave . . . it*] first brought it to my attention; cf. *OED* s.v. 'light' 3,
but there is no example of this construction.
104. *sycophant*] the Essex faction's nickname for Cobham: see p. 42.
*politician*] Cf. III.iv.297n, IV.iv.31n; there is a stronger sense here of
the deviousness usually implied; the suggestion is that one or more contemporary actors were government informers.

*Caesar.* Where is that player?

*Tucca.* He is without here.

*Caesar.* Call him in.

*Tucca.* Call in the player there, Master Aesop, call him.

*Equites.* Player? Where is the player?                        110

[*Enter* HISTRIO *followed by* CRISPINUS *and* DEMETRIUS.]

Bear back! None but the player enter.

*Tucca.* Yes, [*Indicating Crispinus and Demetrius*] this gent'man
and his Achates must.

*Crispinus.* 'Pray you master usher; we'll stand close here.

*Tucca.* [*Indicating Crispinus*] 'Tis a gent'man of quality, this,   115
though he be somewhat out of clothes, I tell ye. Come,
Aesop. Hast a bay-leaf in thy mouth? Well said, be not
out, stinkard. Thou shalt have a monopoly of playing
confirmed to thee and thy covey under the emperor's
broad seal for this service.                                   120

---

110.1. S.D.] *This ed.; Enter* ÆSOP . . . DEMETRIUS. *G; Enter Histrio, Crispinus, Demetrius, Lictors. Parfitt.*

---

109. *Aesop*] Tucca's use of the name caused *G* and most subsequent editors to add an extra non-speaking character to the *dramatis personae*, but it is simply Tucca's inflated name for Histrio, who gave Lupus 'first light' (l. 103) of the banquet also. Histrio is listed in the massed entry at the head of this scene in both *Q* and *F*; Aesop is not.

113. *Achates*] attendant and armour-bearer of Aeneas in the *Aeneid*; here, Demetrius.

114. *usher*] as with Tucca's use in l. 27 above, the anachronistic term underlines Crispinus' unworthiness to be associated with the values of Augustan Rome.

*close*] silent.

115–16. *gent'man . . . clothes*] ridiculing Marston's pretensions to gentility, as in II.i.87–100, III.i.26, III.iii.18, and III.iv.163.

117. *bay-leaf*] recommended by Martial V.iv.1–2: 'Myrtale is wont to reek with much wine, but, to mislead us, she devours laurel leaves'. Cf. III.iv.298.

118. *out*] nervous, put out (*OED*, 5).

118–20. *Thou . . . service*] the granting of trading monopolies by the crown was highly unpopular; for attacks by Martin, Hakewill and others in the Parliament of October 1601, see p. 47; cf. Donne, *Satire IV*, ll. 103–7.

119. *covey*] a brood of game birds, hence figuratively and contemptuously of any group.

120. *broad seal*] the Great Seal of England, not of Rome, and a reminder that the grant of monopolies was a royal prerogative; cf. *CR* V.vi.74.

*Caesar.* Is this he?

*Lupus.* Ay, Caesar, this is he.

*Caesar.* Let him be whipped. Lictors, go take him hence.

        *[Exeunt* Lictors *with* HISTRIO.]

   And Lupus, for your fierce credulity,

   One fit him with a pair of larger ears.       125

   'Tis Caesar's doom, and must not be revoked.

   We hate to have our court and peace disturbed

   With these quotidian clamours. *[To 1 Eques]* See it done.

*Lupus.* Caesar!

*Caesar.*     Gag him, we may have his silence.

        [Equites *gag* LUPUS *and exeunt.*]

*Virgil.* Caesar hath done like Caesar. Fair and just    130

   Is his award against these brainless creatures.

   'Tis not the wholesome sharp morality

   Or modest anger of a satiric spirit

   That hurts or wounds the body of a state,

   But the sinister application          135

   Of the malicious ignorant and base

   Interpreter, who will distort and strain

   The general scope and purpose of an author

   To his particular and private spleen.

---

123.1. S.D.] *This ed.; Exe. some of the Lictors, with Lupus and Æsop.* G, *at l.*
*130.*  *129. Verse in F; 2 lines in Q, which does not normally indicate shared lines
of verse; prose in G.*  we] *Q, F; that we* G.  *129.1. S.D.] This ed.*

---

123–9.] Augustus' lack of concern over 'libels', though not the punishment of informers, is based on Suetonius *Divus Augustus* LV: 'He did
not even dread the lampoons ('famosos libellos') against him which were
scattered in the senate house'.

123. *whipped*] Suetonius records three instances of Augustus punishing
actors, two of them by whipping (*Divus Augustus* XLV).

125. *larger ears*] in keeping with his *praenomen*, Asinius; the punishment
deliberately copies that given to Midas by Apollo when he preferred Pan's
inferior music to his own (Ovid *Met.* XI, 146–93).

126. *doom*] judgement.

128. *quotidian*] commonplace, trivial (*OED*, 3).

132–9.] a recurrent theme in J., answering the authorities' attack on
satire which culminated in the ban of 1599; cf. Ind. 22–54, III.v *passim*,
'Apol. Dial.', 61–75, *EMO*, Ind. 123–46, and *Volp.* Epistle, 44–102.

135. *application*] See Ind. 24n.

139. *particular and private*] Cf. *Volp.* Epistle, 52–3.

*Caesar.* We know it, our dear Virgil, and esteem it                    140
A most dishonest practice in that man
Will seem too witty in another's work.

> *This while the rest* [GALLUS *and* TIBULLUS]
> *whisper* [to] CAESAR.

What would Cornelius Gallus and Tibullus?

*Tucca.* [*To Maecenas*] Nay, but as thou art a man, dost hear? A
man of worship, and honourable: hold, here, take thy            145
chain again. Resume, mad Maecenas. What, dost thou
think I meant t' have kept it, old boy? No, I did it but to
fright thee, I, to try how thou wouldst take it. What, will I
turn shark upon my friends, or my friends' friends? I scorn
it with my three souls. Come, I love bully Horace as well as   150
thou dost, I. 'Tis an honest hieroglyphic. [*Taking his hand*]
Give me thy wrist, Helicon. Dost thou think I'll second

---

142.1. S.D.] *F in margin; not in Q.*    144. S.D.] *G.*    147. old] *Q;* bold
*F.*    151. S.D.] *This ed.*

---

140. *esteem*] consider (*OED*, 5); cf. *MND* III.ii.353: 'this their jangling I
esteem a sport'.

142. *too ... work*] Cf. *ML*, Chorus II, 45–7: 'most unbecomming a
*Gentleman* to appeare malignantly witty in anothers *Worke*', and the 'invading
interpreters' of *Volp*. Epistle, 64; derived from Martial, preface to *Epigrams*,
I, 'it is a shameless business when anyone exercises his ingenuity on another
man's book'.

145. *man of worship*] See I.i.29n.

149. *shark*] cheat, parasite; cf. III.iv.190.

150. *three souls*] a commonplace derived from Aristotle, *De anima*, II.i,
'De plantis', I; the souls are of growth (plants only), motion and growth
(animals) and the rational or immortal soul (mankind). Donne uses the idea
frequently, e.g. 'To the Countesse of Salisbury', ll. 51–4, *Devotions*, XVIII,
and *Paradoxes*, I. *H&S* quote Trevisa, *Bartholomaeus de Proprietatibus Rerum*
(1498), III.vii, p. 53: 'In dyvers bodyes ben thre manere soules: vegetabilis
that yevyth lyfe and noo felinge, as in plantes and rootes; Sensibilis, that
yevyth lyfe and felynge and no reason in unskylfull beastes; Racionalis, that
yevyth lyf, felyng, and reeson in men.'

*bully*] as a title, signifying friendly admiration; cf. *MND* III.i.8:
'What sayest thou, bully Bottom?'.

151. *hieroglyphic*] i.e. the emblem.

152. *wrist*] presumably as in a handshake, though not in *OED* as a
phrase, or as a substitute for 'hand'.

*Helicon*] Mount Helicon was sacred to the Muses; the popular collection
*England's Helicon* had just (1600) been published.

e'er a rhinoceros of them all against thee, ha? Or [*Indicating
Horace*] thy noble Hippocrene here? I'll turn stager first,
and be whipped too: dost thou see, bully?                              155
*Caesar.* [*To Gallus and Tibullus*] You have your will of Caesar.
   Use it Romans.
   Virgil shall be your praetor, and ourself
   Will here sit by, spectator of your sports,
   And think it no impeach of royalty.
   [*To Virgil*] Our ear is now too much profaned, grave Maro     160
   With these distastes, to take thy sacred lines.
   Put up thy book till both the time and we
   Be fitted with more hallowed circumstance
   For the receiving so divine a work.
   [*To Gallus, Tibullus and Maecenas*] Proceed with your
     design.                                                    165
*Maecenas, Gallus, Tibullus.* Thanks to great Caesar.
*Gallus.* Tibullus, draw you the indictment then, whilst
   Horace arrests them on the statute of calumny. Maecenas
   and I will take our places here. Lictors, assist him.

    [*Re-enter* Lictors. *They bring forward* CRISPINUS *and*
            DEMETRIUS.]

---

160. grave Maro] *In parentheses in Q, F.*     164. work] *F;* Labour *Q.*
169.1–2. S.D.] *This ed.*

---

153. *rhinoceros*] suggesting the blundering nature of the attack, as in *CR*
I.iii.17.
   154. *Hippocrene*] a river springing from Mount Helicon, as Horace's poetry
springs from Maecenas' patronage.
   *stager*] actor; cf. I.ii.15n.
   155. *whipped*] as a vagabond under the statutes of 1572 and 1597–8; see
I.ii.54n.
   157. *praetor*] a judge: originally one, the *praetor urbanus*, their number was
increased eventually to 18: see Rosinus VII.xi.
   159. *impeach*] calling in question; cf. *3H6* I.iv.60: 'no impeach of valour'.
   160. *Maro*] Virgil's *cognomen*.
   161. *distastes*] annoyances (*H&S*).
   165. *design*] plan.
   168. *statute of calumny*] 'whosoever should *calumniari,.i.[e.]* forge an
accusation against another, a certaine letter [in fact a K] should be burnt in
his forehead in token of infamy. This law is sometimes called *Lex Rhemnia*'
(Godwyn, p. 160); cf. Cicero *Rep.* IV.x.12. See also V.iii.209 and 558–60,
and the 'just decree' of III.v.132. J. had been branded on the thumb
for killing Gabriel Spencer (see p. 29), as Dekker reminds him in *S-M*
I.ii.116–17.

*Horace.* I am the worst accuser under heaven.                    170
*Gallus.* Tut, you must do't, 'twill be noble mirth.
*Horace.* I take no knowledge that they do malign me.
*Tibullus.* Ay, but the world takes knowledge.
*Horace.*                              'Would the world knew
How heartily I wish a fool should hate me.
*Tucca.* [*Aside*] Body of Jupiter! What, will they arraign my    175
brisk poetaster and his poor journeyman, ha? Would I
were abroad skeldering for a drachma, so I were out
of this labyrinth again. I do feel myself turn stinkard
already. But I must set the best face I have upon't now.
[*To Horace*] Well said, my divine, deft Horace, bring the       180
whoreson detracting slaves to the bar, do. Make 'em hold
up their spread golls. I'll give in evidence for thee if thou
wilt. [*Aside to Crispinus*] Take courage, Crispinus. Would
thy man had a clean band.
*Crispinus.* [*Aside to Tucca*] What must we do, captain?         185
*Tucca.* [*Aside to Crispinus*] Thou shalt see anon: do not make
division with thy legs so.
*Caesar.* [*Indicating Tucca*] What's he, Horace?
*Horace.* I only know him for a motion, Caesar.

---

173. *Nicholson; prose in Q, F.*    175. S.D.] *G (at 179).*    177. a drachma]
*Subst. F;* Twopence *Q.*    178. this] *Q, F;* his *F2.*    183. S.D.] *Nicholson.*

172–4.] the (unconvincing) claim of J. in the 'Apol. Dial.', 10–26 and of
Crites in *CR* III.iii. Cf. Hor. *Sat.* I.x.78–80, quoted below, ll. 448–54n.
177. *abroad*] at large.
178. *turn stinkard*] See I.ii.32n. Here, 'become contemptible': cf. *SW*
IV.ii.108: 'You notorious stinkardly beareward'. Both uses suggest 'stinkard'
had become synonymous with 'coward', but here there is a stronger suggestion of literally stinking through fear, Tucca fearing that he will wet or
'bescumber' (l. 298n) himself.
180. *deft*] spruce, neat.
181–2. *hold . . . golls*] hold up their hands to be indicted, the practice in
English law, as in l. 207 below. Cf. Dekker, *S-M* I.ii.387–8, as Tucca gives
Horace money: 'Holde, hold up thy hand, I ha seene the day thou didst not
scorne to holde up thy golles'.
184. *thy man*] Demetrius.
*band*] collar.
186–7. *make division*] musical term for a rapid melodic passage; cf.
IV.v.191. Crispinus' knees are knocking.
189. *motion*] puppet (see III.iv.319n).

*Tucca.* I am one of thy commanders, Caesar. A man of service    190
    and action. My name is Pantilius Tucca. I have served i'
    thy wars against Mark Antony, I.

*Caesar.* [*Aside to Gallus*] Do you know him, Cornelius?

*Gallus.* [*Aside to Caesar*] He's one that hath had the mustering
    or convoy of a company now and then. I never noted him    195
    by any other employment.

*Caesar.* [*Aside to Gallus*] We will observe him better.

*Tibullus.* Lictor, proclaim silence in the court.

*[1] Lictor.* In the name of Caesar, silence.

*Tibullus.* Let the parties, the accuser and the accused, present    200
    themselves.

*[1] Lictor.* The accuser and the accused, present yourselves in
    court.

*Crispinus, Demetrius.* Here.

*Virgil.* Read the indictment.    205

*Tibullus.* [*Reading*] Rufus Laberius Crispinus and Demetrius
    Fannius, hold up your hands. You are before this time
    jointly and severally indicted, and here presently to be
    arraigned, upon the statute of calumny, or *lex remmia*, the
    one by the name of Rufus Laberius Crispinus, alias    210

---

193. S.D.] *This ed.*    206. S.D.] *Subst. Nicholson.*    206–27.] *Subst.*
*italics in Q, F.*    209–12. the . . . plagiary] *In parentheses in Q, F.*

---

190–6.] Dekker parodies this exchange in *S-M* V.ii.167–71: '*King.* Sir
*Vaughan,* what's this jolly Captaines name? / *Sir Vaugh.* Has a very sufficient
name, and is a man has done God and his Country as good and as hot service
(in conquering this vile Monster-Poet) as ever did Saint *George* his horse-
backe about the Dragon.'

192. *wars . . . Antony*] the uneasy relationship between Octavian and
Antony broke into open war in 32 BC; Antony, defeated at Actium in 31,
harassed by Gallus' army (cf. l. 193), committed suicide in 30 BC.

194–5. *mustering . . . company*] i.e. he has not had a command in the field;
Tucca's activities are comparable with those of Falstaff in *2HIV* III.ii. See
also p. 49.

199.] Augustus appears to have established his own court of law: Suetonius
describes trials presided over by him (*Divus Augustus* XXXIII, LI).

206–27.] parodying English law: cf. the arraignment of Essex and
Southampton 'not having the fear of God before your eyes' (in E. M.
Tenison, *Elizabethan England*, XI (Leamington Spa, 1956), p. 464).

208. *presently*] i.e. now.

209. *statute . . . remmia*] See above, l. 168n.

Crispinas, poetaster and plagiary; the other by the name of
Demetrius Fannius, play-dresser and plagiary, that you,
not having the fear of Phoebus or his shafts before your
eyes, contrary to the peace of our liege lord Augustus
Caesar, his crown and dignity, and against the form of a            215
statute in that case made and provided, have most ignor-
antly, foolishly, and (more like yourselves) maliciously,
gone about to deprave and calumniate the person and
writings of Quintus Horatius Flaccus, here present, poet,
and priest to the Muses. And to that end have mutually             220
conspired and plotted at sundry times, as by several
means, and in sundry places, for the better accomplishing
your base and envious purpose, taxing him falsely of
self-love, arrogancy, impudence, railing, filching by
translation, etcetera. Of all which calumnies, and every           225
of them, in manner and form aforesaid, what answer you?
Are you guilty or not guilty?

*Tucca.* [*Aside to Crispinus and Demetrius*] Not guilty, say.
*Crispinus, Demetrius.* Not guilty.
*Tibullus.* How will you be tried?                                 230

---

213–14. not . . . eyes] *In parentheses in Q, F.*     225. etcetera] *This ed.; &c.*
*Q, F.*     228. S.D.] *Nicholson.*

---

211. *Crispinas*] See II.i.96n.

*plagiary*] plagiarist; for Crispinus' plagiarism, see IV.iii.96–7. J. is
recalling Hor. *Epist.* I.xix.19: 'O you mimics [*imitatores*], you slavish herd!
How often your pother has stirred my spleen, how often my mirth!'

212. *play-dresser*] Cf. III.iv.321n; Dekker had plagiarised *EMO* in *Patient
Grissil* (1600).

218. *deprave*] vilify; cf. *Ado* V.i.95, 'deprave and slander'.

224–5. *self-love . . . translation*] Chrisoganus, in *Hist.* (1599), though presented as an idealist, is an arrogant, censorious translator and satirist (Wood,
III, 257); Brabant Senior in *JD's Ent.* (1600) is a critic 'puft up with arrogant
conceit' (Wood, III, 229); see also *WYW* (*ibid.*, II, 249–50) and the attack
about to be made in *S-M*, e.g. V.ii.218–22: 'Or should we minister strong
pilles to thee: / What lumpes of hard and indigested stuffe, / Of bitter
*Satirisme*, of *Arrogance*, / Of *Selfe-love*, of *Detraction*, of a blacke / And
stinking *Insolence* should we fetch up?' Drummond noted some of these
characteristics in J.: 'He is a great lover and praiser of himself, a contemner
and Scorner of others . . . a bragger of some good that he wanteth' (*Conv.*
680–5).

225–6. *all . . . them*] parodying legal usage. The formula 'all and every'
corresponds to the Latin 'universi et singuli', i.e. 'all of them, and each
separate one of them'; see *OED*, s.v. 'every' 7b.

*Tucca.* [*Aside to Crispinus and Demetrius*] By the Roman gods,
and the noblest Romans.

*Crispinus, Demetrius.* By the Roman gods, and the noblest
Romans.

*Virgil.* Here sits Maecenas and Cornelius Gallus.                        235
Are you contented to be tried by these?

*Tucca.* [*Aside to Crispinus and Demetrius*] Ay, so the noble
captain may be joined with them in commission, say.

*Crispinus, Demetrius.* Ay, so the noble captain may be joined
with them in commission.                                                   240

*Virgil.* What says the plaintiff?

*Horace.* I am content.

*Virgil.* Captain, then take your place.

*Tucca.* Alas my worshipful praetor, 'tis more of thy gent'ness
than of my deserving, iwis. But since it hath pleased the         245
court to make choice of my wisdom and gravity, come, my
calumnious varlets, let's hear you talk for yourselves now
an hour or two. What can you say? Make a noise. Act, act!

*Virgil.* [*To Tucca, Maecenas and Gallus*] Stay, turn and take
an oath first. You shall swear

---

231. S.D.] *Subst. G.*      237. S.D.] *Subst. G.*      245. iwis] *This ed.; Iwusse*
*Q, F.*      249–55. You . . . laws] *Subst. italics in Q, F.*

---

232. *noblest Romans*] Roman juries were chosen from separate panels
(*decuriae*) made up of Senators, *equites* and, later, tribunes and other lower
ranking citizens. The jury (much larger than that presented here) returned a
majority verdict by placing one of three symbols in an urn (see below ll. 336,
374, 399), for guilty, not guilty, or undecided (*non liquet*). The *praetor* did not
vote, but pronounced sentence (as in ll. 519–69 below). The standard work
on Roman law in J.'s time was Sigonius, *De Antiquo Jure Civium Romanorum*
(Paris, 1572) (see esp. Book I, 21 and 28); for the casting of votes, see also
Rosinus IX, 19.
238. *commission*] delegated authority, especially in England that of magistrate (*OED*, 2c, 5).
245. *iwis*] See I.ii.56n.
247. *calumnious*] slandering; cf. *All's W* I.iii.56–7: 'foul-mouth'd and
calumnious knave'. Tucca's prejudgement of the case would not have been
surprising to a contemporary audience: judges were subservient to the
executive, and frequently spoke as if the accused's guilt was already clear;
this was very obvious in the arraignment of Essex and Southampton. J.
implicitly contrasts the unsatisfactory English system with the formal balance
of Roman justice.
248. *Act*] in sense of 'take verbal action', but deception is also implied.

By thunder-darting Jove, the king of gods,                     250
And by the genius of Augustus Caesar,
By your own white and uncorrupted souls,
And the deep reverence of our Roman justice,
To judge this case with truth and equity,
As bound by your religion and your laws.                       255
                              [*They nod assent.*]
Now, read the evidence; but first demand
Of either prisoner if that writ be theirs.
*Tibullus.* [*Giving the papers to 1 Lictor*] Show this unto Cri-
spinus. [*To Crispinus*] Is it yours?
*Tucca.* Say ay. What, dost thou stand upon it, pimp? Do not   260
deny thine own Minerva, thy Pallas, the issue of thy brain.
*Crispinus.* Yes, it is mine.
*Tibullus.* [*To 1 Lictor*] Show that unto Demetrius. [*To Deme-
trius*] Is it yours?
*Demetrius.* It is.                                            265
*Tucca.* There's a father will not deny his own bastard now, I
warrant thee.
*Virgil.* Read them aloud.
*Tibullus.* [*Reads.*] *Ramp up my genius, be not retrograde,*

---

255.1. S.D.] *This ed.*    258. S.D.] *This ed.; Gives him two papers.* G.

250. *thunder-darting*] Englishing *altitonans*; see IV.v.209n. Jove presided
over justice, and the oath to him was thus administered by the *praetor*.
251. *genius . . . Caesar*] the tutelary spirit of the head of family was wor-
shipped in Rome; in Augustus' reign this was extended to worship of the
Emperor's presiding genius by his subjects.
252. *white*] sacred to Jupiter because the light of heaven, as well as
indicating purity.
254. *equity*] fairness, especially in law the application of general principles
of justice (*OED*, 3 and 4).
257. *writ*] writing.
260. *stand upon it*] hesitate.
261. *Minerva . . . Pallas*] both names of Athena, who was born fully
armed from the head of Jove, 'the issue of [his] brain'.
269. Ramp] apparently here to rear up, as in 'rampant', but to ramp was
also to rage violently, and to behave in a crude or sexually loose way (*OED*,
*v.* 1, 4 and 5, *sb.* 1). Marston uses it as a verb in *AR* (acted 1599–1601),
Prol. 1–2: 'The rawish dank of clumsy winter ramps [? 'seizes'] / The fluent
summer's vein'. Cf. also *Scourge* IX, 5, 'O how on tiptoes proudly mounts
my Muse'; *ibid.*, 8, 'Making my sprite mount up to higher straines', and *1
Ant.* IV.i.260, 'mount up your spirits and prepare'.

> But boldly nominate a spade a spade.                     270
> What, shall thy lubrical and glibbery Muse
> Live as she were defunct, like punk in stews?

---

my genius] Marston frequently invokes his genius, his muse, or his spirit,
e.g. in *Scourge*, 'To Detraction', 6–8, 'Know that my spirit scorns *Detractions*
spight. / Know that the *Genius*, which attendeth on, / And guides my powers
intellectuall', and *Scourge* VI, 10, 'Think'st thou that *Genius* that attends my
soule'; cf. also *WYW*, 'what merry *Genius* haunts thee to day' (Wood, II,
231).

retrograde] not found in Marston, but used fairly commonly, initially as
an astrological term, from Chaucer on: J. regarded it as affected, using it
twice in *CR* (V.iii.118, and V.iv.10) in the mouths of Asotus and Amorphus
respectively. Cf. *All's W* I.i.198 (as astrological term) and *Ham.* I.ii.114,
where it is used without irony. As with other words not traced to Marston in
Crispinus' poem, they may have been found in an unrevised version of *WYW*
(not published until 1607; see p. 35 n. 69); but J. almost certainly incorporated what he regarded as pretentious or affected vocabulary, especially
neologisms, from other writers into the 'poems' of both Crispinus and
Demetrius. He had already done this in the 'fustian' spoken by Clove in
*EMO* III.iv.13–40, where the primary target is Marston.

270. nominate] designate (*OED*, 1, first example 1545). Not found in
Marston, but 'nomination' is in his contribution to *Love's Martyr* (1601), 'A
narration and description . . . Perfectioni Hymnus', l. 10, 'All nomination is
too straight of sence'. 'Nominate' is used by Gabriel Harvey (a source of
Juniper's vocabulary in *C is A*: see *H&S*, IX, 310), in *Pierce's Supererogation*
(1593), p. 205, and is ridiculed in *LLL* I.ii.15 and V.i.8; Juniper uses fifteen
'-ate' words, according to King (p. 19). None are from Marston, but it is a
favourite suffix of his: see e.g. *AR*, I.ii.103, 'inamorate', and II.iii.28,
'intimate'; Crispinus vomits *'magnificate'*, *'inflate'* and *'fatuate'* in ll. 473–92
below. Hoskyns mocks 'ruinate', 'insinuate' and 'intimate' in his 'Tufftafity'
speech at the Middle Temple Revels of 1597–8 (*Hoskyns*, pp. 100–2). King
unkindly suggests that Marston favoured them because they were easy to
rhyme (p. 23).

271. lubrical] slippery: this is the first example in *OED*; not found in
Marston, but he is fond of '-al' suffixes, which are ridiculed in *EMO*
III.iv.25–38.

glibbery] a favourite adjective, perhaps a coinage, of Marston's; his is first
recorded use in *OED*, in *JD's Ent.* (Wood, III, 185). See also his use,
probably earlier, in *1 Ant.* I.i.108, II.i.6, and IV.1.70. Marston is also one of
the first to use 'glib', as both adjective and verb (see *OED* examples).

272. defunct] from Latin *defunctus*, discharged, extinct, as in *Oth.*
I.iii.263–4, 'the young affects / In [me] defunct'. Not in Marston, but a
neologism used by Shakespeare in various forms: see also *H5* (1599) IV.i.21
('defunct'), I.ii.58 ('defunction'), *Phoen.* (1601) 14 ('defunctive'). King notes
Marston's liking for 'u-assonance' (pp. 16–17).

punk in stews] a whore in a brothel; cf. *Scourge* III, 53 'O now yee male
stewes'. The phrase means that 'defunct' is being misused.

*Tucca.* [*Aside*] Excellent!
*Tibullus. Alas! That were no modern consequence,*
  *To have cothurnal buskins frighted hence.*          275
  *No, teach thy incubus to poetise,*
  *And throw abroad thy spurious snotteries*

---

273. *Tucca. . . .* Excellent!] *This ed.; (Tucca.* Excellent.) *Q;* (TVCC. Excellent!) *F. Cf. 279, 300, 303, 308–9. F, followed by F2, at first prefixed a dash to Tucca's interjections, except in 273, but cancelled it in a few copies. Q and F put all these interjections in parentheses as in 273.* S.D.] *Nicholson (so 300, 303, 308).*

274. modern] a relatively new word, here meaning 'ordinary, trivial' (*OED*, 4, first example 1591), a sense often hard to distinguish from 'up to date' (*OED*, 2, first example 1585); cf. *Volp.* III.iv.91, *Alc.* IV.i.23, and *BF* V.iii.121. Marston, *Scourge* IX, 44–5, uses it ambiguously: 'O what a tricksie lerned nicking straine / Is this applauded, sencles, modern vain' (*H&S*); cf. also *Scourge* VI, 26, 'moderne Poesies habiliments', *JD's Ent.*, 'our moderne witts' (Wood, III, 221) and 'moderne policie' (*ibid.*, 223).

consequence] result (*OED*, 1, first example 1400); Marston uses 'consequent' pretentiously in *Hist.* (Wood, III, 275): 'In matters of more worthy consequent'; and *JD's Ent.* (Wood, III, 210): 'And now sir for the consequent houres of the day'.

275. cothurnal buskins] Perhaps parodying Marston, *AR* II.v.45, 'O now *Tragoedia Cothurnata* mounts', itself borrowed from *The Spanish Tragedy* IV.i.160, '*Tragoedia Cothurnata*, fitting Kings', but the words are found in the anonymous *Lust's Dominion*, ed. J. le G. Brereton, *Materials for the Study of the Old English Drama* (Louvain, 1931), l. 3511. K.G. Cross, 'The Authorship of *Lust's Dominion*', SP, LV (1958), 39–61, attributes this play to Marston, partly on the evidence of this apparent quotation. The *cothurnus* was the thick-soled boot worn by tragic actors in Roman times, and was synonymous with 'buskin', its normal English translation.

276. incubus] malignant spirit (*OED*, 1) or oppressive nightmare (*OED*, 2) used twice by Marston in *AR* I.i.90: 'I would have told you, if the incubus / That rides your bosom would have patience', and IV.iv.21–2: 'Then death, like to a stifling incubus / Lie on my bosom.'

poetise] compose poetry (*OED*, 1, first example 1581); used by Marston, *Scourge*, 'Proemium in librum secundum', 9: 'Or daine for base reward to Poetize', and by Daniel, *Civil Wars* (1595) I.vi (ed. Laurence Michel, New Haven, 1958, p. 72): 'I versifie the troth, not poetize'. In *EMO* III.iv.34 Clove's 'fustian' includes 'modellizing' and 'diamondizing'.

277. spurious] illegitimate; see *Scourge* II, 35–6: 'Tilting incounters, with some spurious seede / Of marrow pies, and yawning Oysters breede'; first citation in *OED* in this fig. sense (*OED*, 1.b), but used literally (also 1598) by Hall, *Virgidemiarum* VI.i.238 (*Poems*, p. 94).

snotteries] See *Scourge* II, 71: 'To purge the snottery of our slimie time' (*H&S*). This, and J.'s use here, are the only example's in *OED*, which derives it from 'snot', mucus, hence 'filth, filthiness'.

> *Upon that puffed-up lump of barmy froth——*
> *Tucca. [Aside]* Ah ha!
> *Tibullus. Or clumsy chilblained judgement, that with oath*          280
> *Magnificates his merit, and bespawls*
> *The conscious time with humorous foam, and brawls,*

---

279. S.D.] *This ed.*

---

278. puffed-up] See *Scourge*, 'To *Detraction*', 13: 'My spirit is not puft up with fatte fume / Of slimie Ale' (1599 ed. only); *JD's Ent.*, Wood, III, 229: 'puft up with arrogant conceit'. See below, 487n for Marston's use of 'puff' and related words.

barmy froth] 'barm' is the froth formed on fermenting beer (hence yeast); Marston uses the two words commonly to mean either scum or empty-headedness; see e.g. *Scourge*, 'To those that seeme iudiciall perusers', 12–14: 'iudiciall *Torquatus*, (that like some rotten stick in a troubled water, hath gotte a great deale of barmy froth to stick to his sides'; *ibid.*, VI, 1–2: '*Curio*, know'st me? why thou bottle-ale, / Thou barmy froth!'; *JD's Ent.*, Wood, III, 182, 'Ye shall have me an emptie caske thats furd / With nought but barmy froath.'

280. clumsy] numbed with cold, hence awkward, ungainly; used by Hall, *Virgidemiarum* I.iii.42 (*Poems*, p. 15), and probably seen by him and Marston as an appropriate adjective for the satirist. Marston uses it in *AR* Prol. 1 (quoted above, 269n) and (the passage being parodied by J.), in *JD's Ent.*, Wood, III, 199: 'Let clumsie judgements, chilblaind gowtie wits'.

chilblained] Marston's use in *JD's Ent.* antedates the first example in *OED*, which is from this passage.

280–1. with ... merit] referring to the oath that 'magnificates' *CR*, Epilogue, 20, '*By* (—) '*tis good, and if you lik't, you may.*' Cf. Marston, *Scourge*, 'Proemium in librum secundum', 3, 'I cannot with swolne lines magnificate, / Mine own poore worth'; see also *Scourge* III, 192 and *Pigmalion*, Satire II, 66. For 'merit' see p. 24; for Marston's liking for -ate suffixes, see above, l. 270n.

281. bespawls] covers with saliva; cf. *JD's Ent.*, Wood, III, 190: 'Why should your stomacke be so queasie now, / As to bespawle the pleasures of the world?' *OED* wrongly gives *Poetaster* as first example.

282. conscious time] Marston uses 'conscious heart' in *AR* I.i.76, and 'ravenous time', *ibid.*, I.iii.41. He is one of the first to use 'conscious' in any sense (earliest *OED* example is, wrongly, from this passage); see e.g. *Scourge*, VIII, 95: 'conscius of strange villanie' and *WYW*, Wood, II, 240: 'By heaven that once was consious of my love'. *H&S* note that J.'s former collaborator Nashe had objected to Harvey's 'conscious mind' in *Foure Letters Confuted* (*Works*, ed. McKerrow, I, 316). J. used 'conscious feares' in *Und.* IX, l. 11 (*c.* 1619)

humorous] See *Scourge*, IV, 16: 'The backe of humorous Time'; cf. IV.vii.8n.

foam] spittle, especially of the rabid or epileptic; used by Marston frequently, see e.g. *JD's Ent.*, Wood, III, 216; *AR* II.ii.20–1: 'not pierced

As if his organons of sense would crack
The sinews of my patience. Break his back,
O poets all and some: for now we list                    285
Of strenuous venge-ance to clutch the fist.
          Subscribed Crispinus: alias, Innocence.

287. Subscribed Crispinus:] This ed.; Subscri. Cris: Q, Subst. F.    alias,
Innocence] Q; not in F.

---

by savage tooth / Of foaming malice'; II.iii.54 'foamy bubbling of a fleamy
brain' and III.v.17–18, 'reeking the steam / Of foaming vengeance'.
    283. organons of sense] sensory organs; quoting Scourge VIII, 210,
'Abusing all his organons of sense'. Marston uses 'organon' in a different
sense in Scourge IV, 131.
    283–4. crack . . . patience] Cf. JD's Ent., Wood, III, 214: 'Crack not the
sinewes of my patience'.
    284. Break his back] Cf. Hist., Wood, III, 271: 'Mavo. Broke we not
house up, you would breake our backs. / 1. ser. We breake your backs? no
'tis your rich lac'd sutes, / And straight lac'd mutton; those breake all your
backs.'
    285. list] desire; cf. Ham. I.v.177, 'If we list to speak'.
    286. strenuous . . . fist] Cf. AR V.i.3, 'The fist of strenuous Vengeance is
clutched', and AR III.i.45–6, 'grasp the stern-bended front / Of frowning
vengeance with unpeisd clutch'. 'Strenuous' is a coinage of Marston's, first
used in 1 Ant. Ind. 35: 'preserve the sap of more strenuous spirits.' J. has
already ridiculed it in II.i.13. Marston's lines are also mocked in Meas.
III.ii.44–7, 'What, is there none of Pygmalion's images newly made woman
to be had now, for putting the hand in the pocket and extracting it clutch'd?'
H&S note the parody by Fletcher, The Honest Man's Fortune (1613): 'The
strenuous fist of vengeance now is clutcht' (Works, ed. A. R. Waller, X, 233).
    venge-ance] repeated three times in quick succession by Antonio in AR
III.ii.36, 39, 41; as J.'s hyphen mockingly indicates, it is usually a trisyllable in
Marston; see e.g. Sophonisba, Wood, II, 10: 'The winged vengeance of
incensed Jove'.
    clutch] Cf. passages just quoted, and AR I.i.3–4, 'all the earth is clutched
/ In the dull leaden hand of snoring sleep'. See OED, v. 1. 5 (Marston's is
the first example in this sense).
    287. (Q, F) Subscri.] Probably abbreviating English 'subscribed', but
possibly Latin subscriptus, both meaning 'signed'; the subscriptio was anything
written beneath the text of a document; here it is the signature, but there is
also a suggestion of the specific legal usage of the signing of an accusation (cf.
e.g. Cicero Clu. xlvii, 131). J. is also recalling Hor. Sat. I.x.92, where after
attacking Demetrius and Tigellius, Hor. writes 'Go boy and quickly add this
subscription [subscribe] to my little book' (my translation); in Hor., the
subscriptio is the whole satire.
    alias, Innocence] See IV.vii.30 for Crispinus' protestations of innocence;
cf. Scourge, 'To him that hath perused me', 16–17: 'knew they how guiltlesse,
and how free I were from prying into privatnes, they would blush to thinke,
how much they wrong themselves, in seeking to injure me', and 1 Ant.,

*Tucca.* Ay marry, this was written like a Hercules in poetry now.

*Caesar.* Excellently well threatened! 290

*Virgil.* Ay, and as strangely worded Caesar.

*Caesar.* We observe it.

*Virgil* [*To Tibullus*] The other now.

*Tucca.* This's a fellow of a good prodigal tongue too. This'll do well. 295

*Tibullus.* [*Reads.*] *Our Muse is in mind for th' untrussing a poet;*
*I slip by his name, for most men do know it:*
*A critic that all the world bescumbers*
*With satirical humours and lyrical numbers.*

*Tucca.* [*Aside*] Art thou there, boy? 300

*Tibullus.* *And for the most part himself doth advance*
*With much self-love, and more arrogance.*

*Tucca.* [*Aside*] Good again!

---

303. Good again!] *G;* Good: Againe. *Q;* Good againe. *F.*

---

Dedication, 1–3: 'To the . . . most honorably renowned Nobody, bounteous Maecenas of Poetry and Lord Protector of oppressed innocence.' Chrisoganus is self-righteously 'innocent' in *Hist.*, Wood, III, 291: 'Thus Heaven (in spite of fury) can preserve, / The trustfull innocent, and guiltlessse Soule'.

288. *Hercules in poetry*] Cf. Juvenal II, 19–21: 'Far worse are those who denounce evil ways in the language of a Hercules; and after discoursing upon virtue, prepare to practise vice.' The allusion is pertinent since Juvenal is a primary model for Marston's satire. Cf. also *EMO* Ind. 39.

294. *prodigal*] lavish, wasteful; intended as a compliment, the suggestion is that Demetrius (and therefore Dekker) is over-prolific.

296–313.] The parody of Dekker is less specific than that of Marston, but accurately reflects the simplicity (here banality) of Dekker's style in contrast to Marston's.

296. untrussing] unfastening the 'points' of a garment, hence exposing the buttocks to be whipped. Cf. IV.vii.28, V.iii.592, and (as noun) *EMO* II.iii.97. *The Untrussing of the Humorous Poet* was the theatrical title of *S-M* and the running title of the printed version, *Satiro-mastix* appearing on the title-page of 1602 only. J.'s reference is therefore to the title of Dekker's play as he and his audience were to know it, or, by the date of *Poetaster's* publication in 1602, already knew it.

298. bescumbers] fouls, specifically of a dog; cf. Marston, *Scourge* IX, 33–4: 'Ill-tutor'd pedant, *Mortimers* numbers / With muck-pit esculine filth bescumbers.' J. uses it (of dogs) in *S of N* V.iv.62.

300. *Art . . . boy*] Tucca is encouraging Demetrius as he would a hound or terrier.

*Tibullus.* And, but that I would not be thought a prater,
　　I could tell you he were a translator.                               305
　　I know the authors from whence he has stole,
　　And could trace him too, but that I understand 'em not full
　　　and whole.

*Tucca.* [*Aside*] That line is broke loose from all his fellows:
　　chain him up shorter, do.

*Tibullus.* The best note I can give you to know him by           310
　　Is that he keeps gallants company:
　　Whom I would wish in time should him fear,
　　Lest after they buy repentance too dear.
　　　　　　　　　　　　　　　　Subscribed Demetrius Fannius.

*Tucca.* Well said. This carries palm with it.                    315

*Horace.* And why, thou motley gull, why should they fear?
　　When hast thou known us wrong or tax a friend?
　　I dare thy malice to betray it. Speak!
　　Now thou curl'st up, thou poor and nasty snake,
　　And shrink'st thy pois'nous head into thy bosom.               320
　　Out viper, thou that eat'st thy parents, hence.

---

304. *but . . . prater*] *In parentheses in Q, F.*     314. Subscribed . . . Fannius.]
*This ed.;* Subscri. De. Fannius. *Q;* Subscri. DEME. FAN. *F.*

---

304–7.] Anaides (whom Dekker took to be himself) makes the same
charge against Crites in *CR* III.ii.60–2: 'S'lud, Ile give out, all he does is
dictated from other men, and sweare it too (if thou'lt ha' mee) and that I know
the time, and place where he stole it'.

305. translator] here, a plagiarist from other languages; cf. IV.iii.121–2.

311.] The accusation of envy of J.'s friendships amongst the gentry is made
and answered in *S-M* IV.iii.208–26; cf. also *S-M* I.ii.142–4 and especially
V.ii.303–7: 'Besides, you must forsweare to venter on the stage, when your
Play is ended, and to exchange curtezies, and complements with Gallants in
the Lordes roomes, to make all the house rise up in Armes, and to cry that's
*Horace*, that's he, that's he, that's he, that pennes and purges Humours and
diseases.'

315. *carries palm*] wins the prize (*OED*, 3), the palm being an emblem of
victory; cf. l. 360 below.

316. *motley gull*] Cf. *AYL* II.vii.13, 'A motley fool'; motley was the
variegated coat worn by jesters; a gull, a fool or dupe.

319–24.] The serpent imagery echoes that of Envy in the Ind., esp. 5–11
and 44–53.

321. *viper . . . parents*] The young of the viper were believed to eat their way
out of the mother, killing it in the process, see Pliny, *Natural History*,
X.lxxxii.170; *H&S* cite *Sej.* III.385–8.

Rather such specklèd creatures as thyself
Should be eschewed and shunned: such as will bite
And gnaw their absent friends, not cure their fame;
Catch at the loosest laughters and affect                    325
To be thought jesters; such as can devise
Things never seen or heard, t' impair men's names
And gratify their credulous adversaries;
Will carry tales, do basest offices,
Cherish divided fires, and still increase                    330
New flames out of old embers; will reveal
Each secret that's committed to their trust;
These be black slaves: Romans, take heed of these.

*Tucca.* Thou twang'st right, little Horace, they be indeed: a
couple of chap-fallen curs. Come, we of the bench, let's    335
rise to the urn and condemn 'em quickly.

*Virgil.* Before you go together, worthy Romans,
We are to tender our opinion,
And give you those instructions that may add
Unto your even judgement in the cause,                       340
Which thus we do commence: first you must know
That where there is a true and perfect merit

---

330. still] *F; not in Q.*    334–6.] *Subst. G; verse in Q, F, divided at* indeed: /
A . . . bench, / Let's.    337. worthy Romans] *In parentheses in Q, F.*

323–33.] imitating Hor. *Sat.* I.iv.81–5: 'The man who backbites an absent
friend; who fails to defend him when another finds fault; the man who courts
the loud laughter of others, and the reputation of a wit; who can invent what he
never saw; who cannot keep a secret—that man is black of heart; of him
beware, good Roman.' For the accusation in *S-M* that J. himself betrayed
friendships, see App. 1, pp. 283–4.
    324. *cure*] care for (*OED*, 1).
    334. *twang'st*] speak: cf. I.ii.46n; these are the only two citations in *OED*
for this use of the verb (*v.* 1.5b), but J. uses 'twanging' to mean 'wonderful' in
*SW* V.iii.10.
    335. *chap-fallen*] with the jaw hanging down, still parodying Marston, *1
Ant.* IV.ii.1: 'Now come, united force of chapfall'n death'.
    336–7. *rise . . . together*] The Roman jurors put their verdicts into the urn,
but may first have retired to discuss the case.
    337–41.] The *praetor* was responsible for assessing the evidence before the
jurors, and for passing sentence (see also above, 232n).
    342. *perfect*] complete, well finished (*OED*, 3).

There can be no dejection; and the scorn
Of humble baseness oftentimes so works
In a high soul upon the grosser spirit,
That to his blearèd and offended sense                          345
There seems a hideous fault blazed in the object,
When only the disease is in his eyes.
Here-hence it comes our Horace now stands taxed
Of impudence, self-love and arrogance                           350
By these who share no merit in themselves,
And therefore think his portion is as small.
For they from their own guilt assure their souls
If they should confidently praise their works,
In them it would appear inflation;                              355
Which in a full and well-digested man
Cannot receive that foul abusive name,
But the fair title of erection.
And for his true use of translating men,
It still hath been a work of as much palm                       360
In clearest judgements, as t' invent or make.
His sharpness, that is most excusable,

---

343. *dejection*] abasement (*OED*, 2); cf. Ind. 83.

343–8. *scorn . . . eyes*] i.e. the high soul's scorn of the baseness of the grosser spirit so works on the latter that it seems to his distorted vision that the fault is in the 'high soul' when in fact it is in himself. Dekker parodies this complacency in *S-M* I.ii.199–203, applying it to J.'s poetry: 'when my lines are measur'd out as straight / As even Paralels, tis strange that still, / Still some imagine they are drawne awry. / The error is not mine, but in theyr eye, / That cannot take proportions.'

347. *blazed*] set forth (*OED*, 4).

349. *Here-hence*] as a result of this.

*taxed*] accused.

350. *impudence . . . arrogance*] See above, ll. 224–5n.

*impudence*] in this sense of effrontery, this antedates the first *OED* example, from *Wint.* (1611); Lampatho is an 'od impudent' in *WYW* (Wood, II, 250).

355. *inflation*] 'The condition of being puffed up with vanity, pride, or baseless notions' (*OED*, 3).

356. *well-digested*] well ordered, balanced; cf. Tourneur, *Revenger's Tragedy*, ed. Foakes (Revels, 1986) I.i.76–7: 'To seek some strange-digested fellow forth, / Of ill-contented nature.'

358. *erection*] as opposed to inflation, the condition of soundly based self-esteem, a figurative 'standing upright'. Not in *OED* in this sense.

362–4.] Dekker replies to this in *S-M* V.ii.212–17: 'Should I but bid thy *Muse* stand to the *Barre*, / Thy selfe against her wouldst give evidence: / For

As being forced out of a suffering virtue
Oppressèd with the licence of the time.
And howsoever fools or jerking pedants,                    365
Players, or such like buffon, barking wits
May with their beggarly and barren trash
Tickle base vulgar ears in their despite,
This, like Jove's thunder shall their pride control:
The honest satyr hath the happiest soul.                   370
Now Romans, you have heard our thoughts. Withdraw
when you please.

*Tibullus.* Remove the accused from the bar.

*Tucca.* Who holds the urn to us, ha? [*Aside to Crispinus and
Demetrius*] Fear nothing, I'll quit you, mine honest pitiful    375
stinkards. I'll do it.

*Crispinus.* [*Aside to Tucca*] Captain, you shall eternally girt me
to you, as I am generous.

*Tucca.* [*Aside*] Go to.

*Caesar.* [*Aside to Tibullus*] Tibullus, let there be a case of    380
vizards privately provided. We have found a subject to
bestow them on.

---

366. buffon, barking] *Subst. F; Buffonary Q; buffons,* barking *F2.*    369.
like . . . thunder] *In parentheses in Q, F.*    370.] *Subst. italics in Q; gnomic
pointing in Q, F.* satyr] *This ed.;* Satyre *Q, F Subst.*    374–5. S.D.]
*Subst. Nicholson.*    380. S.D.] *This ed.*

---

flat rebellion gainst the Sacred lawes, / Of divine Poesie: heerein most she mist,
/ *Thy pride and scorne made her turne Saterist,* / And not her love to vertue (as thou
Preachest).'

365. *jerking pedants*] schoolmasters who whip their pupils; 'jerking' is a
favourite term of Marston's (see e.g. *Scourge,* 'Proemium in librum primum',
19–20: 'Quake guzzell dogs, that live on putred slime, / Skud from the lashes
of my yerking rime.') In *Conv.* J. dismisses the neo-Latin poet Owen as 'a pure
Pedantique Schoolmaster sweeping his living from the Posteriors of little
children' (223–4).

366. *buffon*] buffoon-like; cf. *S of N* V.vi.10–11: 'with *buffon* licence, ieast
/ At whatsoe'r is serious, if not sacred.'

368. *despite*] malice; 'their' refers to the 'barking wits', not the 'vulgar
ears'.

374. *Who . . . us*] Tucca is looking for the urn in order to cast his verdict
(see above, l. 232n).

375. *quit*] acquit; cf. *SW* I.i.159, *Alc.* V.v.164 (*H&S*).

377. *girt*] bind (*OED* s.v. 'gird' 5).

378. *generous*] of gentle birth; cf. *Ham.* I.iii.74, 'select and generous'.

380–1. *case . . . vizards*] pair of masks; cf. *EMO,* Characters, 100: 'An
inseparable case of Coxcombs, City-borne; The *Gemini* or Twins of foppery.'

381. *privately*] discreetly.

*Tibullus.* It shall be done, Caesar.

[TIBULLUS *speaks to one of the* Equites Romani *who leaves*
*and returns with a pair of masks.*]

*Caesar.* Here be words, Horace, able to bastinado a man's ears.

*Horace.* Ay. Please it great Caesar, I have pills about me,          385
   Mixed with the whitest kind of hellebore,
   Would give him a light vomit that should purge
   His brain and stomach of those tumorous heats
   Might I have leave to minister unto him.

*Caesar.* O be his Aesculapius, gentle Horace;                        390
   You shall have leave, and he shall be your patient.
   Virgil, use your authority, command him forth.

*Virgil.* Caesar is careful of your health, Crispinus,
   And hath himself chose a physician
   To minister unto you: take his pills.                              395

*Horace.* [*Giving Crispinus a pill*] They are somewhat bitter,
   sir, but very wholesome.

---

383.1–2. S.D.] *This ed.*     386. Mixed . . . hellebore] *In parentheses in Q,*
*F.*   390. his] *as Q.*     396. S.D.] *This ed.*     sir,] *F; not in Q.*     very] *F;*
*not in Q.*

---

384. *bastinado*] to beat with a heavy stick or club.

385–549.] Based on Lucian's *Lexiphanes*, in which Lexiphanes ('word-
flaunter') is cured of his addiction to rare and difficult vocabulary by being
given a purge which induces him to vomit up a series of words. *H&S* say this
was first pointed out by James Upton, *Remarks on Three Plays of Benjamin*
*Jonson* (1749), p. 3, but Dekker had already noticed it in *S-M* IV.ii.97–100:
'Thou'lt shoote thy quilles at mee, when my terrible backe's turn'd for all this,
wilt not Porcupine? and bring me and my Heliconistes into thy Dialogues to
make us talke madlie, wut not Lucian?'

386. *hellebore*] *veratrum album*, a remedy for mental disease; cf. *Hor. Sat.*
II.iii.82: 'To the covetous must we give far the largest dose of hellebore'.
Bond's note to this reads 'Elleborus melancholiam purgans, remedium est
insaniae.' *H&S* quote Pliny, *Natural History* XXV.v, trans. Holland (1601), p.
217: 'The white [ellebore purgeth] by vomit upward, and doth evacuat the
offensive humours which cause diseases. In times past it was thought to be a
dangerous purgative, and men were afraid to use it: but afterwards it became
familiar and common, insomuch as many students tooke it ordinarily for to
cleanse the eyes of those fumes which troubled their sight, to the end that
whiles they read or wrote, they might see the better and more clearley.'

388. *tumorous*] swelling, figuratively for bombastic language; cf. *Disc.*
2052–4: 'For that [style] which is high and lofty, declaring excellent matter,
becomes vast and tumorous, speaking of petty and inferiour things.'

390. *Aesculapius*] god of medicine.

396. *somewhat bitter*] Cf. *S-M*, I.ii.219–23, where Crispinus replies: 'when
your dastard wit will strike at men / In corners, and in riddles folde the vices /

Take yet another, so. Stand by, they'll work anon.

*Tibullus.* Romans, return to your several seats. Lictors, bring
    forward the urn and set the accused at the bar.

*Tucca.* Quickly, you whoreson egregious varlets, come for-     400
    ward. What, shall we sit all day upon you? You make no
    more haste now than a beggar upon pattens, or a physician
    to a patient that has no money, you pilchers.

    [*The judges put their verdicts in the urn as* TIBULLUS *speaks.*]

*Tibullus.* Rufus Laberius Crispinus and Demetrius Fannius,
    hold up your hands. You have, according to the Roman     405
    custom, put yourselves upon trial to the urn for divers and
    sundry calumnies, whereof you have before this time been
    indicted, and are now presently arraigned. Prepare
    yourselves to hearken to the verdict of your triers. [*He
    takes the verdicts from the urn.*] Caius Cilnius Maecenas     410
    pronounceth you by this handwriting guilty. Cornelius
    Gallus, guilty. Pantilius Tucca——

*Tucca.* Parcel-guilty I.

*Demetrius.* He means himself, for it was he indeed
    Suborned us to the calumny.                       415

---

397. yet another, so] *F;* another, yet; so *Q.*     398–9.] *F; verse in Q, divided*
at Lictors, / Bring.     403. has] *G;* ha's *Q, F.*     403.1. S.D.] *This ed.*
404–12.] *Subst. italics in Q, F.*     405–6. according . . . custom] *In paren-*
*theses in Q, F.*     409–10. S.D.] *This ed.*     411–13.] *F; Q transposes*
*speech prefix Tuc. thus:* Guiltie. Corneli- / *Tuc.* Gallus, *Guiltie.*
Pantilius Tucca—— / us Parcell guiltie; I.

---

Of your best friends, you must not take to heart, / If they take off all gilding
from their pilles, / And onely offer you the bitter Coare.'

   401. *all . . . you*] all day [in judgement] upon you.

   402. *beggar . . . pattens*] pattens were a form of wood-soled shoe or
overshoe.

   403. *pilchers*] See III.iv.4n.

   411. *handwriting*] referring to the 'writ' (V.iii.257), the offending poems;
since Crispinus and Demetrius have admitted authorship, there is no question
of identification of their handwriting, nor is the reference likely to be to writing
on the verdicts in the urn: J. would probably have known that symbols were
used for the verdicts.

   413. *Parcel-guilty*] i.e. *non liquet*, undecided (see above, l. 232n), with a
play on 'parcel-gilt'; Tucca has presumably voted not guilty, and is now trying
to extricate himself after hearing the other votes (so *H&S*).

   414–15.] Mallory points out that Demetrius had 'first' been suborned to
calumniate Horace by the players (see III.iv.322–4), but the reference here is
to the 'calumny' of the two 'poems'.

*Tucca.* I, you whoreson cantharides? Was't I?

*Demetrius.* I appeal to your conscience, captain.

*Tibullus.* Then you confess it now?

*Demetrius.* I do, and crave the mercy of the court.

*Tibullus.* What saith Crispinus?                                420

*Crispinus.* [*Groaning*] O, the captain, the captain——

*Horace.* My physic begins to work with my patient I see.

*Virgil.* Captain, stand forth and answer.

*Tucca.* Hold thy peace, poet praetor. I appeal from thee to
Caesar, I. Do me right, royal Caesar.                            425

*Caesar.* Marry, and I will, sir. Lictors, gag him, do:
And put a case of vizards o'er his head,
That he may look bi-fronted, as he speaks.

*Tucca.* Gods and fiends! Caesar! Thou wilt not Caesar, wilt
thou? [*The* Lictors *seize him.*] Away you whoreson vultures,    430
away! You think I am a dead corpse now, because Caesar
is disposed to jest with a man of mark or so. Hold your
hooked talons out of my flesh, you inhuman harpies.
Go to, do't. What, will the royal Augustus cast away a
gent'man of worship, a captain and a commander, for a            435
couple of condemned, caitiff, calumnious cargoes?

421. S.D.] *This ed.*    426. him, do:] *This ed.;* him: *Q, ?uncorr. F;* him: doe.
*?corr. F.*    429. fiends!] *?corr. F;* Fiends. *Q;* fiends. *?uncorr. F;* friends!
*F2.*    430. S.D.] *This ed.*    433. harpies] *F;* Gorboduckes *Q.*    436.
cargoes] *This ed.; Cargo's Q, F.*

---

416. *cantharides*] *cantharis vesicatoria*, the 'Spanish fly', a beetle used in its
dried form externally as a vesicant (Demetrius is blistering Tucca's reputation)
and internally as an aphrodisiac.

427–8. *case ... bi-fronted*] symbolising his duplicity. Such masks were
tied together, so the wearer seemed to look both ways at once: J. is adapting
the opening lines of Marston, *Satire I*, in *Pigmalion*: 'I cannot show in strange
proportion / Changing my hew like a Camelion. / But you all-canning wits,
hold water out, / Yee vizarded-bifronted-*Ianian* rout' (*Poems*, p. 67). Cf. also
Guilpin, *Skialetheia* sig. c3v: 'This vizar-fac't . . . dissimulation . . . / This
squynt-eyde slave, which lookes two wayes at once.' 'Bifrons' is the usual
epithet for Janus: cf. Virgil *Aeneid*, VII, 180, XII, 198.

432. *or so*] See III.iv.160n.

433. (*Q*) *Gorboduckes*] referring to the play by Norton and Sackville (1562);
for the change in *F* see App. 1, p. 284. By 1601 Sackville had become Lord
High Treasurer, and as High Steward had presided over the trial of Essex and
Southampton.

436. *cargoes*] probably from the Spanish *cargo*, a burden or bundle; this
contemptuous use is earliest cited in *OED*, antedating the modern usage (first
example 1657).

*Caesar.* Dispatch, lictors.

*Tucca.* Caesar!

[Lictors *place the double-fronted mask over his head; exit* TUCCA.]

*Caesar.* Forward, Tibullus.

*Virgil.* Demand what cause they had to malign Horace.          440

*Demetrius.* In troth, no great cause, not I, I must confess, but
    that he kept better company for the most part than I,
    and that better men loved him than loved me, and that his
    writings thrived better than mine and were better liked
    and graced. Nothing else.          445

*Virgil.* Thus envious souls repine at others' good.

*Horace.* If this be all, faith I forgive thee freely.

    Envy me still, so long as Virgil loves me,

    Gallus, Tibullus, and the best-best Caesar;

    My dear Maecenas. While these, with many more,          450

    Whose names I wisely slip, shall think me worthy

    Their honoured and adored society,

    And read and love, prove and applaud my poems,

    I would not wish but such as you should spite them.

*Crispinus.* [*Groaning*] O——          455

---

438.1. S.D.] *This ed.; The vizards are put upon him.* G.     442. for . . . part]
*In parentheses in* Q, F.     451. Whose . . . slip] *In parentheses in* Q, F.
455. S.D.] *This ed.*

---

448–54.] imitating Hor. *Sat* I.x.78–91, one of the main sources for
*Poetaster*: 'Am I to be troubled by that louse Pantilius? Or tortured because
Demetrius carps at me behind my back, or because silly Fannius, who
sponges on Hermogenes Tigellius, girds at me? Let but Plotius and Varius
approve of these verses; let Maecenas, Virgil, and Valgius . . . also you,
honest Furnius, and many another scholar and friend, whom I purposely
pass over. In their eyes I should like these verses, such as they are, to find
favour, and I should be grieved if their pleasure were to fall short of my
hopes. But you, Demetrius, and you, Tigellius, I bid you go whine amidst
the easy chairs of your pupils in petticoats.'

449. *best-best*] Cf. *Und.* XXV, 63: 'O then, my best-best loved' (*H&S*).

451. *slip*] pass over.

453. *prove*] try out, taste.

455–515.] expanded from Lucian *Lexiphanes* 21: 'Begin now to lighten
yourself. Aha! First, this "prithee," then after it "eftsoons" has come up,
then on their heels his "quoth he" and "in some wise," and "fair sir,"
and "in sooth," and his incessant "sundry." Make an effort, however; put
your fingers down your throat. You have not yet given up "instanter" or
"pandiculation" or "divagation" or "spoliation." Many things still lurk
in hiding and your inwards are full of them. It would be better if some

*Tibullus.* How now, Crispinus?

*Crispinus.* O, I am sick——

*Horace.* A basin, a basin, quickly; our physic works. [*To Crispinus*] Faint not, man.

> [HORACE *holds a basin into which* CRISPINUS *appears to vomit his words.*]

*Crispinus.* O—*retrograde—reciprocal—incubus.*                    460

*Caesar.* What's that Horace?

*Horace.* [*Looking in the basin*] *Retrograde, reciprocal* and *incubus* are come up.

*Gallus.* Thanks be to Jupiter.

*Crispinus.* O—*glibbery—lubrical—defunct—*O——                    465

*Horace.* Well said! Here's some store.

*Virgil.* What are they?

*Horace.* [*Looking*] *Glibbery, lubrical* and *defunct.*

*Gallus.* O, they came up easy.

*Crispinus.* [*Loudly*] O—O——                                     470

*Tibullus.* What's that?

*Horace.* Nothing yet.

*Crispinus. Magnificate.*

*Maecenas. Magnificate?* That came up somewhat hard.

*Horace.* Ay. What cheer, Crispinus?                              475

*Crispinus.* O, I shall cast up my—*spurious—snotteries*——

*Horace.* Good. Again.

---

459.1–2. S.D.] *This ed.*     462–3. *reciprocal* and *incubus*] *Subst. Q; and reciprocall, Incubus ?uncorr. F; and reciprocall Incubus ?corr. F.*     468. S.D.] *This ed.*     470. S.D.] *This ed.*

---

should take the opposite course. Anyhow, "vilipendency" will make a great racket when it comes tumbling out on the wings of the wind.'

460–515.] The following words vomited by Crispinus are dealt with in notes to V.iii.269–86 above: *retrograde, incubus, glibbery, lubrical, defunct, magnificate, spurious, snotteries, chilblained, clumsy, barmy froth, strenuous, conscious, clutched.*

460. reciprocal] not found in Marston; J. uses it ironically in *EMO* IV.iii.90, and *CR* I.iv.77. *H&S* suggest that J.'s point may lie in what they call a 'corrected' reading of F, '*reciprocall / Incubus*', but in fact no copies have this 'correction', and J. probably objected to it as a fashionable neologism (cf. King, p. 27).

462–3.] Horace repeats the words brought up by Crispinus in order to clarify for the audience what might have been lost in the vomiting delivery of the boy playing Crispinus.

*Crispinus.* Chilblained—O—O—*clumsy*——
*Horace.* That *clumsy* stuck terribly.
*Maecenas.* What's all that Horace?                    480
*Horace.* [*Looking*] *Spurious snotteries, chilblained, clumsy.*
*Tibullus.* O Jupiter!
*Gallus.* Who would have thought there should ha' been such a
     deal of filth in a poet?
*Crispinus.* O—*barmy froth*——                          485
*Caesar.* What's that?
*Crispinus.*  —*Puffy—inflate—turgidous—ventositous.*
*Horace.* Barmy froth, puffy, inflate, turgidous and *ventositous* are
     come up.
*Tibullus.* O terrible windy words!                      490
*Gallus.* A sign of a windy brain.
*Crispinus.* O—*oblatrant—furibund—fatuate—strenuous*——

---

481. S.D.] *This   ed.*   487,   488. *ventositous*] *F; Ventosity Q.*   492.
*oblatrant*] *F; Oblatrant—Obcæcate—Q.*

---

487. Puffy] may be a coinage of Marston's (see *OED*, 3) in *Scourge*, 'In
Lectores', 41–2: 'ye vaine fantasticke troupe / Of puffie youthes', and IV, 55:
'Mong puffie Spunges'. Associated forms ('puff', 'puffes') are also common
throughout his work.
     inflate] not in Marston; J. is probably alluding to its Latin meaning of
flatulence (see Lewis and Short, s.v. *inflatio*, II); like the following 'windy
words', it is included as both descriptive of Marston's inflated style, and
parodic of his method of coining words, rather than as a word specifically
used by him.
     turgidous] swollen, inflated; a coinage of J.'s from Latin *turgidus*, swollen;
cf. Hor. *Sat.* I.x.36, 'Turgidus Alpinus' (of a bad poet). Not in Marston; this
is the only example in *OED*.
     ventositous] flatulent, windy; coined by J. from Latin *ventosus*, windy,
bombastic; cf. Hor. *Epist.* II.i.177. Not in Marston, and again the only
example in *OED*.
     (*Q*). ventosity] flatulence, especially belching. Not in Marston, but *H&S*
point out it is used as a Marstonian word in *EMO* III.iv.27; first example in
*OED* dates from 1398.
     490–1.] The relationship between physical flatulence and the brain was
not simply metaphoric in Renaissance medicine; see e.g. Burton, *Anatomy*, I,
222: 'All pulse are naught, beans, pease, fitches etc., they fill the brain (saith
Isaac) with gross fumes, breed black, thick blood, and cause troublesome
dreams.'
     492. oblatrant] coined by J. from Latin *oblatro*, to rail or carp; this is the
only example cited in *OED*, but Marston does coin the more successful
'petulant', *Scourge*, 'To everlasting Oblivion', 2.

*Horace.* Here's a deal: *oblatrant, furibund, fatuate, strenuous.*

*Caesar.* Now all's come up, I trow. What a tumult he had in his
belly!

*Horace.* No, there's the often *conscious damp* behind still.          495

*Crispinus.* O—*conscious—damp.*

*Horace.* It's come up, thanks to Apollo and Aesculapius. Yet
there's another. You were best take a pill more?

*Crispinus.* O no! O—O—O—O——          500

*Horace.* Force yourself then a little with your finger.

            [CRISPINUS *pushes his finger down his throat.*]

*Crispinus.* [*Loudly*] O—O—*prorumped.*

*Tibullus.* *Prorumped?* What a noise it made! As if his spirit
would have prorumped with it.

*Crispinus.* O—O—O——          505

*Virgil.* Help him. It sticks strangely, whatever it is.

            [HORACE *slaps* CRISPINUS *on the back.*]

*Crispinus.* O—*clutched.*

*Horace.* Now it's come: *clutched.*

*Caesar.* *Clutched?* It's well that's come up! It had but a narrow
passage.          510

*Crispinus.* O——

---

493. oblatrant] F; Oblatrant, Obcæcate Q.    496. damp] F; not in Q.
497. conscious—damp] F; Conscious. Q.    498–9.] Subst. G; verse in Q, F,
divided at Aesculapius. / Yet.    501.1. S.D.] This ed.    502. S.D.] This
ed.    506.1. S.D.] This ed.    507. clutched] This ed.; Clutcht Q; clutcht F;
(also 508, 9).

---

(*Q*). obcaecate] blind (mentally or spiritually), from Latin *obcaeco*, to
make blind or obscure; cf. Cicero *De or.* II.80; not in Marston; first example
in *OED*, 1568.

furibund] from Latin *furibundus*, raging; coined by Caxton, 1490, but not
in Marston, though again descriptive of his style; Gabriel Harvey uses
'furibundal', *Pierce's Superogation*, in *Works*, ed. Grosart, II, 17.

fatuate] coined by J. from Latin *fatuor*, to talk foolishly; not in Marston,
but again (in J.'s view) descriptive of his style. This is the only example in
*OED*.

496. often... damp] Cf. Lucian *Lexiphanes* 21, 'his incessant "sundry"';
J. added 'damp' in F, probably feeling that Marston had overused 'damps' in
*AR* I.iii.74, 83, and III.iii.93.

501.] Cf. Lucian *Lexiphanes* 21, 'Make an effort, however; put your
fingers down your throat.'

502. prorumped] from Latin *prorumpo*, to burst forth: not in Marston, but
accurately parodying his coining of Latinate words.

*Virgil.* Again! Hold him, hold his head there!
[HORACE *holds* CRISPINUS's *head over the basin.*]
*Crispinus. Snarling gusts—quaking custard.*
*Horace.* How now, Crispinus?
*Crispinus.* O—*obstupefact.*                                                  515
*Tibullus.* Nay, that are all we, I assure you.
*Horace.* How do you feel yourself?
*Crispinus.* Pretty and well, I thank you.
*Virgil.* These pills can but restore him for a time,
Not cure him quite of such a malady                                            520
Caught by so many surfeits, which have filled
His blood and brain thus full of crudities.
'Tis necessary therefore he observe
A strict and wholesome diet. [*To Crispinus*] Look you take
Each morning of old Cato's principles                                          525

---

512.1. S.D.] *This ed.*     513. *Snarling . . . custard*] *F; Tropologicall—Anago-*
*gicall—Loquacity—Pinnosity Q.*

---

513. Snarling gusts] Cf. *AR*, Prol. 4: 'Whilst snarling gusts nibble the
juiceless leaves.'
   quaking custard] Cf. *Scourge*, II, 4: 'Let Custards quake, my rage must
freely run'; the line is ridiculed again in *Volp.* Prol. 21: 'Nor quaking
custards with fierce teeth affrighted.'
   (*Q*). Tropologicall . . . Anagogicall] not in Marston; both describe methods
of interpreting texts, especially Biblical ones; cf. Tindale, *Obedience of a
christen man* (1528) p. 129: 'They devide ye scripture in to iiij.senses, ye
literall, tropologicall, allegoricall, anagogicall.'
   (*Q*). Loquacity] talkativeness; this example antedates first *OED* citation
by two years. Not in Marston.
   (*Q*). Pinnosity] a nonce word, not in Marston or *OED*, but presumably
derived from 'pinion', which is used by Marston in *AR* IV.v.84–5 and
*Scourge*, 'In Lectores', 72. See also II.i.25.
   515. obstupefact] coined by J. from Latin *obstupefactus*, stupified; not in
Marston, but a sonnet signed 'Il Candido', dated 1599, in Florio's translation
of Montaigne uses 'obstupefying' along with other words reminiscent of
Marston's vocabulary: 'Epileptique', 'lethargic', 'frost benumming' (*Essays*,
ed. Harmer, Everyman, I, 12).
   518. *Pretty and*] the adj. 'pretty' plus 'and' used in place of the adverb,
meaning 'fairly', 'quite': see *OED* s.v. 'pretty' *a.* 5c. Not affected here as
elsewhere in the play (see I.ii.130n).
   524–49. *Look . . . sentence*] Cf. Lucian *Lexiphanes* 23–5, where Lycinus
lectures Lexiphanes on improving his style with a similar programme of
reading and tuition.
   525. *old Cato's*] the elder Cato (234–149 BC), famed for his plain morality,
to whom was attributed the *Catonis Disticha*, a work of the later Imperial

A good draught next your heart. That walk upon
Till it be well digested, then come home
And taste a piece of Terence: suck his phrase
Instead of licorice, and at any hand
Shun Plautus and old Ennius: they are meats                         530
Too harsh for a weak stomach. Use to read
(But not without a tutor) the best Greeks,
As Orpheus, Musaeus, Pindarus,
Hesiod, Callimachus and Theocrite,
High Homer, but beware of Lycophron,                                 535
He is too dark and dangerous a dish.

---

526. That walk upon] *Subst. Q, F;* and walk upon't *F2.*

---

period, which was popular throughout medieval and Renaissance times,
quoted by Chaucer, and edited by Erasmus (so *H&S*).

526. *next your heart*] i.e. on an empty stomach, before breakfast (*H&S*).

528. *Terence*] Publius Terentius Afer, (?190–?159 BC), Latin comic playwright who greatly influenced Renaissance drama, in part through the
commentaries on his plays collected under the name of Donatus. J.'s library
included a fifteenth-century manuscript *Opera* (McPherson, 187).

530. *Shun . . . Ennius*] early Latin writers; Maccius Titus Plautus (died *c.*
190 BC), comic dramatist; his plays (and language) are less realistic than
Terence's; for Ennius see I.i.61n. Surviving fragments of his work suggest a
highly patterned language, with many archaisms (hence he is not a recommended model for Crispinus), but his epic *Annales* is probably the greatest
single loss to Latin literature. J. gives similar advice in an English context in
*Disc.* 1796–802: 'And as it is fit to read the best Authors to youth first, so
let them be of the openest, and clearest. As *Livy* before *Salust, Sydney* before
*Donne:* and beware of letting them taste *Gower,* or *Chaucer* at first, lest falling
too much in love with Antiquity, and not apprehending the weight, they
grow rough and barren in language onely.'

533. *Orpheus, Musaeus*] For Orpheus, see IV.iii.81n; mythical singers of
closely related kind, the latter confused in J.'s time with the late fifth-century
AD Musaeus Grammaticus, who wrote a *Hero and Leander* which influenced
Marlowe, and was translated in 1618 by Chapman.

*Pindarus*] Pindar (518–438 BC), lyric poet; *Und.* LXX is the first attempt
in English at a thoroughgoing 'imitation' of the Pindaric ode.

534. *Hesiod, Callimachus*] See I.i.53–5n.

*Theocrite*] Theocritus (*c.* 300–*c.* 260 BC), pastoral poet who wrote in Greek
about his native Sicily.

535. *Lycophron*] (born *c.* 320 BC), Greek tragedian; none of his plays
survives, but he may have written the obscure epic *Alexandra,* which,
like Marston's work, employs neologisms and vulgarisms; it is this that
Lexiphanes and Crispinus are warned against.

You must not hunt for wild, outlandish terms
To stuff out a peculiar dialect,
But let your matter run before your words.
And if at any time you chance to meet                          540
Some Gallo-Belgic phrase, you shall not straight
Rack your poor verse to give it entertainment,
But let it pass, and do not think yourself
Much damnified if you do leave it out,
When nor your understanding nor the sense                      545
Could well receive it. This fair abstinence
In time will render you more sound and clear;
And this have I prescribed to you in place
Of a strict sentence. [*To Lictors*] Which till he perform
Attire him in that robe. [*To Crispinus*] And henceforth
      learn                                                    550
To bear yourself more humbly, not to swell,
Or breathe your insolent and idle spite
On him whose laughter can your worst affright.
*Tibullus*. [*To Lictors*] Take him away.
*Crispinus*.                        Jupiter guard Caesar.
*Virgil*. And for a week or two, see him locked up             555
      In some dark place, removed from company.
      He will talk idly else after his physic.

---

554. Caesar.] *Some copies of F are defective, printing only* CAE

537. *outlandish*] still 'foreign', but beginning at this time to acquire its
pejorative meaning of bizarre; see *OED*, 1 and 2.
539. *let . . . words*] Cf. *CR*, Prol. 20: 'Words, above action; matter, above
words', and Tucca's joke in IV.v.143–4 (*H&S*). Bacon, *Advancement of
Learning* (1605) sees the 'first distemper of learning' arising 'when men study
words and not matter' (I.iv.3).
541. *Gallo-Belgic*] the *Mercurii Gallo Belgici* was a news 'register' published in Cologne from 1588 to 1630, famous for its Latinisms. Cf. *Ep.* XCII,
15–16: 'They carry in their pockets Tacitus, / And the *Gazetti*, or *Gallo-
Belgicus*' (*G*, *H&S*). Donne attacks it in the epigram 'Mercurius Gallo-
Belgicus' (*Donne*, p. 35).
550. *that robe*] probably the same as the fool's 'coat and cap' given to
Demetrius in l. 565 below; this reading is supported by *S-M* IV.iii.247–8:
''tis not your fooles Cap Master *Horace*, which you covered your Poetasters in'
(so *H&S*).
555–6. *see . . . company*] The usual treatment for lunatics; cf. *Err.*
IV.iv.91, 'They must be bound, and laid in some dark room' and *Tw.N*
III.iv.136–7: 'Come, we'll have him in a dark room and bound.'

[*To Demetrius*] Now to you, sir. Th' extremity of law
Awards you to be branded in the front
For this your calumny. But since it pleaseth                    560
Horace (the party wronged) t' intreat of Caesar
A mitigation of that juster doom,
With Caesar's tongue thus we pronounce your sentence:
Demetrius Fannius, thou shalt here put on
That coat and cap; and henceforth think thyself              565
No other than they make thee. Vow to wear them
In every fair and generous assembly,
Till the best sort of minds shall take to knowledge
As well thy satisfaction as thy wrongs.

*Horace.* Only, grave praetor, here in open court              570
I crave the oath for good behaviour
May be administered unto them both.

*Virgil.* Horace, it shall. Tibullus, give it them.

*Tibullus.* Rufus Laberius Crispinus and Demetrius Fannius,
lay your hands on your hearts. You shall here solemnly       575
attest and swear that never, after this instant, either at
booksellers' stalls, in taverns, twopenny rooms, 'tiring
houses, noblemen's butteries, puisnes' chambers (the best

---

558. S.D.] *G.*    570. grave praetor] *In parentheses in Q, F.*    574–97.]
*Subst. italics in Q, F.*    576. attest] *contest Q.*    after . . . instant] *In parentheses in Q, F.*

---

558–60.] See above, l. 168n.
559. *front*] forehead (*OED*, 1).
565. *coat and cap*] See above, l. 550n.
567. *generous*] See above, l. 378n.
569. *satisfaction*] in the sense of making amends.
574–97.] Dekker makes Asinius Bubo and Horace swear a similar series
of oaths in *S-M* V.ii.270–336.
577. *booksellers' stalls*] meeting places for gallants and intellectuals; in
*EMO* III.i.29–31, Clove 'will sit you a whole afternoone sometimes, in
a booke-sellers shop, reading the *Greeke, Italian,* and *Spanish*; when he
understands not a word of either'.
*twopenny rooms*] See III.iv.130n.
577–8. *'tiring houses*] dressing rooms of the theatres.
578. *noblemen's butteries*] though *OED* does not give this meaning, these
are akin to the butteries of Oxford and Cambridge colleges, places where
wine, beer and provisions were not only stored but dispensed to the humbler
visitors; cf. *Tw.N* I.iii.70, 'bring your hand to th' butt'ry-bar, and let it
drink', and *Shr.* Ind. i.102., where the players are taken 'to the buttery'.

and farthest places where you are admitted to come), you
shall once offer or dare (thereby to endear yourself the     580
more to any player, engle, or guilty gull in your company)
to malign, traduce or detract the person or writings of
Quintus Horatius Flaccus, or any other eminent man
transcending you in merit, whom your envy shall find
cause to work upon, either for that, or for keeping himself   585
in better acquaintance or enjoying better friends. Or if
(transported by any sudden and desperate resolution) you
do, that then you shall not under the baton, or in the next
presence, being an honourable assembly of his favourers,
be brought as voluntary gent. to undertake the forswearing   590
of it. Neither shall you at any time, (ambitiously affecting
the title of the untrussers or whippers of the age) suffer the
itch of writing to overrun your performance in libel, upon
pain of being taken up for lepers in wit, and (losing both

---

588. baton] *This ed.;* Bastoun *Q; bastoun F.*     590. gent.] *Q, F;* Gentlemen *F3, G.*

*puisnes' chambers*] the context does not allow for the meaning of 'junior
judges' chambers', and must therefore be to those of students at the Inns of
Court; cf. III.iv.309, where it is applied to underlings of any kind.

581. *engle . . . gull*] See I.ii.16n.

582. *detract*] disparage.

585. *for that*] for transcending them in merit.

588. *under . . . baton*] The 'baston' of the Fleet was a prison officer who
accompanied prisoners allowed out on licence (*OED*, s.v. 'Baston', 5).

589. *presence*] company (*OED*, 3), but usually indicating a person or
group of superior rank, in this case 'an honourable assembly of his favourers'.

590. *voluntary gent.*] normally a gentleman volunteer on a military expedition (*OED* s.v. 'voluntary' 7b); here meaning either that the assembly give
them the honorary title of gentleman, or referring to Marston's insistence on
his status. It may be that the abbreviation is not significant and should be
opened out as in *F3.*

592. *untrussers*] See V.iii.296n.

*whippers*] referring to Marston's *Scourge* and only secondarily to
Weever's *Whipping of the Satyre.*

593. *itch of writing*] answered firmly in *S-M* V.ii.201–3: 'you Nastie
Tortois, you and your Itchy Poetry breake out like Christmas, but once a
yeare'.

your time and your papers) be irrecoverably forfeited to   595
the Hospital of Fools. So help you our Roman gods, and
the genius of great Caesar.

*Virgil.* So. Now dissolve the court.

*Horace, Tibullus, Gallus, Maecenas, Virgil.* And thanks to
Caesar,

That thus hath exercised his patience.

[*Exeunt* CRISPINUS *and* DEMETRIUS *led out by* Lictors.]

*Caesar.* We have indeed, you worthiest friends of Caesar.   600
It is the bane and torment of our ears
To hear the discords of those jangling rhymers
That with their bad and scandalous practices
Bring all true arts and learning in contempt.
But let not your high thoughts descend so low   605
As these despisèd objects. Let them fall
With their flat, grovelling souls: be you yourselves.
And as with our best favours you stand crowned,
So let your mutual loves be still renowned.
Envy will dwell where there is want of merit,   610
Though the deserving man should crack his spirit.

SONG.

*Blush, folly, blush: here's none that fears*
*The wagging of an ass's ears,*
*Although a wolvish case he wears.*

599.1 S.D.] *This ed.*   611.1. SONG] *F; CANTVS Q.*

595–6. *forfeited . . . Fools*] figuratively, rather than committed to Bedlam
or its Roman equivalent. H&S cite the title of Tommaso Garzoni's *The
Hospitall of Incurable Fooles* (1600).

598. *Horace . . . Virgil*] It is unlikely that all five spoke together. One
actor may have spoken with the rest signifying their agreement.

599. *patience*] pronounced as three syllables.

601. *bane*] agent of woe (*OED*, 4).

611. *crack*] damage irreparably (*OED*, 20).

613–14. *ass's . . . wears*] referring both to the fable of the ass in the lion's
skin, and to Lupus, the wolf who is now wearing ass's ears.

614. *case*] physical exterior, the body, enclosing the soul (*OED, sb.* 2, 3).

*Detraction is but baseness, varlet,*                    615
*And apes are apes, though clothed in scarlet.*

THE END.

Rumpatur, quisquis rumpitur invidia.

616.1. THE END.] *F; Finis Actus quinti & vltimi. / Exeunt. Q.*

---

616.] proverbial; cf. Dent, A263, Erasmus *Adagia* 265A, and (*H&S*)
Lucian *Adversus indoctum*, 4. Though the proverb refers to splendour and
power in general, it must, in the context of the play, have seemed to glance at
judges in particular. Judges' robes varied according to the calendar from
scarlet to violet.
617.] Martial IX.xcvii.12: 'Whoever is bursting with envy, let him burst'
(my trans.). Detraction and envy are confirmed as major moral targets of the
play.

# TO THE READER

If by looking on what is past thou hast deserved that name,
I am willing thou shouldst yet know more by that which
follows, an *Apologetical Dialogue*, which was only once spoken
upon the stage, and all the answer I ever gave to sundry
impotent libels then cast out (and some yet remaining) against     5
me and this play. Wherein I take no pleasure to revive the
times, but that posterity may make a difference between their
manners that provoked me then, and mine that neglected
them ever. For in these strifes, and on such persons, were as
wretched to affect a victory, as it is unhappy to be committed     10
with them. *Non annorum canicies est laudanda, sed morum.*

---

1–11. If . . . morum] *F, subst. in italics; not in Q, which has:* HERE *(Reader)
in place of the* Epilogue, *was meant to thee an* Apology *from the Author, with
his reasons for the publishing of this booke: but (since he is no lesse restrain'd,
then thou depriu'd of it, by Authoritie) hee praies thee to thinke charitably of what
thou hast read, till thou maist heare him speake what hee hath written. /* FINIS.
3. *Apologetical Dialogue*] *This ed.;* apologeticall Dialogue *F.*

---

3–4. *was . . . stage*] The dialogue is probably substantially the same as that
'Apology' which *Q* tells us was 'restrain'd . . . by Authoritie', particularly
since J. there asks the reader to wait 'till thou maist hear him speake', a
statement which also supports the suggestion made by A. W. Ward that
J. spoke the author's part himself (*English Dramatic Literature* (1899), II,
360). The appearance of the author (or an actor representing him) directly
addressing the audience is sanctioned by the *parabasis* of the Greek 'Old
Comedy', to which J. refers below (ll. 173–7), in which the chorus leader
takes on this role. See e.g. Aristophanes *Wasps* 1009–121.

4–6. *sundry . . . play*] The 'once spoken' dialogue was added some time
after the first performance, and was not originally part of the play; it takes
account of S-M in ll. 172 and 181, and so postdates it. S-M is probably,
therefore, the source of most of the 'sundry libels'.

12. Non . . . morum] 'not the grey hairs of the years deserve praise, but
those of character'. Ambrose *Epistles* I.xviii, ed. Migne, *Patrologia Latina*
(*H&S*).

[APOLOGETICAL DIALOGUE]

*The Persons*

NASUTUS, POLYPOSUS, AUTHOR

[*Enter* NASUTUS *and* POLYPOSUS]

*Nasutus.* I pray you, let's go see him, how he looks
 After these libels.
*Polyposus.*                    O, vexed, vexed, I warrant you.
*Nasutus.* Do you think so? I should be sorry for him
 If I found that.
*Polyposus.*                    O, they are such bitter things
 He cannot choose.
*Nasutus.*                    But is he guilty of 'em?                    5
*Polyposus.* Fuh! That's no matter.
*Nasutus.*                    No?
*Polyposus.*                                        No. Here's his lodging.
 We'll steal upon him. Or let's listen; stay:
 He has a humour oft t' talk t' himself.
*Nastutus.* They are your manners lead me, not mine own.
                    [*They come forward; the scene opens,*
                    *and discovers the* AUTHOR *in his study.*]
*Author.* The fates have not spun him the coarsest thread                    10
 That, free from knots of perturbation,

---

0.1–227.] *F; not in Q.*    0.3 *Enter* . . . POLYPOSUS.] *This ed.;* SCENE,
*The* Author's *Lodgings. Enter* NASUTUS *and* POLYPOSUS. *G.*    9.1–2.
S.D.] *G.*    11. free . . . perturbation] *In parentheses in F.*

---

0.2. NASUTUS, POLYPOSUS] taken from Martial XII.xxxvii, used
on the title-page of *CR* in *F*: 'Nasutum volo, nolo Polyposum' ('I approve of
a man with a nose: I object to one with a polypus'). 'Nasutus' means both
large-nosed and witty; 'Polyposus' means a deformed nose, infested by
tumors (polyps): cf. Henry Lyte, *Dodoens' Niewe Herball* (1578), II.cxii.305:
'the Polypus growing in the Nosthrilles'. Hence, Nasutus is a sound critic,
Polyposus a malicious and ignorant one. The nasal metaphor is taken up in
l. 195.
    9.1. S.D.] Cf. *S-M* I.ii.0.1–2: 'Horace *sitting in a study behinde a Cur-
taine, a candle by him burning, bookes lying confusedly*' and *Hist.*: 'So all goe to
*Chrisoganus* study, where they find him reading' (Wood, III, 252).
    10. *fates . . . thread*] i.e. his fate has not been too harsh; J. does not see the
coarser thread as stronger. Cf. *Hadd.* 224–5: 'untill the *Parcae* spunne /
Their whitest wooll'.
    11. *knots*] occuring in the coarser thread of fate.

Doth yet so live, although but to himself,
As he can safely scorn the tongues of slaves,
And neglect Fortune more than she can him.
It is the happiest thing this, not to be          15
Within the reach of malice. It provides
A man so well to laugh off injuries,
And never sends him farther for his vengeance
Than the vexed bosom of his enemy.
Ay, now but think how poor their spite sets off,  20
Who after all their waste of sulphurous terms,
And burst out thunder of their chargèd mouths,
Have nothing left but the unsavoury smoke
Of their black vomit to upbraid themselves.
Whilst I, at whom they shot, sit here shot-free,  25
And as unhurt of envy as unhit.

     [POLYPOSUS *and* NASUTUS *discover themselves.*]
*Polyposus.* Ay, but the multitude, they think not so, sir,
They think you hit and hurt, and dare give out
Your silence argues it, in not rejoining
To this or that late libel.
*Author.*           'Las, good rout!          30
I can afford them leave to err so still,
And, like the barking students of Bears' College,

18. farther] *G;* farder *F.*    23. unsavoury] *G;* vnsau'ry *F.*    26.1. S.D.]
*G.*

12. *live . . . himself*] in self-reliant spiritual or physical isolation; cf. Hor.
*Sat.* II.vii.83: 'Who then is free? The wise man who is lord to himself [sibi
qui imperiosus]' (my trans.); cf. also Rom. xiv.7: 'For none of us liveth to
himselfe, neither doeth any die to himselfe' (Geneva trans.).
20. *sets off*] appears, shows forth (notwithstanding the succeeding imagery
of guns, *OED* does not record 'set off' meaning to cause an explosion until
1881).
25–6. *shot-free . . . unhit*] *H&S* cite Seneca *Constant.* III.3: imitated more
fully by J. in *Und.* XXV, 48–50: 'He is shot-free / From injury / That is not
hurt, not he that is not hit'. Cf. also *NI* IV.iv.205–6.
30. *good rout*] the following lines suggest 'rout' is contemptuous ('a disreputable crowd': *OED*, 5), with 'good' used ironically.
32. *barking . . . College*] the dogs used in bear-baiting, especially at the
Bear Garden (also called Paris Garden), near the Rose Theatre on Bankside.
In *S-M* Tucca tells Horace 'when the Stagerites banisht thee into the Ile of
Dogs, thou turn'dst Ban-dog (villanous Guy) and euer since bitest, therefore
I aske if th'ast been at Parris-garden, because thou hast such a good mouth,
thou baitst well' (IV.i.132–5). Cunningham's edition of J. (1875) notes that

To swallow up the garbage of the time
With greedy gullets, whilst myself sit by
Pleased and yet tortured with their beastly feeding.          35
'Tis a sweet madness runs along with them
To think all that are aimed at still are struck,
Then, where the shaft still lights, make that the mark;
And so each fear- or fever-shaken fool
May challenge Teucer's hand in archery.          .          40
Good troth! If I knew any man so vile
To act the crimes these whippers reprehend,
Or what their servile apes gesticulate,
I should not then much muse their shreds were liked,
Since ill men have a lust t' hear others' sins,          45
And good men have a zeal to hear sin shamed.
But when it is all excrement they vent,
Base filth and offal, or thefts notable
As ocean piracies or highway stands,
And not a crime there taxed, but is their own,          50
Or what their own foul thoughts suggested to them,
And that in all their heat of taxing others
Not one of them but lives himself, if known,
*Improbior satiram scribente cinaedo,*
What should I say more? Then turn stone with wonder!          55
*Nasutus.* I never saw this play bred all this tumult.

---

53. if known] *In parentheses in F.*     54. *satiram*] *G; satyram F.*

---

the 'Agas' map of London (1560–70) shows the dogs chained in their kennels, waiting for the sport.
   33. *garbage*] the dogs were fed on offal provided by the markets of Eastcheap and Newgate.
   36. *sweet*] used ironically (cf. 'fine madness'); *OED*, 5d (first example 1656).
   40. *Teucer's*] the best archer amongst the Greeks in the *Iliad* XII, 350.
   41. *Good troth*] a corruption of 'God's Truth!'
   42. *whippers*] Cf. IV.iii.117–8n and V.iii.592n.
   43. *servile apes*] the actors.
   44. *shreds*] scraps.
   49. *stands*] hold-ups; cf. *EMO* IV.v.36, 'he has beene the only *Bid-stand* that ever kept *New-market, Salisbury-plaine, Hockley* i'the hole, *Gadshill*'.
   54.] Juvenal IV, 106: 'more shameless than a sodomite writing satire' (the Loeb trans. is bowdlerised, as is Mallory's note).
   55. *turn stone*] as at the sight of the Gorgon, Medusa.

What was there in it could so deeply offend,
And stir so many hornets?
*Author.*                                  Shall I tell you?
*Nasutus.* Yes, and ingenuously.
*Author.*                                  Then by the hope
Which I prefer unto all other objects,                              60
I can profess I never writ that piece
More innocent, or empty of offence.
Some salt it had, but neither tooth nor gall,
Nor was there in it any circumstance
Which, in the setting down, I could suspect                          65
Might be perverted by an enemy's tongue.
Only it had the fault to be called mine.
That was the crime.
*Polyposus.*                     No? Why, they say you taxed
The law and lawyers, captains, and the players
By their particular names.
*Author.*                          It is not so.                      70

---

59. *ingenuously*] frankly; cf. *EMI* IV.v.16–17: 'but, tell me, ingenuously, dost thou affect my sister BRIDGET, as thou pretend'st?'.

59–60. *by . . . objects*] a serious oath, referring to the hope of seeing Christ; cf. I Tim. i.i: 'our Lord Jesus Christ our hope' (Geneva trans.).

63. *salt*] Cf. IV.iii.89n.

*tooth . . . gall*] Cf. IV.iii.115–6n.

64–6.] Cf. V.iii.132–9.

69. *law and lawyers*] See I.ii., especially 115–34. Cf. *S-M* IV.iii.184–8: 'th'ast entred Actions of assault and battery, against a companie of honourable and worshipfull Fathers of the law: you wrangling rascall, law is one of the pillers ath land, and if thou beest bound too't (as I hope thou shalt bee) thou't prove a skip-Iacke, thou't be whipt.'

70. *particular names*] The punctuation of *F* makes it clear that this refers only to the players, who are 'named' in III.iv.280–307. They are also attacked in I.ii.36–56 and III.iv.125–43. Dekker replies in an intriguing passage in *S-M* that J. 'shouldst have been hang'd, but for one of these part-takers, these charitable Copper-lac'd Christians, that fetcht thee out of Purgatory, (Players I meane) Theaterians pouch-mouth, Stage-walkers' (IV.iii.202–5). This may refer to the *Isle of Dogs* affair (1597), when J. was imprisoned with the actors Gabriel Spencer and Robert Shaa, but is more likely to refer to J.'s trial for killing Spencer in 1598. The 'duel' was fought at about the time of the opening of *EMI*, very close to the Curtain, where it was being performed. It may well have been connected with the new play, written for the Chamberlain's Men and not for Henslowe, to whose company Spencer belonged, and could thus have been witnessed by actors. If J. was, as he claimed, not the aggressor, the evidence of witnesses could have saved him,

I used no name. My books have still been taught
To spare the persons and to speak the vices.
These are mere slanders, and enforced by such
As have no safer ways to men's disgraces
But their own lies and loss of honesty.                    75
Fellows of practised and most laxative tongues,
Whose empty and eager bellies i' the year
Compel their brains to many desp'rate shifts.
(I spare to name 'em, for their wretchedness
Fury itself would pardon.) These, or such,                 80
Whether of malice or of ignorance
Or itch t' have me their adversary (I know not),
Or all these mixed: but sure I am, three years
They did provoke me with their petulant styles
On every stage. And I at last, unwilling,                  85
But weary, I confess, of so much trouble,
Thought I would try if shame could win upon 'em.
And therefore chose Augustus Caesar's times,
When wit and arts were at their height in Rome,
To show that Virgil, Horace, and the rest                  90
Of those great master spirits did not want

since the judge had discretion over allowing him to plead benefit of clergy
(see pp. 30–1).

72.] Martial X.xxiii. 9–10, already quoted in III.v.133–4.

76. *laxative*] unable to contain themselves; the first example in *OED* of this figurative use.

77–8.] This appears to refer to writers rather than actors; as such it is more appropriate to Dekker than Marston, who is not so likely to be motivated by poverty.

77. *i'the year*] during the year, with the sense of 'as the year goes by'.

80–3. *These . . . mixed*] The cramped syntax is seeking to separate Marston's motivation from Dekker's; 'ignorance' allows for the portrait of Chrisoganus in *Hist.*, probably intended by Marston to be complimentary.

83–5. *three . . . stage*] See pp. 30–1.

84. *styles*] See III.v.65n; *H&S* note its repetition in *Volp*. Epistle, l. 70.

85. *every stage*] *Hist.*, *JD's Ent.* and *WYW* were all acted at Paul's, while *S-M* was acted at the Globe and Paul's. It is argued above (pp. 36–8) that *Tw.N* should be added to this list. No other surviving play before *Poetaster* has been convincingly shown to contain an attack on J. *Troil.* may also mock J. as Ajax, but probably postdates *Poetaster*.

91. *master spirits*] Cf. *Caes.* III.i.163: 'The choice and master spirits of this age', and *Volp*. Epistle, 125–6: 'all the great and master spirits of our world.'

Detractors then, or practisers against them.
And by this line (although no parallel)
I hoped at last they would sit down and blush.
But nothing could I find more contrary.                    95
And though the impudence of flies be great,
Yet this hath so provoked the angry wasps,
Or as you said, of the next nest, the hornets,
That they fly buzzing, mad, about my nostrils;
And like so many screaming grasshoppers                   100
Held by the wings, fill every ear with noise.
And what? Those former calumnies you mentioned:
First, of the law; indeed, I brought in Ovid,
Chid by his angry father for neglecting
The study of their laws for poetry;                        105
And I am warranted by his own words:
*Saepe pater dixit, studium quid inutile tentas?*
   *Maeonides nullas ipse reliquit opes.*
And in far harsher terms elsewhere, as these:
*Non me verbosas leges ediscere, non me*                   110
   *Ingrato voces prostituisse foro.*
But how this should relate unto our laws
Or their just ministers with least abuse,
I reverence both too much to understand!
   Then for the captain, I will only speak                 115
An Epigram I here have made. It is

---

107–8.] *Trist. lib.* 4 / *Eleg.* 10. *Marginal note in F.*       107. *Saepe*] *F2; Sape*
*F.*      108, 111.] *F2 insets the pentameter lines; F lines them up with the*
*hexameters.*      110–11.] *Amo. lib.* I. / *Eleg.* I.5. *Marginal note in F.*

---

93. *parallel*] See I.ii.29n.

100–1. *screaming . . . noise*] Dent, G425; *H&S* note this proverb in Lucian
*Pseudologistes* (Loeb ed., V.373); cf. also Erasmus *Adagia* 345D and *Volp.*
III.iv.55. 'Ay me, I have ta'en a grasshopper by the wing!'

107–8.] Cf. I.ii.79–95n.

110–11.] *Amores* I.xv.5–6: 'Nor learning garrulous legal lore, nor set my
voice for common case in the ungrateful forum.' Modern editors read 'nec'
for 'non'.

116. *Epigram*] reprinted as *Ep.* CVIII, 'To True Souldiers', with minor
changes in punctuation. It follows *Ep.* CVII, 'To Captayne Hungry'. In *S-M*
Horace distributes a number of parody epigrams attacking Tucca (III.i.237–
59).

> *Unto true soldiers.* That's the *lemma.* Mark it.
> *Strength of my country, whilst I bring to view*
> *Such as are miscalled captains, and wrong you*
> *And your high names, I do desire that thence*                   120
> *Be nor put on you, nor you take offence.*
> *I swear by your true friend, my Muse, I love*
> *Your great profession, which I once did prove,*
> *And did not shame it with my actions then,*
> *No more than I dare now do with my pen.*                        125
> *He that not trusts me, having vowed thus much,*
> *But's angry for the captain still, is such.*

Now, for the players, it is true I taxed 'em,
And yet but some, and those so sparingly
As all the rest might have sat still, unquestioned,              130
Had they but had the wit or conscience
To think well of themselves. But impotent, they
Thought each man's vice belonged to their whole tribe:
And much good do't 'em. What th' ave done 'gainst me
I am not moved with. If it gave 'em meat                         135
Or got 'em clothes, 'tis well. That was their end.
Only amongst them I am sorry for
Some better natures, by the rest so drawn
To run in that vile line.

---

136. clothes, 'tis] *G;* clothes. 'Tis *F.*

---

117. lemma] here, a title; cf. Martial XIV.ii.3–4: 'If you ask why headings [*lemmata*] are added, I will explain: it is that, if you prefer, you may read the headings only.'

121. put on you] applied to you.

123–4. which . . . then] J. told Drummond he had served 'in the Low Countries' and 'had in the face of both the Campes Killed ane Enimie & taken opima spolia from him' (*Conv.* 242–6).

127. is such] i.e. is like the captain.

130–2. all . . . themselves] Cf. Martial, preface to *Epigrams*: 'none who forms a right judgment of himself can complain of them'. Cf. *BF*, Ind. 82–4: 'made to delight all, and to offend none. Provided they have either, the wit, or the honesty to thinke well of themselves.' *H&S* note J. echoes the same passage in his letter to Cecil of 1605 (*H&S*, I.195, ll. 18–19).

135–6. If . . . end] Cf. III.iv.326–9, and 341–3.

137–8. Only . . . natures] Commentators predictably identify Shakespeare, but without evidence; *G*, however, was over-compensating when he noted 'there is no allusion whatever to Shakspeare, or to the company with which he was connected. The commentators are absolutely mad.'

*Polyposus.*                    And is this all?
  Will you not answer then the libels?
*Author.*                              No.                    140
*Polyposus.* Nor the untrussers?
*Author.*                        Neither.
*Polyposus.*                          Y'are undone then.
*Author.* With whom?
*Polyposus.*        The world.
*Author.*                      The bawd!
*Polyposus.*                              It will be taken
  To be stupidity or tameness in you.
*Author.* But they that have incensed me can in soul
  Acquit me of that guilt. They know I dare              145
  To spurn or baffle 'em, or squirt their eyes
  With ink or urine. Or I could do worse,
  Armed with Archilochus' fury write iambics
  Should make the desperate lashers hang themselves;
  Rhyme 'em to death, as they do Irish rats              150
  In drumming tunes. Or, living, I could stamp

---

141. *untrussers*] Cf. IV. vii.28 and V.iii.296n.
142. *world . . . bawd*] Cf. *T of T* II.v.38–9: 'Well, fortune, / Thou art a blind Bawd'.
145–51] See Elliott, *Satire*, pp. 3–48 for the historical background to this passage.
146. *baffle*] disgrace, treat with contumely (*OED, v.* 2).
146–7. *squirt . . . urine*] Cf. Cicero *Nat. D.* II.49. 127, 'effusio atramenti'; Hor. *Sat.* I.iv.100–1: 'Here is the very ink of the cuttlefish; here is venom unadulterate'; *Volp.* Epistle, 131–2: 'to spout ink in their faces, that shall eat, farther than their marrow, into their fames', and Dekker, *S-M* IV.ii.77–9: ''tis fashion to flirt Inke in everie mans face; and then to craule into his bosome, and damne thy selfe to wip't off agen'.
148–9.] Cf. Hor. *Ars P*, 79: 'Rage armed Archilochus with his own *iambus*', and *Epist.* I.xix.23–5: 'I was the first to show to Latium the iambics of Paros, following the rhythms and spirit of Archilochus, not the themes or the words that hounded Lycambes'. Lycambes supposedly hanged himself because of Archilochus' lampoons. See Elliott, *Satire*, pp. 3–13.
150–1. *Rhyme . . . tunes*] According to Reginald Scott, *Discoverie of Witchcraft* (1584), III, 15, Irish wizards claimed 'they can rime either man or beast to death'. The belief that the Irish anathematised rats is mentioned by Sidney, *Apology* p. 142; cf. also *AYL* III.ii.176–7: 'I was never so berhym'd since Pythagoras' time, that I was an Irish rat'. See also Elliott, *Satire*, pp. 18–48.
151–4. *Or . . . plasters*] imitating Martial VI.lxiv.24–6: 'But if the heat of my wrath sets a brand upon you, that will remain and cling to you and be

Their foreheads with those deep and public brands
That the whole company of Barber-Surgeons
Should not take off, with all their art and plasters.
And these my prints should last still to be read                       155
In their pale fronts, when what they write 'gainst me
Shall, like a figure drawn in water, fleet,
And the poor wretched papers be employed
To clothe tobacco, or some cheaper drug.
This I could do, and make them infamous.                               160
But to what end? When their own deeds have marked
    'em,
And that I know within his guilty breast
Each slanderer bears a whip that shall torment him
Worse than a million of these temporal plagues?
Which to pursue were but a feminine humour,                            165

---

read all over the town, and Cinnamus, for all his cunning skill, will not efface
the marks.' Cf. *Volp.* Epistle, 131–5. Cinnamus was a barber-surgeon (cf.
III.iv.106); the depth of branding was still important in J.'s time, since a
felon could plead benefit of clergy only once. Eight year's after J.'s branding
a hangman was whipped 'for burning a fellow in the hand with a cold iron' so
that the brand could be removed (quoted in Marchette Chute, *Ben Jonson of
Westminster* (New York, 1953), p. 78).

157. *figure . . . water*] Cf. Erasmus *Adagia* 170F: 'You write in water, that
is, you achieve nothing' (my trans.).

*fleet*] hurry away.

158–9. *poor . . . drug*] echoing Hor. *Epist.* II.i.269–70: 'the street where
they sell frankincense and pepper and everything else that is wrapped in
sheets of useless paper', and Martial III.ii.2–5 (to his book): 'Haste to get to
yourself a protector, lest, hurried off to a sooty kitchen, you wrap tunny-fry
in your sodden papyrus, or be a cornet [*cucullus*] for incense or pepper.' Cf.
*Ep.* III.12, *Und.* XLII, 52 and *Disc.* 589–92: 'wee shall heare those things
commended, and cry'd up for the best writings, which a man would scarce
vouchsafe, to wrap any wholsome drug in; hee would never light his *Tobacco*
with them'.

159. *tobacco . . . drug*] tobacco, a new and expensive drug, was sold like
other drugs by apothecaries in cone-shaped twills of paper. The use of such
drugs was beginning to increase in J.'s time.

161–6. *When . . . man*] *H&S* note the echo of Juvenal XIII, 189–95: 'For
vengeance is always the delight of a little, weak, and petty mind; of which
you may straightaway draw proof from this—that no one so rejoices in
vengeance as a woman. But why should you suppose that a man escapes
punishment whose mind is ever kept in terror by the consciousness of an evil
deed which lashes him with unheard blows, his own soul ever shaking over
him the unseen whip of torture?'

And far beneath the dignity of a man.
*Nasutus.* 'Tis true, for to revenge their injuries
    Were to confess you felt 'em. Let 'em go
    And use the treasure of the fool, their tongues,
    Who makes his gain by speaking worst of best.                 170
*Polyposus.* O, but they lay particular imputations——
*Author.* As what?
*Polyposus.*                    That all your writing is mere railing.
*Author.* Ha! If all the salt in the old comedy
    Should be so censured, or the sharper wit
    Of the bold satire termèd scolding rage,                      175
    What age could then compare with those for buffoons?
    What should be said of Aristophanes,
    Persius or Juvenal, whose names we now
    So glorify in schools, at least pretend it?
    Ha' they no other?
*Polyposus.*                    Yes, they say you are slow,        180
    And scarce bring forth a play a year.

---

166. a] *F; not in F2.*    175. satire] *G; satyre F.*

---

167–8. *to revenge . . . felt 'em*] Cf. Seneca *De Ira* III.v.7–8 (*H&S*).
169. *treasure . . . tongues*] From Plautus *Poenulus* 625, quoted in *Disc.*
392–3: 'The treasure of a foole is alwayes in his tongue (said the witty *comick Poet*)'; cf. also *Volp.* I.ii.71–3.
172. *railing*] Cf. Hor. *Sat.* I.iv.78–9 ' "You like to give pain" says one, "and you do so with spiteful intent" '; Dekker, *S-M*, IV.iii.159–60, 'your Muse leanes upon nothing but filthy rotten railes', and V.ii.236: 'your tongue you know is full of blisters with rayling'. J. returns to the accusation in *Volp.* Epistle, 44–7: 'And, howsoever I cannot escape from some the imputation of sharpness, but that they will say I have taken a pride, or lust, to be bitter, and not my youngest infant but hath come into the world with all his teeth'.
173. *old comedy*] *Vetus Comoedia*, Greek comedy of the fifth century BC, of which the only complete examples are the earlier plays of Aristophanes. J. had turned to it in the Ind. to *EMO* for the theoretical justification of his new satiric comedy (ll. 232–70). Cf. *H&S*, I, 376, and Campbell, pp. 4–6.
174–5. *sharper . . . satire*] referring to Roman satire, especially Juvenal and Persius.
181. *scarce . . . year*] Cf. *S-M* V.ii.201–3: 'you Nastie Tortois, you and your Itchy Poetry breake out like Christmas, but once a yeare'. In The *Return From Parnassus, II,* 296–7 (see p. 36) J. is 'so slow an Inventor, that he were better betake himselfe to his old trade of Bricklaying.' *H&S* quote Jasper Mayne, 'To the Memory of BEN. IOHNSON': 'Scorne then their censures, who gav't out, *thy Witt* / As long upon a *Comoedie* did sit / As *Elephants* bring forth' (ll. 49–50, *H&S*, XI, 452). Dekker, by contrast, had some part

*Author.*                                            'Tis true.
I would they could not say that I did that:
There's all the joy that I take i' their trade,
Unless such scribes as they might be proscribed
Th' absèd theatres. They would think it strange now        185
A man should take but coltsfoot for one day
And between whiles spit out a better poem
Than e'er the master of art or giver of wit,
Their belly, made. Yet this is possible,
If a free mind had but the patience                         190
To think so much together, and so vile.
But that these base and beggarly conceits
Should carry it by the multitude of voices
Against the most abstracted work, opposed
To the stuffed nostrils of the drunken rout!                195
O this would make a learn'd and liberal soul

---

in at least forty-four plays between 1598 and 1602. Kay (pp. 106–7) argues
convincingly that J. was not a particularly slow writer.

182–3] Cf. the letter to Cecil of 1605, where J. regrets that their fortune
has 'necessitated' him and Chapman 'to so despisd a Course' as writing a play
(*H&S*, I, p. 195, 16–18).

186. *coltsfoot*] a plant whose leaves were usually smoked or drunk as an
infusion, to treat asthma or as a general expectorant. Cf. Middleton and
?Fletcher, *Nice Valour*, III.ii.82–4: 'our moderne Kick / Which has been
mightily in use of late / Since our young men drank Coltsfoot' (*Dramatic
Works*, ed. Bowers, VII, 1989). Such herbs were smoked like tobacco in the
theatre: 'tobacco or a species of wound-wort . . . This they regard as a curious
medicine for defluctions . . . and the habit is so common with them that they
. . . light up on all occasions, at the play, in the taverns' (Platter, *Travels in
England*, quoted in Gurr, p. 39). In *BF* II.ii.91–2 it is mixed with tobacco
'to itch it out'.

188–9. *master . . . belly*] from Persius, *Sat.*, Prologue, 9–11: 'Who taught
the magpie to ape the language of man? It was that master of the arts, that
dispenser of genius, the Belly'; cf. *PR* 13–15 (so *H&S*).

192. *conceits*] inventions, with a secondary sense of trifles, as in *MND*
I.i.33: 'With bracelets of thy hair, rings, gawds, conceits'.

193.] i.e. should be preferred by popular acclaim.

195. *stuffed nostrils*] from idiomatic Latin, meaning to be stupid; Hor.
speaks of the satirist Lucilius having 'keen-scented nostrils' (*Sat.* I.iv.8),
while Nasutus' name means the same: Lewis and Short give *nares* as 'an
organ expressive of sagacity'. Cf. *Sej.* III. 248.

196. *liberal*] generous, but also large, as in *D is A* I.vi.179: 'his liberall
eares'.

To rive his stainèd quill up to the back,
And damn his long-watched labours to the fire—
Things that were born when none but the still night
And his dumb candle saw his pinching throes— 200
Were not his own free merit a more crown
Unto his travails than their reeling claps.
This 'tis that strikes me silent, seals my lips,
And apts me rather to sleep out my time
Than I would waste it in contemnèd strifes 205
With these vile ibids, these unclean birds,
That make their mouths their clysters, and still purge
From their hot entrails. But I leave the monsters
To their own fate. And since the Comic Muse
Hath proved so ominous to me, I will try 210

198. fire—] *This ed.;* fire; *F.* 200. throes—] *This ed.;* throes: *F.*

---

197–200.] based on Juvenal VII, 27–30: 'Break your pen, poor wretch; destroy the battles that have robbed you of your sleep—you that are inditing lofty strains in a tiny garret, that you may come forth worthy of a scraggy bust wreathed with ivy!' Cf. *Ode,* 'Yff Men, and tymes were nowe' (*UV,* XLVIII), 19–20: 'Breake then thie quills, blott out / Thie long watch'[d] verse / And rather to the ffyre, then to the Rowte / Their labour'd tunes reherse'. This poem, like *Und.* XXIII (see below ll. 225–6n), was probably written at about the same time as the 'Apol. Dial.'.
197. *rive . . . back*] split it from top to bottom; cf. *Troil.* I.iii.316, 'Blunt wedges rive hard knots'.
199–200.] Cf. *CR* III.ii.2–3, and 9–11, where Crites 'smells all lampoyle, with studying by candle-light', an image taken up by Marston, *WYW,* Wood, II, 258: 'I wasted lampoile, baited my flesh, / Shrunk up my veines, and still my spaniel slept.'
201. *more crown*] used thus with a noun in *SW* I.ii.20, 'How! that's a more portent' and *Cat.* IV.688: 'for the more authoritie' (so *H&S*).
202. *reeling*] drunken, cf. *Tp.* V.i.279: 'And Trinculo is reeling ripe'.
204. *apts*] See I.ii.99n.
206–8. *ibids . . . entrails*] ibises, a heron-like stork; Nicholson cites Pliny, *Natural History,* trans. Holland (1601), VIII.xxvii: 'The . . . device . . . of clystres, we learned first of a foule in . . . Ægypt, called Ibis (or the black Storke). This bird having a crooked and hooked bill, useth it in steed of a syringe or pipe, to squirt water into that part, whereby it is most kind and holsome to void the doung and excrements of meat, and so purgeth and cleanseth her bodie.' This fourth echo of Holland's translation late in the play (cf. IV.vi.11–12 and V.iii.321, 386n) suggests that Jonson had just read it; it was entered May 1600, so could have been published at any time in 1601. A clyster was either an enema or the pipe used to administer it. Here J. reverses Pliny's process, the 'doung and excrements' being sucked out by his opponents, and then spewed far and wide.

If Tragedy have a more kind aspect.
Her favours in my next I will pursue,
Where, if I prove the pleasure but of one,
So he judicious be, he shall be alone
A theatre unto me. Once I'll say                                    215
To strike the ear of time, in those fresh strains
    As shall, beside the cunning of their ground,
Give cause to some of wonder, some despite,
    And unto more, despair to imitate their sound.
I that spend half my nights and all my days          220
    Here in a cell, to get a dark, pale face,
To come forth worth the ivy or the bays,
    And in this age can hope no other grace—
Leave me. There's something come into my thought

---

214. be alone] *G;* b'alone *F.*

212. *next*] *Sejanus* (1603). J. received a £10 advance in June 1602 for
'A Boocke called Richard crockbacke & for new adicyons for Jeronymo'
(Henslowe, *Diary,* p. 203), but his *Richard III,* if it was ever written, is lost;
he must have begun work on *Sejanus* soon after *Poetaster.*
213–15. *if . . . me*] Foremost in J.'s mind is probably Hor. *Sat.* I.x.76,
'Tis enough if the knights applaud me', and Marston's reversal of this:
'Thinke you if that his sceanes tooke stampe in mint / Of three or foure
deem'd most juditious, / It must inforce the world to currant them?' (*WYW,*
Wood, II, 232). *H&S* cite Seneca *Ep.* I.vii.11, and *Ham.* III.ii.26–8: 'the
censure of which one must in your allowance o'erweigh a whole theatre of
others.' The passage in *Ham.* was probably inserted after the writing of
*Poetaster:* see Arden ed., pp. 1–2.
215–19. *Once . . . sound*] Cf. *Ode* (*UV* XLVIII) 32–6: 'And once more
stryke the eare of tyme wth those ffresh straynes: / As shall besides delyght /
And Cunninge of their grownde / Give cause to some of wonnder, some
despite, / But unto more despayre to Imitate their sounde.'
215. *say*] try; cf. II.i.19n.
217. *ground*] subject-matter, plot; cf. *Conv.* 148: 'for a heroik poeme he
saide ther was no such Ground as King Arthurs fiction'.
218. *despite*] envy.
219, 226.] alexandrines, to add emphasis and dignity to the subject of
tragedy. Cf. *EMI* II.i.87, and *Alc.* III.iv.4.
220–3] Cf. Juvenal VII, 27–30, quoted above, ll. 197–202n, and *Ode*
(*UV* XLVIII), 24–7: 'Thou that doest spend thie dayes / to gett the[e] a
leane fface, / And come fforth worthie Ivye, or the Bayes, / And in this Age,
canst hope no [other] grace.' The 'dark pale face' corresponds to the 'saffron-
cheeke sunburnt Gipsie' and 'leane . . . hollow-cheekt scrag' of *S-M* I.ii.367–
8 and V.ii.262.

That must and shall be sung, high and aloof,                225
Safe from the wolf's black jaw and the dull ass's hoof.
*Nasutus.* I reverence these raptures, and obey 'em.

[*Exeunt* NASUTUS *and* POLYPOSUS.]


This
Comical Satire was first
acted in the year
1601

*By the then Children of Queen*                             5
ELIZABETH'S
Chapel.

The principal Comedians were,
NATHANIEL FIELD.  JOHN UNDERWOOD.

---

227.1. S.D.] *This ed.;* The scene closes. G.   1–12. This . . . REVELS.]
*F; not in Q, or F2 which places l. 12 (With . . .* REVELS) *on title-page, and ll.*
*8–11 (list of Comedians) following* THE SCENE. ROME. *before half-title*
*and   Induction.*   9–11.   NATHANIEL . . . MARTON.] NAT.   FIELD.   IOH.
VNDERWOOD. / SAL. PAVY. WILL. OSTLER. / THO. DAY. THO. MARTON. *F.*

---

225–6. *high . . . hoof*] Cf. *Ode. To himself, Und.,* XXIII, 35–6, probably
written at the same period.
    9. *NATHANIEL FIELD*] 1587–1633, Nathaniel, Nathan or Ned, son
of Rev. John Field, who wrote a violent attack on the theatre (*A Godly
Exhortation &c.,* 1583); Nathaniel Field was probably a pupil of St Paul's
School when he was pressed forcibly into service with the Children of the
Chapel. He had acted in *CR*; his first recorded part (though possibly not in
the original 1604 production) is as Bussy in *Bussy d'Ambois.* He leads the cast
list in *SW* (1609), still at the Blackfriars aged twenty-two, moved with the
rest of the company to merge with the Lady Elizabeth's Men in 1613, and
was in *BF* (V.iii.86–8: 'which is your *Burbage* now? . . . Your best *Actor.*
Your *Field*?') in 1614. He transferred to the King's Men about 1615, and his
name appears in the Shakespeare first Folio as one of the 'Principall Actors'.
J. told Drummond that he was 'his Schollar & he had read to him the Satyres
of Horace & some Epigrames of Martiall' (*Conv.* 164–5). Field wrote nine
plays, beginning with *A Woman is a Weathercock* (1609–10).
    *JOHN UNDERWOOD*] at the Blackfriars until about 1608, when he
transferred to the King's Men; he acted in *Alc.* (1610), *Cat.* (1611), and
continued to appear in their actor lists until his death in 1624.

SALAMON PAVY.     WILLIAM OSTLER.          10
THOMAS DAY.       THOMAS MARTON.

*With the allowance of the Master of* REVELS.

---

10. *SALAMON PAVY*] *c.* 1590–1602; variously Salamon, Solomon, Salathiel and Salmon. According to J.'s epitaph in *Ep.* CXX, 'Yeeres he numbred scarse thirteene'; with the Paul's boys in 1600, then moved to Blackfriars to act in *CR*, also 1600. See Gair, p. 64.

*WILLIAM OSTLER*] died 1614, having transferred to the King's Men about the same time as Underwood; he is first recorded with them in *Alc.* (1610), and continues to appear in actor lists until his death. John Davies of Hereford, *Scourge of Folly* (*c.* 1611) calls him 'Sole King of Actors.'

11. *THOMAS DAY*] also acted in *CR*, otherwise unknown.

*THOMAS MARTON*] known only in this play.

12. Master . . . *REVELS*] Edmund Tilney when *Poetaster* was performed; Sir George Buc when *F* was published in 1616. Originally a Court official, he became responsible for licensing plays for performance, and after 1607, for publishing. Dekker implies that J. had hopes of the post himself: Horace's Welsh patron, Sir Vaughan, says 'I have some cossens Garman at Court, shall beget you the reversion of the Master of the Kings Revels, or else be his Lord of Mis-rule nowe at Christmas' (*S-M* IV.i.188–91). In fact J. did get the reversion of the post in 1621 (Riggs, p. 271).

# APPENDIX I
## Textual History of the Play

*The Quarto*

*Poetaster Or The Arraignment* was entered in the Stationers' Register on 21 December 1601 by Matthew Lownes as 'A booke called. Poetaster or his arrainement'.[1] Lownes had entered Marston's *Antonio and Mellida* and *Antonio's Revenge* two months earlier, jointly with Thomas Fisher, but this, Jonson's fourth published play, was the first with which he was associated. He was to retain his rights when Stansby printed the *Workes* of 1616, bequeathing them to his son in 1627.[2] *Poetaster*, like the two *Antonio* plays, was published in 1602, and all three books were to be sold in Lownes's shop in St Dunstan's Churchyard in Fleet Street.[3] The title-page of 1602 is reproduced as Plate 2, p. 61.

Greg surmised rightly that the printer of *Poetaster*, as of the Antonio plays, was Richard Bradock: he uses the title-page ornament and the *H* initial and first ornament on N1v in books claimed by him on the title-page at this period.[4] *Poetaster* was the first book of Jonson's that Bradock had printed.[5] Copy was cast off for setting by formes, which had also been the procedure when Bradock printed *A Midsummer Night's Dream* for Fisher in 1600.[6] As there, two compositors were involved: one, called here 'A', favours long, sometimes unabbreviated, speech prefixes; the other ('B') normally abbreviates. This is a far from infallible identifier, but an unmistakable pattern emerges once the tendency is noticed. This shows both compositors working together on the same forme throughout, normally setting two pages each: in C outer, for example, compositor A set the two pages on the right-hand side of the forme as printed (1r and 2v) and B the two on the left (4v and 3r). This right/left division occurs in fourteen of the twenty formes where there are sufficient speech prefixes to assign the setting. In B outer and M outer the division was top/bottom, with compositor B setting the top two pages (i.e. 2v and 3r).[7] Only their different treatment of speech prefixes distinguishes the compositors: both use sticks of the same length (8.75–8.8 cm), and neither page depth and layout nor distribution of errors shows any obvious pattern. Punctuation, spelling and the use of italic and capitals are all consistent throughout,

277

probably reflecting the copy rather than the habits of the compositors.

The copy was almost certainly prepared by Jonson himself: his characteristic spellings occur frequently,[8] and the text shows none of the usual signs of being derived from either foul papers or prompt book, or from copy 'intermediate' between the two. It is light on stage directions: only exits are given, and those not always; characters are given massed entrances at the beginning of each scene, a practice Parker relates to early humanist editions of Terence and Plautus[9] but which probably also owed something to neo classical examples like Kyd's *Cornelia*, Gager's *Meleager* or even *Gorboduc*. A liberal use of italic adds to the literary aspect of the text, as do the marginal reference notes: some notes appear in the Induction to *Cynthia's Revels* to gloss names; such notes are also found in *Poetaster*, but the notes to sources accompanying translations from Ovid, Horace and Virgil are a new feature, the first of their kind in Jonson, and probably in any English play taken from the popular stage, anticipating the more copious apparatus of the masques and entertainments of the immediately following years, and of *Sejanus* (printed 1605). They are evidence of the literary status Jonson sought for his text, and of the distance the copy for *Q* has moved away from the stage, and from the usual play quarto, a distance emphasised by the motto on the title-page and the epigram 'Ad Lectorem' on A1v, both taken from Martial, VII.xii.

*Q* is relatively rare: eight copies have been collated for this edition, and only one genuine variant has emerged, 'rarher' being corrected to 'rather' on C1v (II.i.35).[10] Other variants listed in de Vocht's over-pedantic collation are merely the results of wear during printing. The lack of variants suggests that correction was made by taking proofs at an early stage.[11] There are signs of changes to the text at a late stage of composition: at the foot of F1r the catchword 'I.*Pyr.*' is incorrect. 'I.*Pyr.*' now begins the second line of F1v; these two sides also contain thirty-four lines instead of the more usual thirty-five. Evidently the first line of F1v has been moved there after F1r, and the whole of F outer, has been set. The explanation is found in the 1616 Folio, where there are three additional passages of about four lines in total referring to the players (III.iv.130–1, 157–9, 173–4) which would, had they been in *Q*, have been on F1r and F1v. The presumption must be that these lines were in the copy, were set and then removed. This is also suggested by the generous spacing given to Tucca's speech on F1v (III.iv.163–74), followed by the now unnecessary compression of the line following it, which includes a turn-over, the latter a saving of space only needed had the page originally contained its full thirty-five lines.[12]

If these lines were in Jonson's fair copy, were others now only found in F? Jonson says 'An Apology *from the Author*' should have stood in place of the short address 'To the Reader' with which Q now closes. It is probable that, as Chambers and Simpson[13] suggest (*ES*, III, 366, *H&S*, IV, 193), this was a version of the 'Apologetical Dialogue' that appears in F as 'only once spoken upon the stage'. While this could have been dropped before Jonson made his fair copy, the final page of Q has the air of a hastily composed substitute: there is no catchword on N1r, and N1v is set askew, the tailpiece at an angle to the text. This is not a compelling argument in the case of a printer who can set the title-page ornament upside down, but since the 227 lines of the present 'Apologetical Dialogue' would, with a prefatory address to the reader, have filled the seven spare pages available from gathering N very neatly, and since Jonson says his Apology 'with his reasons for the publishing of this book' was 'meant' to begin 'Here' on N1v, it seems probable that Bradock originally cast off copy to run into thirteen full quires, intending to fill N with the 'Apologetical Dialogue' more or less as we now have it.

Of the other passages found first in F, the dedication, with its references to a fairly distant past ('once' and 'then') must have been written for it. Act III scene v, a translation of Horace, *Satires* I.ii, is also unlikely to have been in the original copy.[14] Jonson (or the bookseller) was keen to publish 'more than hath been Publickely Spoken or Acted' in the quartos,[15] and had it been available in 1602 it would probably have gone in, despite its undramatic qualities, and its politically contentious defence of satire. Given its more formal style, however, in particular the unusual use of couplets, it seems likely that this was a translation made some time after 1601–2, with or without a view to inclusion in a later edition.[16] Some innocuous lines spoken by Crispinus (II.i.103–5) were probably omitted by compositor A: they would have come near the foot of a crowded page, C2r, probably the last page of C inner to be set. Their loss would pass unnoticed by a reader, and Jonson can hardly have written them specially for F, where they were probably reinstated by a compositor working from a copy of Q marked up by Jonson from his original MS. Six lines on the players (III.iv.307–14) may also have been dropped from that MS, rather than added for F: F3v,

*Tuc.* Doeſt thou ſweare? To morrowe then ; ſay, and holde
ſlaue. There are ſome of you Players honeſt Gent'man-like
Scoundrels : A man may skelder yee, now and than, of halfe a
dozen ſhillinges, or ſo. Doeſt thou not know that *Caprichio*
there?

*Hiſt.* No, I aſſure you, Captaine.

*Tuc.* Goe, and be acquainted with him, then; hee is a Gent'-
man, parcell-*Poet*, you ſlaue: his Father was a man of worſhip,
I tell thee : goe, he. pens high, loftie, in a newe ſtalking ſtraine;
bigger then halfe the Rimers i'the towne againe: he was borne
to fill thy mouth , *Minotaurus*; he was: he will teach thee to
teare and rand , Raſcall; to him : cheriſh his *Muſe*; goe : thou
haſt fortie , fortie ; ſhillings, I meane , Stinkard; giue him in
earneſt ; doe : hee ſhall write for thee, ſlaue . If hee penne
for thee once., thou ſhalt not neede to trauell , with thy
pumpes full of grauell, any more , after a blinde Ladt. and a
Hamper. (taine.

*Hiſtrio.* Troth, I thinke I ha' not ſo much about mee, Cap-
*Tuc.* It's no matter: giue him what thou haſt : *Paunch* , I'le
giue my word for the reſt : though it lack a ſhilling or two , it
ſkilles not: Go, thou art an honeſt *Twentie i'the hundred*; I'le ha'
the Statute repeal'd for thee, *Minos*: I muſt tel thee, *Minos*, thou

---

Tvcc. Doeſt thou 'ſweare ? to morrow then ; ſay , and hold ſlaue.
There are ſome of you plaiers honeſt gent'man-like ſcoundrels and ſuſpe-
ſted to ha' ſome wit , as well as your *poets*; both at drinking , and breaking of ieſts : and are companions for gallants. A man may skelder yee,
now and then, of halfe a dozen ſhillings, or ſo. Doeſt thou not know that
PANTALABVS there ?

HIST. No, I aſſure you, Captaine.

Tvcc. Goe, and bee acquainted with him, then ; hee is a gent'man,
parcell-*poet*, you ſlaue : his father was a man of worſhip, I tell thee. Goe,
he pens high, loftie, in a new ſtalking thaine; bigger then halfe the rimers
i' the towne, againe : he was borne to fill thy mouth, MINOTAVRVS, he
was : hee will teach thee to teare, and rand, Raſcall, to him, cheriſh his
*muſe*, goe : thou haſt fortie, fortie, ſhillings, I meane, ſtinkard, giue him in
earneſt, doe, he ſhall write for thee, ſlaue. If hee pen for thee once, thou
ſhalt not need to trauell, with thy pumps full of grauell, any more, after a
blinde iade and a hamper: and ſtalke vpon boords, and barrell heads, to an
old crackt trumpet———

HIST. Troth, I thinke I ha' not ſo much about me, Captaine.

Tvcc. It's no matter : giue him what thou haſt : *Stiffe toe*, I'le giue
my word for the reſt : though it lacke a ſhilling, or two, it skils not : Goe,
thou art an honeſt ſhifter, I'le ha' the *ſtatute* repeal'd for thee. MINOS,
I muſt

---

3   Above: from *Q*, sig. FIV. Below: from *F*, sig. 2C2V. Both two-
thirds actual size

where they would occur, shows signs, unusually, of two compositors in its mixture of full and abbreviated speech headings, while the catchword '*Pyrg.*' of F2r, set next to it on the inner forme of F, does not correspond to the 'I. *Pyr*' at the top of F2v. There are only thirty-four lines on F2r, and very generous spacing of prose speeches in the centre of the page. There are also signs of two compositors in F2r, suggesting that they were faced with the sudden loss from copy already set of six lines felt to constitute too virulent an attack on the players, 'defending' them against charges of being thieves, usurers, pimps, and 'the common retreats for punks decayed i'their practice'.

A long passage attacking lawyers (I.ii.93–5, 97–134), which would have appeared on B2r and v, coincides with a pause in the presswork which analysis of running titles reveals. Skeletons for both formes of B, almost certainly the first sheet printed, were dismantled, and two new skeletons made up, using some of the running titles from B; one was used to print formes C–M (outer), another C–K (inner), with the inner formes of L and M being adjusted only slightly. Clearly B was perfected before the running titles of C were set, with the implication that there was a greater delay between B and C than between subsequent sheets. This may have nothing to do with the attack on lawyers: B was the first sheet printed, and it would not be unreasonable to check it before going on; or another, more urgent job may have intervened. But it is possible that the passage of thirty-seven lines found in *F* was originally set then cut during or after printing of B outer and setting of B inner. This does not explain why the running titles themselves should have been changed, and it is open to the objection made to a similar reconstruction of the printing of *Eastward Ho!* that such late changes to a text are uneconomical, and a careful printer would edit a MS before casting it off.[17] Against this, the idea that printers read copy carefully smacks of academic unworldliness, and changes *were* made elsewhere after casting off. The mixing-up of running titles could easily occur in confusion over hurried cancellation. Regardless of the printing history, it is more likely that the passage was in Jonson's original copy, and was reinstated in *F*, than that he composed a new passage for *F* stylistically very close to the rest of the scene, and intensifying satire that had already brought him close to serious trouble.[18] Presswork continued normally after the pause, with sheets C to M printed in straightforward sequence. One running title from M outer was then used to print N1r (N1v has no running title), and A outer was set up next using the rest of that skeleton, except that one running title from the inner of M was substituted on A2v, and another dropped for the title-page itself. Forme A inner was printed last, using two running titles from M inner and one from M outer.

## The Folio

The second edition of *Poetaster*, now subtitled 'His Arraignment', is the fourth play in the *Workes* of 1616, on sigs Z4r–2G3v.[19] The printer, William Stansby, registered copy that he owned on 20 January 1615, and printing probably began late that year at the earliest.[20] Thirty-three copies have been examined, and a list and a tabulated collation by formes is given as Appendix 2. The copy was a marked-up version of *Q* together with additional MS copy from Jonson. A single error in *F* confirms that *Q* was used: in III.iv.155 a mark left by a space in *Q* between *thou* and *sweare* is set as an apostrophe ('Doest thou 'sweare') (see Plate 3). This could be derived only from the printed text, whereas the numerous other errors which *F* takes over from *Q* could in theory (though hardly in practice) all be derived from a common MS source. With the evidence of the apostrophe, other errors in *F* fall into place as derived directly from *Q*: for example, two pieces of punctuation unnecessary even by Jonson's standards are incorporated in IV.iv.23–4, while V.iii.334–6, which is undoubtedly prose, is printed in *Q* and, following it, in *F* as verse. The opposite happens in III.i.84–5, III.iv.261–2, and IV.viii.1–2, while in I.iii.29–30 *F* first misreads *Q* because of crowding, and then corrects during printing. *F* also takes over *Q*'s curious setting of the speech prefix *'Demet. Histrio.'* for two interjections (III.iv.230, 247) which should be attributed to Histrio alone; this error must be derived in some way from Jonson's original copy for *Q*.[21] Stop-press corrections also point firmly to *Q* as the copy: they often alter minor points of punctuation that have been correctly set from *Q*, but with which (at what must have been an irritatingly late stage) Jonson was no longer satisfied. Shorter additional passages in *F* and other minor changes could easily have been written into a copy of *Q*, but this cannot hold for the longer additions, and compositors must have worked from printed copy interleaved with, or alongside, MS. The spellings of the long additions in I.ii.93–134, III.v and the 'Apologetical Dialogue' all point to holograph copy, notably in preferring final *y* over final *ie*. The compositors were apparently less willing to impose their own spellings on these passages set from MS than on those taken from *Q*.

A puzzling change in F is the deletion of all references to knighthood. The problem is peculiar to *Poetaster*: knights are mocked in *The Alchemist, Volpone, Epicoene* and *Every Man Out*. Jonson may have considered them anachronistic. This would explain the dropping of uncontentious uses, as when Caesar calls Gallus and Tibullus 'knights' (V.i.7), which in F becomes 'gentlemen', the word used by the contemporary historian of Rome, Thomas Godwyn, in generalising about the equestrian order. Elsewhere, however, Godwyn is happy to refer to 'Knights and Gentlemen of Rome', while *Rider's Dictionarie* and Minsheu's *Ductor* give *eques* and *miles* as the Latin equivalents (s.v. 'knight').[22] 'Knight' was and is a better translation of *eques* than 'gentleman'. Straightforward censorship also presents problems: the knighthood references were not left out of Q, whereas other offensive passages were, to be reinstated in F. If there had been objections to Jonson's treatment of knights in 1601 one would have expected to see evidence of it in Q, rather than F. Such objections might, moreover, be expected to have been confronted in the 'Apologeticall Dialogue'. Although after *Eastward Ho!* (1605) Jonson might have developed greater caution over the treatment of knights, James I's enthusiastic distribution of knighthoods being a delicate issue, Puntarvolo, Sir Politick Would-Be, Sir John Daw, Sir Amorous La Foole and Sir Epicure Mammon all survive in F. What may have happened is self-censorship as a result of *Satiromastix*, which was printed later than *Poetaster* (see p. 28 n. 53), and which, on the evidence of the 'Apologetical Dialogue', hurt Jonson deeply. Dekker dwells on knights and knighthood throughout that play, and in particular ridicules Horace/Jonson's relations with his Welsh patron, Sir Vaughan ap Rees, whose generosity he betrays. In June 1601 Jonson's Welsh patron, Sir John Salusbury, was knighted. Salusbury was a member of the Middle Temple; he had been the recipient of *Love's Martyr* during 1601, with poems by Jonson and Marston, as well as Shakespeare, Chapman and Chester. Jonson's contributions (reprinted in *The Forrest* X and XI) suggest that for him 'both Turtle and Phoenix [i.e. Salusbury and his wife] were living persons . . . with whom he stood on terms of acquaintance, perhaps even friendship'.[23] The Salusbury family papers contain a holograph copy of Jonson's 'Ode to James Earl of Desmond' (like Jonson, and some of Salusbury's family, a Catholic), written in 1600–1, bound between poems by Salusbury himself.[24] Dekker parodies this very poem in *Satiromastix* I.ii.1–20. By the end of 1601, when *Poetaster* was on the stage, Salusbury's fortunes had taken a sharp downward turn from which they never recovered.[25] Accusations of ingratitude towards a patron such as that made in *Satiromastix* IV.i.61–3 ('Art not famous enough yet ... for killing a Player, but thou must eate men alive? thy friends? Sirra wildeman, thy Patrons? thou Anthropophagite, thy Maecenasses?') would have stung, becoming more embarrassing if the patron was in difficulties as Salusbury was in 1602–3. They would, moreover, have been difficult to counter in the Apologetical Dialogue. Marston's own connections with Salusbury may have been an extra, complicating factor, as may have been the knighting in 1603 of two more patrons, Sir Robert Cotton and Sir Robert Townshend, the latter of whom Jonson was 'living upon' by February 1603, and possibly earlier.[26] This argument is supported by three minor changes in *F* that are best explained as a reaction to Dekker: in *Satiromastix* I.ii.339 Horace is 'King Gorboduck'; in *Poetaster* V.iii.433 *Q*'s 'Gorboduckes' is changed to 'harpies'; in I.ii.249 *Q*'s 'dudgeon Censures stab' becomes 'desp'rate censures stab', reacting to Dekker's 'stab'd with his dudgion wit' (I.ii.135); and in II.i.102 *Q*'s 'Flat-cappe' is altered to 'trades-man', perhaps in response to Dekker's 'thou cryest ptrooh at worshipfull Cittizens, and cals't them Flat-caps' (*S-M* IV.iii.194–5). I have not returned here to *Q*'s reading for these minor revisions, but I have reinstated 'knight', 'knighthood' and cognate words on the grounds that their deletion seems to be a form of self-censorship, a departure from Jonson's preferred version, and certainly a departure from the play that was performed at the Blackfriars. Other substantive changes in *F* are listed in the apparatus, and where necessary discussed in the commentary; none makes it possible to guess at a date for the revision.

Typographical changes in *F* include more dashes, exclamation marks and hyphens, the use of small capitals for proper nouns, where *Q* had used italic, and a decrease in the use of initial capitals used in *Q* for emphasis. Simpson talks of Jonson's 'minute care' (*H&S*, IV, 190), but that routine changes were left to the compositors is confirmed by the change from *Q*'s *Helicon* and *Castalian* to *helicon* and *castalian* (I.i.10 and 36); Jonson could not have marked these as corrections to lower case unless he was very drunk. That he did mark up substantive changes to *Q* himself is confirmed by a series of alterations in I.ii: here, in l. 134, setting from MS copy (the whole long passage is not in *Q*) the compositor has set 'Boy'; he has done the same thing in l. 149 where, this time almost certainly writing directly on to a copy of $Q$, Jonson has substituted 'old boy' for $Q$'s 'knight errant'. In both cases Jonson has corrected to lower case $b$. All examples of Jonson's hand that I have seen show an idiosyncratic $b$, with a marked downward loop at the top, which is always likely to be mistaken for $B$.

Because Stansby had plenty of type (Gerritsen estimates that thirty-seven folio pages were standing towards the end of $F$) he did not have to set by formes, but he did.[27] A cluster of spelling preferences, none reliable on their own, suggests that one compositor set most of quire Z and half of 2A (2A1r–6v, 1v–6r, 2r–5v). The spelling *Ile* is not found after 2B3v, nor *verie/euerie* after 2A6r. After this, too, the balance between *y* and *ie* endings becomes more even, though if we discount final *ly* in words like *heavenly* (always spelt thus) it is almost always in favour of *ie* endings until the last few pages. Here quire G shows a strong preference for final *y*: this may indicate a third compositor, or reflect greater fidelity to the MS copy, G containing the previously unpublished 'Apologeticall Dialogue'. Up to this point, $Q$'s *y* endings have frequently been changed to *ie*. Analysis of headlines shows that no fewer than sixteen different skeleton formes were used to print the 48 formes used for *Poetaster*. Of these, five were used in the first quire (Z), which includes the final pages of *Cynthia's Revels*, each forme needing a different set of headlines. The outer sheet of this quire includes the most striking printing error in $F$, the use of the running title for *Cynthia's Revels* at the head of the second page of text of *Poetaster* (p. 276, Z6v). The final quire (2G) also needed new running-titles for the 'Apologeticall Dialogue' (headed 'To the Reader'), the list of comedians and the opening pages of *Sejanus*. Here again a new skeleton—or at least, a new headline—was made up for each forme. For the bulk of the play, quires 2A–2F, six skeleton formes were used; either four or five different skeletons were used for the six formes needed for each quire. This contrasts starkly with the use of one skeleton for the bulk of the Shakespeare first folio.[28] Stop-press correction was less systematic than Herford and Simpson supposed, and the statement that 'most of the corrections are the author's, made at the printing-office where he would present himself for this purpose every morning' (*H&S*, IX, 72) is partly fiction. Only ten of the forty-eight formes show variants, while some of the non-variant formes contain errors that Simpson's careful author should have noticed, whether or not he was on Stansby's doorstep every morning.

Stop-press correction as it appears in variants is set out in Appendix 2: the heaviest correction is found in six formes, involving changes of punctuation, italicisation and capitalisation that a printer's reader would not make at this late stage. They are, moreover, changes in the main from $Q$'s copy, which has been correctly set. Here, therefore, Simpson is right: they *are* Jonson's corrections, but the evidence suggests he did not correct the sheets at all systematically.

*Later editions*

The third edition of *Poetaster* appears in the second folio of the *Workes* (1640, Stationers' Register, 4 March 1639), in which it is printed by Robert Young for Richard Bishop.[29] The few variant readings are unlikely to be Jonson's: 'improvements' such as 'enforce' for 'enforme' (Ind. 54), and 'savours' for 'labours' (V.i.129) seem those of an intelligent printer.[30] The third folio of 1692 was largely a reprint of the second (and therefore, for *Poetaster*, of the first). The first real if inefficient attempt at editing Jonson was undertaken by Peter Whalley (1756). Whalley's inconsistency and self-congratulation aroused the derision of the most important single figure in Jonson studies, the irascible William Gifford, whose edition of *The Works* (9 vols, 1816) was a wholehearted attempt to re-establish Jonson as a major dramatist rather than as the malignant enemy of Shakespeare, a role which Gifford, with some reason, believed had been thrust on him by eighteenth-century Shakespeare scholars. In the case of *Poetaster*, Gifford's importance lies in his identification of Marston and Dekker with Crispinus and Demetrius (see III.iv.161n). The first separate editions of *Poetaster* since 1602 were those of H.S. Mallory (*Yale Studies in English*, XXVII (1905)), whose accurate text is offset by an introduction and notes which evince his dislike of the play, and of J.H. Penniman (usefully combined with *Satiromastix*, Boston and London, 1913). Both were essentially reprints of *F*; George Parfitt (Nottingham, 1979) also based his text on *F*, though less closely. In 1932, *Poetaster* appeared in volume IV of the Oxford *Ben Jonson* edited by C.H. Herford and Percy Simpson. The dignity of this magisterial edition has received some dents over recent years, but all editors, indeed all readers, of Jonson still owe a huge debt to it. In 1934 Henry de Vocht edited an accurate type-facsimile edition of *Q* (*Materials for the Study of the Old English Drama*, IX), with a wildly unintelligent and partisan commentary in favour of *Q* which did nothing to rehabilitate the latter in the face of the Oxford editors' over-strong preference for *F*.

*This edition*

The clear supremacy of *F* over the quartos which was assumed by Herford and Simpson has rightly been called into question, as, more recently, has the whole concept of a final, authoritative copy-text. It is thus no longer possible for an editor of Jonson to take *F* as the definitive text it once seemed to be.[31] In the case of *Poetaster*, however, the fact that *Q* was subject to censorship, and is intended as much as *F* to be a 'literary' text, means that *F* does have greater authority: it contains censored material the inclusion of which gives a text closer to that originally performed, and closer to Jonson's original intentions, than does *Q*; and, however much we may question the extent of Jonson's supervision of the printing of *F*, he clearly gave substantive revision to the copy used. If this were an old-spelling edition the problem of copy-text would be more complex, and there would be a strong case for retaining *Q*'s accidentals while incorporating *F*'s substantive revisions;[32] for a modernised edition of *Poetaster*, as opposed to *Sejanus*, the argument for using *Q* as copy-text is weaker, and I have returned to it only in such matters as the knighthood references, the sub title and in the case of obvious errors in *F*. I have also retained IV.v.123–7, cut from *F* because it involved 'business' with the hands not readily intelligible to the reader. It was in the play performed at the Blackfriars, and should at least be available for a modern director. I have not considered following Gifford in relegating III.v, which was probably not in the original production, to an appendix: if undramatic, it is an important addition to the play, appropriate as comment on the satirist's function in general, and on Jonson's strong identification with Horace in particular.

As this is a modernised text, punctuation and orthography, which are the real problem areas as regards the authority of *F*, are rarely crucial; wherever they affect meaning or metre, however, they are recorded in the apparatus. A particular problem for the moderniser is presented by the word 'satyre', deeply important to this play, and spelt thus throughout *F* and *Q* because supposedly derived from the Greek satyr plays (see III.iv.366n and III.v.2n): on the eighteen occasions the word or its derivatives occur (always italicised except in the description 'Comicall Satyre' on the last page of *F*), the reader is reminded of this etymology by the spelling (hence also Horace is a 'goat-footed envious slave' in IV.vii.8–9); not only does modernising relinquish this dual association, but in five of these cases (e.g. V.iii.370, 'The honest *Satyre* hath the happiest soule') the satirist and the goat-footed satyr are bound inextricably together. In these latter cases, therefore, I have used the spelling 'satyr'; where the reference is to the literary or dramatic form alone, I have spelt 'satire'.

I have followed Jonson's scene divisions with one exception: in IV.vii the stage clears at line 30, with four new characters entering. Elsewhere in *Poetaster* this would merit a new scene, and I have accordingly started one here. There is some crowding in *Q* at this point (I2r, probably the last of the inner forme to be set) and it is possible that the scene division was dropped to save space; if so, failure to reinstate it in *F* would be another sign that Jonson revised less thoroughly than has been thought. The massed entries at the beginning of each scene have been distributed throughout at the appropriate points. Where *Q* gives exits (the only stage directions in *Q*) these are incorporated without square brackets, and recorded in the apparatus. The marginal stage directions added in *F* (which gives no exits) are also incorporated, but it has been impossible to print them as marginalia, and their translation to the main body of the text is recorded in the apparatus; Jonson's marginal notes are similarly recorded, but not printed in the text. Stage directions added by myself or earlier editors are in square brackets; those new to this edition are only recorded where they affect interpretation or involve important action: any stage directions not noted in the apparatus, therefore, appear for the first time here. Gifford's scene headings, which are still found in many modern editions of Jonson, are recorded, but *Q*'s Latin headings and endings of acts (ACTVS PRIMVS./SCENA PRIMA.) are not. The speech prefix for the first speaker in each scene, always omitted in *F* (but not in *Q*) is silently restored. Also modernised without being recorded in the apparatus are *u* for *v* and *vice versa*, *j* for *i*, *-st*, *ha*'s, *'hem*, *then* (for *than*), *I* (for *Ay*), *yfaith*, *mary* (for *marry*), *your selves*, *them selves* etc.; *F*'s small capitals and *Q*'s italics for proper nouns; capitals after colons and semicolons, and question marks for exclamation marks. I have added an apostrophe before 'pothecary'; and used the modern 'Maecenas' for 'Mecoenas' or 'Mecaenas'. Since press corrections in *F* are in Appendix 2, they are noted only if they involve a substantive variant from *Q* or are otherwise significant. *F*'s parentheses (less frequent than *Q*'s) are retained where a liberal interpretation of modern usage could justify them, and noted in the apparatus where they are omitted. I have abandoned my initial attempt to incorporate as much as possible of *F*'s punctuation, which (ignoring the question of how far it really does reflect Jonson's copy) provides a considerable stumbling block to the modern reader.

NOTES

1  Arber, *SR*, III, 77v.
2  Subsequent transfers are summarised by Greg, *BEPD*, I, 297.
3  Title-pages in *BEPD*, I, 294–6; Fisher was 'at the White Hart, in Fleete Street' (title-page of *Midsummer Night's Dream*).
4  *BEPD*, I, 296; for ornaments, see e.g. Breton's *Melancholike Humours* (1600) and *An Apologie of the Earle of Essex* (1603); cf. F. S. Ferguson's card index in the British Library, and Lavin, pp. 331–8.
5  Greg was wrong in crediting him with the first quarto of *Every Man Out* (*STC* 14767), which was probably printed by Islip (see Lavin, pp. 331–3).
6  See Robert K. Turner Jr, 'Printing Methods and Textual Problems in *A Midsummer Night's Dream* Q1', *SB*, XV (1962), 33–55; Turner's conclusions are questioned by Peter W. M. Blayney, *The Texts of King Lear and their Origins*, I (Cambridge, 1982), 91–3, but this part of his argument remains valid.
7  This pattern contrasts with that at Cambridge in the late seventeenth century, where 'even when two or more compositors worked on a book, they did not work together setting sheet and sheet about. What usually happened was that one took over where the other left off', D. F. McKenzie, 'Printers of the Mind: Some Notes on Bibliographical Theories and Printing-House Practices', *SB*, XXII (1969), 1–75. It follows that McKenzie's argument that concurrent production was the norm may not hold for Bradock's shop, the more so as *STC* III records only eight books printed by Bradock in 1602, none of them large.
8  Of those charted by C. G. Petter in his edition of *Eastward Ho!* (1973), p. xx, *Q* has thirty-seven instances of *'hem*, twenty-four of *ha'* and ten of *i'the*; *F* perpetuates these, and adds a few more in the additional passages it contains.
9  *Volpone*, ed. R. B. Parker (Revels, Manchester, 1983), p. 2.
10  Copies examined: British Library 644.b.52 and Ashley 954; V&A, Dyce D.25.A.Y9; Nat. Lib. Scotland, Bute 300; Bodleian, Malone 213 (1); Huntington Library; Harvard College Library; Folger Shakespeare Library (last three on microfilm). None appears to have N2. T.J. Wise's copy (Ashley) has N1 skilfully extended from the gutter, possibly a leaf taken from another copy, but otherwise seems reliable. Ashley, Dyce, Huntington, Harvard and Folger copies have 'rarher', the rest 'rather'.
11  For correction at an early stage of imposition in another shop see W. Craig Ferguson, *Valentine Simmes* (Charlottesville, Va, 1968), pp. 84–5.
12  For a list of trivial variations of catchwords in *Q*, see *H&S*, IV, 188 n. 1.
13  Charles Herford died while vol. IV of the Oxford *Ben Jonson* was in press, but seems in any case to have been responsible only for the general introduction to the edition; Percy Simpson undertook the text and commentary, being helped in later volumes by his wife, Evelyn. I have

assumed therefore that Percy Simpson is the real editor of *Poetaster* in the Oxford edition.

14 Richard Dutton, *Ben Jonson: to the First Folio* (Cambridge, 1983) is doubly mistaken in writing that III.v is 'the Apologetical Dialogue originally printed at the end of the quarto, but inserted at the end of act III in the folio' (p. 49); the 'Apology', not called a dialogue in *Q*, never was printed there; and the Horace–Trebatius dialogue could never have been described as '*an* Apology *from the Author, with his reasons for the publishing of this booke*'.

15 See the title-pages of the quartos of *Every Man Out*.

16 Couplets are used for the other two avowed pieces of translation, Ovid's poem in I.i.43–84 and Virgil's reading in V.ii.56–97, but these are formal recitations, not dramatic dialogue.

17 See *Eastward Ho!*, ed. Petter, xxiii–xxiv.

18 This is also the view of Simpson, *H&S*, IV, 193 and Clare, pp. 86–9.

19 The collation within *F* is: Z4r, title-page (three variants, see Appendix 2); Z4v, blank; Z5r, the dedicatory epistle; Z5v, 'The Persons of the Play' and The Scene; Z6r–2A1r, the Induction; 2A1r–2F6v, the text of the play; 2F6v–2G3r 'To the Reader' and 'Apologeticall Dialogue'; 2G3v date of first performance and list of principal comedians. The running title from 2A1r to 2F6v is '*Poetaster*'.

20 Johan Gerritsen, review of *H&S*, *ES*, XXXVIII (1957), 120–6, p. 123. Gerritsen promised a longer study in 'Stansby and Jonson Produce a Folio: A Preliminary Account', *ES*, XL (1959), 52–5, but it has not yet appeared; *H&S*, IX, 13–86 is still the fullest description; see also Greg, 'Some Notes on Ben Jonson's Works', *RES*, II (1926), 129–45, and his reviews of *H&S* in *RES*, IX (1933), 102–4, XIV (1938), 216–18 and XVIII (1942), 144–66; James A. Riddell, 'Variant Title-Pages of the 1616 Jonson Folio', *Library* 6, VIII (1986), 152–6; Kevin J. Donovan, 'The Final Quires of the Jonson 1616 Workes', *SB*, XL (1987), 106–20, and 'Jonson's Texts in the First Folio' in *Ben Jonson's 1616 Folio*, ed. Jennifer Brady and W. H. Herenden (Newark, London and Toronto, 1991), pp. 23–37.

21 Another seemingly conclusive piece of evidence, the repetition of 'and' in IV.vii.6, is ambiguous since it could be an example of Tucca's stutter, a possibility increased because it remains in a line of *F* corrected, in all probability, by Jonson. Simpson suggests that the heavy punctuation of Tucca's speech in *Q*, which is largely normalised in *F*, was also an attempt to reproduce his stutter (*H&S*, IV, 191–2).

22 Godwyn, pp. 24, 15; John Holyoke, *Rider's Dictionarie Corrected and Augmented* (1606); John Minsheu, *Ductor in Linguas, The Guide Into Tongues* (London, 1617).

23 For Salusbury's biography, see *Poems by Sir John Salusbury and Robert Chester*, ed. Carleton Brown, *Early English Text Society*, CXII (London, 1914), pp. xi–xxvii, and E. A. J. Honigmann, *Shakespeare: The 'Lost Years'* (Manchester, 1985), pp. 91–113.

24 *Poems by Sir John Salusbury*, pp. xxxvii and 5–7; Salusbury's brother had been executed for his part in the Catholic Babington conspiracy.

25 *Ibid.*, pp. xviii–xxvi; cf. Honigmann, '*The Lost Years*', pp. 93–7 and 110–13.

26 Riggs, p. 92; for discussion of the patronage aspect of the Poetomachia, see Robert C. Evans, *Ben Jonson and the Poetics of Patronage* (Lewisburg, London and Toronto, 1989), pp. 146–7.

27 Gerritsen, 'Stansby and Jonson Produce a Folio', pp. 52–5.

28 Charlton Hinman, *The Printing and Proof-Reading of the First Folio of Shakespeare* (Oxford, 1963), I, 153–4.

29 Bishop was the printer for the whole volume, and Young uses Bishop's device on the title-page of *Poetaster*.

30 Brinsley Nicholson, 'Ben Jonson's Folios and the Bibliographers', *N&Q*, 4, V (1870), 573–5, argues differently. For a full description of the second folio and subsequent early editions, see Greg, *BEPD* III, 1073–84, and *H&S*, IX, 88–159.

31 See Greg, 'The Rationale of Copy-Text', *SB*, III (1950–1), 19–36, Fredson Bowers, 'Greg's Rationale of Copy-Text Revisited', *SB*, XXXI (1978), 109–18, and Donovan, 'Jonson's Texts in the First Folio'.

32 The position is set out with reference to *Sejanus* in Bowers's long 'Note' in 'Greg's Rationale of Copy-Text Revisited', pp. 115–19; it is a question of 'the extent to which within the areas of unchanged substantives the differences in accidentals in a revised edition may be referred to the author' (p. 115).

# APPENDIX 2
# 1616 Folio Collation: arranged by formes

1. Avon County Library (SLC 553/SR84)
2. Blackburn Museum, Hart Collection (1)
3. Blackburn Museum, Hart Collection (2)
4. Bodleian Library (AA, 83 Art)
5. Bodleian Library (Douce I 302)
6. British Library (G.11630)
7. British Library (C.39.K.9)
8. T. G. S. Cain copy
9. Durham University Library (1)
10. Durham University Library (2)
11. Eton College Library
12. Liverpool University Library
13. University of London (SLC I 516)
14. University of London (D-L.L xvii Bc)
15. University of London (BS 1272)
16. University College, London (Ogden A294)
17. University College, London (Ogden A295)
18. University College, London (Ogden A300)
19. Manchester University, John Rylands Library
20. University of Newcastle-upon-Tyne, Robinson Library
21. Oriel College, Oxford
22. Oxford University, English Faculty Library (YK1 26765) ('S1' in H&S)
23. Oxford University, English Faculty Library (YK1 26766) ('S2')
24. Oxford University, English Faculty Library (YK1 26764) ('S3')
25. Shakespeare Institute Library (SR 80 Jon.4616) (lacks all Dd & Ee)
26. Shakespeare Institute Library (SR 80 Jon.4615)
27. Ushaw College Library
28. Victoria and Albert Museum, Forster collection
29. Wadham College Library
30. Warrington Public Library
31. Westminster School

32. Wigan Public Library
33. Winchester College Library

**1. Sig. Z4r (title-page)**
State 1: 3, 5, 9, 13, 14, 15, 16, 17, 18, 19, 22, 26, 28, 31, 32, 33
State 2: 1, 2, 4, 7, 8, 10, 11, 12, 20, 21, 23, 27, 29, 30
State 3: 6, 24

State 1: engraved, in compartment: Printed *W. Stansby*, / for *M. Lownes.*
State 2: plain: Printed by WILLIAM STANSBY, / for *Matthew Lownes.* / M. DC. XVI.
State 3: plain: Printed by WILLIAM STANSBY. / M. DC. XVI.

**2. Sig. Z5r**
*Uncorrected*: 5, 22
*Corrected*: The rest

| | *Uncorrected* | *Corrected* |
|---|---|---|
| Dedication, 4 | FRIEND. | FRIEND, |

**3. Sig. Z6r**
*Uncorrected*: 1, 3, 4, 10, 11, 13, 15, 20, 23, 27, 29, 31
*Corrected*: The rest

| | *Uncorrected* | *Corrected* |
|---|---|---|
| Induction, 1 | thee; | thee, |
| Induction, 11 | Stay: | Stay! |
| Induction, 14 | not if I stare: These | not, if I stare: these |
| Induction, 16 | lights | lights, |

**4. Sig. Aa2v and Aa5r**
*Uncorrected*: 1, 2, 5, 9, 11, 14, 17, 19, 20, 23, 27, 29, 31, 32, 33
*Corrected*: The rest

| | *Uncorrected* | *Corrected* |
|---|---|---|
| Aa2v: I.ii.25 | Master | Master, |
| I.ii.30 | OVID.SE. | OVID.*se*. |
| (so 57, 69, 72) | | |
| I.ii.35 | *camrades* | *cam'rades* |
| I.ii.48 | 'hem, | 'hem: |
| I.ii.49 | *punke* | punke |

| | | | |
|---|---|---|---|
| | I.ii.57 | Me thinkes | Mee thinkes |
| | I.ii.57 | alone; | alone, |
| | I.ii.62 | OVID.IV. | OVID.*iu*. |
| | (so 71) | | |
| | I.ii.62 | me, | mee, |
| | I.ii.74 | reuennew | reuenew |
| Aa5r: | I.iii.29–30 | house, The jewellers, / where | house, / The jewellers where |
| | I.iii.41 | *elyzium* | *elyzian* |
| | I.iii.51 | new | now |

## 5. Sigs Aa3r and Aa4v

*Uncorrected*:   1, 3, 8, 12, 13, 15, 16, 17, 18, 19, 21, 22, 25, 26, 27, 28, 29, 30
*Corrected*:   The rest

| | | *Uncorrected* | *Corrected* |
|---|---|---|---|
| Aa4v: | I.ii.250 | knowledge | knowledge, |

## 6. Sigs Aa3v and Aa4r

*Uncorrected*:   1, 8, 15, 21, 22, 27
*Corrected*:   The rest

| | | *Uncorrected* | *Corrected* |
|---|---|---|---|
| Aa3v: | I.ii.131 | himself | himselfe, |
| | I.11.134 | Boy | boy |
| | I.ii.139 | *law*; Intend that: I | *law*: Intend that, I |
| | I.ii.149 | Boy | boy |
| | I.ii.150 | I, | I—— |
| | I.ii.154 | Now, captaine | Now Captaine |
| | I.ii.181 | nut-cracker: | nut-cracker |
| | I.ii.184 | him and | him, an' |
| Aa4r: | I.ii.187 | now: | now, |
| | I.ii.191 | *Sixe* | *sixe* |
| | I.ii.193 | *Time* | Time |
| | I.ii.204 | CALLIMACHVS. Thy | CALLIMACHVS, thy |
| | I.ii.205 | so: | so, |
| | I.ii.206 | must: They | must, they |
| | I.ii.207 | starued | staru'd |
| | I.ii.208 | linnen: | linnen; |

| I.ii.210 | No: | No, |
| I.ii.210 | Lawyer | lawyer |
| I.ii.212 | Ist | ist |
| I.ii.228 | me | me, |
| I.ii.220 | horse | horse, |
| I.ii.232 | *Romane artes* | artes |

## 7. Sigs Bb3r and Bb4v

*Uncorrected*:  4, 5, 6, 7, 8, 9, 10, 11, 14, 15, 16, 17, 20, 21, 22, 23, 24, 26, 27, 28, 29, 30, 31
*Corrected*:  The rest

|  | *Uncorrected* | *Corrected* |
| Bb3r: II.ii.188 | hat | that |

## 8. Sigs Dd1v and Dd6r

*Uncorrected?*:  5, 6, 7, 8, 13, 17, 18, 19, 21, 24, 29
*Corrected?*:  The rest (except 25, in which these pages are missing)

|  | *Uncorrected?* | *Corrected?* |
| Dd1v: IV.ii.45 | A God, but | A God; but |
| IV.ii.52 | Court: | Court; |
| Dd6r: IV.v.214 | OVID: | OVID; |

## 9. Sigs Ee1r and Ee6v

*Uncorrected*:  7, 16
*Corrected*:  The rest (except 25, in which these pages are missing)

|  | *Uncorrected* | *Corrected* |
| Ee1r: IV.vii.6 | lockt vp: | lockt vp. |
| IV.vii.6 | 'Hart; | 'Hart, |
| IV.vii.8 | humours | *humours* |
| IV.vii.14 | truncheon; | truncheon. |
| IV.viii.19 | arse, | arse; |
| IV.viii.2–3 | Stay, ASINIVS; you ... LICTORS: | Stay, ASINIVS;/You ... *Lictors* |
| Ee6v: V.iii.29 | LICTORS | Lictors |

## 10. Sigs Ee3r and Ee4v

*Uncorrected*:  5, 8, 12, 14, 21, 22, 23, 26, 28, 30
*Corrected*:  The rest (except 25, in which these pages are missing)

|            |             | Uncorrected   | Corrected                           |
|------------|-------------|---------------|-------------------------------------|
| Ee3r:      | IV.x.79.1   | *no s.d.*     | *Shee calls / him / backe.*         |
|            |             |               | *(in margin)*                       |
|            | IV.x.81     | vndescern'd   | vndiscern'd                         |
|            | IV.x.85     | descerne      | discerne                            |
|            | IV.x.88     | *no s.d.*     | *He calls / her backe. (in margin)* |
| Ee4v:      | V.i.102     | reason        | reasons                             |
|            | V.i.105     | bodie;        | bodie:                              |
|            | V.i.106     | himselfe:     | himselfe.                           |

## 11. Sigs Ff2r and Ff5v
*Damaged:*    4, 7, 8, 9, 11, 12, 21, 23, 25, 26, 27, 29
*Undamaged:* The rest

|            |             | Damaged       | Undamaged   |
|------------|-------------|---------------|-------------|
| Ff5v:      | V.iii.554   | CAE           | CAESAR      |

## 12. Sigs Ff3r and Ff4v
*Uncorrected?*: All but those below
*Corrected?*:    5, 6, 7, 24

|         |              | Uncorrected?          | Corrected?            |
|---------|--------------|-----------------------|-----------------------|
| Ff3r:   | V.iii.276    | *No*;                 | *No,*                 |
|         | V.iii.279    | ——(TVCCA              | (TVCCA                |
|         | (so 300, 303, 308) |                 |                       |
|         | V.iii.280    | *iudgement*;          | *iudgement*:          |
|         | V.iii.282    | *brawles.*            | *brawles,*            |
|         | V.iii.294    | too;                  | too,                  |
|         | V.iii.296    | *poet*:               | *poet,*               |
|         | V.iii.299    | *numbers*:            | *numbers,*            |
|         | V.iii.302    | *arrogance*:          | *arrogance.*          |
|         | V.iii.319    | snake;                | snake,                |
| Ff4v:   | V.iii.423    | Captaine;             | Captaine,             |
|         | V.iii.426    | him:                  | him: doe              |
|         | V.iii.429    | fiends.               | fiends!               |
|         | V.iii.431    | now;                  | now,                  |
|         | V.iii.435    | Commander;            | Commander,            |
|         | V.iii.448    | still;                | still,                |
|         | V.iii.460    | *incubus*             | *Incubus*             |
|         | V.iii.462    | and *reciprocall,*    | and *reciprocall*     |

# Glossarial Index to the Commentary

An asterisk indicates that the note contains information which supplements that in the *OED*